STOCK
TRADER'S
ALMANAC
2014

Jeffrey A. Hirsch & Yale Hirsch

D1532396

WILEY

www.stocktradersalmanac.com

Copyright © 2014 by John Wiley & Sons, Inc. All rights reserved.

Published by John Wiley & Sons, Inc., Hoboken, New Jersey

Editor in Chief	Jeffrey A. Hirsch
Editor at Large	Yale Hirsch
Director of Research	Christopher Mistal
Production Editor	Melissa Lopez

No part of this publication may be reproduced, stored in a retrieval system, or transmitted in any form or by any means, electronic, mechanical, photocopying, recording, scanning, or otherwise, except as permitted under Section 107 or 108 of the 1976 United States Copyright Act, without either the prior written permission of the Publisher, or authorization through payment of the appropriate per-copy fee to the Copyright Clearance Center, 222 Rosewood Drive, Danvers, MA 01923, 978-750-8400, fax 978-646-8600, or on the Web at www.copyright.com. Requests to the Publisher for permission should be addressed to the Permissions Department, John Wiley & Sons, Inc., 111 River Street, Hoboken, NJ 07030, 201-748-6011, fax 201-748-6008.

Limit of Liability/Disclaimer of Warranty: While the publisher and the author have used their best efforts in preparing this book, they make no representations or warranties with respect to the accuracy or completeness of the contents of this book and specifically disclaim any implied warranties of merchantability or fitness for a particular purpose. No warranty may be created or extended by sales representatives or written sales materials. The advice and strategies contained herein may not be suitable for your situation. You should consult with a professional where appropriate. Neither the publisher nor the author shall be liable for any loss of profit or any other commercial damages, including but not limited to special, incidental, consequential, or other damages.

For general information about our other products and services, please contact our Customer Care Department within the United States at 800-762-2974, outside the United States at 317-572-3993 or fax 317-572-4002.

Wiley also publishes its books in a variety of electronic formats. Some content that appears in print may not be available in electronic books. For more information about Wiley products, visit our Web site at www.wiley.com.

ISBN: 978-1-118-65945-8 (cloth)
ISBN: 978-1-118-80504-6 (ebk)
ISBN: 978-1-118-80502-2 (ebk)
10 9 8 7 6 5 4 3 2 1

Printed in the U.S.A.

This Forty-Seventh Edition is respectfully dedicated to:

John L. Person

John is a 34-year market veteran and industry icon, a brilliant speaker, educator, author, and a crack trader. He started on the floor of the Chicago Mercantile Exchange in 1979. He was the first ever to use the powerful combination of candlesticks and pivot points. His Person's Pivots and other technical indicators are on numerous trading platforms, including TD Ameritrade, TradeStation, Trade Navigator, and others.

We first became acquainted with John in 2002 at the New York Traders Expo, but it was not until we hit it off at the February 2007 Expo that we began exploring ways we could work together. John's deep knowledge of market history, cycles, seasonality, economics, stocks, options, futures, forex, and, most of all, technical analysis was mind-blowing. Our similar musical and movie tastes made it that much easier to work together. John and his wife, Mary, are gracious hosts and a joy to work with.

In 2009, we joined forces to revamp and produce the *Commodity Trader's Almanac* in what has become an invaluable partnership. For the past five years we have improved, tweaked, and beefed up the CTA. For 2014, it is morphing into a quarterly digital-only product. We look forward to its continued success. On page 36 we share some highlights.

On page 52 we have selected John's latest opus, *Mastering the Stock Market: High Probability Market Timing & Stock Selection Tools* as the Best Investment Book of the Year. On page 22 we impart some of John's trading tools and techniques.

Find out more at http://www.personsplanet.com/.

INTRODUCTION TO THE FORTY-SEVENTH EDITION

We are pleased and proud to introduce the Forty-Seventh Edition of the *Stock Trader's Almanac*. The *Almanac* provides you with the necessary tools to invest successfully in the twenty-first century.

J. P. Morgan's classic retort, "Stocks will fluctuate," is often quoted with a wink-of-the-eye implication that the only prediction one can make about the stock market is that it will go up, down, or sideways. Many investors agree that no one ever really knows which way the market will move. Nothing could be further from the truth.

We discovered that while stocks do indeed fluctuate, they do so in well-defined, often predictable patterns. These patterns recur too frequently to be the result of chance or coincidence. How else do we explain that since 1950 all the gains in the market were made during November through April, compared to a loss May through October? (See page 48.)

The *Almanac* is a practical investment tool. It alerts you to those little-known market patterns and tendencies on which shrewd professionals enhance profit potential. You will be able to forecast market trends with accuracy and confidence when you use the *Almanac* to help you understand:

- How our presidential elections affect the economy and the stock market—just as the moon affects the tides. Many investors have made fortunes following the political cycle. You can be sure that money managers who control billions of dollars are also political cycle watchers. Astute people do not ignore a pattern that has been working effectively throughout most of our economic history.

- How the passage of the Twentieth Amendment to the Constitution fathered the January Barometer. This barometer has an outstanding record for predicting the general course of the stock market each year, with only seven major errors since 1950, for a 88.9% accuracy ratio. (See page 16.)

- Why there is a significant market bias at certain times of the day, week, month, and year.

Even if you are an investor who pays scant attention to cycles, indicators, and patterns, your investment survival could hinge on your interpretation of one of the recurring patterns found within these pages. One of the most intriguing and important patterns is the symbiotic relationship between Washington and Wall Street. Aside from the potential profitability in seasonal patterns, there's the pure joy of seeing the market very often do just what you expected.

The *Stock Trader's Almanac* is also an organizer. Its wealth of information is presented on a calendar basis. The *Almanac* puts investing in a business framework and makes investing easier because it:

- Updates investment knowledge and informs you of new techniques and tools.

- Is a monthly reminder and refresher course.

- Alerts you to both seasonal opportunities and dangers.

- Furnishes a historical viewpoint by providing pertinent statistics on past market performance.

- Supplies forms necessary for portfolio planning, record keeping, and tax preparation.

The WITCH icon signifies THIRD FRIDAY OF THE MONTH on calendar pages and alerts you to extraordinary volatility due to the expiration of equity and index options and index futures contracts. Triple-witching days appear during March, June, September, and December.

The BULL icon on calendar pages signifies favorable trading days based on the S&P 500 rising 60% or more of the time on a particular trading day during the 21-year period January 1992 to December 2012.

A BEAR icon on calendar pages signifies unfavorable trading days based on the S&P falling 60% or more of the time for the same 21-year period.

Also, to give you even greater perspective, we have listed next to the date of every day that the market is open the Market Probability numbers for the same 21-year period for the Dow (D), S&P 500 (S) and NASDAQ (N). You will see a "D," "S," and "N" followed by a number signifying the actual Market Probability number for that trading day, based on the recent 21-year period. On pages 121–128 you will find complete Market Probability Calendars, both long-term and 21-year for the Dow, S&P, and NASDAQ, as well as for the Russell 1000 and Russell 2000 indices.

Other seasonalities near the ends, beginnings, and middles of months—options expirations, around holidays, and other significant times—as well as all FOMC Meeting dates are noted for *Almanac* investors' convenience on the weekly planner pages. All other important economic releases are provided in the Strategy Calendar every month in our e-newsletter, *Almanac Investor*, available at our website *www.stocktradersalmanac.com*.

New in this edition, we have included one-year seasonal pattern charts for Dow, S&P 500, NASDAQ, Russell 1000, and Russell 2000 on pages 171 to 173. There are three charts each for Dow and S&P 500 spanning our entire database starting in 1901 and one each for the younger indices. As 2014 is a midterm election year, each chart contains typical midterm election year performance compared to all years.

The Notable Events on page 6 provides a handy list of major events of the past year that can be helpful when evaluating things that may have moved the market. Over the past few years, our research had been restructured to flow better with the rhythm of the year. This has also allowed us more room for added data. Again, we have included historical data on the Russell 1000 and Russell 2000 indices. The Russell 2K is an excellent proxy for small and mid caps, which we have used over the years, and the Russell 1K provides a broader view of large caps. Annual highs and lows for all five indices covered in the *Almanac* appear on pages 149–151 and we've tweaked the Best & Worst section.

In order to cram in all this material, some of our Record Keeping section was cut. We have converted many of these paper forms into computer spreadsheets for our own internal use. As a service to our faithful readers, we are making these forms available at our website *www.stocktradersalmanac.com*.

Midterm election years are historically prone to bottoms, especially in October (page 30). 2014 is also a "fourth" year, which has the fourth best record in the decennial cycle for 132 years (pages 24 and 129). Of the last four midterm election years since the start of the Great Depression (1934, 1954, 1974, 1994) that were also fourth years, only 1954 was impressive. If the 2013 bull rally powers ahead without much of a pause, 2014 becomes more vulnerable to another sizable downturn. But *Almanac* readers can take some solace in the fact that the Dow has gained nearly 50% on average from the midterm low to the pre-election year high (page 74).

Among the research you will find especially pertinent to 2014 are Market Charts of Midterm Years (page 26), Prosperity More Than Peace Determines the Outcome of Midterm Elections (page 32), and that Midterm Election Time Is Unusually Bullish (page 100). Since 1934, the eight trading days surrounding midterm election days have produced an impressive 2.7% average gain.

Sector seasonalities include several consistent shorting opportunities and appear on pages 92–96. In response to many reader inquiries about how and what to trade when implementing the Best Months Switching Strategies, we detail some simple techniques, including a sampling of tradable mutual funds and ETFs on page 34.

We are constantly searching for new insights and nuances about the stock market and welcome any suggestions from our readers.

Have a healthy and prosperous 2014!

NOTABLE EVENTS

2012

Jul 13	JPMorgan Trading Loss reaches $5.8 billion
July 27	Moody's AAA Corp bond yield falls 3.26, lowest in over 50 years
Aug 31	Federal debt exceeds $16 trillion
Sep 11	American diplomatic mission attacked in Benghazi, Libya
Sep 13	Fed commits to buy $40 billion/month MBS
Sep 18	Apple shares top $700
Oct 29	Hurricane Sandy makes landfall in NJ, storm surge closes NYSE for 2 days
Dec 12	QE four-ever, additional $45 billion in Treasury securities/month until unemployment falls below 6.5%
Dec 14	Sandy Hook Elementary School shooting

2013

Jan 1	Payroll tax cut expires
Jan 2	American Taxpayer Relief Act of 2012 enacted, Bush tax cuts extended for most
Jan 5	Michael Dell announces bid to take Dell private
Jan 23	Europe bans Iranian oil imports, effective July 1
Mar 1	Federal sequester begins spending cut $85 billion/year
Mar 5	Dow closes at all-time high, first time since 2007
Mar 25	Cyprus bailed out, uninsured bank deposits taxed
Mar 28	S&P 500 closes at all-time high, first time since 2007
Apr 15	Boston Marathon bombing
May 9	U.S. dollar/Japanese yen breaks 100
May 10	Audit report confirms IRS targeting political groups
May 20	EF5 tornado strikes Moore, OK

2013 OUTLOOK

With the Dow above 15,000 in mid-May we addressed the prospects of a new secular bull market underway and revisited our Super Boom forecast and 15-year projection for DJIA to reach 38,820 around the year 2025, but for the current secular bear market that began in 2000 to drag on until 2017 or so before the next boom and secular bull commences. Two months of new highs is not enough to declare a new secular bull market. The war on terror still rages, a paradigm-shifting technology has yet to emerge, and inflation is subdued. The low point of the economy and the bottom of the stock market now clearly appear to be behind us. But other factors have yet to align. CPI has risen just 31% since 2001. President Obama has not tacked to the center, and we have yet to see him exhibit unwavering leadership and inspire the country. If the Republican leadership in Congress and the White House can't get the country rolling again, new leaders with new ideas will be voted in and a properly functioning federal government will evolve over the next four to six years.

Our 15-year projection (2012 STA, page 74) was based upon nearly 50 years of research and analysis into stock market cycles, patterns, and seasonality. Drawn in March 2011, we anticipated that the market would at least challenge its previous all-time highs before failing and falling to a low in midterm election year 2014 with another low in 2017–2018 before the next super-boom truly began. Now that DJIA has modestly exceeded the high end of the range, the final low of this secular bear is likely to be higher, in the 9,000–10,000 range or a 30–40% decline from current levels.

With President Obama on the defensive against a plethora of issues, midterm politics will likely rear its ugly head again in 2014. Midterm election years are notoriously weaker for Democrats (2013 STA, page 32). But midterm elections have a history of being a bottom picker's paradise. In the last 13 quadrennial cycles since 1961, 9 of the 16 bear markets bottomed in the midterm year. In the last 13 midterm election years, bear markets began or were in progress nine times—we experienced bull years in 1986, 2006, and 2010 while 1994 was flat. However, this has provided excellent buying opportunities. By the third, pre-election, year the administration's focus shifts to "priming the pump." Policies are enacted to improve the economic well-being of the country and its electorate. From the midterm low to the pre-election year high, the Dow has gained nearly 50% on average since 1914.

Bulls are currently getting cockier, upping their forecasts and pounding their chests. Bears are dwindling and running for cover. Retail investors are beginning to get back into the market. While we expect a modest correction in Q2–Q3 2013, a bear market will likely be staved off until late 2013 or early 2014 when the Fed is likely to begin draining the QE punchbowl and Chairman Bernanke likely steps down in January 2014. We suspect a good hunk of the next major downturn to transpire in 2014, though it is also likely to provide an ample buying opportunity. A 2014 low in the DJIA 12,000 range is likely, while we expect DJIA 10,000 to be breached at least one more time in the next 4–6 years.

— *Jeffrey A. Hirsch, May 24, 2013*

THE 2014 STOCK TRADER'S ALMANAC

CONTENTS

DIRECTORY OF TRADING PATTERNS & DATABANK

STRATEGY PLANNING AND RECORD SECTION

2014 STRATEGY CALENDAR
(Option expiration dates circled)

	MONDAY	TUESDAY	WEDNESDAY	THURSDAY	FRIDAY	SATURDAY	SUNDAY
JANUARY	30	31	1 JANUARY New Year's Day	2	3	4	5
	6	7	8	9	10	11	12
	13	14	15	16	(17)	18	19
	20 Martin Luther King Day	21	22	23	24	25	26
	27	28	29	30	31	1 FEBRUARY	2
FEBRUARY	3	4	5	6	7	8	9
	10	11	12	13	14 ♥	15	16
	17 Presidents' Day	18	19	20	(21)	22	23
	24	25	26	27	28	1 MARCH	2
MARCH	3	4	5 Ash Wednesday	6	7	8	9 Daylight Saving Time Begins
	10	11	12	13	14	15	16
	17 ☘ St. Patrick's Day	18	19	20	(21)	22	23
	24	25	26	27	28	29	30
	31	1 APRIL	2	3	4	5	6
APRIL	7	8	9	10	11	12	13
	14	15 Tax Deadline Passover	16	(17)	18 Good Friday	19	20 Easter
	21	22	23	24	25	26	27
	28	29	30	1 MAY	2	3	4
MAY	5	6	7	8	9	10	11 Mother's Day
	12	13	14	15	(16)	17	18
	19	20	21	22	23	24	25
	26 Memorial Day	27	28	29	30	31	1 JUNE
JUNE	2	3	4	5	6	7	8
	9	10	11	12	13	14	15 Father's Day
	16	17	18	19	(20)	21	22
	23	24	25	26	27	28	29

Market closed on shaded weekdays; closes early when half-shaded.

2014 STRATEGY CALENDAR

(Option expiration dates circled)

MONDAY	TUESDAY	WEDNESDAY	THURSDAY	FRIDAY	SATURDAY	SUNDAY	
30	1 JULY	2	3	4 Independence Day	5	6	JULY
7	8	9	10	11	12	13	
14	15	16	17	(18)	19	20	
21	22	23	24	25	26	27	
28	29	30	31	1 AUGUST	2	3	
4	5	6	7	8	9	10	AUGUST
11	12	13	14	(15)	16	17	
18	19	20	21	22	23	24	
25	26	27	28	29	30	31	
1 SEPTEMBER Labor Day	2	3	4	5	6	7	SEPTEMBER
8	9	10	11	12	13	14	
15	16	17	18	(19)	20	21	
22	23	24	25 Rosh Hashanah	26	27	28	
29	30	1 OCTOBER	2	3	4 Yom Kippur	5	OCTOBER
6	7	8	9	10	11	12	
13 Columbus Day	14	15	16	(17)	18	19	
20	21	22	23	24	25	26	
27	28	29	30	31	1 NOVEMBER	2 Daylight Saving Time Ends	
3	4 Election Day	5	6	7	8	9	NOVEMBER
10	11 Veterans' Day	12	13	14	15	16	
17	18	19	20	(21)	22	23	
24	25	26	27 Thanksgiving	28	29	30	
1 DECEMBER	2	3	4	5	6	7	DECEMBER
8	9	10	11	12	13	14	
15	16	17 Chanukah	18	(19)	20	21	
22	23	24	25 Christmas	26	27	28	
29	30	31	1 JANUARY New Year's Day	2	3	4	

11

JANUARY ALMANAC

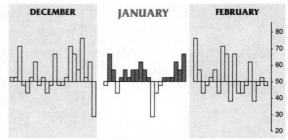

JANUARY						
S	M	T	W	T	F	S
				1	2	3	4
5	6	7	8	9	10	11
12	13	14	15	16	17	18
19	20	21	22	23	24	25
26	27	28	29	30	31	

FEBRUARY						
S	M	T	W	T	F	S
						1
2	3	4	5	6	7	8
9	10	11	12	13	14	15
16	17	18	19	20	21	22
23	24	25	26	27	28	

Market Probability Chart above is a graphic representation of the S&P 500 Recent Market Probability Calendar on page 124.

◆ January Barometer predicts year's course with .762 batting average (page 16) ◆ 10 of last 16 midterm election years followed January's direction ◆ Every down January on the S&P since 1950, without exception, preceded a new or extended bear market, a flat market, or a 10% correction (page 42) ◆ S&P gains January's first five days preceded full-year gains 85.0% of the time, 8 of last 16 midterm years followed first five days' direction (page 14) ◆ November, December, and January constitute the year's best three-month span, a 4.4% S&P gain (pages 44 & 147) ◆ January NASDAQ powerful 3.0% since 1971 (pages 56 & 148) ◆ "January Effect" now starts in mid-December and favors small-cap stocks (pages 106 & 110) ◆ 2009 has the dubious honor of the worst S&P 500 January on record.

January Vital Statistics

	DJIA		S&P 500		NASDAQ		Russell 1K		Russell 2K	
Rank	5		5		1		4		2	
Up	42		40		29		23		20	
Down	22		24		14		12		15	
Average % Change	1.1%		1.2%		3.0%		1.3%		2.0%	
Midterm Year	−0.6%		−0.9%		−0.6%		−1.0%		−0.7%	
Best & Worst January										
	% Change		% Change		% Change		% Change		% Change	
Best	1976	14.4	1987	13.2	1975	16.6	1987	12.7	1985	13.1
Worst	2009	−8.8	2009	−8.6	2008	−9.9	2009	−8.3	2009	−11.2
Best & Worst January Weeks										
Best	1/9/76	6.1	1/2/09	6.8	1/12/01	9.1	1/2/09	6.8	1/9/87	7.0
Worst	1/24/03	−5.3	1/28/00	−5.6	1/28/00	−8.2	1/28/00	−5.5	1/4/08	−6.5
Best & Worst January Days										
Best	1/17/91	4.6	1/3/01	5.0	1/3/01	14.2	1/3/01	5.3	1/21/09	5.3
Worst	1/8/88	−6.9	1/8/88	−6.8	1/2/01	−7.2	1/8/88	−6.1	1/20/09	−7.0
First Trading Day of Expiration Week: 1980–2013										
Record (#Up–#Down)	24–10		21–13		20–14		20–14		20–14	
Current streak	U4		D1		D1		D1		D1	
Avg % Change	0.15		0.14		0.19		0.12		0.19	
Options Expiration Day: 1980–2013										
Record (#Up–#Down)	17–17		18–16		18–16		18–16		19–15	
Current streak	U3		U3		D4		U3		U2	
Avg % Change	−0.10		−0.09		−0.15		−0.11		−0.12	
Options Expiration Week: 1980–2013										
Record (#Up–#Down)	18–16		15–19		19–15		15–19		18–16	
Current streak	U3		U2		U2		U2		U2	
Avg % Change	−0.16		−0.07		0.25		−0.08		0.25	
Week After Options Expiration: 1980–2012										
Record (#Up–#Down)	18–16		21–13		19–15		21–13		23–11	
Current streak	U1		U2		U2		U2		U3	
Avg % Change	0.04		0.22		0.10		0.19		0.22	
First Trading Day Performance										
% of Time Up	59.4		50.0		58.1		45.7		48.6	
Avg % Change	0.29		0.19		0.25		0.21		0.14	
Last Trading Day Performance										
% of Time Up	57.8		62.5		65.1		60.0		77.1	
Avg % Change	0.23		0.26		0.3		0.34		0.29	

Dow & S&P 1950–April 2013, NASDAQ 1971–April 2013, Russell 1K & 2K 1979–April 2013.

20th Amendment made "lame ducks" disappear.
Now, "As January goes, so goes the year."

DECEMBER 2013/JANUARY 2014

MONDAY
D 42.9
S 61.9
N 52.4
30

The symbol of all relationships among such men, the moral symbol of respect for human beings, is the trader.
— Ayn Rand (Russian-born American novelist and philosopher, from Galt's Speech, *Atlas Shrugged*, 1957, 1905–1982)

Last Trading Day of the Year, NASDAQ Down 11 of last 13
NASDAQ Was Up 29 Years in a Row 1971–1999

TUESDAY
D 38.1
S 28.6
N 47.6
31

One machine can do the work of fifty ordinary men. No machine can do the work of one extraordinary man.
— Elbert Hubbard (American author, *A Message To Garcia*, 1856–1915)

New Years Day (Market Closed)

WEDNESDAY
1

Things may come to those who wait, but only the things left by those who hustle.
— Abraham Lincoln (16th U.S. President, 1809–1865)

Small Caps Punished First Trading Day of Year
Russell 2000 Down 14 of Last 24, But Up Last 5

THURSDAY
D 71.4
S 47.6
N 66.7
2

While markets often make double bottoms, three pushes to a high is the most common topping pattern.
— John Bollinger (Bollinger Capital Management, *Capital Growth Letter, Bollinger on Bollinger Bands*)

Second Trading Day of the Year, Dow Up 14 of Last 20
Santa Claus Rally Ends (Page 114)

FRIDAY
D 71.4
S 66.7
N 66.7
3

The man who can master his time can master nearly anything.
— Winston Churchill (British statesman, 1874–1965)

SATURDAY
4

January Almanac Investor Seasonalities: See Pages 92, 94, and 96

SUNDAY
5

JANUARY'S FIRST FIVE DAYS: AN EARLY WARNING SYSTEM

The last 40 up First Five Days were followed by full-year gains 34 times for an 85.0% accuracy ratio and a 13.6% average gain in all 40 years. The five exceptions include flat 1994 and four related to war. Vietnam military spending delayed start of 1966 bear market. Ceasefire imminence early in 1973 raised stocks temporarily. Saddam Hussein turned 1990 into a bear. The war on terrorism, instability in the Mideast, and corporate malfeasance shaped 2002 into one of the worst years on record. The 23 down First Five Days were followed by 12 up years and 11 down (47.8% accurate) and an average gain of 0.2%.

In Midterm Election Years this indicator has had a spotty record—almost a contrary indicator. In the last 16 Midterm Years only eight full years followed the direction of the First Five Days and only two of the last nine (2006, 2010). The full-month January Barometer (page 16) has a better Midterm record.

THE FIRST-FIVE-DAYS-IN-JANUARY INDICATOR

	Chronological Data					Ranked By Performance		
	Previous Year's Close	January 5th Day	5-Day Change	Year Change		Rank	5-Day Change	Year Change
1950	16.76	17.09	2.0%	21.8%		1	1987	6.2%	2.0%
1951	20.41	20.88	2.3	16.5		2	1976	4.9	19.1
1952	23.77	23.91	0.6	11.8		3	1999	3.7	19.5
1953	26.57	26.33	−0.9	−6.6		4	2003	3.4	26.4
1954	24.81	24.93	0.5	45.0		5	2006	3.4	13.6
1955	35.98	35.33	−1.8	26.4		6	1983	3.3	17.3
1956	45.48	44.51	−2.1	2.6		7	1967	3.1	20.1
1957	46.67	46.25	−0.9	−14.3		8	1979	2.8	12.3
1958	39.99	40.99	2.5	38.1		9	2010	2.7	12.8
1959	55.21	55.40	0.3	8.5		10	1963	2.6	18.9
1960	59.89	59.50	−0.7	−3.0		11	1958	2.5	38.1
1961	58.11	58.81	1.2	23.1		12	1984	2.4	1.4
1962	71.55	69.12	−3.4	−11.8		13	1951	2.3	16.5
1963	63.10	64.74	2.6	18.9		14	2013	2.2	??
1964	75.02	76.00	1.3	13.0		15	1975	2.2	31.5
1965	84.75	85.37	0.7	9.1		16	1950	2.0	21.8
1966	92.43	93.14	0.8	−13.1		17	2004	1.8	9.0
1967	80.33	82.81	3.1	20.1		18	2012	1.8	13.4
1968	96.47	96.62	0.2	7.7		19	1973	1.5	−17.4
1969	103.86	100.80	−2.9	−11.4		20	1972	1.4	15.6
1970	92.06	92.68	0.7	0.1		21	1964	1.3	13.0
1971	92.15	92.19	0.04	10.8		22	1961	1.2	23.1
1972	102.09	103.47	1.4	15.6		23	1989	1.2	27.3
1973	118.05	119.85	1.5	−17.4		24	2011	1.1	−0.003
1974	97.55	96.12	−1.5	−29.7		25	2002	1.1	−23.4
1975	68.56	70.04	2.2	31.5		26	1997	1.0	31.0
1976	90.19	94.58	4.9	19.1		27	1980	0.9	25.8
1977	107.46	105.01	−2.3	−11.5		28	1966	0.8	−13.1
1978	95.10	90.64	−4.7	1.1		29	1994	0.7	−1.5
1979	96.11	98.80	2.8	12.3		30	1965	0.7	9.1
1980	107.94	108.95	0.9	25.8		31	2009	0.7	23.5
1981	135.76	133.06	−2.0	−9.7		32	1970	0.7	0.1
1982	122.55	119.55	−2.4	14.8		33	1952	0.6	11.8
1983	140.64	145.23	3.3	17.3		34	1954	0.5	45.0
1984	164.93	168.90	2.4	1.4		35	1996	0.4	20.3
1985	167.24	163.99	−1.9	26.3		36	1959	0.3	8.5
1986	211.28	207.97	−1.6	14.6		37	1995	0.3	34.1
1987	242.17	257.28	6.2	2.0		38	1992	0.2	4.5
1988	247.08	243.40	−1.5	12.4		39	1968	0.2	7.7
1989	277.72	280.98	1.2	27.3		40	1990	0.1	−6.6
1990	353.40	353.79	0.1	−6.6		41	1971	0.04	10.8
1991	330.22	314.90	−4.6	26.3		42	2007	−0.4	3.5
1992	417.09	418.10	0.2	4.5		43	1960	−0.7	−3.0
1993	435.71	429.05	−1.5	7.1		44	1957	−0.9	−14.3
1994	466.45	469.90	0.7	−1.5		45	1953	−0.9	−6.6
1995	459.27	460.83	0.3	34.1		46	1974	−1.5	−29.7
1996	615.93	618.46	0.4	20.3		47	1998	−1.5	26.7
1997	740.74	748.41	1.0	31.0		48	1988	−1.5	12.4
1998	970.43	956.04	−1.5	26.7		49	1993	−1.5	7.1
1999	1229.23	1275.09	3.7	19.5		50	1986	−1.6	14.6
2000	1469.25	1441.46	−1.9	−10.1		51	2001	−1.8	−13.0
2001	1320.28	1295.86	−1.8	−13.0		52	1955	−1.8	26.4
2002	1148.08	1160.71	1.1	−23.4		53	2000	−1.9	−10.1
2003	879.82	909.93	3.4	26.4		54	1985	−1.9	26.3
2004	1111.92	1131.91	1.8	9.0		55	1981	−2.0	−9.7
2005	1211.92	1186.19	−2.1	3.0		56	1956	−2.1	2.6
2006	1248.29	1290.15	3.4	13.6		57	2005	−2.1	3.0
2007	1418.30	1412.11	−0.4	3.5		58	1977	−2.3	−11.5
2008	1468.36	1390.19	−5.3	−38.5		59	1982	−2.4	14.8
2009	903.25	909.73	0.7	23.5		60	1969	−2.9	−11.4
2010	1115.10	1144.98	2.7	12.8		61	1962	−3.4	−11.8
2011	1257.64	1271.50	1.1	−0.003		62	1991	−4.6	26.3
2012	1257.60	1280.70	1.8	13.4		63	1978	−4.7	1.1
2013	1426.19	1457.15	2.2	??		64	2008	−5.3	−38.5

Based on S&P 500

JANUARY

January Ends "Best Three-Month Span" (Pages 44, 56, 147, and 148)

MONDAY

D 47.6
S 57.1
N 57.1

6

The difference between life and the movies is that a script has to make sense, and life doesn't.
— Joseph L. Mankiewicz (Film director, writer, producer, 1909–1993)

TUESDAY

D 52.4
S 42.9
N 57.1

7

The secret to business is to know something that nobody else knows.
— Aristotle Onassis (Greek shipping billionaire)

January's First Five Days Act as an "Early Warning" (Page 14)

WEDNESDAY

D 38.1
S 52.4
N 57.1

8

A good new chairman of the Federal Reserve Bank is worth a $10 billion tax cut.
— Paul H. Douglas (U.S. Senator Illinois, 1949–1967, 1892–1976)

THURSDAY

D 57.1
S 57.1
N 71.4

9

If banking institutions are protected by the taxpayer and they are given free reign to speculate, I may not live long enough to see the crisis, but my soul is going to come back and haunt you.
— Paul A. Volcker (Fed Chairman, 1979–1987, Chair Economic Recovery Advisory Board, 2/2/2010, b. 1927)

FRIDAY

D 47.6
S 52.4
N 52.4

10

Banking establishments are more dangerous than standing armies; and that the principle of spending money to be paid by posterity, under the name of funding, is but swindling futurity on a large scale.
— Thomas Jefferson (3rd U.S. President, 1743–7/4/1826, 1816 letter to John Taylor of Caroline)

SATURDAY

11

SUNDAY

12

THE INCREDIBLE JANUARY BAROMETER (DEVISED 1972): ONLY SEVEN SIGNIFICANT ERRORS IN 63 YEARS

Devised by Yale Hirsch in 1972, our January Barometer states that as the S&P 500 goes in January, so goes the year. The indicator has registered **only seven major errors since 1950 for an 88.9% accuracy ratio**. Vietnam affected 1966 and 1968; 1982 saw the start of a major bull market in August; two January rate cuts and 9/11 affected 2001; the anticipation of military action in Iraq held down the market in January 2003; 2009 was the beginning of a new bull market following the second worst bear market on record; and the Fed saved 2010 with QE2 (*Almanac Investor* newsletter subscribers receive full analysis of each reading as well as its potential implications for the full year.)

Including the eight flat-year errors (less than +/- 5%) yields a 76.2% accuracy ratio. A full comparison of all monthly barometers for the Dow, S&P, and NASDAQ in our January 18, 2013 blog post at *blog.stocktradersalmanac.com* details January's market forecasting prowess. Bear markets began or continued when Januarys suffered a loss *(see page 42)*. Full years followed January's direction in 10 of the last 16 midterm election years. *See page 18 for more.*

AS JANUARY GOES, SO GOES THE YEAR

Market Performance In January

Year	Previous Year's Close	January Close	January Change	Year Change	
1950	16.76	17.05	1.7%	21.8%	
1951	20.41	21.66	6.1	16.5	
1952	23.77	24.14	1.6	11.8	
1953	26.57	26.38	-0.7	-6.6	
1954	24.81	26.08	5.1	45.0	
1955	35.98	36.63	1.8	26.4	
1956	45.48	43.82	-3.6	2.6	flat
1957	46.67	44.72	-4.2	-14.3	
1958	39.99	41.70	4.3	38.1	
1959	55.21	55.42	0.4	8.5	
1960	59.89	55.61	-7.1	-3.0	flat
1961	58.11	61.78	6.3	23.1	
1962	71.55	68.84	-3.8	-11.8	
1963	63.10	66.20	4.9	18.9	
1964	75.02	77.04	2.7	13.0	
1965	84.75	87.56	3.3	9.1	
1966	92.43	92.88	0.5	-13.1	X
1967	80.33	86.61	7.8	20.1	
1968	96.47	92.24	-4.4	7.7	X
1969	103.86	103.01	-0.8	-11.4	
1970	92.06	85.02	-7.6	0.1	flat
1971	92.15	95.88	4.0	10.8	
1972	102.09	103.94	1.8	15.6	
1973	118.05	116.03	-1.7	-17.4	
1974	97.55	96.57	-1.0	-29.7	
1975	68.56	76.98	12.3	31.5	
1976	90.19	100.86	11.8	19.1	
1977	107.46	102.03	-5.1	-11.5	
1978	95.10	89.25	-6.2	1.1	flat
1979	96.11	99.93	4.0	12.3	
1980	107.94	114.16	5.8	25.8	
1981	135.76	129.55	-4.6	-9.7	
1982	122.55	120.40	-1.8	14.8	X
1983	140.64	145.30	3.3	17.3	
1984	164.93	163.41	-0.9	1.4	flat
1985	167.24	179.63	7.4	26.3	
1986	211.28	211.78	0.2	14.6	
1987	242.17	274.08	13.2	2.0	flat
1988	247.08	257.07	4.0	12.4	
1989	277.72	297.47	7.1	27.3	
1990	353.40	329.08	-6.9	-6.6	
1991	330.22	343.93	4.2	26.3	
1992	417.09	408.79	-2.0	4.5	flat
1993	435.71	438.78	0.7	7.1	
1994	466.45	481.61	3.3	-1.5	flat
1995	459.27	470.42	2.4	34.1	
1996	615.93	636.02	3.3	20.3	
1997	740.74	786.16	6.1	31.0	
1998	970.43	980.28	1.0	26.7	
1999	1229.23	1279.64	4.1	19.5	
2000	1469.25	1394.46	-5.1	-10.1	
2001	1320.28	1366.01	3.5	-13.0	X
2002	1148.08	1130.20	-1.6	-23.4	
2003	879.82	855.70	-2.7	26.4	X
2004	1111.92	1131.13	1.7	9.0	
2005	1211.92	1181.27	-2.5	3.0	flat
2006	1248.29	1280.08	2.5	13.6	
2007	1418.30	1438.24	1.4	3.5	flat
2008	1468.36	1378.55	-6.1	-38.5	
2009	903.25	825.88	-8.6	23.5	X
2010	1115.10	1073.87	-3.7	12.8	X
2011	1257.64	1286.12	2.3	-0.003	flat
2012	1257.60	1312.41	4.4	13.4	
2013	1426.19	1498.11	5.0	??	

January Performance By Rank

Rank	Year	January Change	Year's Change	
1	1987	13.2%	2.0%	flat
2	1975	12.3	31.5	
3	1976	11.8	19.1	
4	1967	7.8	20.1	
5	1985	7.4	26.3	
6	1989	7.1	27.3	
7	1961	6.3	23.1	
8	1997	6.1	31.0	
9	1951	6.1	16.5	
10	1980	5.8	25.8	
11	1954	5.1	45.0	
12	2013	5.0	??	
13	1963	4.9	18.9	
14	2012	4.4	13.4	
15	1958	4.3	38.1	
16	1991	4.2	26.3	
17	1999	4.1	19.5	
18	1971	4.0	10.8	
19	1988	4.0	12.4	
20	1979	4.0	12.3	
21	2001	3.5	-13.0	X
22	1965	3.3	9.1	
23	1983	3.3	17.3	
24	1996	3.3	20.3	
25	1994	3.3	-1.5	flat
26	1964	2.7	13.0	
27	2006	2.5	13.6	
28	1995	2.4	34.1	
29	2011	2.3	-0.003	flat
30	1972	1.8	15.6	
31	1955	1.8	26.4	
32	1950	1.7	21.8	
33	2004	1.7	9.0	
34	1952	1.6	11.8	
35	2007	1.4	3.5	flat
36	1998	1.0	26.7	
37	1993	0.7	7.1	
38	1966	0.5	-13.1	X
39	1959	0.4	8.5	
40	1986	0.2	14.6	
41	1953	-0.7	-6.6	
42	1969	-0.8	-11.4	
43	1984	-0.9	1.4	flat
44	1974	-1.0	-29.7	
45	2002	-1.6	-23.4	
46	1973	-1.7	-17.4	
47	1982	-1.8	14.8	X
48	1992	-2.0	4.5	flat
49	2005	-2.5	3.0	flat
50	2003	-2.7	26.4	X
51	1956	-3.6	2.6	flat
52	2010	-3.7	12.8	X
53	1962	-3.8	-11.8	
54	1957	-4.2	-14.3	
55	1968	-4.4	7.7	X
56	1981	-4.6	-9.7	
57	1977	-5.1	-11.5	
58	2000	-5.1	-10.1	
59	2008	-6.1	-38.5	
60	1978	-6.2	1.1	flat
61	1990	-6.9	-6.6	
62	1960	-7.1	-3.0	flat
63	1970	-7.6	0.1	flat
64	2009	-8.6	23.5	X

X = major error   **Based on S&P 500**

JANUARY

First Trading Day of January Expiration Week, Dow Up 16 of Last 21

MONDAY
D 52.4
S 57.1
N 61.9
13

We are like tenant farmers chopping down the fence around our house for fuel when we should be using Nature's inexhaustible sources of energy—sun, wind and tide. I'd put my money on the sun and solar energy. What a source of power! I hope we don't have to wait until oil and coal run out before we tackle that.
— Thomas Alva Edison (American inventor, 1093 patents, 1847–1931)

TUESDAY
D 52.4
S 57.1
N 57.1
14

If you are ready to give up everything else to study the whole history of the market as carefully as a medical student studies anatomy and you have the cool nerves of a great gambler, the sixth sense of a clairvoyant, and the courage of a lion, you have a ghost of a chance.
— Bernard Baruch (Financier, speculator, statesman, presidential adviser, 1870–1965)

January Expiration Week Horrible Since 1999, Dow Down 9 of Last 15
Average Dow loss: –1.4%

WEDNESDAY
D 61.9
S 61.9
N 52.4
15

The future now belongs to societies that organize themselves for learning. What we know and can do holds the key to economic progress.
— Ray Marshall (b. 1928) and Marc Tucker (b. 1939) (*Thinking for a Living: Education and the Wealth of Nations*, 1992)

THURSDAY
D 57.1
S 57.1
N 66.7
16

The only function of economic forecasting is to make astrology look respectable.
— John Kenneth Galbraith (Canadian/American economist and diplomat, 1908–2006)

January Expiration Day, Dow Down 10 of Last 15 With Big Losses
Off 2.1% in 2010, Off 2.0% in 2006, and 1.3% in 2003

FRIDAY
D 33.3
S 52.4
N 61.9
17

We can guarantee cash benefits as far out and at whatever size you like, but we cannot guarantee their purchasing power.
— Alan Greenspan (Fed Chairman, 1987–2006, on funding Social Security to Senate Banking Committee, 2/15/05)

SATURDAY
18

SUNDAY
19

JANUARY BAROMETER IN GRAPHIC FORM SINCE 1950

% Loss JANUARY CHANGE % Gain   % Loss FULL-YEAR CHANGE % Gain

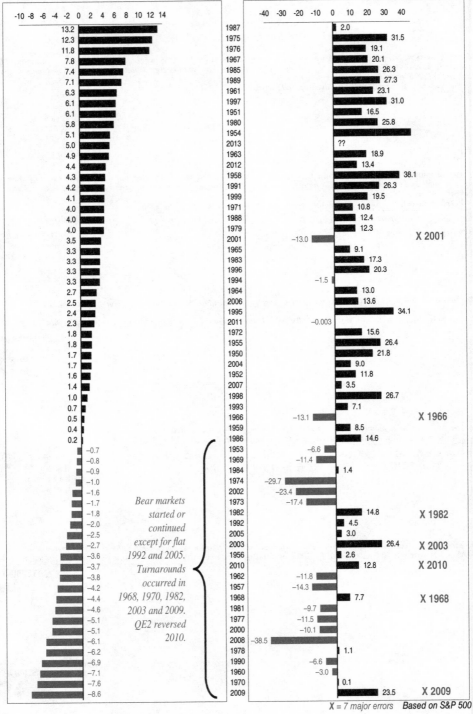

Year	January Change	Full-Year Change
1987	13.2	2.0
1975	12.3	31.5
1976	11.8	19.1
1967	7.8	20.1
1985	7.4	26.3
1989	7.1	27.3
1961	6.3	23.1
1997	6.1	31.0
1951	6.1	16.5
1980	5.8	25.8
1954	5.1	
2013	5.0	??
1963	4.9	18.9
2012	4.4	13.4
1958	4.3	38.1
1991	4.2	26.3
1999	4.1	19.5
1971	4.0	10.8
1988	4.0	12.4
1979	4.0	12.3
2001	3.5	−13.0 X 2001
1965	3.3	9.1
1983	3.3	17.3
1996	3.3	20.3
1994	3.3	−1.5
1964	2.7	13.0
2006	2.5	13.6
1995	2.4	34.1
2011	2.3	−0.003
1972	1.8	15.6
1955	1.8	26.4
1950	1.7	21.8
2004	1.7	9.0
1952	1.6	11.8
2007	1.4	3.5
1998	1.0	26.7
1993	0.7	7.1
1966	0.5	−13.1 X 1966
1959	0.4	8.5
1986	0.2	14.6
1953	−0.7	−6.6
1969	−0.8	−11.4
1984	−0.9	1.4
1974	−1.0	−29.7
2002	−1.6	−23.4
1973	−1.7	−17.4
1982	−1.8	14.8 X 1982
1992	−2.0	4.5
2005	−2.5	3.0
2003	−2.7	26.4 X 2003
1956	−3.6	2.6
2010	−3.7	12.8 X 2010
1962	−3.8	−11.8
1957	−4.2	−14.3
1968	−4.4	7.7 X 1968
1981	−4.6	−9.7
1977	−5.1	−11.5
2000	−5.1	−10.1
2008	−6.1	−38.5
1978	−6.2	1.1
1990	−6.9	−6.6
1960	−7.1	−3.0
1970	−7.6	0.1
2009	−8.6	23.5 X 2009

Bear markets started or continued except for flat 1992 and 2005. Turnarounds occurred in 1968, 1970, 1982, 2003 and 2009. QE2 reversed 2010.

X = 7 major errors *Based on S&P 500*

18

JANUARY

Martin Luther King Jr. Day (Market Closed)

The years teach much which the days never know.
— Ralph Waldo Emerson (American author, poet and philosopher, *Self-Reliance*, 1803–1882)

TUESDAY
21

D 28.6
S 28.6
N 28.6

We like what's familiar, and we dislike change. So, we push the familiar until it starts working against us big-time—a crisis. Then, MAYBE we can accept change.
— Kevin Cameron (Journalist, *Cycle World*, April 2013)

WEDNESDAY
22

D 33.3
S 42.9
N 33.3

It is totally unproductive to think the world has been unfair to you. Every tough stretch is an opportunity.
— Charlie Munger (Vice-Chairman Berkshire Hathaway, 2007 Wesco Annual Meeting, b. 1924)

THURSDAY
23

D 42.9
S 47.6
N 47.6

When investment decisions need to consider the speed of light, something is seriously wrong.
— Frank M. Bifulco (Senior Portfolio Manager Alcott Capital Management, *Barron's Letters to the Editor*, 5/24/2010)

FRIDAY
24

D 38.1
S 52.4
N 61.9

Every man who knows how to read has it in his power to magnify himself, to multiply the ways in which he exists, to make his life full, significant and interesting.
— Aldous Huxley (English author, *Brave New World*, 1894–1963)

SATURDAY
25

February Almanac Investor Seasonalities: See Pages 92, 94, and 96

SUNDAY
26

FEBRUARY ALMANAC

FEBRUARY						
S	M	T	W	T	F	S
						1
2	3	4	5	6	7	8
9	10	11	12	13	14	15
16	17	18	19	20	21	22
23	24	25	26	27	28	

MARCH						
S	M	T	W	T	F	S
						1
2	3	4	5	6	7	8
9	10	11	12	13	14	15
16	17	18	19	20	21	22
23	24	25	26	27	28	29
30	31					

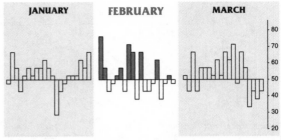

Market Probability Chart above is a graphic representation of the S&P 500 Recent Market Probability Calendar on page 124.

◆ February is the weak link in "Best Six Months" (pages 44, 48, & 147) ◆ RECENT RECORD: S&P up 7, down 8, average change −1.4% last 15 years ◆ Fifth best NASDAQ month in midterm election years average gain 0.6%, up 5, down 5 (page 157), #6 Dow, up 11, down 5, and #6 S&P, up 9, down 7 (pages 153 & 155) ◆ Day before Presidents' Day weekend S&P down 17 of 22, 11 straight 1992–2002, day after down 7 of last 13 (see pages 86 & 133) ◆ Many technicians modify market predictions based on January's market.

February Vital Statistics

	DJIA	S&P 500	NASDAQ	Russell 1K	Russell 2K
Rank	8	11	9	11	7
Up	37	35	23	21	20
Down	27	29	20	14	15
Average % Change	0.1%	−0.1%	0.5%	0.1%	1.0%
Midterm Year	0.9%	0.5%	0.6%	1.0%	1.6%
Best & Worst February					
	% Change	% Change	% Change	% Change	% Change
Best	1986 8.8	1986 7.1	2000 19.2	1986 7.2	2000 16.4
Worst	2009 −11.7	2009 −11.0	2001 −22.4	2009 −10.7	2009 −12.3
Best & Worst February Weeks					
Best	2/1/08 4.4	2/6/09 5.2	2/4/00 9.2	2/6/09 5.3	2/1/91 6.6
Worst	2/20/09 −6.2	2/20/09 −6.9	2/9/01 −7.1	2/20/09 −6.9	2/20/09 −8.3
Best & Worst February Days					
Best	2/24/09 3.3	2/24/09 4.0	2/11/99 4.2	2/24/09 4.1	2/24/09 4.5
Worst	2/10/09 −4.6	2/10/09 −4.9	2/16/01 −5.0	2/10/09 −4.8	2/10/09 −4.7
First Trading Day of Expiration Week: 1980–2013					
Record (#Up–#Down)	20–14	23–11	18–16	23–11	19–15
Current streak	D1	D1	D1	D1	D1
Avg % Change	0.28	0.23	0.01	0.20	0.04
Options Expiration Day: 1980–2013					
Record (#Up–#Down)	17–17	14–20	13–21	15–19	14–20
Current streak	U4	D1	D2	D1	D2
Avg % Change	−0.07	−0.15	−0.30	−0.15	−0.11
Options Expiration Week: 1980–2013					
Record (#Up–#Down)	20–14	18–16	17–17	17–17	21–13
Current streak	D1	U4	D1	U4	U4
Avg % Change	0.33	0.11	−0.05	0.11	0.15
Week After Options Expiration: 1980–2013					
Record (#Up–#Down)	15–19	15–19	18–16	15–19	17–17
Current streak	U2	D1	D1	D1	D6
Avg % Change	−0.37	−0.28	−0.26	−0.24	−0.17
First Trading Day Performance					
% of Time Up	62.5	62.5	72.1	68.6	68.6
Avg % Change	0.16	0.18	0.39	0.24	0.43
Last Trading Day Performance					
% of Time Up	50.0	56.3	53.5	57.1	60.0
Avg % Change	0.01	−0.01	−0.05	−0.05	0.12

Dow & S&P 1950–April 2013, NASDAQ 1971–April 2013, Russell 1K & 2K 1979–April 2013.

Either go short, or stay away the day before Presidents' Day.

JANUARY/FEBRUARY

MONDAY
D 61.9
S 52.4
N 42.9
27

Today's Ponzi-style acute fragility and speculative dynamics dictate that he who panics first panics best.
— Doug Noland (Prudent Bear Funds, *Credit Bubble Bulletin*, 10/26/07)

FOMC Meeting (2 Days)

TUESDAY
D 66.7
S 52.4
N 76.2
28

The worst crime against working people is a company that fails to make a profit.
— Samuel Gompers

🐂 **WEDNESDAY**
D 57.1
S 61.9
N 71.4
29

Foolish consistency is the hobgoblin of little minds.
— Ralph Waldo Emerson (American author, poet, and philosopher, *Self-Reliance*, 1803–1882)

THURSDAY
D 52.4
S 57.1
N 47.6
30

Even being right 3 or 4 times out of 10 should yield a person a fortune, if he has the sense to cut his losses quickly on the ventures where he has been wrong.
— Bernard Baruch (Financier, speculator, statesman, presidential adviser, 1870–1965)

"January Barometer" 88.9% Accurate (Page 16)
Almanac Investor Subscribers Emailed Official Results (See Insert)

🐻 **FRIDAY**
D 61.9
S 66.7
N 61.9
31

We're not believers that the government is bigger than the business cycle.
— David Rosenberg (Economist, Merrill Lynch, *Barron's*, 4/21/2008)

SATURDAY
1

SUNDAY
2

JOHN PERSON'S TOP TEN MARKET TIMING & STOCK SELECTION TOOLS

Excerpted from his most recent book effort, *Mastering the Stock Market: High Probability Market Timing & Stock Selection Tools* (Wiley, 2013), our 2014 Best Investment Book of the Year (see page 52), are John Person's (http://www.personsplanet.com/) top non-correlated, yet corroborating market timing and stock selection tools—in order of importance. We have summarized them here for handy reference, but you will still want to read the book to learn how to implement them and how to use them to their maximum capacity.

#1 SECTOR ANALYSIS
Smart money watches the various sectors for changes during the year and throughout a business cycle, as money rotates in and out of large capitalized dividend-yielding stocks, small-cap or mid-cap stocks, technology-weighted indexes, and other sectors such as transportation, pharmaceuticals, healthcare, consumer discretionary, and the many subsectors that each sector represents as described in the first two chapters of the book.

#2 SEASONAL TREND ANALYSIS
Various commodities and stocks undergo changes in supply and demand, which dictates prices. Traders often forget and need to understand these typical annual price swings. That is why it is important to use seasonal trend analysis to get into markets as the smart money is reentering—before the rest of the crowd.

#3 CONTRARIAN INDICATORS
If the adage is true that 80% of traders lose, then it follows that a trader would want to do the opposite of the masses. One of the best indicators for this purpose is the CFTC COT report. In a nutshell, it categorizes and measures the professional traders, commercial hedgers, and small speculators who are long or short the markets with actual money on the line with open positions.

#4 PRICE PATTERNS
Knowing when to hold or fold a trade is an age-old problem; that is why it is important to learn to identify bottoming, topping, and continuation patterns. Markets typically go from a trend condition into a consolidation pattern. Besides looking for these patterns in one time period, one technique is to look at higher-degree timeframes for these types of price patterns that are typical formations before a reversal or a resumption of a price move.

#5 MOMENTUM INDICATORS
Most of the popular indicators and oscillators are based on price components, specifically the closing price. Therefore, it is imperative to identify where the close of a current timeframe is in relationship to past price action. Higher closing prices attract more buyers, and the pace of price change adds fuel to the fire; the bottom line is traders need to utilize momentum indicators to find where money is flowing.

#6 VOLUME STUDIES
Higher prices should attract new buyers, which are reflected in an increase in volume. If a market moves without a surge in volume, then it could be assumed it may not be a sustainable move. That is why it is critical to incorporate volume analysis is one's trading.

#7 BREADTH INDICATORS
Most stock indices are capitalization weighted, meaning a small number of stocks can influence the daily price change of an index. To gauge the overall health of a market's move, it is imperative to see if a broad-based move is underway as the majority of stocks are moving in tandem with the specific index. This is why we use breadth or market internal indicators that measure the relationship of advancing and declining shares and those making new highs or lows.

#8 MOVING AVERAGE TOOLS
Moving averages are simply a trendline tool. Most traders simply look at a longer term closing price average like the 50-, 100-, and 200-day time period. We have so many other components available to us to give a quicker or more reliable response to price changes, such as the average of the high, low, and close, a moving average of percentage changes, rather than price changes, or an average of just the highs or lows, which gives us a view of channeling prices and breakouts or consolidations.

#9 SUPPORT AND RESISTANCE
Another old adage for traders is in bull markets buy pullbacks and in bear markets sell rallies. But there are not too many concrete methods to define what a *pullback* or a *rally* is and at what price level. That is why professional traders use support and resistance analysis. One of the best tools for identifying support and resistance areas that incorporates the timeframe as well as a specific level that the price might reach is the Person's Pivot Point Indicator.

#10 RISK MANAGEMENT, TRADE MANAGEMENT, AND POSITION SIZE
The market tends to let you in every loser, yet seldom lets people into winners; and it seems whenever you are wrong it is on a heavy position. That is why it is imperative to identify a correctly weighted position size and an exit strategy for every trade or investment you make.

FEBRUARY

First Day Trading in February, Dow and S&P Up 10 of Last 11
NASDAQ Up 9 Years in a Row

MONDAY
D 76.2
S 76.2
N 81.0
3

Any fool can buy. It is the wise man who knows how to sell.
— Albert W. Thomas (Trader, investor, *Over My Shoulder*, mutualfundmagic.com, *If It Doesn't Go Up, Don't Buy* It!, b. 1927)

TUESDAY
D 47.6
S 57.1
N 61.9
4

There is no one who can replace America. Without American leadership, there is no leadership. That puts a tremendous burden on the American people to do something positive. You can't be tempted by the usual nationalism.
— Lee Hong-koo (South Korean prime minister, 1994–1995, and ambassador to U.S., 1998–2000, *NY Times*, 2/25/2009)

WEDNESDAY
D 42.9
S 42.9
N 47.6
5

The principles of successful stock speculation are based on the supposition that people will continue in the future to make the mistakes that they have made in the past.
— Thomas F. Woodlock (*Wall Street Journal* editor and columnist, quoted in *Reminiscences of a Stock Operator*, 1866–1945)

THURSDAY
D 47.6
S 47.6
N 57.1
6

We are all born originals; why is it so many die copies?
— Edward Young (English poet, 1683–1765)

FRIDAY
D 57.1
S 52.4
N 57.1
7

Nothing is more uncertain than the favor of the crowd.
— Marcus Tullius Cicero (Great Roman orator, politician, 106–43 B.C.)

SATURDAY
8

SUNDAY
9

THE FOURTH YEAR OF DECADES

Fourth years have the fourth best record, but 2014 is a midterm election year, which has the second worst record of the four-year presidential election cycle. Of the last four midterm election years since the start of the Great Depression (1934, 1954, 1974, 1994) that were also fourth years, only 1954 was impressive.

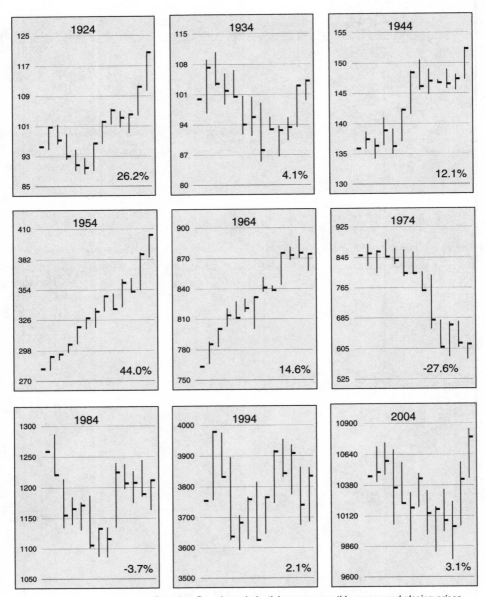

Based on Dow Jones industial average monthly ranges and closing prices

FEBRUARY

When new money is created on a grand scale, it must go somewhere and have some major consequences. One of these will be greatly increased volatility and instability in the economy and financial system.
— J. Anthony Boeckh, Ph.D (Chairman Bank Credit Analyst, 1968–2002, *The Great Reflation, Boeckh Investment Letter*)

Week Before February Expiration Week, NASDAQ Down 9 of Last 13, 2010 Up 2.0%, 2011 Up 1.5%

TUESDAY
D 57.1
S 42.9
N 42.9
11

I'm very big on having clarified principles. I don't believe in being reactive. You can't do that in the markets effectively. I can't. I need perspective. I need a game plan.
— Ray Dalio (Money manager, founder Bridgewater Associates, *Fortune*, 3/16/2009, b. 1949)

WEDNESDAY
D 57.1
S 71.4
N 57.1
12

You know a country is falling apart when even the government will not accept its own currency.
— Jim Rogers (Financier, *Adventure Capitalist*, b. 1942)

THURSDAY
D 61.9
S 66.7
N 57.1
13

If you want to raise a crop for one year, plant corn. If you want to raise a crop for decades, plant trees. If you want to raise a crop for centuries, raise men. If you want to plant a crop for eternities, raise democracies.
— Carl A. Schenck (German forester, 1868–1955)

Valentine's Day ♥
Day Before Presidents' Day Weekend, S&P Down 17 of Last 22

FRIDAY
D 42.9
S 38.1
N 57.1
14

Pretend that every single person you meet has a sign around his or her neck that says, "Make me feel important." Not only will you succeed in sales, you will succeed in life.
— Mary Kay Ash (Mary Kay Cosmetics)

SATURDAY
15

SUNDAY
16

MARKET CHARTS OF MIDTERM ELECTION YEARS

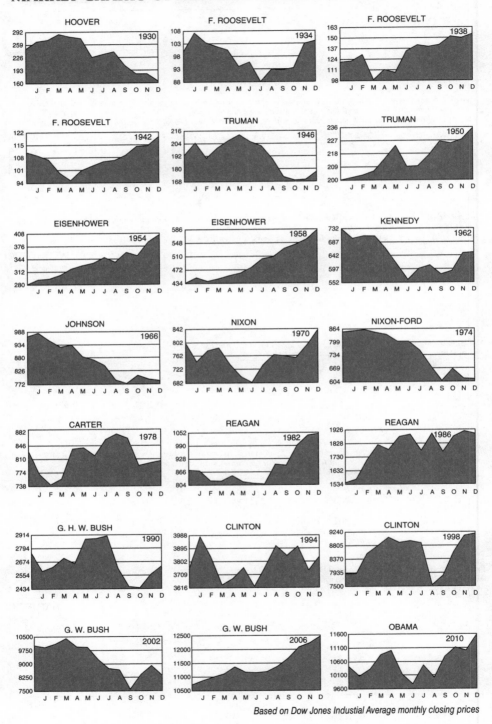

Based on Dow Jones Industial Average monthly closing prices

FEBRUARY

MONDAY

17

The only title in our democracy superior to that of president is the title of citizen.
— Louis D. Brandeis (U.S. Supreme Court Justice, 1916–1939, 1856–1941)

Day After Presidents' Day, S&P Down 7 of Last 13
First Trading Day of February Expiration Week, Dow Down 5 of Last 8

TUESDAY

D 61.9
S 66.7
N 52.4

18

Let me tell you the secret that has led me to my goal. My strength lies solely in my tenacity.
— Louis Pasteur (French chemist, founder of microbiology, 1822–1895)

WEDNESDAY

D 52.4
S 42.9
N 38.1

19

Another factor contributing to productivity is technology, particularly the rapid introduction of new microcomputers based on single-chip circuits.... The results over the next decade will be a second industrial revolution.
— Yale Hirsch (Creator of *Stock Trader's Almanac, Smart Money Newsletter*, 9/22/1976, b. 1923)

THURSDAY

D 38.1
S 42.9
N 47.6

20

Don't be overly concerned about your heirs. Usually, unearned funds do them more harm than good.
— Gerald M. Loeb (E.F. Hutton, *The Battle for Investment Survival*, predicted 1929 Crash, 1900–1974)

February Expiration Day, Dow Down 7 of Last 14, But Up Last 4

FRIDAY

D 52.4
S 47.6
N 38.1

21

To an imagination of any scope the most far-reaching form of power is not money, it is the command of ideas.
— Oliver Wendell Holmes Jr. (U.S. Supreme Court Justice, 1902–1932, *The Mind and Faith of Justice Holmes*, edited by Max Lerner, 1841–1935)

SATURDAY

22

March Almanac Investor Seasonalities: See Pages 92, 94, and 96

SUNDAY

23

MARCH ALMANAC

MARCH						
S	M	T	W	T	F	S
						1
2	3	4	5	6	7	8
9	10	11	12	13	14	15
16	17	18	19	20	21	22
23	24	25	26	27	28	29
30	31					

APRIL						
S	M	T	W	T	F	S
		1	2	3	4	5
6	7	8	9	10	11	12
13	14	15	16	17	18	19
20	21	22	23	24	25	26
27	28	29	30			

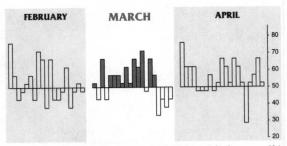

Market Probability Chart above is a graphic representation of the S&P 500 Recent Market Probability Calendar on page 124.

- ◆ Mid-month strength and late-month weakness are most evident above
- ◆ RECENT RECORD: S&P 20 up, 10 down, average gain 1.4%, third best
- ◆ Rather turbulent in recent years with wild fluctuations and large gains and losses ◆ March has been taking some mean end-of-quarter hits (page 134), down 1469 Dow points March 9–22, 2001 ◆ Last three or four days Dow a net loser 14 out of last 24 years ◆ NASDAQ hard hit in 2001, down 14.5% after 22.4% drop in February ◆ Third best NASDAQ month during midterm election years average gain 2.1%, up 7, down 3.

March Vital Statistics

	DJIA	S&P 500	NASDAQ	Russell 1K	Russell 2K
Rank	6	4	5	5	5
Up	42	42	28	24	26
Down	22	22	15	11	9
Average % Change	1.1%	1.2%	0.9%	1.2%	1.4%
Midterm Year	1.3%	1.4%	2.1%	2.2%	3.3%
Best & Worst March					
	% Change	% Change	% Change	% Change	% Change
Best	2000 7.8	2000 9.7	2009 10.9	2000 8.9	1979 9.7
Worst	1980 −9.0	1980 −10.2	1980 −17.1	1980 −11.5	1980 −18.5
Best & Worst March Weeks					
Best	3/13/09 9.0	3/13/09 10.7	3/13/09 10.6	3/13/09 10.7	3/13/09 12.0
Worst	3/16/01 −7.7	3/6/09 −7.0	3/16/01 −7.9	3/6/09 −7.1	3/6/09 −9.8
Best & Worst March Days					
Best	3/23/09 6.8	3/23/09 7.1	3/10/09 7.1	3/23/09 7.0	3/23/09 8.4
Worst	3/2/09 −4.2	3/2/09 −4.7	3/12/01 −6.3	3/2/09 −4.8	3/27/80 −6.0
First Trading Day of Expiration Week: 1980–2013					
Record (#Up–#Down)	22–12	22–12	15–19	20–14	17–17
Current streak	U2	U2	U1	U1	U1
Avg % Change	0.14	0.01	−0.35	−0.04	−0.37
Options Expiration Day: 1980–2013					
Record (#Up–#Down)	18–16	20–14	16–18	18–16	15–18
Current streak	D2	D1	D2	D1	D2
Avg % Change	0.06	0.001	−0.04	0.001	−0.06
Options Expiration Week: 1980–2013					
Record (#Up–#Down)	23–10	22–12	20–14	21–13	18–16
Current streak	U2	U2	U2	U2	U2
Avg % Change	0.86	0.70	−0.04	0.63	0.13
Week After Options Expiration: 1980–2013					
Record (#Up–#Down)	15–19	12–22	18–16	12–22	17–17
Current streak	D2	D2	D1	D2	D2
Avg % Change	−0.20	−0.09	0.17	−0.09	0.13
First Trading Day Performance					
% of Time Up	67.2	64.1	62.8	60.0	65.7
Avg % Change	0.15	0.15	0.22	0.11	0.18
Last Trading Day Performance					
% of Time Up	42.2	40.6	65.1	48.6	82.9
Avg % Change	−0.10	0.001	0.18	0.10	0.37

Dow & S&P 1950–April 2013, NASDAQ 1971–April 2013, Russell 1K & 2K 1979–April 2013.

March has Ides and St. Patrick's Day;
Begins bullishly, then fades away.

🦬 **MONDAY**
D 57.1
S 61.9
N 57.1 **24**

Some men see things as they are and say "why?" I dream things that never were and say "why not?"
— George Bernard Shaw (Irish dramatist, 1856–1950)

End of February Miserable in Recent Years (Pages 20 and 133)

🐻 **TUESDAY**
D 33.3
S 38.1
N 52.4 **25**

Always grab the reader by the throat in the first paragraph, sink your thumbs into his windpipe in the second, and hold him against the wall until the tag line.
— Paul O'Neil (Marketer, *Writing Changes Everything*)

WEDNESDAY
D 42.9
S 47.6
N 52.4 **26**

The market is a voting machine, whereon countless individuals register choices which are the product partly of reason and partly of emotion.
— Graham & Dodd

Week After February Expiration Week, Dow Down 10 of Last 15

THURSDAY
D 42.9
S 52.4
N 52.4 **27**

The facts are unimportant! It's what they are perceived to be that determines the course of events.
— R. Earl Hadady (*Bullish Consensus, Contrary Opinion*)

FRIDAY
D 42.9
S 47.6
N 38.1 **28**

The words "I am…" are potent words; be careful what you hitch them to. The thing you're claiming has a way of reaching back and claiming you.
— A. L. Kitselman (Author, math teacher)

SATURDAY
1

SUNDAY
2

MIDTERM ELECTION YEARS: WHERE BOTTOM PICKERS FIND PARADISE

American presidents have danced the Quadrennial Quadrille over the past two centuries. After the midterm congressional election and the invariable seat loss by his party, the president during the next two years jiggles fiscal policies to get federal spending, disposable income, and social security benefits up and interest rates and inflation down. By Election Day, he will have danced his way into the wallets and hearts of the electorate and, hopefully, will have choreographed four more years in the White House for his party.

After the Inaugural Ball is over, however, we pay the piper. Practically all bear markets began and ended in the two years after presidential elections. Bottoms often occurred in an air of crisis: the Cuban Missile Crisis in 1962, tight money in 1966, Cambodia in 1970, Watergate and Nixon's resignation in 1974, and threat of international monetary collapse in 1982. But remember, the word for "crisis" in Chinese is composed of two characters: the first, the symbol for danger; the second, opportunity. In the last 13 quadrennial cycles since 1961, 9 of the 14 bear markets bottomed in the midterm year. *See pages 131–132 for further detail.*

THE RECORD SINCE 1914

1914	Wilson (D)	Bottom in July. War closed markets.
1918	Wilson (D)	**Bottom 12 days prior to start of year.**
1922	Harding (R)	**Bottom 4-1/2 months prior to start of year.**
1926	Coolidge (R)	Only drop (7 wks, −17%) ends Mar. 30.
1930	Hoover (R)	**'29 Crash continues through 1930. No bottom.**
1934	Roosevelt (D)	1st Roosevelt bear, Feb to July 26 bottom (−23%).
1938	Roosevelt (D)	Big 1937 break ends in March, DJI off 49%.
1942	Roosevelt (D)	World War II bottom in April.
1946	Truman (D)	Market tops in May, bottoms in October.
1950	Truman (D)	June 1949 bottom, June 1950 Korean War outbreak causes 14% drop.
1954	Eisenhower (R)	**September 1953 bottom, then straight up.**
1958	Eisenhower (R)	**October 1957 bottom, then straight up.**
1962	Kennedy (D)	Bottoms in June and October.
1966	Johnson (D)	Bottom in October.
1970	Nixon (R)	Bottom in May.
1974	Nixon, Ford (R)	December Dow bottom, S&P bottom in October.
1978	Carter (D)	March bottom, despite October massacre later.
1982	Reagan (R)	Bottom in August.
1986	Reagan (R)	**No bottom in 1985 or 1986.**
1990	Bush (R)	Bottom October 11 (Kuwaiti Invasion).
1994	Clinton (D)	Bottom April 4 after 10% drop.
1998	Clinton (D)	October 8 bottom (Asian currency crisis, hedge fund debacle).
2002	Bush, GW (R)	October 9 bottom (Corp. malfeasance, terrorism, Iraq).
2006	Bush, GW (R)	**No bottom in 2006** (Iraq success, credit bubble).
2010	Obama (D)	**No bear**, July low, −13.6% from April high.

Bold = No bottom in midterm election year

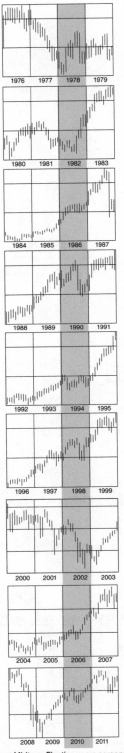

Graph shows Midterm-Election years screened
Based on Dow Jones industial average monthly ranges

First Trading Day in March, Dow Down 4 of Last 7, −4.2% in 2009, 1996–2006 Up 9 of 11

MONDAY
D 57.1
S 52.4
N 52.4
3

Don't delay! A good plan, violently executed now, is better than a perfect plan next week. War is a very simple thing, [like stock trading] and the determining characteristics are self-confidence, speed, and audacity.
— General George S. Patton, Jr. (U.S. Army field commander WWII, 1885–1945)

March Historically Strong Early in the Month (Pages 28 and 134)

TUESDAY
D 47.6
S 42.9
N 33.3
4

Ideas are easy; it's execution that's hard.
— Jeff Bezos (Amazon.com)

Ash Wednesday

WEDNESDAY
D 57.1
S 66.7
N 66.7
5

If we did all the things we are capable of doing, we would literally astound ourselves.
— Thomas Alva Edison (American inventor, 1093 patents, 1847–1931)

THURSDAY
D 38.1
S 42.9
N 38.1
6

It doesn't pay to anticipate the correction; there are already plenty who have been carried out on their shields trying to do that. Rather, we will wait for some confirmed sell signals before altering our still-bullish view.
— Lawrence G. McMillan (Professional trader, author, Registered Investment Advisor, speaker, educator, OptionStrategist.com, b. 1946)

FRIDAY
D 61.9
S 57.1
N 47.6
7

I have a simple philosophy. Fill what's empty. Empty what's full. And scratch where it itches.
— Alice Roosevelt Longworth

SATURDAY
8

Daylight Saving Time Begins

SUNDAY
9

PROSPERITY MORE THAN PEACE DETERMINES OUTCOME OF MIDTERM CONGRESSIONAL RACES

Though the stock market in presidential election years very often is able to predict if the party in power will retain or lose the White House, the outcome of congressional races in midterm years is another matter entirely. Typically, the President's party will lose a number of House seats in these elections (1934, 1998, and 2002 were exceptions). It is considered a victory for the President when his party loses a small number of seats, and a repudiation of sorts when a large percentage of seats is lost.

The table below would seem to indicate that there is no relationship between the stock market's behavior in the ten months prior to the midterm election and the magnitude of seats lost in the House. Roaring bull markets preceded the elections of 1954 and 1958, yet Republicans lost few seats during one, and a huge number in the other.

If the market does not offer a clue to the outcome of House races, does anything besides the popularity and performance of the Administration? Yes! In the two years prior to the elections in the first ten midterm years listed, no war or major recession began. As a result, the percentage of House seats lost was minimal. A further observation is that the market gained ground in the last seven weeks of the year, except 2002.

Our five major wars began under four Democrats and one Republican in the shaded area. The percentage of seats lost was greater during these midterm elections. But the eight worst repudiations of the President are at the bottom of the list. These were preceded by: the sick economy in 1930, the botched health proposals in 1994, the severe recession in 1937, the post-war contraction in 1946, the recession in 1957, financial crisis and the second worst bear market in history from 2007 to 2009, Watergate in 1974, and rumors of corruption (Teapot Dome) in 1922. **Obviously, prosperity is of greater importance to the electorate than peace!**

LAST 24 MIDTERM ELECTIONS RANKED BY % LOSS OF SEATS BY PRESIDENT'S PARTY

	% Seats Gained or Lost	Year	President	Dow Jones Industrials Jan 1 to Elec Day	Elec Day to Dec 31	Year's CPI % Change
1	3.6 %	2002	R: G.W. Bush	−14.5 %	−2.7 %	1.6 %
2	2.9	1934	D: Roosevelt	−3.8	8.3	1.5
3	2.4	1998	D: Clinton	10.1	5.5	1.6
4	−1.5	1962	D: Kennedy	−16.5	6.8	1.3
5	−2.7	1986	R: Reagan	22.5	0.1	1.1
6	−4.0	1926	R: Coolidge	−3.9	4.4	−1.1
7	−4.6	1990	R: G.H.W. Bush	−9.1	5.3	6.1
8	−5.1	1978	D: Carter	−3.7	0.6	9.0
9	−6.3	1970	R: Nixon	−5.3	10.7	5.6
10	−8.1	1954	R: Eisenhower	26.0	14.2	−0.7
11	−9.0	1918	D: Wilson (WW1)	15.2	−4.1	20.4
12	−11.0	1950	D: Truman (Korea)	11.2	−5.8	5.9
13	−12.9	2006	R: G.W. Bush (Iraq)	13.4	2.5	2.6
14	−13.5	1982	R: Reagan	14.9	4.1	3.8
15	−15.9	1966	D: Johnson (Vietnam)	−17.2	−2.1	3.5
16	−16.9	1942	D: Roosevelt (WW2)	3.4	4.1	9.0
17	−18.4	1930	R: Hoover	−25.4	−11.2	−6.4
18	−20.9	1994	D: Clinton	1.5	0.7	2.7
19	−21.3	1938	D: Roosevelt	28.2	−0.1	−2.8
20	−22.6	1946	D: Truman	−9.6	1.6	18.1
21	−23.9	1958	R: Eisenhower	25.1	7.1	1.8
22	−24.6	2010	D: Obama	7.3	3.5	1.5
23	−25.0	1974	R: Ford	−22.8	−6.2	12.3
24	−25.0	1922	R: Harding	21.4	0.3	−2.3

Try it FREE for 30 Days!

Profit from History with The Almanac Investor The #1 Authority on Stock Market Cycles

Make the most of every trade with The Almanac Investor, including:

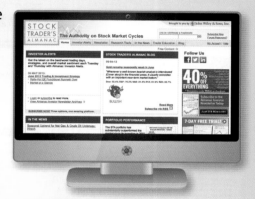

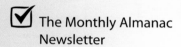 The Monthly Almanac Newsletter

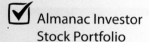 Almanac Investor Stock Portfolio

☑ 2x a week Almanac Alert

Rely on the #1 expert of market history, trends, and tradeable insights to guide you through today's dynamic markets. Start improving your entries and exits, learn to see cyclical trends hidden in signal data, and gain trading confidence with detailed weekly email Alerts, website calculators and tools, and so much more.

Stock Trader's Almanac editor Jeffrey Hirsch appears regularly on CNBC, Yahoo! Finance, and other financial media.

Get started with 30 Days FREE today!
>go to **stocktradersalmanac.com/30daysfree**

TRY IT FREE for 30 DAYS!
>go to **stocktradersalmanac.com/30daysfree**

☑ Model Portfolio up 322% since inception

☑ 40+ years of proven market analysis

☑ Trading Alerts reveal opportunities/dangers

☑ And much more!

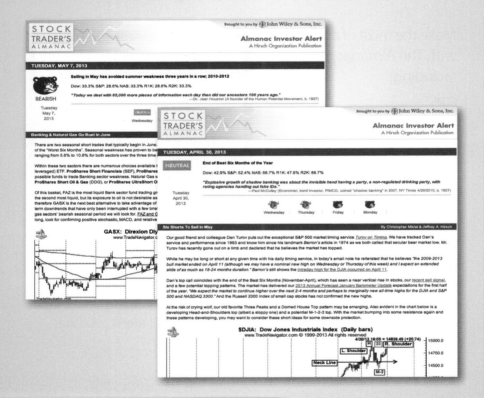

"I know of no other market timing system that comes close to that strong of a statistical foundation."

—Mark Hubert

STOCK
TRADER'S
ALMANAC

MARCH

Monday Before March Triple Witching, Dow Up 19 of Last 26

MONDAY
D 47.6
S 57.1
N 47.6
10

What's money? A man is a success if he gets up in the morning and goes to bed at night and in between does what he wants to do.
— Bob Dylan (American singer-songwriter, musician, and artist, b. 1941)

TUESDAY
D 66.7
S 57.1
N 52.4
11

Individualism, private property, the law of accumulation of wealth and the law of competition…are the highest result of human experience, the soil in which, so far, has produced the best fruit.
— Andrew Carnegie (Scottish-born U.S. industrialist, philanthropist, *The Gospel of Wealth*, 1835–1919)

Dow Down 1469 Points March 9–22 in 2001

WEDNESDAY
D 61.9
S 52.4
N 47.6
12

The four horsemen of the Investment Apocalypse are fear, greed, hope and ignorance. And notice, only one of the four is not an emotion – ignorance. These four things have accounted for more losses in the market than any recession or depression, and they will never change. Even if you correct ignorance, the other three will get you every time.
— James P. O'Shaughnessy (Chairman and CEO at O'Shaughnessy Asset Management, b. 1960)

THURSDAY
D 47.6
S 61.9
N 66.7
13

Cannot people realize how large an income is thrift?
— Marcus Tullius Cicero (Great Roman orator, politician, 106–43 B.C.)

FRIDAY
D 66.7
S 52.4
N 52.4
14

All free governments are managed by the combined wisdom and folly of the people.
— James A. Garfield (20th U.S. President, 1831–1881)

SATURDAY
15

SUNDAY
16

HOW TO TRADE BEST MONTHS SWITCHING STRATEGIES

Our Best Months Switching Strategies found on pages 48, 50, 58, and 60 are simple and reliable with a proven 63-year track record. Thus far we have failed to find a similar trading strategy that even comes close over the past six decades. And to top it off, the strategy has only been improving since we first discovered it in 1986.

Exogenous factors and cultural shifts must be considered. "Backward" tests that go back to 1925 or even 1896 and conclude that the pattern does not work are best ignored. They do not take into account these factors. Farming made August the best month from 1900–1951. Since 1987 it is the second worst month of the year for Dow and S&P. Panic caused by financial crisis in 2007–08 caused every asset class aside from U.S. Treasuries to decline substantially. But the bulk of the major decline in equities in the worst months of 2008 was sidestepped using these strategies.

Our Best Months Switching Strategy will not make you an instant millionaire as other strategies claim they can do. What it will do is steadily build wealth over time with half the risk (or less) of a "buy and hold" approach.

A sampling of tradable funds for the Best and Worst Months appears in the table below. These are just a starting point and only skim the surface of possible trading vehicles currently to take advantage these strategies. Your specific situation and risk tolerance will dictate a suitable choice. If you are trading in a tax-advantaged account such as a company-sponsored 401(k) or Individual Retirement Account (IRA), your investment options may be limited to what has been selected by your employer or IRA administrator. But if you are a self-directed trader with a brokerage account, then you likely have unlimited choices (perhaps too many).

TRADABLE BEST AND WORST MONTHS SWITCHING STRATEGY FUNDS

Best Months		Worst Months	
Exchange Traded Funds (ETF)		**Exchange Traded Funds (ETF)**	
Symbol	Name	Symbol	Name
DIA	SPDR Dow Jones Industrial Average	SHY	iShares Barclays 1–3 Year Treasury Bond
SPY	SPDR S&P 500	IEI	iShares Barclays 3–7 Year Treasury Bond
QQQ	PowerShares QQQ	IEF	iShares Barclays 7–10 Year Treasury Bond
IWM	iShares Russell 2000	TLT	iShares Barclays 20+ Year Treasury Bond
Mutual Funds		**Mutual Funds**	
Symbol	Name	Symbol	Name
VWNDX	Vanguard Windsor Fund	VFSTX	Vanguard Short-Term Investment-Grade Bond Fund
FMAGX	Fidelity Magellan Fund	FBNDX	Fidelity Investment Grade Bond Fund
AMCPX	American Funds AMCAP Fund	ABNDX	American Funds Bond Fund of America
FKCGX	Franklin Flex Cap Growth Fund	FKUSX	Franklin U.S. Government Securities Fund
SECEX	Guggenheim Large Cap Core Fund	SIUSX	Guggenheim U.S. Intermediate Bond Fund

Generally speaking, during the Best Months you want to be invested in equities that offer similar exposure to the companies that constitute Dow, S&P 500, and NASDAQ indices. These would typically be large-cap growth and value stocks as well as technology concerns. Reviewing the holdings of a particular ETF or mutual fund and comparing them to the index members is an excellent way to correlate.

During the Worst Months switch into Treasury bonds, money market funds, or a bear/short fund. **Grizzly Short** (GRZZX) and **Ranger Equity Bear** (HDGE) are two possible choices. Money market funds will be the safest, but are likely to offer the smallest return, while bear/short funds offer potentially greater returns, but more risk. If the market moves sideways or higher during the Worst Months, a bear/short fund is likely to lose money. Treasuries offer a combination of decent returns with limited risk.

Additional Worst Month possibilities include precious metals and the companies that mine them. **SPDR Gold Shares** (GLD), **Market Vectors Gold Miners** (GDX), and **ETF Securities Physical Swiss Gold** (SGOL) are a few well recognized names available from the ETF universe.

Become an *Almanac Investor*

Almanac Investor subscribers receive specific buy and sell recommendations based upon the Best Months Switching Strategies online and via email. Sector Index Seasonalities, found on page 92, are also put into action throughout the year with ETF recommendations. Buy limits, stop losses, and auto-sell price points for the majority of seasonal trades are delivered directly to your inbox. Visit www.stocktradersalmanac.com or see the insert for details and a special offer for new subscribers.

St. Patrick's Day ☘

Bullish Cluster Highlights March's "Sweet Spot"

MONDAY
D 66.7
S 66.7
N 47.6
17

A cynic is a man who knows the price of everything and the value of nothing.
— Oscar Wilde (Irish-born writer and wit, 1845–1900)

FOMC Meeting (2 Days)

TUESDAY
D 57.1
S 61.9
N 61.9
18

It is the growth of total government spending as a percentage of gross national product—not the way it is financed—that crowds out the private sector.
— Paul Craig Roberts (*Business Week*, 1984)

WEDNESDAY
D 61.9
S 71.4
N 66.7
19

It is a funny thing about life; if you refuse to accept anything but the best, you very often get it.
— W. Somerset Maugham

THURSDAY
D 61.9
S 47.6
N 61.9
20

With respect to trading Sugar futures, if they give it away for free at restaurants you probably don't want to be trading it.
— John L. Person (Professional trader, author, and speaker, *Commodity Trader's Almanac*, nationalfutures.com, 2/22/2011, TradersExpo, b. 1961)

March Triple Witching Day Mixed Last 12 Years
Dow Down 4 of Last 5

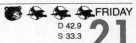
FRIDAY
D 42.9
S 33.3
N 52.4
21

English stocks…are springing up like mushrooms this year…forced up to a quite unreasonable level and then, for the most part, collapse. In this way, I have made over 400 pounds…[Speculating] makes small demands on one's time, and it's worth while running some risk in order to relieve the enemy of his money.
— Karl Marx (German social philosopher and revolutionary, in an 1864 letter to his uncle, 1818–1883)

SATURDAY
22

SUNDAY
23

NEW MILLENNIUM SEASONAL & SECTOR TRADES

After seven lucky years of producing the *Commodity Trader's Almanac* with our co-author John Person (see pages 3, 22, and 52) in conjunction with Wiley we are responding to the more fast-paced active trading marketplace and in the process of converting it from an annual almanac to a digital-only report issued four times per year.

The *Seasonal & Sector Swing Trader* will provide timely and actionable trade recommendations and research, alerting active traders to major swing trades each month. It will include the preeminent aspects and features of the *Commodity Trader's Almanac* without the desk calendar components. Each issue will provide a precise map of which sectors, markets, stocks, ETFs, and strategies market history suggests are poised for large moves and have set up well for the current period. Here are two examples of the top trades we expect to deliver to readers.

A DIFFERENT "SELL IN MAY" SEASONAL TRADE

You can take advantage of seasonal May–October weakness using an option strategy on a leveraged inverse ETF. These are the hybrid products of the 21st century. The **Direxion Daily Small Cap Bear 3X** (TZA) correlates to three times the daily move of the small-cap index, but moves opposite of the underlying market. TZA tracks the Russell 2000 index of small-cap stocks, which means if the Russell 2000 declines, then TZA would move up in value.

TZA often provides a solid risk/reward opportunity to apply risk capital for a seasonal short trade for the overall stock market. If the Advanced–Decline line on the Russell 2000 flashes a significant bearish divergence pattern and the small-cap sector begins to significantly underperform the overall market as indicated by a breakdown in the relative strength chart as we enter the seasonally weak time period for stocks, you can consider an advanced options trading strategy such as a vertical bull call spread on TZA.

CRUDE OIL STRIKES A WINNER IN FEBRUARY

Crude oil has a tendency to bottom in mid-February and then rally through mid-May. It is that early February break that can give traders an edge by buying low in a seasonally strong period. In the 30-year history, this trade has worked 24 years for an 80.0% win ratio with a cumulative profit of $88,790 (based upon a single futures contract excluding commissions and taxes). This trade has the second highest win ratio of all our commodity-based sector seasonality swing trades.

Seasonal influence that causes crude oil to move higher in this time period is partly due to continuing demand for heating oil and diesel fuel in the northern states and partly due to the shutdown of refinery operations in order to switch production facilities from producing heating oil to reformulated unleaded gasoline in anticipation of heavy demand for the upcoming summer driving season. This has refiners buying crude oil in order to ramp up the production for gasoline.

An outright long futures position (July contract) is the direct method to take advantage of crude oil's seasonal strength, and of course, there are plenty other alternatives for traders without futures accounts. Stock traders can use exchange-traded funds (ETF) such as **United States Oil Fund** (USO) or **PowerShares DB Oil** (DBO), which both hold actual crude oil futures contracts and offer a direct path to trade this commodity-based seasonality. **SPDR Energy** (XLE) and **iShares S&P Global Energy** (IXC) track the **Amex Oil index** (XOI), which is a stock index and not the actual commodity. Options on these ETFs or highly-correlated stocks like **Exxon** (XOM) and **Chevron** (CVX) or other refinery stocks that have a direct price correlation to the underlying futures market also make excellent choices.

MARCH

Week After Triple Witching, Dow Down 17 of Last 26, 2000 Up 4.9%,
2007 Up 3.1%, 2009 Up 6.8%, 2011 Up 3.1%, Up 6 of Last 10

MONDAY
D 42.9
S 66.7
N 61.9
24

Life is like riding a bicycle. You don't fall off unless you stop peddling.
— Claude D. Pepper (U.S. Senator, Florida, 1936–1951, 1900–1989)

TUESDAY
D 57.1
S 57.1
N 66.7
25

The higher a people's intelligence and moral strength, the lower will be the prevailing rate of interest.
— Eugen von Bohm-Bawerk (Austrian economist, *Capital and Interest*, 1851–1914)

March Historically Weak Later in the Month (Pages 28 and 134)

WEDNESDAY
D 28.6
S 33.3
N 38.1
26

Establish a no excuse environment—you will find your own quality will increase as well.
— Jordan Kimmel (Portfolio manager Magnet AE Fund, b. 1958)

THURSDAY
D 47.6
S 42.9
N 38.1
27

There have been three great inventions since the beginning of time: fire, the wheel, and central banking.
— Will Rogers (American humorist and showman, 1879–1935)

FRIDAY
D 57.1
S 38.1
N 42.9
28

Age is a question of mind over matter. If you don't mind, it doesn't matter.
— Leroy Robert "Satchel" Paige (Negro League and Hall of Fame pitcher, 1906–1982)

SATURDAY
29

April Almanac Investor Seasonalities: See Pages 92, 94, and 96

SUNDAY
30

APRIL ALMANAC

APRIL						
S	M	T	W	T	F	S
		1	2	3	4	5
6	7	8	9	10	11	12
13	14	15	16	17	18	19
20	21	22	23	24	25	26
27	28	29	30			

MAY						
S	M	T	W	T	F	S
				1	2	3
4	5	6	7	8	9	10
11	12	13	14	15	16	17
18	19	20	21	22	23	24
25	26	27	28	29	30	31

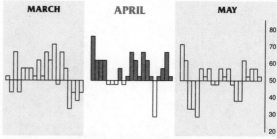

Market Probability Chart above is a graphic representation of the S&P 500 Recent Market Probability Calendar on page 124.

◆ April is still the best Dow month (average 2.0%) since 1950 (page 44) ◆ April 1999, first month ever to gain 1000 Dow points, 856 in 2001, knocked off its high horse in 2002, down 458, 2003 up 488 ◆ Up eight straight, average gain 3.4% ◆ Prone to weakness after mid-month tax deadline ◆ Stocks anticipate great first-quarter earnings by rising sharply before earnings are reported, rather than after ◆ Rarely a dangerous month, recent exceptions are 2002, 2004, and 2005 ◆ "Best Six Months" of the year end with April (page 48) ◆ Midterm year Aprils weaker since 1950 (Dow 0.8%, S&P 0.2%, NASDAQ 0.04%) ◆ End of April NASDAQ strength (pages 125 & 126).

April Vital Statistics

	DJIA		S&P 500		NASDAQ		Russell 1K		Russell 2K	
Rank	1		2		3		1		3	
Up	42		44		28		23		22	
Down	22		20		15		12		13	
Average % Change	2.0%		1.5%		1.5%		1.6%		1.7%	
Midterm Year	0.8%		0.2%		0.04%		−0.1%		1.3%	
Best & Worst April										
		% Change		% Change		% Change		% Change		% Change
Best	1978	10.6	2009	9.4	2001	15.0	2009	10.0	2009	15.3
Worst	1970	−6.3	1970	−9.0	2000	−15.6	2002	−5.8	2000	−6.1
Best & Worst April Weeks										
Best	4/11/75	5.7	4/20/00	5.8	4/12/01	14.0	4/20/00	5.9	4/3/09	6.3
Worst	4/14/00	−7.3	4/14/00	−10.5	4/14/00	−25.3	4/14/00	−11.2	4/14/00	−16.4
Best & Worst April Days										
Best	4/5/01	4.2	4/5/01	4.4	4/5/01	8.9	4/5/01	4.6	4/9/09	5.9
Worst	4/14/00	−5.7	4/14/00	−5.8	4/14/00	−9.7	4/14/00	−6.0	4/14/00	−7.3
First Trading Day of Expiration Week: 1980–2013										
Record (#Up–#Down)	21–13		19–15		18–16		18–16		14–20	
Current streak	D1		D3		D3		D3		D1	
Avg % Change	0.19		0.11		0.10		0.09		−0.04	
Options Expiration Day: 1980–2013										
Record (#Up–#Down)	24–10		23–11		20–14		23–11		22–12	
Current streak	U3		U3		U1		U3		U3	
Avg % Change	0.24		0.22		0.001		0.21		0.24	
Options Expiration Week: 1980–2013										
Record (#Up–#Down)	27–7		24–10		22–12		22–12		25–9	
Current streak	D1		D1		D3		D1		D1	
Avg % Change	1.08		0.85		0.90		0.82		0.74	
Week After Options Expiration: 1980–2013										
Record (#Up–#Down)	23–11		23–11		25–9		23–11		23–11	
Current streak	U4		U4		U7		U4		U4	
Avg % Change	0.43		0.41		0.68		0.42		0.89	
First Trading Day Performance										
% of Time Up	59.4		62.5		46.5		60.0		48.6	
Avg % Change	0.17		0.14		−0.14		0.17		−0.09	
Last Trading Day Performance										
% of Time Up	51.6		56.3		67.4		57.1		68.6	
Avg % Change	0.10		0.09		0.19		0.09		0.14	

Dow & S&P 1950–April 2013, NASDAQ 1971–April 2013, Russell 1K & 2K 1979–April 2013.

April "Best Month" for Dow since 1950;
Day-before-Good Friday gains are nifty.

Last Trading Day of March, Dow Down 15 of Last 25
Russell 2000 Up 14 of Last 19

MONDAY

D 38.1
S 42.9
N 57.1

31

Whatever method you use to pick stocks…, your ultimate success or failure will depend on your ability to ignore the worries of the world long enough to allow your investments to succeed. It isn't the head but the stomach that determines the fate of the stockpicker.
— Peter Lynch (Fidelity Investments, *Beating the Street*, 1994)

First Trading Day in April, Dow Up 15 of Last 19

TUESDAY

D 81.0
S 76.2
N 61.9

1

In the history of the financial markets, arrogance has destroyed far more capital than stupidity.
— Jason Trennert (Managing Partner, Strategas Research Partners, March 27, 2006)

Start Looking for the Dow and S&P MACD SELL Signal (Pages 48 and 50)
Almanac Investor Subscribers Emailed When It Triggers (See Insert)

WEDNESDAY

D 61.9
S 61.9
N 52.4

2

The most important lesson in investing is humility.
— Sir John Templeton (Founder Templeton Funds, philanthropist, 1912–2008)

THURSDAY

D 52.4
S 61.9
N 71.4

3

Some people say we can't compete with Intel. I say, like hell you can't….Dominant companies usually don't change unless they're forced to do so.
— David Patterson (Chip designing force behind R.I.S.C. and R.A.I.D., *WSJ*, 8/28/98)

FRIDAY

D 66.7
S 61.9
N 57.1

4

War is God's way of teaching Americans geography.
— Ambrose Bierce (Writer, satirist, Civil War hero, *The Devil's Dictionary*, 1842–1914?)

SATURDAY

5

SUNDAY

6

THE DECEMBER LOW INDICATOR: A USEFUL PROGNOSTICATING TOOL

When the Dow closes below its December closing low in the first quarter, it is frequently an excellent warning sign. Jeffrey Saut, managing director of investment strategy at Raymond James, brought this to our attention a few years ago. The December Low Indicator was originated by Lucien Hooper, a *Forbes* columnist and Wall Street analyst back in the 1970s. Hooper dismissed the importance of January and January's first week as reliable indicators. He noted that the trend could be random or even manipulated during a holiday-shortened week. Instead, said Hooper, "Pay much more attention to the December low. If that low is violated during the first quarter of the New Year, watch out!"

Eighteen of the 32 occurrences were followed by gains for the rest of the year—and 16 full-year gains—after the low for the year was reached. For perspective we've included the January Barometer readings for the selected years. Hooper's "Watch Out" warning was absolutely correct, though. All but two of the instances since 1952 experienced further declines, as the Dow fell an additional 10.9% on average when December's low was breached in Q1.

Only three significant drops occurred (not shown) when December's low was not breached in Q1 (1974, 1981, and 1987). Both indicators were wrong only five times, and nine years ended flat. If the December low is not crossed, turn to our January Barometer for guidance. It has been virtually perfect, right nearly 100% of these times (view the complete results at *www.stocktradersalmanac.com*).

YEARS DOW FELL BELOW DECEMBER LOW IN FIRST QUARTER

Year	Previous Dec Low	Date Crossed	Crossing Price	Subseq. Low	% Change Cross-Low	Rest of Year % Change	Full Year % Change	Jan Bar
1952	262.29	2/19/52	261.37	256.35	−1.9%	11.7%	8.4%	1.6%[2]
1953	281.63	2/11/53	281.57	255.49	−9.3	−0.2	−3.8	−0.7[3]
1956	480.72	1/9/56	479.74	462.35	−3.6	4.1	2.3	−3.6[1, 2, 3]
1957	480.61	1/18/57	477.46	419.79	−12.1	−8.7	−12.8	−4.2
1960	661.29	1/12/60	660.43	566.05	−14.3	−6.7	−9.3	−7.1
1962	720.10	1/5/62	714.84	535.76	−25.1	−8.8	−10.8	−3.8
1966	939.53	3/1/66	938.19	744.32	−20.7	−16.3	−18.9	0.5[1]
1968	879.16	1/22/68	871.71	825.13	−5.3	8.3	4.3	−4.4[1, 2, 3]
1969	943.75	1/6/69	936.66	769.93	−17.8	−14.6	−15.2	−0.8
1970	769.93	1/26/70	768.88	631.16	−17.9	9.1	4.8	−7.6[2, 3]
1973	1000.00	1/29/73	996.46	788.31	−20.9	−14.6	−16.6	−1.7
1977	946.64	2/7/77	946.31	800.85	−15.4	−12.2	−17.3	−5.1
1978	806.22	1/5/78	804.92	742.12	−7.8	0.01	−3.1	−6.2[3]
1980	819.62	3/10/80	818.94	759.13	−7.3	17.7	14.9	5.8[2]
1982	868.25	1/5/82	865.30	776.92	−10.2	20.9	19.6	−1.8[1, 2]
1984	1236.79	1/25/84	1231.89	1086.57	−11.8	−1.6	−3.7	−0.9[3]
1990	2687.93	1/15/90	2669.37	2365.10	−11.4	−1.3	−4.3	−6.9[3]
1991	2565.59	1/7/91	2522.77	2470.30	−2.1	25.6	20.3	4.2[2]
1993	3255.18	1/8/93	3251.67	3241.95	−0.3	15.5	13.7	0.7[2]
1994	3697.08	3/30/94	3626.75	3593.35	−0.9	5.7	2.1	3.3[2, 3]
1996	5059.32	1/10/96	5032.94	5032.94	NC	28.1	26.0	3.3[2]
1998	7660.13	1/9/98	7580.42	7539.07	−0.5	21.1	16.1	1.0[2]
2000	10998.39	1/4/00	10997.93	9796.03	−10.9	−1.9	−6.2	−5.1
2001	10318.93	3/12/01	10208.25	8235.81	−19.3	−1.8	−7.1	3.5[1]
2002	9763.96	1/16/02	9712.27	7286.27	−25.0	−14.1	−16.8	−1.6
2003	8303.78	1/24/03	8131.01	7524.06	−7.5	28.6	25.3	−2.7[1, 2]
2005	10440.58	1/21/05	10392.99	10012.36	−3.7	3.1	−0.6	−2.5[3]
2006	10717.50	1/20/06	10667.39	10667.39	NC	16.8	16.3	2.5
2007	12194.13	3/2/07	12114.10	12050.41	−0.5	9.5	6.4	1.4[2]
2008	13167.20	1/2/08	13043.96	7552.29	−42.1	−32.7	−33.8	−6.1
2009	8149.09	1/20/09	7949.09	6547.05	−17.6	31.2	18.8	−8.6[1, 2]
2010	10285.97	1/22/10	10172.98	9686.48	−4.8	13.8	11.0	−3.7[1, 2]
			Average Drop		−10.9%			

[1] *January Barometer wrong* [2] *December Low Indicator wrong* [3] *Year Flat*

APRIL

MONDAY 7

D 42.9
S 47.6
N 38.1

There are ways for the individual investor to make money in the securities markets. Buying value and holding long term while collecting dividends has been proven over and over again.
— Robert M. Sharp (Author, *The Lore and Legends of Wall Street*)

April is the Best Month for the Dow, Average 2.0% Gain Since 1950

TUESDAY 8

D 42.9
S 47.6
N 52.4

All great truths begin as blasphemies.
— George Bernard Shaw (Irish dramatist, 1856–1950)

WEDNESDAY 9

D 52.4
S 47.6
N 47.6

There are two kinds of people who lose money: those who know nothing and those who know everything.
— Henry Kaufman (German-American economist, b. 1927, to Robert Lenzner in *Forbes*, 10/19/98, who added, "With two Nobel Prize winners in the house, Long-Term Capital clearly fits the second case.")

April is 2nd Best Month for S&P, 3rd Best for NASDAQ (Since 1971)

THURSDAY 10

D 66.7
S 57.1
N 61.9

In nature there are no rewards or punishments; there are consequences.
— Horace Annesley Vachell (English writer, *The Face of Clay*, 1861–1955)

FRIDAY 11

D 57.1
S 47.6
N 47.6

Never will a man penetrate deeper into error than when he is continuing on a road that has led him to great success.
— Friedrich von Hayek (*Counterrevolution of Science*)

SATURDAY 12

SUNDAY 13

DOWN JANUARYS: A REMARKABLE RECORD

In the first third of the twentieth century, there was no correlation between January markets and the year as a whole (page 24). Then, in 1972 Yale Hirsch discovered that the 1933 "lame duck" Amendment to the Constitution changed the political calendar, and the January Barometer was born. Its record has been quite accurate (page 16).

Down Januarys are harbingers of trouble ahead, in the economic, political, or military arenas. Eisenhower's heart attack in 1955 cast doubt on whether he could run in 1956—a flat year. Two other election years with down Januarys were also flat (1984 and 1992). Twelve bear markets began, and ten continued into second years with poor Januarys. 1968 started down, as we were mired in Vietnam, but Johnson's "bombing halt" changed the climate. Imminent military action in Iraq held January 2003 down before the market triple-bottomed in March. After Baghdad fell, pre-election and recovery forces fueled 2003 into a banner year. 2005 was flat, registering the narrowest Dow trading range on record. 2008 was the worst January on record and preceded the worst bear market since the Great Depression. A negative reading in 2010 preceded a 16% April-July correction, which was quickly reversed by QE2.

Unfortunately, bull and bear markets do not start conveniently at the beginnings and ends of months or years. Though some years ended higher, **every down January since 1950 was followed by a new or continuing bear market, a 10% correction or a flat year**. **Down Januarys were followed by substantial declines averaging** *minus* **13.9%**, providing excellent buying opportunities later in most years.

FROM DOWN JANUARY S&P CLOSES TO LOW NEXT 11 MONTHS

Year	January Close	% Change	11-Month Low	Date of Low	Jan Close to Low %	% Feb to Dec	Year % Change	
1953	26.38	−0.7%	22.71	14-Sep	−13.9%	−6.0%	−6.6%	bear
1956	43.82	−3.6	43.42	14-Feb	−0.9	6.5	2.6	FLAT/bear
1957	44.72	−4.2	38.98	22-Oct	−12.8	−10.6	−14.3	Cont. bear
1960	55.61	−7.1	52.30	25-Oct	−6.0	4.5	−3.0	bear
1962	68.84	−3.8	52.32	26-Jun	−24.0	−8.3	−11.8	bear
1968	92.24	−4.4	87.72	5-Mar	−4.9	12.6	7.7	−10%/bear
1969	103.01	−0.8	89.20	17-Dec	−13.4	−10.6	−11.4	Cont. bear
1970	85.02	−7.6	69.20	26-May	−18.6	8.4	0.1	Cont. bear/FLAT
1973	116.03	−1.7	92.16	5-Dec	−20.6	−15.9	−17.4	bear
1974	96.57	−1.0	62.28	3-Oct	−35.5	−29.0	−29.7	Cont. bear
1977	102.03	−5.1	90.71	2-Nov	−11.1	−6.8	−11.5	bear
1978	89.25	−6.2	86.90	6-Mar	−2.6	7.7	1.1	Cont. bear/bear
1981	129.55	−4.6	112.77	25-Sep	−13.0	−5.4	−9.7	bear
1982	120.40	−1.8	102.42	12-Aug	−14.9	16.8	14.8	Cont. bear
1984	163.42	−0.9	147.82	24-Jul	−9.5	2.3	1.4	Cont. bear/FLAT
1990	329.07	−6.9	295.46	11-Oct	−10.2	0.4	−6.6	bear
1992	408.79	−2.0	394.50	8-Apr	−3.5	6.6	4.5	FLAT
2000	1394.46	−5.1	1264.74	20-Dec	−9.3	−5.3	−10.1	bear
2002	1130.20	−1.6	776.76	9-Oct	−31.3	−22.2	−23.4	bear
2003	855.70	−2.7	800.73	11-Mar	−6.4	29.9	26.4	Cont. bear
2005	1181.27	−2.5	1137.50	20-Apr	−3.7	5.7	3.0	FLAT
2008	1378.55	−6.1	752.44	20-Nov	−45.4	−34.5	−38.5	Cont. bear
2009	825.88	−8.6	676.53	9-Mar	−18.1	35.0	23.5	Cont. bear
2010	1073.87	−3.7	1022.58	2-Jul	−4.8	17.1	12.8	−10%/no bear
		Totals			−334.4%	−1.1%	−96.2%	
		Average			−13.9%	−0.05%	−4.0%	

APRIL

Monday Before Expiration, Dow Up 17 of Last 25, Down 5 of Last 9

MONDAY
D 71.4
S 52.4
N 52.4
14

Patriotism is when love of your own people comes first. Nationalism is when hate for people other than your own comes first.
— Charles De Gaulle (French president and WWII General, 1890–1970, May 1969)

Passover
Income Tax Deadline, *Generally Bullish, Dow Down Only Six Times Since 1981*

TUESDAY
D 71.4
S 66.7
N 47.6
15

When you're one step ahead of the crowd, you're a genius. When you're two steps ahead, you're a crackpot.
— Shlomo Riskin (Rabbi, author, b. 1940)

April Prone to Weakness After Tax Deadline (Pages 36 and 134)

WEDNESDAY
D 57.1
S 61.9
N 47.6
16

That's the American way. If little kids don't aspire to make money like I did, what the hell good is this country?
— Lee Iacocca (American industrialist, former Chrysler CEO, b. 1924)

April Expiration Day, Dow Up 14 of Last 17,
NASDAQ Up 13 Straight Day Before Good Friday

THURSDAY
D 52.4
S 52.4
N 47.6
17

Government is like fire—useful when used legitimately, but dangerous when not.
— David Brooks (*N Y Times* columnist, 10/5/07)

Good Friday (Market Closed)

FRIDAY
18

The greatest good you can do for another is not just to share your riches, but to reveal to him his own.
— Benjamin Disraeli (British prime minister, 1804–1881)

SATURDAY
19

Easter

SUNDAY
20

TOP PERFORMING MONTHS PAST 63⅓ YEARS: STANDARD & POOR'S 500 AND DOW JONES INDUSTRIALS

Monthly performance of the S&P and the Dow are ranked over the past 63⅓ years. NASDAQ monthly performance is shown on page 56.

April, November, and December still hold the top three positions in both the Dow and the S&P. March has reclaimed the fourth spot on the S&P. Two disastrous Januarys in 2008 and 2009 knocked January into fifth. This, in part, led to our discovery in 1986 of the market's most consistent seasonal pattern. You can divide the year into two sections and have practically all the gains in one six-month section and very little in the other. September is the worst month on both lists. (See "Best Six Months" on page 48.)

MONTHLY % CHANGES (JANUARY 1950 TO APRIL 2013)

	Standard & Poor's 500					Dow Jones Industrials			
Month	Total % Change	Avg. % Change	# Up	# Down	Month	Total % Change	Avg. % Change	# Up	# Down
Jan	74.6%	1.2%	40	24	Jan	72.2%	1.1%	42	22
Feb	−6.3	−0.1	35	29	Feb	4.2	0.1	37	27
Mar	77.8	1.2	42	22	Mar	71.8	1.1	42	22
Apr	97.0	1.5	44	20	Apr	126.0	2.0	42	22
May	7.8	0.1	35	28	May	−5.2	−0.1	31	32
Jun	−0.5	−0.01	33	30	Jun	−19.0	−0.3	29	34
Jul	59.1	0.9	34	29	Jul	73.1	1.2	39	24
Aug	−0.4	−0.01	35	28	Aug	−4.2	−0.1	36	27
Sep*	−33.0	−0.5	28	34	Sep	−50.5	−0.8	25	38
Oct	47.2	0.7	37	26	Oct	30.0	0.5	37	26
Nov	93.6	1.5	41	22	Nov	92.8	1.5	41	22
Dec	106.5	1.7	48	15	Dec	106.5	1.7	45	18
% Rank					**% Rank**				
Dec	106.5%	1.7%	48	15	Apr	126.0%	2.0%	42	22
Apr	97.0	1.5	44	20	Dec	106.5	1.7	45	18
Nov	93.6	1.5	41	22	Nov	92.8	1.5	41	22
Mar	77.8	1.2	42	22	Jul	73.1	1.2	39	24
Jan	74.6	1.2	40	24	Jan	72.2	1.1	42	22
Jul	59.1	0.9	34	29	Mar	71.8	1.1	42	22
Oct	47.2	0.7	37	26	Oct	30.0	0.5	37	26
May	7.8	0.1	35	28	Feb	4.2	0.1	37	27
Aug	−0.4	−0.01	35	28	Aug	−4.2	−0.1	36	27
Jun	−0.5	−0.01	33	30	May	−5.2	−0.1	31	32
Feb	−6.3	−0.1	35	29	Jun	−19.0	−0.3	29	34
Sep*	−33.0	−0.5	28	34	Sep	−50.5	−0.8	25	38
Totals	523.4%	8.2%			**Totals**	497.7%	7.9%		
Average		0.68%			**Average**		0.66%		

*No change 1979

Anticipators, shifts in cultural behavior, and faster information flow have altered seasonality in recent years. Here is how the months ranked over the past 15⅓ years (184 months) using total percentage gains on the S&P 500: March 35.9, April 32.6, October 27.6, December 25.9, November 16.1, July −3.4, January −4.4, May −7.0, June −8.7, February −13.5, August −14.5, September −16.2.

During the last 15⅓ years front-runners of our Best Six Months may have helped push October into the number-three spot. January has declined in 7 of the last 14 years. Sizeable turnarounds in "bear killing" October were a common occurrence from 1998 to 2007. Recent big Dow losses in the period were: August 1998 (SE Asia crisis), off 15.1%; September 2001 (9/11 attack), off 11.1%; September 2002 (Iraq war drums), off 12.4%; October 2008, off 14.1%, and February 2009 (financial crisis), off 11.7%.

Day After Easter, Second Worst Post-Holiday (Page 86)

MONDAY
D 71.4
S 66.7
N 61.9
21

A weak currency is the sign of a weak economy, and a weak economy leads to a weak nation.
— H. Ross Perot (American businessman, *The Dollar Crisis*, 2-time 3rd-party presidential candidate, 1992 and 1996, b. 1930)

TUESDAY
D 57.1
S 61.9
N 61.9
22

Corporate guidance has become something of an art. The CFO has refined and perfected his art, gracefully leading on the bulls with the calculating grace and cunning of a great matador.
— Joe Kalinowski (I/B/E/S)

April 1999 First Month Ever to Gain 1000 Dow Points

WEDNESDAY
D 57.1
S 52.4
N 52.4
23

Never overpay for a stock. More money is lost than in any other way by projecting above-average growth and paying an extra multiple for it.
— Charles Neuhauser (Bear Stearns)

THURSDAY
D 42.9
S 28.6
N 47.6
24

There are many people who think they want to be matadors [or money managers or traders] only to find themselves in the ring with two thousand pounds of bull bearing down on them, and then discover that what they really wanted was to wear tight pants and hear the crowd roar.
— Terry Pearce (Founder and President of Leadership Communication, b. 1941)

FRIDAY
D 57.1
S 52.4
N 47.6
25

Most periodicals and trade journals are deadly dull, and indeed full of fluff provided by public relations agents.
— Jim Rogers (Financier, b. 1942)

SATURDAY
26

May Almanac Investor Seasonalities: See Pages 92, 94, and 96

SUNDAY
27

MAY ALMANAC

MAY						
S	M	T	W	T	F	S
					1	2	3
4	5	6	7	8	9	10
11	12	13	14	15	16	17
18	19	20	21	22	23	24
25	26	27	28	29	30	31

JUNE						
S	M	T	W	T	F	S
1	2	3	4	5	6	7
8	9	10	11	12	13	14
15	16	17	18	19	20	21
22	23	24	25	26	27	28
29	30					

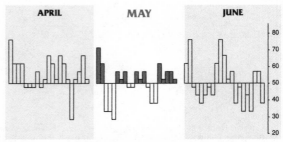

Market Probability Chart above is a graphic representation of the S&P 500 Recent Market Probability Calendar on page 124.

◆ "May/June disaster area" between 1965 and 1984 with S&P down 15 out of 20 Mays ◆ Between 1985 and 1997 May was the best month with 13 straight gains, gaining 3.3% per year on average, up 7, down 8 since ◆ Worst six months of the year begin with May (page 48) ◆ A $10,000 investment compounded to $765,055 for November–April in 63 years compared to a $1,105 loss for May–October ◆ Dow Memorial Day week record: up 12 years in a row (1984–1995), down 10 of the last 17 years ◆ Since 1950, midterm-year Mays rank poorly, #9 Dow, #11 S&P, and #9 NASDAQ.

May Vital Statistics

	DJIA	S&P 500	NASDAQ	Russell 1K	Russell 2K
Rank	10	8	7	6	6
Up	31	35	24	22	21
Down	32	28	18	12	13
Average % Change	–0.1%	0.1%	0.7%	0.9%	1.3%
Midterm Year	–0.8%	–1.1%	–1.6%	–0.4%	–2.2%

	Best & Worst May									
	% Change		% Change		% Change		% Change		% Change	
Best	1990	8.3	1990	9.2	1997	11.1	1990	8.9	1997	11.0
Worst	2010	–7.9	1962	–8.6	2000	–11.9	2010	–8.1	2010	–7.7

	Best & Worst May Weeks									
Best	5/29/70	5.8	5/2/97	6.2	5/17/02	8.8	5/2/97	6.4	5/14/10	6.3
Worst	5/25/62	–6.0	5/25/62	–6.8	5/7/10	–8.0	5/7/10	–6.6	5/7/10	–8.9

	Best & Worst May Days									
Best	5/27/70	5.1	5/27/70	5.0	5/30/00	7.9	5/10/10	4.4	5/10/10	5.6
Worst	5/28/62	–5.7	5/28/62	–6.7	5/23/10	–5.9	5/20/10	–3.9	5/20/10	–5.1

First Trading Day of Expiration Week: 1980–2012					
Record (#Up–#Down)	21–12	21–12	17–16	20–13	16–17
Current streak	D2	D2	D2	D2	D2
Avg % Change	0.18	0.16	0.11	0.13	–0.08

Options Expiration Day: 1980–2012					
Record (#Up–#Down)	14–19	17–16	15–18	17–16	15–18
Current streak	D2	D2	D2	D2	D2
Avg % Change	–0.15	–0.16	–0.18	–0.15	–0.07

Options Expiration Week: 1980–2012					
Record (#Up–#Down)	17–16	16–17	16–17	15–18	17–16
Current streak	D4	D4	D4	D4	D4
Avg % Change	0.03	–0.04	0.10	–0.04	–0.23

Week After Options Expiration: 1980–2012					
Record (#Up–#Down)	18–15	20–13	22–11	20–13	24–9
Current streak	U1	U1	U1	U1	U4
Avg % Change	–0.05	0.11	0.12	0.14	0.27

First Trading Day Performance					
% of Time Up	57.8	57.8	60.5	54.3	60.0
Avg % Change	0.20	0.23	0.30	0.25	0.25

Last Trading Day Performance					
% of Time Up	61.9	63.5	71.4	58.8	70.6
Avg % Change	0.23	0.30	0.25	0.28	0.41

Dow & S&P 1950–April 2013, NASDAQ 1971–April 2013, Russell 1K & 2K 1979–April 2013.

May's new pattern, a smile or a frown, Odd years UP and even years DOWN.

MONDAY
D 57.1
S 57.1
N 66.7
28

[A contrarian's opportunity] If everybody is thinking alike, then somebody isn't thinking.
— General George S. Patton, Jr. (U.S. Army field commander WWII, 1885–1945)

FOMC Meeting (2 Days)

TUESDAY
D 71.4
S 66.7
N 76.2
29

There is a habitual nature to society and human activity. People's behavior and what they do with their money and time bears upon economics and the stock market.
— Jeffrey A. Hirsch (Chief Market Strategist Magnet AE Fund, editor *Stock Trader's Almanac*, b. 1966)

End of"Best Six Months" of the Year (Pages 44, 48, 50, and 147)

WEDNESDAY
D 42.9
S 52.4
N 66.7
30

Markets are constantly in a state of uncertainty and flux and money is made by discounting the obvious and betting on the unexpected.
— George Soros (Financier, philanthropist, political activist, author, and philosopher, b. 1930)

First Trading Day in May, Dow Up 12 of Last 16

THURSDAY
D 71.4
S 71.4
N 71.4
1

"Sell in May and go away." However, no one ever said it was the beginning of the month.
— John L. Person (Professional trader, author, and speaker, *Commodity Trader's Almanac*, nationalfutures.com, 6/19/2009, b. 1961)

FRIDAY
D 66.7
S 61.9
N 61.9
2

Financial markets will find and exploit hidden flaws, particularly in untested new innovations—and do so at a time that will inflict the most damage to the most people.
— Raymond F. DeVoe, Jr. (Market strategist, Jesup & Lamont, *The DeVoe Report*, 3/30/07)

SATURDAY
3

SUNDAY
4

"BEST SIX MONTHS": STILL AN EYE-POPPING STRATEGY

Our Best Six Months Switching Strategy consistently delivers. Investing in the Dow Jones Industrial Average between November 1st and April 30th each year and then switching into fixed income for the other six months has produced reliable returns with reduced risk since 1950.

The chart on page 147 shows November, December, January, March, and April to be the top months since 1950. Add February, and an excellent strategy is born! These six consecutive months gained 16397.61 Dow points in 63 years, while the remaining May-through-October months lost 1772.14 points. The S&P gained 1662.96 points in the same best six months versus a loss of 83.46 points in the worst six.

Percentage changes are shown along with a compounding $10,000 investment. The November–April $765,055 gain overshadows May–October's $1,105 loss. (S&P results were $575,846 to $5,356.) Just three November–April losses were double-digit: April 1970 (Cambodian invasion), 1973 (OPEC oil embargo), and 2008 (financial crisis). Similarly, Iraq muted the Best Six and inflated the Worst Six in 2003. When we discovered this strategy in 1986, November–April outperformed May–October by $88,163 to minus $1,522. Results improved substantially these past 27 years, $676,892 to $417. A simple timing indicator triples results (page 50).

	SIX-MONTH SWITCHING STRATEGY			
	DJIA % Change May 1–Oct 31	Investing $10,000	DJIA % Change Nov 1–Apr 30	Investing $10,000
1950	5.0%	$10,500	15.2%	$11,520
1951	1.2	10,626	−1.8	11,313
1952	4.5	11,104	2.1	11,551
1953	0.4	11,148	15.8	13,376
1954	10.3	12,296	20.9	16,172
1955	6.9	13,144	13.5	18,355
1956	−7.0	12,224	3.0	18,906
1957	−10.8	10,904	3.4	19,549
1958	19.2	12,998	14.8	22,442
1959	3.7	13,479	−6.9	20,894
1960	−3.5	13,007	16.9	24,425
1961	3.7	13,488	−5.5	23,082
1962	−11.4	11,950	21.7	28,091
1963	5.2	12,571	7.4	30,170
1964	7.7	13,539	5.6	31,860
1965	4.2	14,108	−2.8	30,968
1966	−13.6	12,189	11.1	34,405
1967	−1.9	11,957	3.7	35,678
1968	4.4	12,483	−0.2	35,607
1969	−9.9	11,247	−14.0	30,622
1970	2.7	11,551	24.6	38,155
1971	−10.9	10,292	13.7	43,382
1972	0.1	10,302	−3.6	41,820
1973	3.8	10,693	−12.5	36,593
1974	−20.5	8,501	23.4	45,156
1975	1.8	8,654	19.2	53,826
1976	−3.2	8,377	−3.9	51,727
1977	−11.7	7,397	2.3	52,917
1978	−5.4	6,998	7.9	57,097
1979	−4.6	6,676	0.2	57,211
1980	13.1	7,551	7.9	61,731
1981	−14.6	6,449	−0.5	61,422
1982	16.9	7,539	23.6	75,918
1983	−0.1	7,531	−4.4	72,578
1984	3.1	7,764	4.2	75,626
1985	9.2	8,478	29.8	98,163
1986	5.3	8,927	21.8	119,563
1987	−12.8	7,784	1.9	121,835
1988	5.7	8,228	12.6	137,186
1989	9.4	9,001	0.4	137,735
1990	−8.1	8,272	18.2	162,803
1991	6.3	8,793	9.4	178,106
1992	−4.0	8,441	6.2	189,149
1993	7.4	9,066	0.03	189,206
1994	6.2	9,628	10.6	209,262
1995	10.0	10,591	17.1	245,046
1996	8.3	11,470	16.2	284,743
1997	6.2	12,181	21.8	346,817
1998	−5.2	11,548	25.6	435,602
1999	−0.5	11,490	0.04	435,776
2000	2.2	11,743	−2.2	426,189
2001	−15.5	9,923	9.6	467,103
2002	−15.6	8,375	1.0	471,774
2003	15.6	9,682	4.3	492,060
2004	−1.9	9,498	1.6	499,933
2005	2.4	9,726	8.9	544,427
2006	6.3	10,339	8.1	588,526
2007	6.6	11,021	−8.0	541,444
2008	−27.3	8,012	−12.4	474,305
2009	18.9	9,526	13.3	537,388
2010	1.0	9,621	15.2	619,071
2011	−6.7	8,976	10.5	684,073
2012	−0.9	8,895	13.3	775,055
Average/Gain	0.3%	($1,105)	7.6%	$765,055
# Up/Down	37/26		49/14	

MAY

🐻 **MONDAY**

D 28.6
S 33.3
N 52.4

5

The men who can manage men manage the men who manage only things, and the men who can manage money manage all.
— Will Durant

🐻 **TUESDAY**

D 38.1
S 33.3
N 47.6

6

A statistician is someone who can draw a straight line from an unwarranted assumption to a foregone conclusion.
— Anonymous

🐻 **WEDNESDAY**

D 33.3
S 28.6
N 33.3

7

Entrepreneurs who believe they're in business to vanquish the competition are less successful than those who believe their goal is to maximize profits or increase their company's value.
— Kaihan Krippendorff (Business consultant, strategist, author, *The Art of the Advantage*, The Strategic Learning Center, b. 1971)

THURSDAY

D 66.7
S 57.1
N 71.4

8

Experience is helpful, but it is judgment that matters.
— General Colin Powell (Chairman Joint Chiefs, 1989–93, Secretary of State, 2001–05, *NY Times*, 10/22/2008, b. 1937)

Friday Before Mother's Day, Dow Up 12 of Last 19

FRIDAY

D 61.9
S 52.4
N 52.4

9

Get inside information from the president and you will probably lose half your money. If you get it from the chairman of the board, you will lose all your money.
— Jim Rogers (Financier, b. 1942)

SATURDAY

10

Mother's Day

SUNDAY

11

MACD-TIMING TRIPLES "BEST SIX MONTHS" RESULTS

Using the simple MACD (Moving Average Convergence Divergence) indicator developed by our friend Gerald Appel to better time entries and exits into and out of the Best Six Months (page 48) period nearly triples the results. Several years ago, Sy Harding enhanced our Best Six Months Switching Strategy with MACD triggers, dubbing it the "best mechanical system ever." In 2006, we improved it even more, achieving similar results with just four trades every four years (page 60).

Our *Almanac Investor Newsletter* (see insert) implements this system with quite a degree of success. Starting October 1, we look to catch the market's first hint of an uptrend after the summer doldrums, and beginning April 1, we prepare to exit these seasonal positions as soon as the market falters.

In up-trending markets, MACD signals get you in earlier and keep you in longer. But if the market is trending down, entries are delayed until the market turns up, and exit points can come a month earlier.

The results are astounding, applying the simple MACD signals. Instead of $10,000 gaining $765,055 over the 63 recent years when invested only during the Best Six Months (page 48), the gain nearly tripled to 2,067,413. The $1,105 loss during the Worst Six Months expanded to a loss of 6,713.

Impressive results for being invested during only 6.3 months of the year on average! For the rest of the year consider money markets, bonds, puts, bear funds, covered calls, or credit call spreads. See page 34 for more executable trades employing ETFs and mutual funds.

Updated signals are e-mailed to our *Almanac Investor eNewsletter* subscribers as soon as they are triggered. Visit *www.stocktradersalmanac.com,* or see the insert for details and a special offer for new subscribers.

SIX-MONTH SWITCHING STRATEGY+TIMING

| | DJIA | | DJIA | |
| | % Change | Investing | % Change | Investing |
	May 1–Oct 31*	$10,000	Nov 1–Apr 30*	$10,000
1950	7.3%	$10,730	13.3%	$11,330
1951	0.1	10,741	1.9	11,545
1952	1.4	10,891	2.1	11,787
1953	0.2	10,913	17.1	13,803
1954	13.5	12,386	16.3	16,053
1955	7.7	13,340	13.1	18,156
1956	−6.8	12,433	2.8	18,664
1957	−12.3	10,904	4.9	19,579
1958	17.3	12,790	16.7	22,849
1959	1.6	12,995	−3.1	22,141
1960	−4.9	12,358	16.9	25,883
1961	2.9	12,716	−1.5	25,495
1962	−15.3	10,770	22.4	31,206
1963	4.3	11,233	9.6	34,202
1964	6.7	11,986	6.2	36,323
1965	2.6	12,298	−2.5	35,415
1966	−16.4	10,281	14.3	40,479
1967	−2.1	10,065	5.5	42,705
1968	3.4	10,407	0.2	42,790
1969	−11.9	9,169	−6.7	39,923
1970	−1.4	9,041	20.8	48,227
1971	−11.0	8,046	15.4	55,654
1972	−0.6	7,998	−1.4	54,875
1973	−11.0	7,118	0.1	54,930
1974	−22.4	5,524	28.2	70,420
1975	0.1	5,530	18.5	83,448
1976	−3.4	5,342	−3.0	80,945
1977	−11.4	4,733	0.5	81,350
1978	−4.5	4,520	9.3	88,916
1979	−5.3	4,280	7.0	95,140
1980	9.3	4,678	4.7	99,612
1981	−14.6	3,995	0.4	100,010
1982	15.5	4,614	23.5	123,512
1983	2.5	4,729	−7.3	114,496
1984	3.3	4,885	3.9	118,961
1985	7.0	5,227	38.1	164,285
1986	−2.8	5,081	28.2	210,613
1987	−14.9	4,324	3.0	216,931
1988	6.1	4,588	11.8	242,529
1989	9.8	5,038	3.3	250,532
1990	−6.7	4,700	15.8	290,116
1991	4.8	4,926	11.3	322,899
1992	−6.2	4,621	6.6	344,210
1993	5.5	4,875	5.6	363,486
1994	3.7	5,055	13.1	411,103
1995	7.2	5,419	16.7	479,757
1996	9.2	5,918	21.9	584,824
1997	3.6	6,131	18.5	693,016
1998	−12.4	5,371	39.9	969,529
1999	−6.4	5,027	5.1	1,018,975
2000	−6.0	4,725	5.4	1,074,000
2001	−17.3	3,908	15.8	1,243,692
2002	−25.2	2,923	6.0	1,318,314
2003	16.4	3,402	7.8	1,421,142
2004	−0.9	3,371	1.8	1,446,723
2005	−0.5	3,354	7.7	1,558,121
2006	4.7	3,512	14.4	1,782,490
2007	5.6	3,709	−12.7	1,556,114
2008	−24.7	2,793	−14.0	1,338,258
2009	23.8	3,458	10.8	1,482,790
2010	4.6	3,617	7.3	1,591,034
2011	−9.4	3,277	18.7	1,888,557
2012	0.3	3,287	10.0	2,077,413
Average	**−1.2%**		**9.3%**	
# Up	**33**		**54**	
# Down	**30**		**9**	
63-Year Gain (Loss)	**($6,713)**			**$2,067,413**

*MACD generated entry and exit points (earlier or later) can lengthen or shorten six-month periods.

MAY

Monday After Mother's Day, Dow Up 14 of Last 19
Monday Before May Expiration, Dow Up 20 of Last 26, Average Gain 0.4%

MONDAY
D 66.7
S 57.1
N 38.1
12

To succeed in the markets, it is essential to make your own decisions. Numerous traders cited listening to others as their worst blunder.
— Jack D. Schwager (Investment manager, author, *Stock Market Wizards: Interviews with America's Top Stock Traders*, b. 1948)

TUESDAY
D 47.6
S 47.6
N 52.4
13

When an old man dies, a library burns down.
— African proverb

WEDNESDAY
D 52.4
S 47.6
N 42.9
14

You have to keep digging, keep asking questions, because otherwise you'll be seduced or brainwashed into the idea that it's somehow a great privilege, an honor, to report the lies they've been feeding you.
— David Halberstam (Amercian writer, war reporter, 1964 Pulitzer Prize, 1934–2007)

THURSDAY
D 57.1
S 57.1
N 52.4
15

There is only one corner of the universe you can be certain of improving, and that's yourself.
— Aldous Huxley (English author, *Brave New World*, 1894–1963)

May Expiration Day, Dow Down 14 of Last 24

FRIDAY
D 47.6
S 52.4
N 57.1
16

Being uneducated is sometimes beneficial. Then you don't know what can't be done.
— Michael Ott (Venture capitalist)

SATURDAY
17

SUNDAY
18

BEST INVESTMENT BOOK OF THE YEAR

Mastering the Stock Market: High Probability Market Timing & Stock Selection Tools

By John L. Person

We have known John Person for over a decade now and this year's Forty-Seventh Edition of the *Stock Trader's Almanac* is humbly dedicated to him (page 3) for his meritorious service to traders and investors worldwide, invaluable contributions to market analysis, exemplary efforts over the past five years on our *Commodity Trader's Almanac* (page 36), groundbreaking work combining the many disciplines of market analysis, and outstanding trading methods (page 22) and results. In *Mastering the Stock Market: High Probability Market Timing & Stock Selection Tools*, John reveals all he has learned in the past three and half decades and shows you precisely how to put them to work in your trading account or investment portfolio to increase returns, reduce risk, and limit losses.

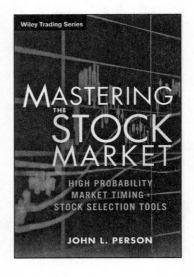

We agree with Jake Bernstein, who wrote the foreword, that this is "John's best book yet." *Mastering the Stock Market* is the culmination of John's 30+ years of real market experience as a floor trader, broker, analyst, author, and educator. Through the years of both big wins and losses he never quits and never ceases learning and developing techniques in an effort to constantly hone and improve his skills as a trader. Nobody knows more about seasonals, sectors, stocks, options, and futures than John and no one combines technical and fundamental analysis better.

On May 20, 2010, we had the privilege to watch him in rare form. We were together with John to finalize our work on the *Commodity Trader's Almanac 2011*. This was two weeks after the infamous May 6, 2010, "Flash Crash." When we set out first thing in the morning the market began to collapse in what ended up being a "mini-crash." John gave us a steely look and said, "Sorry, I've got to trade this market today. We'll get to the CTA after the close." By the end of the day he had scalped most of the downdraft trading the E-Mini S&P 500 Futures in and out, short and long, all day.

Mastering the Stock Market covers all of John's proven tools and techniques. In his down-to-earth and captivating style, John takes the reader step-by-step through the process of identifying worthy trades and how to perfect your timing of entries and exits using his reliable technical indicators and chart analysis methods. He really covers everything you need to know about the stock market but did not necessarily know to ask. This invaluable book runs the gamut, covering the key factors to successful trading and investing from sector and seasonal analysis to using sentiment readings, relative strength, market breadth, volume analysis, price patterns, indicators, pivot points, candlesticks, stops, risk and trade management, and proper position sizing.

Read *Mastering the Stock Market* carefully and you will be well-equipped to increase your returns in the market with better trade selections, enhanced executions, risk control, and appropriate position size, whether you trade stocks, indexes, ETFs, options, futures, or Forex.

Wiley, $90.00, *http://www.personsplanet.com/*. **2014 Best Investment Book of the Year.**

MAY

MONDAY

D 57.1
S 57.1
N 66.7

19

Become more humble as the market goes your way.
— Bernard Baruch (Financier, speculator, statesman, presidential adviser, 1870–1965)

TUESDAY

D 47.6
S 47.6
N 42.9

20

You know you're right when the other side starts to shout.
— I. A. O'Shaughnessy (American oilman, 1885–1973)

WEDNESDAY

D 33.3
S 38.1
N 42.9

21

To achieve satisfactory investment results is easier than most people realize. The typical individual investor has a great advantage over the large institutions.
— Benjamin Graham (Economist, investor, *Securities Analysis*, 1934, *The Intelligent Investor*, 1949, 1894–1976)

THURSDAY

D 33.3
S 38.1
N 42.9

22

I have but one lamp by which my feet (or "investments") are guided, and that is the lamp of experience. I know of no way of judging the future but by the past.
— Patrick Henry (U.S. Founding Father, twice Govenor of VA, 1736–1799, March 23, 1775 speech)

Friday Before Memorial Day Tends to Be Lackluster with Light Trading, Dow Down 8 of Last 13, Average –0.3%

FRIDAY

D 52.4
S 61.9
N 47.6

23

Bear markets don't act like a medicine ball rolling down a smooth hill. Instead, they behave like a basketball bouncing down a rock-strewn mountainside; there's lots of movement up and sideways before the bottom is reached.
— Daniel Turov (*Turov on Timing, Barron's*, May 21, 2001, b. 1947)

SATURDAY

24

June Almanac Investor Seasonalities: See Pages 92, 94, and 96

SUNDAY

25

JUNE ALMANAC

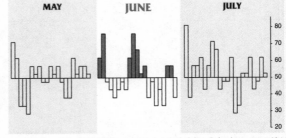

handwritten: A LAST FEW DAYS BAD 90%

	JUNE					
S	M	T	W	T	F	S
1	2	3	4	5	6	7
8	9	10	11	12	13	14
15	16	17	18	19	20	21
22	23	24	25	26	27	28
29	30					

	JULY					
S	M	T	W	T	F	S
		1	2	3	4	5
6	7	8	9	10	11	12
13	14	15	16	17	18	19
20	21	22	23	24	25	26
27	28	29	30	31		

Market Probability Chart above is a graphic representation of the S&P 500 Recent Market Probability Calendar on page 124.

♦ The "summer rally" in most years is the weakest rally of all four seasons (page 70)
♦ Week after June Triple-Witching Day Dow down 20 of last 22 (page 76)
♦ RECENT RECORD: S&P up 11, down 7, average loss 0.1%, ranks tenth ♦ Stronger for NASDAQ, average gain 1.4% last 18 years ♦ Watch out for end-of-quarter "portfolio pumping" on last day of June, Dow down 15 of last 22, NASDAQ down 6 of last 8 ♦ Midterm election year Junes: #12 S&P, #10 NASDAQ, Dow ranks #12 ♦ June ends NASDAQ's Best Eight Months.

June Vital Statistics

	DJIA	S&P 500	NASDAQ	Russell 1K	Russell 2K
Rank	11	10	6	10	8
Up	29	33	24	20	21
Down	34	30	18	14	13
Average % Change	−0.3%	−0.01%	0.8%	0.2%	0.5%
Midterm Year	−1.9%	−2.1%	−2.1%	−1.8%	−2.5%
Best & Worst June					
	% Change	% Change	% Change	% Change	% Change
Best	1955 6.2	1955 8.2	2000 16.6	1999 5.1	2000 8.6
Worst	2008 −10.2	2008 −8.6	2002 −9.4	2008 −8.5	2010 −7.9
Best & Worst June Weeks					
Best	6/7/74 6.4	6/2/00 7.2	6/2/00 19.0	6/2/00 8.0	6/2/00 12.2
Worst	6/30/50 −6.8	6/30/50 −7.6	6/15/01 −8.4	6/15/01 −4.2	6/9/06 −4.9
Best & Worst June Days					
Best	6/28/62 3.8	6/28/62 3.4	6/2/00 6.4	6/10/10 3.0	6/2/00 4.2
Worst	6/26/50 −4.7	6/26/50 −5.4	6/29/10 −3.9	6/4/10 −3.5	6/4/10 −5.0
First Trading Day of Expiration Week: 1980–2012					
Record (#Up–#Down)	17–16	19–14	14–19	17–16	12–20
Current streak	D13	D1	D2	D4	D2
Avg % Change	−0.03	−0.11	−0.29	−0.13	−0.38
Options Expiration Day: 1980–2012					
Record (#Up–#Down)	20–13	21–12	19–14	21–12	19–14
Current streak	U3	U4	U1	U4	U4
Avg % Change	−0.05	0.04	0.001	0.003	0.002
Options Expiration Week: 1980–2012					
Record (#Up–#Down)	19–14	17–16	14–19	15–18	15–18
Current streak	U3	U3	U1	U1	U3
Avg % Change	−0.05	−0.09	−0.32	−0.15	−0.30
Week After Options Expiration: 1980–2012					
Record (#Up–#Down)	10–23	16–17	19–14	16–17	16–17
Current streak	D14	D10	U2	D8	U2
Avg % Change	−0.47	−0.18	0.13	−0.15	−0.11
First Trading Day Performance					
% of Time Up	52.4	50.8	57.1	55.9	61.8
Avg % Change	0.13	0.10	0.11	0.04	0.11
Last Trading Day Performance					
% of Time Up	54.0	50.8	66.7	50.0	67.6
Avg % Change	0.05	0.09	0.32	0.02	0.41

Dow & S&P 1950–April 2013, NASDAQ 1971–April 2013, Russell 1K & 2K 1979–April 2013.

Last Day of June not hot for the Dow;
Down 15 of 22, WOW!

MAY/JUNE

Memorial Day (Market Closed)

MONDAY
26

The way a young man spends his evenings is a part of that thin area between success and failure.
— Robert R. Young (U.S. financier and railroad tycoon, 1897–1958)

Day After Memorial Day, Dow Up 19 of Last 27

TUESDAY
27

D 47.6
S 52.4
N 47.6

Don't be the last bear or last bull standing, let history guide you, be contrary to the crowd, and let the tape tell you when to act.
— Jeffrey A. Hirsch (Chief Market Strategist Magnet AE Fund, editor *Stock Trader's Almanac*, b. 1966)

Memorial Day Week, Dow Down 10 of Last 17, Up 12 Straight 1984–1995

WEDNESDAY
28

D 52.4
S 57.1
N 61.9

Those that forget the past are condemned to repeat its mistakes, and those that mis-state the past should be condemned.
— Eugene D. Cohen (Letter to the Editor, *Financial Times*, 10/30/06)

THURSDAY
29

D 66.7
S 57.1
N 71.4

Laws are like sausages. It's better not to see them being made.
— Otto von Bismarck (German-Prussian politician, 1st Chancellor of Germany, 1815–1898)

Start Looking for NASDAQ MACD SELL Signal (Page 58)
Almanac Investor Subscribers Emailed When It Triggers (See Insert)

FRIDAY
30

D 47.6
S 52.4
N 61.9

I don't know where speculation got such a bad name, since I know of no forward leap which was not fathered by speculation.
— John Steinbeck

SATURDAY
31

SUNDAY
1

TOP PERFORMING NASDAQ MONTHS PAST 42⅓ YEARS

NASDAQ stocks continue to run away during three consecutive months, November, December, and January, with an average gain of 6.5% despite the slaughter of November 2000, down 22.9%, December 2000, −4.9%, December 2002, −9.7%, November 2007, −6.9%, January 2008, −9.9%, November 2008, −10.8%, January 2009, −6.4%, and January 2010, −5.4%. Solid gains in November and December 2004 offset January 2005's 5.2% Iraq-turmoil-fueled drop.

You can see the months graphically on page 148. January by itself is impressive, up 3.0% on average. April, May, and June also shine, creating our NASDAQ Best Eight Months strategy. What appears as a Death Valley abyss occurs during NASDAQ's bleakest four months: July, August, September, and October. NASDAQ's Best Eight Months seasonal strategy using MACD timing is displayed on page 58.

MONTHLY % CHANGES (JANUARY 1971 TO APRIL 2013)

NASDAQ Composite*					Dow Jones Industrials				
Month	Total % Change	Avg. % Change	# Up	# Down	Month	Total % Change	Avg. % Change	# Up	# Down
Jan	127.3%	3.0%	29	14	Jan	62.5%	1.5%	28	15
Feb	19.7	0.5	23	20	Feb	9.8	0.2	25	18
Mar	38.2	0.9	28	15	Mar	50.6	1.2	29	14
Apr	65.0	1.5	28	15	Apr	95.0	2.2	27	16
May	30.3	0.7	24	18	May	8.2	0.2	21	21
Jun	32.4	0.8	24	18	Jun	−1.8	−0.04	21	21
Jul	1.0	0.02	21	21	Jul	29.6	0.7	23	19
Aug	7.5	0.2	23	19	Aug	−6.9	−0.2	24	18
Sep	−26.1	−0.6	23	19	Sep	−46.6	−1.1	15	27
Oct	20.3	0.5	22	20	Oct	18.6	0.4	25	17
Nov	63.7	1.5	27	15	Nov	48.8	1.2	27	15
Dec	84.0	2.0	25	17	Dec	70.2	1.7	30	12
% Rank					**% Rank**				
Jan	127.3%	3.0%	29	14	Apr	95.0%	2.2%	27	16
Dec	84.0	2.0	25	17	Dec	70.2	1.7	30	12
Apr	65.0	1.5	28	15	Jan	62.5	1.5	28	15
Nov	63.7	1.5	27	15	Mar	50.6	1.2	29	14
Mar	38.2	0.9	28	15	Nov	48.8	1.2	27	15
Jun	32.4	0.8	24	18	Jul	29.6	0.7	23	19
May	30.3	0.7	24	18	Oct	18.6	0.4	25	17
Oct	20.3	0.5	22	20	Feb	9.8	0.2	25	18
Feb	19.7	0.5	23	20	May	8.2	0.2	21	21
Aug	7.5	0.2	23	19	Jun	−1.8	−0.04	21	21
Jul	1.0	0.02	21	21	Aug	−6.9	−0.2	24	18
Sep	−26.1	−0.6	23	19	Sep	−46.6	−1.1	15	27
Totals	**463.3%**	**11.0%**			**Totals**	**338.0%**	**8.0%**		
Average		**0.92%**			**Average**		**0.66%**		

Based on NASDAQ composite, prior to Feb. 5, 1971 based on National Quotation Bureau indices

For comparison, Dow figures are shown. During this period, NASDAQ averaged a 0.92% gain per month, 39 percent more than the Dow's 0.66% per month. Between January 1971 and January 1982, NASDAQ's composite index doubled in twelve years, while the Dow stayed flat. But while NASDAQ plummeted 77.9% from its 2000 highs to the 2002 bottom, the Dow only lost 37.8%. The Great Recession and bear market of 2007–2009 spread its carnage equally across Dow and NASDAQ. Recent market moves are increasingly more correlated.

JUNE

First Trading Day in June, Dow Up 18 of Last 25,
Down 2008/2010 −1.1%, 2011/12 −2.2%

MONDAY

D 66.7
S 61.9
N 57.1

2

Every successful enterprise requires three people—a dreamer, a businessman, and a son-of-a-bitch.
— Peter McArthur (1904)

TUESDAY

D 52.4
S 76.2
N 81.0

3

Drawing on my fine command of language, I said nothing.
— Robert Benchley (American writer, actor, and humorist, 1889–1945)

WEDNESDAY

D 52.4
S 47.6
N 57.1

4

In the stock market those who expect history to repeat itself exactly are doomed to failure.
— Yale Hirsch (Creator of *Stock Trader's Almanac*, b. 1923)

June Ends NASDAQ's "Best Eight Months" (Pages 56, 58, and 148)

THURSDAY

D 52.4
S 42.9
N 47.6

5

The reasonable man adapts himself to the world; the unreasonable one persists in trying to adapt the world to himself.
Therefore, all progress depends on the unreasonable man.
— George Bernard Shaw (Irish dramatist, 1856–1950)

FRIDAY

D 52.4
S 38.1
N 33.3

6

Six words that spell business success: create concept, communicate concept, sustain momentum.
— Yale Hirsch (Creator of *Stock Trader's Almanac*, b. 1923)

SATURDAY

7

SUNDAY

8

GET MORE OUT OF NASDAQ'S "BEST EIGHT MONTHS" WITH MACD TIMING

NASDAQ's amazing eight-month run from November through June is hard to miss on pages 56 and 148. A $10,000 investment in these eight months since 1971 gained $460,316 versus a loss of $3,101 during the void that is the four-month period July–October (as of May 17, 2013).

Using the same MACD timing indicators on the NASDAQ as is done for the Dow (page 50) has enabled us to capture much of October's improved performance, pumping up NASDAQ's results considerably. Over the 42 years since NASDAQ began, the gain on the same $10,000 more than doubles to $1,070,376, and the loss during the four-month void increases to $7,046. Only four sizeable losses occurred during the favorable period, and the bulk of NASDAQ's bear markets were avoided, including the worst of the 2000–2002 bear. See page 34 for more executable trades employing ETFs and mutual funds.

Updated signals are e-mailed to our monthly newsletter subscribers as soon as they are triggered. Visit *www.stocktradersalmanac.com*, or see insert for details and a special offer for new subscribers.

BEST EIGHT MONTHS STRATEGY + TIMING

MACD Signal Date	Worst 4 Months July 1–Oct 31* NASDAQ	% Change	Investing $10,000	MACD Signal Date	Best 8 Months Nov 1–June 30* NASDAQ	% Change	Investing $10,000
22-Jul-71	109.54	−3.6	$9,640	4-Nov-71	105.56	24.1	$12,410
7-Jun-72	131.00	−1.8	9,466	23-Oct-72	128.66	−22.7	9,593
25-Jun-73	99.43	−7.2	8,784	7-Dec-73	92.32	−20.2	7,655
3-Jul-74	73.66	−23.2	6,746	7-Oct-74	56.57	47.8	11,314
11-Jun-75	83.60	−9.2	6,125	7-Oct-75	75.88	20.8	13,667
22-Jul-76	91.66	−2.4	5,978	19-Oct-76	89.45	13.2	15,471
27-Jul-77	101.25	−4.0	5,739	4-Nov-77	97.21	26.6	19,586
7-Jun-78	123.10	−6.5	5,366	6-Nov-78	115.08	19.1	23,327
3-Jul-79	137.03	−1.1	5,307	30-Oct-79	135.48	15.5	26,943
20-Jun-80	156.51	26.2	6,697	9-Oct-80	197.53	11.2	29,961
4-Jun-81	219.68	−17.6	5,518	1-Oct-81	181.09	−4.0	28,763
7-Jun-82	173.84	12.5	6,208	7-Oct-82	195.59	57.4	45,273
1-Jun-83	307.95	−10.7	5,544	3-Nov-83	274.86	−14.2	38,844
1-Jun-84	235.90	5.0	5,821	15-Oct-84	247.67	17.3	45,564
3-Jun-85	290.59	−3.0	5,646	1-Oct-85	281.77	39.4	63,516
10-Jun-86	392.83	−10.3	5,064	1-Oct-86	352.34	20.5	76,537
30-Jun-87	424.67	−22.7	3,914	2-Nov-87	328.33	20.1	91,921
8-Jul-88	394.33	−6.6	3,656	29-Nov-88	368.15	22.4	112,511
13-Jun-89	450.73	0.7	3,682	9-Nov-89	454.07	1.9	114,649
11-Jun-90	462.79	−23.0	2,835	2-Oct-90	356.39	39.3	159,706
11-Jun-91	496.62	6.4	3,016	1-Oct-91	528.51	7.4	171,524
11-Jun-92	567.68	1.5	3,061	14-Oct-92	576.22	20.5	206,686
7-Jun-93	694.61	9.9	3,364	1-Oct-93	763.23	−4.4	197,592
17-Jun-94	729.35	5.0	3,532	11-Oct-94	765.57	13.5	224,267
1-Jun-95	868.82	17.2	4,140	13-Oct-95	1018.38	21.6	272,709
3-Jun-96	1238.73	1.0	4,181	7-Oct-96	1250.87	10.3	300,798
4-Jun-97	1379.67	24.4	5,201	3-Oct-97	1715.87	1.8	306,212
1-Jun-98	1746.82	−7.8	4,795	15-Oct-98	1611.01	49.7	458,399
1-Jun-99	2412.03	18.5	5,682	6-Oct-99	2857.21	35.7	622,047
29-Jun-00	3877.23	−18.2	4,648	18-Oct-00	3171.56	−32.2	421,748
1-Jun-01	2149.44	−31.1	3,202	1-Oct-01	1480.46	5.5	444,944
3-Jun-02	1562.56	−24.0	2,434	2-Oct-02	1187.30	38.5	616,247
20-Jun-03	1644.72	15.1	2,802	6-Oct-03	1893.46	4.3	642,746
21-Jun-04	1974.38	−1.6	2,757	1-Oct-04	1942.20	6.1	681,954
8-Jun-05	2060.18	1.5	2,798	19-Oct-05	2091.76	6.1	723,553
1-Jun-06	2219.86	3.9	2,907	5-Oct-06	2306.34	9.5	792,291
7-Jun-07	2541.38	7.9	3,137	1-Oct-07	2740.99	−9.1	724,796
2-Jun-08	2491.53	−31.3	2,155	17-Oct-08	1711.29	6.1	769,009
15-Jun-09	1816.38	17.8	2,539	9-Oct-09	2139.28	1.6	781,313
7-Jun-10	2173.90	18.6	3,011	4-Nov-10	2577.34	7.4	839,130
1-Jun-11	2769.19	−10.5	2,695	7-Oct-11	2479.35	10.8	929,756
1-Jun-12	2747.48	9.6	2,954	6-Nov-12	3011.93	16.2	1,080,376
17-May-13	3498.97						

As of 5/17/2013, MACD Sell Signal not triggered at press time

42-Year Loss ($7,046)   **42-Year Gain $1,070,376**

* MACD-generated entry and exit points (earlier or later) can lengthen or shorten eight-month periods.

JUNE

If you spend more than 14 minutes a year worrying about the market, you've wasted 12 minutes.
— Peter Lynch (Fidelity Investments, *One Up on Wall Street*, b. 1944)

In an uptrend, if a higher high is made but fails to carry through, and prices dip below the previous high, the trend is apt to reverse. The converse is true for downtrends.
— Victor Sperandeo (*Trader Vic—Methods of a Wall Street Master*)

2008 Second Worst June Ever, Dow −10.2%, S&P −8.6%,
Only 1930 Was Worse, NASDAQ −9.1%, June 2002 −9.4%

Doubt is the father of invention.
— Galileo Galilei (Italian physicist and astronomer, 1564–1642)

As for it being different this time, it is different every time. The question is in what way, and to what extent.
— Tom McClellan (*The McClellan Market Report*)

If you can ever buy with a P/E equivalent to growth, that's a good starting point.
— Alan Lowenstein (co-portfolio manager, John Hancock Technology Fund, *TheStreet.com*, 3/12/2001)

Father's Day

TRIPLE RETURNS, FEWER TRADES: BEST 6 + 4-YEAR CYCLE

We first introduced this strategy to *Almanac Investor* newsletter subscribers in October 2006. Recurring seasonal stock market patterns and the four-year Presidential Election/Stock Market Cycle (page 130) have been integral to our research since the first Almanac 47 years ago. Yale Hirsch discovered the Best Six Months in 1986 (page 48), and it has been a cornerstone of our seasonal investment analysis and strategies ever since.

Most of the market's gains have occurred during the Best Six Months, and the market generally hits a low point every four years in the first (post-election) or second (midterm) year and exhibits the greatest gains in the third (pre-election) year. This strategy combines the best of these two market phenomena, the Best Six Months and the four-year cycle, timing entries and exits with MACD (pages 50 and 58).

We've gone back to 1949 to include the full four-year cycle that began with post-election year 1949. Only four trades every four years are needed to nearly triple the results of the Best Six Months. Buy and sell during the post-election and midterm years and then hold from the mid-term MACD seasonal buy signal sometime after October 1 until the post-election MACD seasonal sell signal sometime after April 1, approximately 2.5 years: better returns, less effort, lower transaction fees, and fewer taxable events. See page 34 for more executable trades employing ETFs and mutual funds.

BEST SIX MONTHS+TIMING+4-YEAR CYCLE STRATEGY			
DJIA % Change May 1–Oct 31*	DJIA Investing $10,000	DJIA % Change Nov 1–Apr 30*	DJIA Investing $10,000
1949 3.0%	$10,300	17.5%	$11,750
1950 7.3	$11,052	19.7	$14,065
1951	$11,052		$14,065
1952	$11,052		$14,065
1953 0.2	$11,074	17.1	$16,470
1954 13.5	$12,569	35.7	$22,350
1955	$12,569		$22,350
1956	$12,569		$22,350
1957 −12.3	$11,023	4.9	$23,445
1958 17.3	$12,930	27.8	$29,963
1959	$12,930		$29,963
1960	$12,930		$29,963
1961 2.9	$13,305	−1.5	$29,514
1962 −15.3	$11,269	58.5	$46,780
1963	$11,269		$46,780
1964	$11,269		$46,780
1965 2.6	$11,562	−2.5	$45,611
1966 −16.4	$9,666	22.2	$55,737
1967	$9,666		$55,737
1968	$9,666		$55,737
1969 −11.9	$8,516	−6.7	$52,003
1970 −1.4	$8,397	21.5	$63,184
1971	$8,397		$63,184
1972	$8,397		$63,184
1973 −11.0	$7,473	0.1	$63,247
1974 −22.4	$5,799	42.5	$90,127
1975	$5,799		$90,127
1976	$5,799		$90,127
1977 −11.4	$5,138	0.5	$90,578
1978 −4.5	$4,907	26.8	$114,853
1979	$4,907		$114,853
1980	$4,907		$114,853
1981 −14.6	$4,191	0.4	$115,312
1982 15.5	$4,841	25.9	$145,178
1983	$4,841		$145,178
1984	$4,841		$145,178
1985 7.0	$5,180	38.1	$200,491
1986 −2.8	$5,035	33.2	$267,054
1987	$5,035		$267,054
1988	$5,035		$267,054
1989 9.8	$5,528	3.3	$275,867
1990 −6.7	$5,158	35.1	$372,696
1991	$5,158		$372,696
1992	$5,158		$372,696
1993 5.5	$5,442	5.6	$393,455
1994 3.7	$5,643	88.2	$740,482
1995	$5,643		$740,482
1996	$5,643		$740,482
1997 3.6	$5,846	18.5	$877,471
1998 −12.4	$5,121	36.3	$1,195,993
1999	$5,121		$1,195,993
2000	$5,121		$1,195,993
2001 −17.3	$4,235	15.8	$1,384,960
2002 −25.2	$3,168	34.2	$1,858,616
2003	$3,168		$1,858,616
2004	$3,168		$1,858,616
2005 −0.5	$3,152	7.7	$2,001,729
2006 4.7	$3,300	−31.7	$1,367,181
2007	$3,300		$1,367,181
2008	$3,300		$1,367,181
2009 23.8	$4,085	10.8	$1,514,738
2010 4.6	$4,273	27.4	$1,929,777
Average −1.0%		9.9%	
# Up 16		28	
# Down 16		4	
64-Year Gain (Loss)	($5,727)		$1,919,777

* MACD and 2.5-year hold lengthen and shorten six-month periods

FOUR TRADES EVERY FOUR YEARS		
	Worst Six Months	Best Six Months
Year	May–Oct	Nov–April
Post-election	Sell	Buy
Midterm	Sell	Buy
Pre-election	Hold	Hold
Election	Hold	Hold

JUNE

Monday of Triple Witching Week, Dow Down 10 of Last 16

🐂 **MONDAY**
D 57.1
S 66.7
N 66.7
16

When everbody thinks alike, everyone is likely to be wrong.
— Humphrey B. Neill (Investor, analyst, author, *Art of Contrary Thinking*, 1954, 1895–1977)

FOMC Meeting (2 Days)

TUESDAY
D 52.4
S 52.4
N 42.9
17

There is no tool to change human nature…people are prone to recurring bouts of optimism and pessimism that manifest themselves from time to time in the buildup or cessation of speculative excesses.
— Alan Greenspan (Fed Chairman, 1987–2006, July 18, 2001, monetary policy report to the Congress)

Triple Witching Week Often Up in Bull Markets and Down in Bears
(Page 76)

WEDNESDAY
D 57.1
S 57.1
N 57.1
18

Make it idiot-proof and someone will make a better idiot.
— Bumper sticker

🐻 **THURSDAY**
D 42.9
S 38.1
N 42.9
19

I'm not nearly so concerned about the return on my capital as I am the return of my capital.
— Will Rogers (American humorist and showman, 1879–1935)

June Triple Witching Day, Dow Mixed Down 7 of Last 14,
Average Loss 0.4%

🐻🐻🐻 **FRIDAY**
D 38.1
S 47.6
N 33.3
20

Women are expected to do twice as much as men in half the time and for no credit. Fortunately, this isn't difficult.
— Charlotte Whitton (Former Ottawa Mayor, feminist, 1896–1975)

SATURDAY
21

SUNDAY
22

FIRST MONTH OF QUARTERS IS THE MOST BULLISH

We have observed over the years that the investment calendar reflects the annual, semiannual, and quarterly operations of institutions during January, April, and July. The opening month of the first three quarters produces the greatest gains in the Dow Jones Industrials and the S&P 500. NASDAQ's record differs slightly.

The fourth quarter had behaved quite differently, since it is affected by year-end portfolio adjustments and presidential and congressional elections in even-numbered years. Since 1991, major turnarounds have helped October join the ranks of bullish first months of quarters. October transformed into a bear-killing-turnaround month, posting some mighty gains in nine of the last 15 years, 2008 was a significant exception. (See pages 152–160.)

After experiencing the most powerful bull market of all time during the 1990s, followed by the ferocious bear market early in the millennium, we divided the monthly average percentage changes into two groups: before 1991 and after. Comparing the month-by-month quarterly behavior of the three major U.S. averages in the table, you'll see that first months of the first three quarters perform best overall. Nasty sell-offs in April 2000, 2002, 2004, and 2005, and July 2000–2002 and 2004, hit the NASDAQ hardest. The bear market of October 2007–March 2009, which more than cut the markets in half, took a toll on every first month except April. October 2008 was the worst month in a decade. January was also a difficult month in 2008, 2009, and 2010. (See pages 152–160.)

Between 1950 and 1990, the S&P 500 gained 1.3% (Dow, 1.4%) on average in first months of the first three quarters. Second months barely eked out any gain, while third months, thanks to March, moved up 0.23% (Dow, 0.07%) on average. NASDAQ's first month of the first three quarters averages 1.67% from 1971–1990, with July being a negative drag.

DOW JONES INDUSTRIALS, S&P 500, AND NASDAQ
AVERAGE MONTHLY % CHANGES BY QUARTER

	DJIA 1950–1990			S&P 500 1950–1990			NASDAQ 1971–1990		
	1st Mo	2nd Mo	3rd Mo	1st Mo	2nd Mo	3rd Mo	1st Mo	2nd Mo	3rd Mo
1Q	1.5%	−0.01%	1.0%	1.5%	−0.1%	1.1%	3.8%	1.2%	0.9%
2Q	1.6	−0.4	0.1	1.3	−0.1	0.3	1.7	0.8	1.1
3Q	1.1	0.3	−0.9	1.1	0.3	−0.7	−0.5	0.1	−1.6
Tot	4.2%	−0.1%	0.2%	3.9%	0.1%	0.7%	5.0%	2.1%	0.4%
Avg	1.40%	−0.04%	0.07%	1.30%	0.03%	0.23%	1.67%	0.70%	0.13%
4Q	−0.1%	1.4%	1.7%	0.4%	1.7%	1.6%	−1.4%	1.6%	1.4%
	DJIA 1991–April 2013			S&P 500 1991–April 2013			NASDAQ 1991–April 2013		
1Q	0.5%	0.2%	1.3%	0.6%	−0.1%	1.4%	2.2%	−0.2%	0.9%
2Q	2.6	0.5	−1.0	1.9	0.6	−0.5	1.4	0.6	0.5
3Q	1.3	−0.8	−0.7	0.6	−0.5	−0.3	0.5	0.3	0.2
Tot	4.4%	−0.1%	−0.4%	3.1%	0.0%	0.6%	4.1%	0.7%	1.6%
Avg	1.47%	−0.03%	−0.13%	1.03%	0.00%	0.20%	1.37%	0.23%	0.53%
4Q	1.6%	1.6%	1.7%	1.4%	1.2%	1.9%	2.2%	1.5%	2.5%
	DJIA 1950–April 2013			S&P 500 1950–April 2013			NASDAQ 1971–April 2013		
1Q	1.1%	0.07%	1.1%	1.2%	−0.1%	1.2%	3.0%	0.5%	0.9%
2Q	2.0	−0.08	−0.3	1.5	0.1	−0.01	1.5	0.7	0.8
3Q	1.2	−0.1	−0.8	0.9	−0.01	−0.5	0.02	0.2	−0.6
Tot	4.3%	−0.1%	0.0%	3.6%	−0.01%	0.7%	4.5%	1.4%	1.1%
Avg	1.43%	−0.04%	0.00%	1.20%	−0.003%	0.23%	1.51%	0.46%	0.37%
4Q	0.5%	1.5%	1.7%	0.7%	1.5%	1.7%	0.5%	1.5%	2.0%

JUNE

 MONDAY

D 33.3
S 33.3
N 33.3
23

If you can buy more of your best idea, why put [the money] into your 10th-best idea or your 20th-best idea? The more positions you have, the more average you are.
— Bruce Berkowitz (Fairholme Fund, *Barron's*, 3/17/08)

TUESDAY

D 42.9
S 42.9
N 42.9
24

Never tell people how to do things. Tell them what to do and they will surprise you with their ingenuity.
— General George S. Patton, Jr. (U.S. Army field commander WWII, 1885–1945)

Week After June Triple Witching, Dow Down 14 in a Row and 21 of Last 23
Average Loss Since 1990, 1.2% **WEDNESDAY**

D 42.9
S 33.3
N 42.9
25

The market can stay irrational longer than you can stay solvent.
— John Maynard Keynes (British economist, 1883–1946)

THURSDAY

D 52.4
S 57.1
N 66.7
26

What is conservatism? Is it not adherence to the old and tried, against the new and untried?
— Abraham Lincoln (16th U.S. President, 1809–1865)

FRIDAY

D 47.6
S 57.1
N 66.7
27

We spend $500 million a year just in training our people. We've developed some technology that lets us do simulations. Think of Flight Simulation. What we've found is that the retention rate from simulation is about 75%, opposed to 25% from classroom work.
— Joe Forehand (CEO, Accenture, *Forbes*, 7/7/03)

SATURDAY

28

July Almanac Investor Seasonalities: See Pages 92, 94, and 96

SUNDAY

29

Buy end of JUNE sell July 2nd *30% SPY OPTION GAIN*

JULY ALMANAC

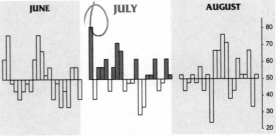

Market Probability Chart above is a graphic representation of the S&P 500 Recent Market Probability Calendar on page 124.

JULY						
S	M	T	W	T	F	S
		1	2	3	4	5
6	7	8	9	10	11	12
13	14	15	16	17	18	19
20	21	22	23	24	25	26
27	28	29	30	31		

AUGUST						
S	M	T	W	T	F	S
					1	2
3	4	5	6	7	8	9
10	11	12	13	14	15	16
17	18	19	20	21	22	23
24	25	26	27	28	29	30
31						

◆ July is the best month of the third quarter except for NASDAQ (page 62) ◆ Start of 2nd half brings an inflow of retirement funds ◆ First trading day Dow up 19 of last 24 ◆ Graph above shows strength in the beginning and end of July ◆ Huge gain in July usually provides better buying opportunity over next 4 months ◆ Start of NASDAQ's worst four months of the year (page 58) ◆ Midterm election Julys are ranked #5 Dow (up 10, down 6), #5 S&P (up 9, down 7), and #11 NASDAQ (up 3, down 7).

July Vital Statistics

	DJIA		S&P 500		NASDAQ		Russell 1K		Russell 2K	
Rank	4		6		11		8		11	
Up	39		34		21		15		16	
Down	24		29		21		19		18	
Average % Change	1.2%		0.9%		0.02%		0.5%		−0.5%	
Midterm Year	1.2%		0.8%		−2.4%		−1.0%		−4.3%	
Best & Worst July										
	% Change		% Change		% Change		% Change		% Change	
Best	1989	9.0	1989	8.8	1997	10.5	1989	8.2	1980	11.0
Worst	1969	−6.6	2002	−7.9	2002	−9.2	2002	−7.5	2002	−15.2
Best & Worst July Weeks										
Best	7/17/09	7.3	7/17/09	7.0	7/17/09	7.4	7/17/09	7.0	7/17/09	8.0
Worst	7/19/02	−7.7	7/19/02	−8.0	7/28/00	−10.5	7/19/02	−7.4	7/2/10	−7.2
Best & Worst July Days										
Best	7/24/02	6.4	7/24/02	5.7	7/29/02	5.8	7/24/02	5.6	7/29/02	4.9
Worst	7/19/02	−4.6	7/19/02	−3.8	7/28/00	−4.7	7/19/02	−3.6	7/23/02	−4.1
First Trading Day of Expiration Week: 1980–2012										
Record (#Up–#Down)	19–14		20–13		21–12		19–14		17–16	
Current streak	D2		D2		D2		D3		D3	
Avg % Change	0.07		−0.002		−0.01		−0.03		−0.12	
Options Expiration Day: 1980–2012										
Record (#Up–#Down)	15–16		16–17		14–19		16–17		12–21	
Current streak	D1		D1		D1		D1		D1	
Avg % Change	−0.29		−0.35		−0.51		−0.36		−0.54	
Options Expiration Week: 1980–2012										
Record (#Up–#Down)	20–13		17–16		17–16		17–16		17–16	
Current streak	U1		U1		U1		U1		D3	
Avg % Change	0.40		0.06		−0.03		0.01		−0.19	
Week After Options Expiration: 1980–2012										
Record (#Up–#Down)	17–16		16–17		14–19		16–17		13–20	
Current streak	U4		U4		U5		U4		U5	
Avg % Change	0.04		−0.14		−0.47		−0.16		−0.32	
First Trading Day Performance										
% of Time Up	63.5		69.8		59.5		70.6		61.8	
Avg % Change	0.25		0.24		0.08		0.29		0.03	
Last Trading Day Performance										
% of Time Up	52.4		63.5		50.0		58.8		64.7	
Avg % Change	0.06		0.10		0.001		0.03		0.02	

Dow & S&P 1950–April 2013, NASDAQ 1971–April 2013, Russell 1K & 2K 1979–April 2013.

When Dow and S&P in July are inferior, NASDAQ days tend to be even drearier.

Last Day of Q2 Bearish for Dow, Down 15 of Last 22
But Bullish for NASDAQ, Up 14 of 21, Although Down 6 of Last 8

MONDAY

D 33.3
S 38.1
N 66.7

30

Those who cannot remember the past are condemned to repeat it.
— George Santayana (American philosopher, poet, 1863–1952)

First Trading Day in July, Dow Up 19 of Last 24

TUESDAY

D 76.2
S 81.0
N 71.4

1

People do not change when you tell them they should; they change when they tell themselves they must.
— Michael Mandelbaum (Johns Hopkins foreign policy specialist, *NY Times*, 6/24/2009, b. 1946)

WEDNESDAY

D 38.1
S 38.1
N 42.9

2

Today we deal with 65,000 more pieces of information each day than did our ancestors 100 years ago.
— Dr. Jean Houston (A founder of the Human Potential Movement, b. 1937)

(Shortened Trading Day)

THURSDAY

D 52.4
S 57.1
N 47.6

3

Have not great merchants, great manufacturers, great inventors done more for the world than preachers and philanthropists?
Can there be any doubt that cheapening the cost of necessities and conveniences of life is the most powerful agent of
civilization and progress?
— Charles Elliott Perkins (Railroad magnate, 1888, 1840–1907)

Independence Day (Market Closed)

FRIDAY

4

Throughout the centuries there were men who took first steps down new roads armed with nothing but their own vision.
— Ayn Rand (Russian-born American novelist and philosopher, *The Fountainhead*, 1957, 1905–1982)

SATURDAY

5

SUNDAY

6

2012 DAILY DOW POINT CHANGES
(DOW JONES INDUSTRIAL AVERAGE)

Week #		Monday**	Tuesday	Wednsday	Thursday	Friday**	Weekly Dow Close	Net Point Change
						2011 Close	12217.56	
1		Holiday	179.82	21.04	−2.72	−55.78	12359.92	142.36
2	J	32.77	69.78	−13.02	21.57	−48.96	12422.06	62.14
3	A	Holiday	60.01	96.88	45.03	96.50	12720.48	298.42
4	N	−11.66	−33.07	81.21	−22.33	−74.17	12660.46	−60.02
5		−6.74	−20.81	83.55	−11.05	156.82	12862.23	201.77
6	F	−17.10	33.07	5.75	6.51	−89.23	12801.23	−61.00
7	E	72.81	4.24	−97.33	123.13	45.79	12949.87	148.64
8	B	Holiday	15.82	−27.02	46.02	−1.74	12982.95	33.08
9		−1.44	23.61	−53.05	28.23	−2.73	12977.57	−5.38
10	M	−14.76	−203.66	78.18	70.61	14.08	12922.02	−55.55
11	A	37.69	217.97	16.42	58.66	−20.14	13232.62	310.60
12	R	6.51	−68.94	−45.57	−78.48	34.59	13080.73	−151.89
13		160.90	−43.90	−71.52	19.61	66.22	13212.04	131.31
14		52.45	−64.94	−124.80	−14.61	Holiday	13060.14	−151.90
15	A	−130.55	−213.66	89.46	181.19	−136.99	12849.59	−210.55
16	P	71.82	194.13	−82.79	−68.65	65.16	13029.26	179.67
17	R	−102.09	74.39	89.16	113.90	23.69	13228.31	199.05
18		−14.68	65.69	−10.75	−61.98	−168.32	13038.27	−190.04
19	M	−29.74	−76.44	−97.03	19.98	−34.44	12820.60	−217.67
20	A	−125.25	−63.35	−33.45	−156.06	−73.11	12369.38	−451.22
21	Y	135.10	−1.67	−6.66	33.60	−74.92	12454.83	85.45
22		Holiday	125.86	−160.83	−26.41	−274.88	12118.57	−336.26
23		−17.11	26.49	286.84	46.17	93.24	12554.20	435.63
24	J	−142.97	162.57	−77.42	155.53	115.26	12767.17	212.97
25	U	−25.35	95.51	−12.94	−250.82	67.21	12640.78	−126.39
26	N	−138.12	32.01	92.34	−24.75	277.83	12880.09	239.31
27		−8.70	72.43*	Holiday	−47.15	−124.20	12772.47	−107.62
28	J	−36.18	−83.17	−48.59	−31.26	203.82	12777.09	4.62
29	U	−49.88	78.33	103.16	34.66	−120.79	12822.57	45.48
30	L	−101.11	−104.14	58.73	211.88	187.73	13075.66	253.09
31		−2.65	−64.33	−37.62	−92.18	217.29	13096.17	20.51
32		21.34	51.09	7.04	−10.45	42.76	13207.95	111.78
33	A	−38.52	2.71	−7.36	85.33	25.09	13275.20	67.25
34	U	−3.56	−68.06	−30.82	−115.30	100.51	13157.97	−117.23
35	G	−33.30	−21.68	4.49	−106.77	90.13	13090.84	−67.13
36		Holiday	−54.90	11.54	244.52	14.64	13306.64	215.80
37	S	−52.35	69.07	9.99	206.51	53.51	13593.37	286.73
38	E	−40.27	11.54	13.32	18.97	−17.46	13579.47	−13.90
39	P	−20.55	−101.37	−44.04	72.46	−48.84	13437.13	−142.34
40		77.98	−32.75	12.25	80.75	34.79	13610.15	173.02
41	O	−26.50	−110.12	−128.56	−18.58	2.46	13328.85	−281.30
42	C	95.38	127.55	5.22	−8.06	−205.43	13343.51	14.66
43	T	2.38	−243.36	−25.19	26.34	3.53	13107.21	−236.30
44		Holiday†	Holiday†	−10.75	136.16	−139.46	13093.16	−14.05
45	N	19.28	133.24	−312.95	−121.41	4.07	12815.39	−277.77
46	O	−0.31	−58.90	−185.23	−28.57	45.93	12588.31	−227.08
47	V	207.65	−7.45	48.38	Holiday	172.79*	13009.68	421.37
48		−42.31	−89.24	106.98	36.71	3.76	13025.58	15.90
49		−59.98	−13.82	82.71	39.55	81.09	13155.13	129.55
50	D	14.75	78.56	−2.99	−74.73	−35.71	13135.01	−20.12
51	E	100.38	115.57	−98.99	59.75	−120.88	13190.84	55.83
52	C	−51.76*	Holiday	−24.49	−18.28	−158.20	12938.11	−252.73
53		166.03				Year's Close	13104.14	166.03
TOTALS		**245.59**	**−49.28**	**−456.37**	**847.34**	**299.30**		**886.58**

Bold Color: Down Friday, Down Monday   * Shortened trading day: Jul 3, Nov 23, Dec 24
** Monday denotes first trading day of week, Friday denotes last trading day of week † Hurricane Sandy

JULY

Market Subject to Elevated Volatility After July 4th

MONDAY

D 57.1
S 57.1
N 57.1

7

Anyone who believes that exponential growth can go on forever in a finite world is either a madman or an economist.
— Kenneth Ewart Boulding (Economist, activist, poet, scientist, philosopher, cofounder General Systems Theory, 1910–1993)

TUESDAY

D 61.9
S 61.9
N 66.7

8

In most admired companies, key priorities are teamwork, customer focus, fair treatment of employees, initiative, and innovation. In average companies the top priorities are minimizing risk, respecting the chain of command, supporting the boss, and making budget.
— Bruce Pfau (*Fortune*)

July Begins NASDAQ's "Worst Four Months" (Pages 56, 58, and 148)

WEDNESDAY

D 47.6
S 42.9
N 57.1

9

At the age of 24, I began setting clear, written goals for each area of my life. I accomplished more in the following year than I had in the previous 24.
— Brian Tracy (Motivational speaker)

THURSDAY

D 61.9
S 57.1
N 61.9

10

We will have to pay more and more attention to what the funds are doing. They are the ones who have been contributing to the activity, especially in the high-fliers.
— Humphrey B. Neill (Investor, analyst, author, *NY Times*, 6/11/1966, 1895–1977)

July is the Best Performing Dow and S&P Month of the Third Quarter

FRIDAY

D 61.9
S 71.4
N 71.4

11

A "tired businessman" is one whose business is usually not a successful one.
— Joseph R. Grundy (U.S. Senator, Pennsylvania, 1929–1930, businessman, 1863–1961)

SATURDAY

12

SUNDAY

13

DON'T SELL STOCKS ON MONDAY OR FRIDAY

Since 1989, Monday*, Tuesday, and Wednesday have been the most consistently bullish days of the week for the Dow; Thursday and Friday* the most bearish, as traders have become reluctant to stay long going into the weekend. Since 1989, Mondays, Tuesdays, and Wednesdays gained 13,221.84 Dow points, while Thursday and Friday combined for a total loss of 847.55 points. Also broken out are the last twelve and a third years to illustrate Monday's and Friday's poor performance in bear market years 2001–2002 and 2008–2009. During uncertain market times, traders often sell before the weekend and are reluctant to jump in on Monday. See pages 66, 78, and 141–144 for more.

ANNUAL DOW POINT CHANGES FOR DAYS OF THE WEEK SINCE 1953

Year	Monday*	Tuesday	Wednesday	Thursday	Friday*	Year's DJIA Closing	Year's Point Change
1953	−36.16	−7.93	19.63	5.76	7.70	280.90	−11.00
1954	15.68	3.27	24.31	33.96	46.27	404.39	123.49
1955	−48.36	26.38	46.03	−0.66	60.62	488.40	84.01
1956	−27.15	−9.36	−15.41	8.43	64.56	499.47	11.07
1957	−109.50	−7.71	64.12	3.32	−14.01	435.69	−63.78
1958	17.50	23.59	29.10	22.67	55.10	583.65	147.96
1959	−44.48	29.04	4.11	13.60	93.44	679.36	95.71
1960	−111.04	−3.75	−5.62	6.74	50.20	615.89	−63.47
1961	−23.65	10.18	87.51	−5.96	47.17	731.14	115.25
1962	−101.60	26.19	9.97	−7.70	−5.90	652.10	−79.04
1963	−8.88	47.12	16.23	22.39	33.99	762.95	110.85
1964	−0.29	−17.94	39.84	5.52	84.05	874.13	111.18
1965	−73.23	39.65	57.03	3.20	68.48	969.26	95.13
1966	−153.24	−27.73	56.13	−46.19	−12.54	785.69	−183.57
1967	−68.65	31.50	25.42	92.25	38.90	905.11	119.42
1968†	6.41	34.94	25.16	−72.06	44.19	943.75	38.64
1969	−164.17	−36.70	18.33	23.79	15.36	800.36	−143.39
1970	−100.05	−46.09	116.07	−3.48	72.11	838.92	38.56
1971	−2.99	9.56	13.66	8.04	23.01	890.20	51.28
1972	−87.40	−1.23	65.24	8.46	144.75	1020.02	129.82
1973	−174.11	10.52	−5.94	36.67	−36.30	850.86	−169.16
1974	−149.37	47.51	−20.31	−13.70	−98.75	616.24	−234.62
1975	39.46	−109.62	56.93	124.00	125.40	852.41	236.17
1976	70.72	71.76	50.88	−33.70	−7.42	1004.65	152.24
1977	−65.15	−44.89	−79.61	−5.62	21.79	831.17	−173.48
1978	−31.29	−70.84	71.33	−64.67	69.31	805.01	−26.16
1979	−32.52	9.52	−18.84	75.18	0.39	838.74	33.73
1980	−86.51	135.13	137.67	−122.00	60.96	963.99	125.25
1981	−45.68	−49.51	−13.95	−14.67	34.82	875.00	−88.99
1982	5.71	86.20	28.37	−1.47	52.73	1046.54	171.54
1983	30.51	−30.92	149.68	61.16	1.67	1258.64	212.10
1984	−73.80	78.02	−139.24	92.79	−4.84	1211.57	−47.07
1985	80.36	52.70	51.26	46.32	104.46	1546.67	335.10
1986	−39.94	97.63	178.65	29.31	83.63	1895.95	349.28
1987	−559.15	235.83	392.03	139.73	−165.56	1938.83	42.88
1988	268.12	166.44	−60.48	−230.84	86.50	2168.57	229.74
1989	−53.31	143.33	233.25	90.25	171.11	2753.20	584.63
SubTotal	*−1937.20*	*941.79*	*1708.54*	*330.82*	*1417.35*		*2461.30*
1990	219.90	−25.22	47.96	−352.55	−9.63	2633.66	−119.54
1991	191.13	47.97	174.53	254.79	−133.25	3168.83	535.17
1992	237.80	−49.67	3.12	108.74	−167.71	3301.11	132.28
1993	322.82	−37.03	243.87	4.97	−81.65	3754.09	452.98
1994	206.41	−95.33	29.98	−168.87	108.16	3834.44	80.35
1995	262.97	210.06	357.02	140.07	312.56	5117.12	1282.68
1996	626.41	155.55	−34.24	268.52	314.91	6448.27	1331.15
1997	1136.04	1989.17	−590.17	−949.80	−125.26	7908.25	1459.98
1998	649.10	679.95	591.63	−1579.43	931.93	9181.43	1273.18
1999	980.49	−1587.23	826.68	735.94	1359.81	11497.12	2315.69
2000	2265.45	306.47	−1978.34	238.21	−1542.06	10786.85	−710.27
SubTotal	*7098.52*	*1594.69*	*−327.96*	*−1299.41*	*967.81*		*8033.65*
2001	−389.33	336.86	−396.53	976.41	−1292.76	10021.50	−765.35
2002	−1404.94	−823.76	1443.69	−428.12	−466.74	8341.63	−1679.87
2003	978.87	482.11	−425.46	566.22	510.55	10453.92	2112.29
2004	201.12	523.28	358.76	−409.72	−344.35	10783.01	329.09
2005	316.23	−305.62	27.67	−128.75	24.96	10717.50	−65.51
2006	95.74	573.98	1283.87	193.34	−401.28	12463.15	1745.65
2007	278.23	−157.93	1316.74	−766.63	131.26	13264.82	801.67
2008	−1387.20	1704.51	−3073.72	−940.88	−791.14	8776.39	−4488.43
2009	−45.22	161.76	617.56	932.68	−15.12	10428.05	1651.66
2010	1236.88	−421.80	1019.66	−76.73	−608.55	11577.51	1149.46
2011	−571.02	1423.66	−776.05	246.27	317.19	12217.56	640.05
2012	254.59	−49.28	−456.37	847.34	299.30	13104.14	886.58
2013	−437.98	1119.01	224.02	217.39	891.91		
Subtotal	*−874.03*	*4566.78*	*1163.84*	*1228.82*	*−1744.77*		*231729*
Totals	**4287.29**	**7103.26**	**2544.42**	**260.23**	**640.39**		**12812.24**

* Monday denotes first trading day of week, Friday denotes last trading day of week
† Most Wednesdays closed last 7 months of 1968 ‡ Partial year through May 10, 2013

Monday Before July Expiration, Dow Up 7 of Last 10

 MONDAY
D 61.9
S 66.7
N 71.4
14

Industrial capitalism has generated the greatest productive power in human history. To date, no other socioeconomic system has been able to generate comparable productive power.
— Peter L. Berger (*The Capitalist Revolution*)

TUESDAY
D 47.6
S 42.9
N 57.1
15

If you torture the data long enough, it will confess to anything.
— Darrell Huff (*How to Lie With Statistics*, 1954)

WEDNESDAY
D 57.1
S 47.6
N 52.4
16

Buy when you are scared to death; sell when you are tickled to death.
— Market Maxim (*The Cabot Market Letter*, April 12, 2001)

THURSDAY
D 52.4
S 47.6
N 52.4
17

Let me end my talk by abusing slightly my status as an official representative of the Federal Reserve. I would like to say to Milton [Friedman]: regarding the Great Depression, you're right; we did it. We're very sorry. But thanks to you, we won't do it again.
— Ben Bernanke (Fed Chairman, 2006–, 11/8/02 speech as Fed Govenor)

July Expiration Day, Dow Down 8 of Last 13, −4.6% in 2002 and −2.5% in 2010

FRIDAY
D 61.9
S 61.9
N 61.9
18

Knowing others is intelligence; knowing yourself is true wisdom. Mastering others is strength; mastering yourself is true power.
— Lau Tzu (Shaolin monk, founder of Taoism, circa 6th–4th century B.C.)

SATURDAY
19

SUNDAY
20

A RALLY FOR ALL SEASONS

Most years, especially when the market sells off during the first half, prospects for the perennial summer rally become the buzz on the street. Parameters for this "rally" were defined by the late Ralph Rotnem as the lowest close in the Dow Jones Industrials in May or June to the highest close in July, August, or September. Such a big deal is made of the summer rally that one might get the impression the market puts on its best performance in the summertime. Nothing could be further from the truth! Not only does the market "rally" in every season of the year, but it does so with more gusto in the winter, spring, and fall than in the summer.

Winters in 50 years averaged a 13.2% gain, as measured from the low in November or December to the first quarter closing high. Spring rose 11.5% followed by fall with 10.9%. Last and least was the average 9.3% summer rally. Even 2009's impressive 19.7% summer rally was outmatched by spring. Nevertheless, no matter how thick the gloom or grim the outlook, don't despair! There's always a rally for all seasons, statistically.

SEASONAL GAINS IN DOW JONES INDUSTRIALS

	WINTER RALLY Nov/Dec Low to Q1 High	SPRING RALLY Feb/Mar Low to Q2 High	SUMMER RALLY May/Jun Low to Q3 High	FALL RALLY Aug/Sep Low to Q4 High
1964	15.3%	6.2%	9.4%	8.3%
1965	5.7	6.6	11.6	10.3
1966	5.9	4.8	3.5	7.0
1967	11.6	8.7	11.2	4.4
1968	7.0	11.5	5.2	13.3
1969	0.9	7.7	1.9	6.7
1970	5.4	6.2	22.5	19.0
1971	21.6	9.4	5.5	7.4
1972	19.1	7.7	5.2	11.4
1973	8.6	4.8	9.7	15.9
1974	13.1	8.2	1.4	11.0
1975	36.2	24.2	8.2	8.7
1976	23.3	6.4	5.9	4.6
1977	8.2	3.1	2.8	2.1
1978	2.1	16.8	11.8	5.2
1979	11.0	8.9	8.9	6.1
1980	13.5	16.8	21.0	8.5
1981	11.8	9.9	0.4	8.3
1982	4.6	9.3	18.5	37.8
1983	15.7	17.8	6.3	10.7
1984	5.9	4.6	14.1	9.7
1985	11.7	7.1	9.5	19.7
1986	31.1	18.8	9.2	11.4
1987	30.6	13.6	22.9	5.9
1988	18.1	13.5	11.2	9.8
1989	15.1	12.9	16.1	5.7
1990	8.8	14.5	12.4	8.6
1991	21.8	11.2	6.6	9.3
1992	14.9	6.4	3.7	3.3
1993	8.9	7.7	6.3	7.3
1994	9.7	5.2	9.1	5.0
1995	13.6	19.3	11.3	13.9
1996	19.2	7.5	8.7	17.3
1997	17.7	18.4	18.4	7.3
1998	20.3	13.6	8.2	24.3
1999	15.1	21.6	8.2	12.6
2000	10.8	15.2	9.8	3.5
2001	6.4	20.8	1.7	23.1
2002	14.8	7.9	2.8	17.6
2003	6.5	23.9	14.3	15.7
2004	11.6	5.2	4.4	10.6
2005	9.0	2.1	5.6	5.3
2006	8.8	8.3	9.5	13.0
2007	6.7	13.5	6.6	10.3
2008	2.5	11.2	3.8	4.5
2009	19.6	34.4	19.7	15.5
2010	11.6	13.1	11.1	16.0
2011	12.6	10.3	7.0	14.7
2012	18.0	4.5	12.4	5.7
2013	16.2	11.4*		
Totals	**658.2%**	**572.7%**	**455.5%**	**533.3%**
Average	**13.2%**	**11.5%**	**9.3%**	**10.9%**

* As of 5/17/2013

70

MONDAY

D 33.3
S 28.6
N 28.6

21

I have always picked people's brains. That's the only way you can grow. Ninety-percent of the information I throw out immediately; five-percent I try and discard; and five-percent I retain.
— Tiger Woods (Top-ranked golfer, on his swing, April 2004)

Week After July Expiration Prone to Wild Swings, Dow Up 8 of Last 11 years1998 –4.3%, 2002 +3.1%, 2006 +3.2%, 2007 –4.2%, 2009 +4.0%, 2010 +3.2

TUESDAY

D 38.1
S 33.3
N 38.1

22

I've continued to recognize the power individuals have to change virtually anything and everything in their lives in an instant. I've learned that the resources we need to turn our dreams into reality are within us, merely waiting for the day when we decide to wake up and claim our birthright.
— Anthony Robbins (Motivator, advisor, consultant, author, entrepreneur, philanthropist, b. 1960)

WEDNESDAY

D 47.6
S 52.4
N 52.4

23

It's a buy when the 10-week moving average crosses the 30-week moving average and the slope of both averages is up.
— Victor Sperandeo (*Trader Vic—Methods of a Wall Street Master*)

Beware the "Summer Rally" Hype
Historically the Weakest Rally of All Seasons (Page 70)

THURSDAY

D 52.4
S 52.4
N 52.4

24

The game is lost only when we stop trying.
— Mario Cuomo (Former NY Governor, *C-Span*)

FRIDAY

D 66.7
S 61.9
N 66.7

25

Discipline always makes hard work easy.
— Jordan Kimmel (Portfolio manager, Magnet AE Fund, b. 1958)

SATURDAY

26

August Almanac Investor Seasonalities: See Pages 92, 94, and 96

SUNDAY

27

AUGUST ALMANAC

AUGUST						
S	M	T	W	T	F	S
					1	2
3	4	5	6	7	8	9
10	11	12	13	14	15	16
17	18	19	20	21	22	23
24	25	26	27	28	29	30
31						

SEPTEMBER						
S	M	T	W	T	F	S
	1	2	3	4	5	6
7	8	9	10	11	12	13
14	15	16	17	18	19	20
21	22	23	24	25	26	27
28	29	30				

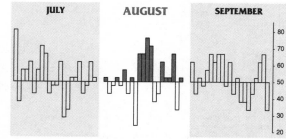

Market Probability Chart above is a graphic representation of the S&P 500 Recent Market Probability Calendar on page 124.

◆ Harvesting made August the best stock market month 1901–1951 ◆ Now that about 2% farm, August is the worst Dow, S&P, and second worst NASDAQ (2000 up 11.7%, 2001 down 10.9) month since 1987 ◆ Shortest bear in history (45 days), caused by turmoil in Russia, currency crisis, and hedge fund debacle, ended here in 1998, 1344.22-point drop in the Dow, second worst behind October 2008, off 15.1% ◆ Saddam Hussein triggered a 10.0% slide in 1990 ◆ Best Dow gains: 1982 (11.5%) and 1984 (9.8%) as bear markets ended ◆ Next to last day S&P up only three times last 17 years ◆ Midterm election year Augusts' rankings #9 S&P, #10 Dow, and #12 NASDAQ.

August Vital Statistics

	DJIA		S&P 500		NASDAQ		Russell 1K		Russell 2K	
Rank	9		9		10		9		9	
Up	36		35		23		22		20	
Down	27		28		19		12		14	
Average % Change	–0.1%		–0.01%		0.2%		0.4%		0.4%	
Midterm Year	–0.9%		–0.7%		–2.4%		–0.6%		–2.8%	
	Best & Worst August									
	% Change		% Change		% Change		% Change		% Change	
Best	1982	11.5	1982	11.6	2000	11.7	1982	11.3	1984	11.5
Worst	1998	–15.1	1998	–14.6	1998	–19.9	1998	–15.1	1998	–19.5
	Best & Worst August Weeks									
Best	8/20/82	10.3	8/20/82	8.8	8/3/84	7.4	8/20/82	8.5	8/3/84	7.0
Worst	8/23/74	–6.1	8/5/11	–7.2	8/28/98	–8.8	8/5/11	–7.7	8/5/11	–10.3
	Best & Worst August Days									
Best	8/17/82	4.9	8/17/82	4.8	8/9/11	5.3	8/9/11	5.0	8/9/11	6.9
Worst	8/31/98	–6.4	8/31/98	–6.8	8/31/98	–8.6	8/8/11	–6.9	8/8/11	–8.9
	First Trading Day of Expiration Week: 1980–2012									
Record (#Up–#Down)	21–12		24–9		24–9		24–9		20–13	
Current streak	D1		D1		U3		D1		D1	
Avg % Change	0.28		0.29		0.30		0.26		0.23	
	Options Expiration Day: 1980–2012									
Record (#Up–#Down)	18–15		19–14		19–14		19–14		21–12	
Current streak	U1		U1		U1		U1		U1	
Avg % Change	–0.05		0.01		–0.07		0.01		0.13	
	Options Expiration Week: 1980–2012									
Record (#Up–#Down)	17–16		20–13		19–14		20–13		21–12	
Current streak	U1		U1		U1		U1		U1	
Avg % Change	0.26		0.44		0.60		0.46		0.69	
	Week After Options Expiration: 1980–2012									
Record (#Up–#Down)	20–13		21–12		20–13		21–12		20–13	
Current streak	D1		D1		D1		D1		D1	
Avg % Change	0.26		0.29		0.43		0.28		0.01	
	First Trading Day Performance									
% of Time Up	47.6		50.8		52.4		47.1		50.0	
Avg % Change	0.02		0.04		–0.09		0.09		–0.02	
	Last Trading Day Performance									
% of Time Up	61.9		65.1		69.0		61.8		73.5	
Avg % Change	0.14		0.14		0.07		–0.03		0.09	

Dow & S&P 1950–April 2013, NASDAQ 1971–April 2013, Russell 1K & 2K 1979–April 2013.

August's a good month to go on vacation;
Trading stocks will likely lead to frustration.

JULY/AUGUST

MONDAY

D 42.9
S 42.9
N 52.4

28

I would rather be positioned as a petrified bull rather than a penniless bear.
— John L. Person (Professional trader, author, speaker, *Commodity Trader's Almanac*, nationalfutures.com, 11/3/2010, b. 1961)

FOMC Meeting (2 Days)

TUESDAY

D 42.9
S 47.6
N 47.6

29

All there is to investing is picking good stocks at good times and staying with them as long as they remain good companies.
— Warren Buffett (CEO Berkshire Hathaway, investor and philanthropist, b. 1930)

WEDNESDAY

D 57.1
S 61.9
N 66.7

30

To affect the quality of the day, that is the highest of the arts.
— Henry David Thoreau (American writer, naturalist, and philosopher, 1817–1862)

Last Trading Day in July, NASDAQ Down 7 of Last 8

THURSDAY

D 42.9
S 52.4
N 42.9

31

News on stocks is not important. How the stock reacts to it is important.
— Michael L. Burke (*Investors Intelligence*)

First Trading Day in August, Dow Down 11 of Last 16
Russell 2000 Up 6 of Last 9

FRIDAY

D 42.9
S 52.4
N 52.4

1

The first human who hurled an insult instead of a stone was the founder of civilization.
— Sigmund Freud (Austrian neurologist, psychiatrist, "father of psychoanalysis," 1856–1939)

SATURDAY

2

SUNDAY

3

WHY A 50% GAIN IN THE DOW IS POSSIBLE FROM ITS 2014 LOW TO ITS 2015 HIGH

Normally, major corrections occur sometime in the first or second years following presidential elections. In the last 13 midterm election years, bear markets began or were in progress nine times—we experienced bull years in 1986, 2006, and 2010, while 1994 was flat.

The puniest midterm advance, 14.5% from the 1946 low, was during the industrial contraction after World War II. The next four smallest advances were: 1978 (OPEC–Iran) 21.0%, 1930 (economic collapse) 23.4%, 1966 (Vietnam) 26.7%, and 2010 (European debt) 32.3%.

Since 1914, the Dow has gained 48.6% on average from its midterm election year low to its subsequent high in the following pre-election year. A swing of such magnitude is equivalent to a move from 9000 to 13500 or from 12000 to 18000.

POST-ELECTION HIGH TO MIDTERM LOW: –20.9%

Conversely, since 1913, the Dow has dropped –20.9% on average from its post-election-year high to its subsequent low in the following midterm year. At press-time the Dow's 2013 post-election year high is 15387.58. A 20.9% decline would put the Dow back at 12171.58 at the 2014 midterm bottom. Persistently sluggish global growth, despite unprecedented global monetary policy accommodation, at press-time, makes a decline back to this level or lower certainly not out of the question. Whatever the level, the rally off the 2014 midterm low could be another great buying opportunity.

Pretty impressive seasonality! There is no reason to think the quadrennial Presidential Election/Stock Market Cycle will not continue. Page 130 shows how effectively most presidents "managed" to have much stronger economies in the third and fourth years of their terms than in their first two.

% CHANGE IN DOW JONES INDUSTRIALS BETWEEN THE MIDTERM YEAR LOW AND THE HIGH IN THE FOLLOWING YEAR

	Midterm Year Low			Pre-Election Year High			
	Date of Low		Dow	Date of High		Dow	% Gain
1	Jul 30	1914*	52.32	Dec 27	1915	99.21	89.6%
2	Jan 15	1918**	73.38	Nov 3	1919	119.62	63.0
3	Jan 10	1922**	78.59	Mar 20	1923	105.38	34.1
4	Mar 30	1926*	135.20	Dec 31	1927	202.40	49.7
5	Dec 16	1930*	157.51	Feb 24	1931	194.36	23.4
6	Jul 26	1934*	85.51	Nov 19	1935	148.44	73.6
7	Mar 31	1938*	98.95	Sep 12	1939	155.92	57.6
8	Apr 28	1942*	92.92	Jul 14	1943	145.82	56.9
9	Oct 9	1946	163.12	Jul 24	1947	186.85	14.5
10	Jan 13	1950**	196.81	Sep 13	1951	276.37	40.4
11	Jan 11	1954**	279.87	Dec 30	1955	488.40	74.5
12	Feb 25	1958**	436.89	Dec 31	1959	679.36	55.5
13	Jun 26	1962*	535.74	Dec 18	1963	767.21	43.2
14	Oct 7	1966*	744.32	Sep 25	1967	943.08	26.7
15	May 26	1970*	631.16	Apr 28	1971	950.82	50.6
16	Dec 6	1974*	577.60	Jul 16	1975	881.81	52.7
17	Feb 28	1978*	742.12	Oct 5	1979	897.61	21.0
18	Aug 12	1982*	776.92	Nov 29	1983	1287.20	65.7
19	Jan 22	1986	1502.29	Aug 25	1987	2722.42	81.2
20	Oct 11	1990*	2365.10	Dec 31	1991	3168.84	34.0
21	Apr 4	1994	3593.35	Dec 13	1995	5216.47	45.2
22	Aug 31	1998*	7539.07	Dec 31	1999	11497.12	52.5
23	Oct 9	2002*	7286.27	Dec 31	2003	10453.92	43.5
24	Jan 20	2006	10667.39	Oct 9	2007	14164.53	32.8
25	Jul 2	2010**	9686.48	Apr 29	2011	12810.54	32.3

*Bear Market ended **Bear previous year   **Average   48.6%**

AUGUST

First Nine Trading Days of August Are Historically Weak (Pages 72 and 124)

MONDAY
D 52.4
S 42.9
N 38.1
4

If the market does not rally, as it should during bullish seasonal periods, it is a sign that other forces are stronger and that when the seasonal period ends those forces will really have their say.
— Edson Gould (Stock market analyst, *Findings & Forecasts*, 1902–1987)

TUESDAY
D 47.6
S 47.6
N 42.9
5

My best shorts come from research reports where there are recommendations to buy stocks on weakness; also, where a brokerage firm changes its recommendation from a buy to a hold.
— Marc Howard (Hedge fund manager, *New York Magazine*, 1976, b. 1941)

WEDNESDAY
D 47.6
S 52.4
N 52.4
6

When you get to the end of your rope, tie a knot and hang on.
— Franklin D. Roosevelt (32nd U.S. President, 1882–1945)

August Worst Dow and S&P Month 1988–2012
Harvesting Made August Best Dow Month 1901–1951

THURSDAY
D 57.1
S 47.6
N 42.9
7

The power to tax involves the power to destroy.
— John Marshall (U. S. Supreme Court, 1819)

FRIDAY
D 47.6
S 57.1
N 33.3
8

What's going on… is the end of Silicon Valley as we know it. The next big thing ain't computers… it's biotechnology.
— Larry Ellison (Oracle CEO, quoted in the *Wall Street Journal*, April 8, 2003)

SATURDAY
9

SUNDAY
10

AURA OF THE TRIPLE WITCH—4TH QUARTER MOST BULLISH: DOWN WEEKS TRIGGER MORE WEAKNESS WEEK AFTER

Options expire the third Friday of every month, but in March, June, September, and December, a powerful coven gathers. Since the S&P index futures began trading on April 21, 1982, stock options, index options, as well as index futures all expire at the same time four times each year—known as Triple Witching. Traders have long sought to understand and master the magic of this quarterly phenomenon.

The market for single-stock and ETF futures continues to grow. However, their impact on the market has thus far been subdued. As their availability continues to expand, trading volumes and market influence are also likely to broaden. Until such time, we do not believe the term "quadruple witching" is applicable just yet.

We have analyzed what the market does prior, during, and following Triple Witching expirations in search of consistent trading patterns. Here are some of our findings of how the Dow Jones Industrials perform around Triple-Witching Week (TWW).

- TWWs became more bullish since 1990, except in the second quarter.
- Following weeks became more bearish. Since Q1 2000, only 17 of 52 were up, and 8 occurred in December, 6 in March, 3 in September, none in June.
- TWWs have tended to be down in flat periods and dramatically so during bear markets.
- DOWN WEEKS TEND TO FOLLOW DOWN TWWs is a most interesting pattern. Since 1991, of 30 down TWWs, 22 following weeks were also down. This is surprising, inasmuch as the previous decade had an exactly opposite pattern: There were 13 down TWWs then, but 12 up weeks followed them.
- TWWs in the second and third quarter (Worst Six Months May through October) are much weaker, and the weeks following, horrendous. But in the first and fourth quarter (Best Six Months period November through April), only the week after Q1 expiration is negative.

Throughout the *Almanac* you will also see notations on the performance of Mondays and Fridays of TWW, as we place considerable significance on the beginnings and ends of weeks (pages 66, 68, 78, and 141–144).

TRIPLE WITCHING WEEK AND WEEK AFTER DOW POINT CHANGES

	Expiration Week Q1	Week After	Expiration Week Q2	Week After	Expiration Week Q3	Week After	Expiration Week Q4	Week After
1991	−6.93	−89.36	−34.98	−58.81	33.54	−13.19	20.12	167.04
1992	40.48	−44.95	−69.01	−2.94	21.35	−76.73	9.19	12.97
1993	43.76	−31.60	−10.24	−3.88	−8.38	−70.14	10.90	6.15
1994	32.95	−120.92	3.33	−139.84	58.54	−101.60	116.08	26.24
1995	38.04	65.02	86.80	75.05	96.85	−33.42	19.87	−78.76
1996	114.52	51.67	55.78	−50.60	49.94	−15.54	179.53	76.51
1997	−130.67	−64.20	14.47	−108.79	174.30	4.91	−82.01	−76.98
1998	303.91	−110.35	−122.07	231.67	100.16	133.11	81.87	314.36
1999	27.20	−81.31	365.05	−303.00	−224.80	−524.30	32.73	148.33
2000	666.41	517.49	−164.76	−44.55	−293.65	−79.63	−277.95	200.60
2001	−821.21	−318.63	−353.36	−19.05	−1369.70	611.75	224.19	101.65
2002	34.74	−179.56	−220.42	−10.53	−326.67	−284.57	77.61	−207.54
2003	662.26	−376.20	83.63	−211.70	173.27	−331.74	236.06	46.45
2004	−53.48	26.37	6.31	−44.57	−28.61	−237.22	106.70	177.20
2005	−144.69	−186.80	110.44	−325.23	−36.62	−222.35	97.01	7.68
2006	203.31	0.32	122.63	−25.46	168.66	−52.67	138.03	−102.30
2007	−165.91	370.60	215.09	−279.22	377.67	75.44	110.80	−84.78
2008	410.23	−144.92	−464.66	−496.18	−33.55	−245.31	−50.57	−63.56
2009	54.40	497.80	−259.53	−101.34	214.79	−155.01	−142.61	191.21
2010	117.29	108.38	239.57	−306.83	145.08	252.41	81.59	81.58
2011	−185.88	362.07	52.45	−69.78	516.96	−737.61	−317.87	427.61
2012	310.60	−151.89	212.97	−126.39	−13.90	−142.34	55.83	−252.73
2013	117.04	−2.08						
Up	16	9	13	2	13	5	17	15
Down	7	14	9	20	9	17	5	7

AUGUST

Monday Before August Expiration, Dow Up 12 of Last 18, Average Gain 0.4%

MONDAY

D 42.9
S 42.9
N 42.9

11

Let us have the courage to stop borrowing to meet the continuing deficits. Stop the deficits.
— Franklin D. Roosevelt (32nd U.S. President, 1932, 1882–1945)

TUESDAY

D 52.4
S 52.4
N 47.6

12

You don't learn to hold your own in the world by standing on guard, but by attacking and getting well hammered yourself.
— George Bernard Shaw (Irish dramatist, 1856–1950)

Mid-August Stronger Than Beginning and End

WEDNESDAY

D 23.8
S 23.8
N 42.9

13

The whole problem with the world is that fools and fanatics are always so certain of themselves, but wiser people so full of doubts.
— Bertrand Russell (British mathematician and philosopher, 1872–1970)

THURSDAY

D 71.4
S 66.7
N 66.7

14

A generation from now, Americans may marvel at the complacency that assumed the dollar's dominance would never end.
— Floyd Norris (Chief financial correspondent, *NY Times*, 2/2/07)

August Expiration Day Bullish Lately, Dow Up 8 of Last 10
Up 156 Points (1.7%) in 2009

FRIDAY

D 47.6
S 66.7
N 66.7

15

Every truth passes through three stages before it is recognized. In the first it is ridiculed; in the second it is opposed; in the third it is regarded as self-evident.
— Arthur Schopenhauer (German philosopher, 1788–1860)

SATURDAY

16

SUNDAY

17

TAKE ADVANTAGE OF DOWN FRIDAY/ DOWN MONDAY WARNING

Fridays and Mondays are the most important days of the week. Friday is the day for squaring positions—trimming longs or covering shorts before taking off for the weekend. Traders want to limit their exposure (particularly to stocks that are not acting well) since there could be unfavorable developments before trading resumes two or more days later.

Monday is important because the market then has the chance to reflect any weekend news, plus what traders think after digesting the previous week's action and the many Monday morning research and strategy comments.

For over 30 years, a down Friday followed by down Monday has frequently corresponded to important market inflection points that exhibit a clearly negative bias, often coinciding with market tops and, on a few climactic occasions, such as in October 2002 and March 2009, near major market bottoms.

One simple way to get a quick reading on which way the market may be heading is to keep track of the performance of the Dow Jones Industrial Average on Fridays and the following Mondays. Since 1995, there have been 186 occurrences of Down Friday/ Down Monday (DF/DM), with 57 falling in the bear market years of 2001, 2002, 2008, and 2011, producing an average decline of 12.8%.

To illustrate how Down Friday/ Down Monday can telegraph market inflection points we created the chart below of the Dow Jones Industrials from November 2011 to May 17, 2013 with arrows pointing to occurrences of DF/DM. Use DF/DM as a warning to examine market conditions carefully. Unprecedented central bank liquidity has tempered subsequent pullbacks, but has not eliminated them.

DOWN FRIDAY/DOWN MONDAYS

Year	Total Number Down Friday/ Down Monday	Subsequent Average % Dow Loss*	Average Number of Days it took
1995	8	−1.2%	18
1996	9	−3.0%	28
1997	6	−5.1%	45
1998	9	−6.4%	47
1999	9	−6.4%	39
2000	11	−6.6%	32
2001	13	−13.5%	53
2002	18	−11.9%	54
2003	9	−3.0%	17
2004	9	−3.7%	51
2005	10	−3.0%	37
2006	11	−2.0%	14
2007	8	−6.0%	33
2008	15	−17.0%	53
2009	10	−8.7%	15
2010	7	−3.1%	10
2011	11	−9.0%	53
2012	11	−4.0%	38
2013**	2	−1.0%	3
Average	**10**	**−6.0%**	**34**

* Over next 3 months, ** Ending May 17, 2013

DOW JONES INDUSTRIALS (NOVEMBER 2011–MAY 17, 2013)

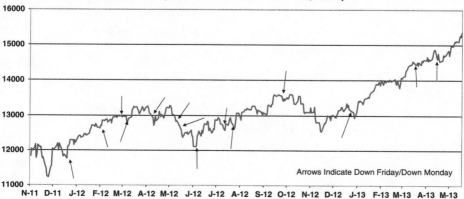

Arrows Indicate Down Friday/Down Monday

N-11 D-11 J-12 F-12 M-12 A-12 M-12 J-12 J-12 A-12 S-12 O-12 N-12 D-12 J-13 F-13 M-13 A-13 M-13

AUGUST

MONDAY 18
D 66.7
S 76.2
N 71.4

I'd be a bum on the street with a tin cup, if the markets were always efficient.
— Warren Buffett (CEO Berkshire Hathaway, investor, and philanthropist, b. 1930)

TUESDAY 19
D 66.7
S 71.4
N 66.7

Based on my own personal experience—both as an investor in recent years and an expert witness in years past—rarely do more than three or four variables really count. Everything else is noise.
— Martin J. Whitman (Founder Third Avenue Funds, b. 1924)

End of August Stronger Last 10 Years

WEDNESDAY 20
D 42.9
S 38.1
N 38.1

Civility is not a sign of weakness, and sincerity is always subject to proof. Let us never negotiate out of fear. But let us never fear to negotiate.
— John F. Kennedy (35th U.S. President, Inaugural Address, 1/20/1961, 1917–1963)

THURSDAY 21
D 42.9
S 42.9
N 47.6

There are no secrets to success. Don't waste your time looking for them. Success is the result of perfection, hard work, learning from failure, loyalty to those for whom you work, and persistence.
— General Colin Powell (Chairman, Joint Chiefs, 1989–1993, secretary of state, 2001–2005, *NY Times*, 10/22/2008, b. 1937)

FRIDAY 22
D 57.1
S 61.9
N 47.6

Sometimes the best investments are the ones you don't make.
— Donald Trump (Real estate mogul and entrepreneur, *Trump: How to Get Rich*, 2004)

SATURDAY 23

SUNDAY 24

SEPTEMBER ALMANAC

SEPTEMBER							OCTOBER						
S	M	T	W	T	F	S	S	M	T	W	T	F	S
			1	2	3	4					1	2	3
5	6	7	8	9	10	11	4	5	6	7	8	9	10
12	13	14	15	16	17	18	11	12	13	14	15	16	17
19	20	21	22	23	24	25	18	19	20	21	22	23	24
26	27	28	29	30	31		25	26	27	28	29	30	

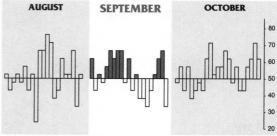

SEPTEMBER							OCTOBER						
S	M	T	W	T	F	S	S	M	T	W	T	F	S
		1	2	3	4	5						1	2
7	8	9	10	11	12	13	3	4	5	6	7	8	9
14	15	16	17	18	19	20	10	11	12	13	14	15	16
21	22	23	24	25	26	27	17	18	19	20	21	22	23
28	29	30					24	25	26	27	28	29	30
							31						

Market Probability Chart above is a graphic representation of the S&P 500 Recent Market Probability Calendar on page 124.

◆ Start of business year, end of vacations, and back-to-school made September a leading barometer month in first 60 years of 20th century; now portfolio managers back after Labor Day tend to clean house ◆ Biggest % loser on the S&P, Dow, and NASDAQ since 1950 (pages 44 & 56) ◆ Streak of four great Dow Septembers averaging 4.2% gains ended in 1999 with six losers in a row averaging –.9% (see page 152), up three straight 2005–2007, down 6% in 2008 and 2011 ◆ Day after Labor Day Dow up 13 of last 19 ◆ S&P opened strong 12 of last 18 years but tends to close weak due to end-of-quarter mutual fund portfolio restructuring, last trading day: S&P down 14 of past 20 ◆ September Triple-Witching Week can be dangerous; week after is pitiful (see page 76).

September Vital Statistics

	DJIA	S&P 500	NASDAQ	Russell 1K	Russell 2K
Rank	12	12	12	12	10
Up	25	28	23	17	19
Down	38	34	19	17	15
Average % Change	–0.8%	–0.5%	–0.6%	–0.7%	–0.5%
Midterm Year	–1.0%	–0.3%	–0.7%	–1.0%	0.1%

Best & Worst September									
		% Change		% Change		% Change		% Change		% Change
Best	2010	7.7	2010	8.8	1998	13.0	2010	9.0	2010	12.3
Worst	2002	–12.4	1974	–11.9	2001	–17.0	2002	–10.9	2001	–13.6

Best & Worst September Weeks									
Best	9/28/01	7.4	9/28/01	7.8	9/16/11	6.3	9/28/01	7.6	9/28/01	6.9
Worst	9/21/01	–14.3	9/21/01	–11.6	9/21/01	–16.1	9/21/01	–11.7	9/21/01	–14.0

Best & Worst September Days									
Best	9/8/98	5.0	9/30/08	5.4	9/8/98	6.0	9/30/08	5.3	9/18/08	7.0
Worst	9/17/01	–7.1	9/29/08	–8.8	9/29/08	–9.1	9/29/08	–8.7	9/29/08	–6.7

First Trading Day of Expiration Week: 1980–2012				
Record (#Up–#Down)	21–12	18–15	13–20	18–15	13–20
Current streak	D1	D1	D1	D1	D1
Avg % Change	–0.11	–0.15	–0.33	–0.17	–0.23

Options Expiration Day: 1980–2012				
Record (#Up–#Down)	17–16	19–14	23–10	20–13	23–10
Current streak	D1	D1	U9	U9	U8
Avg % Change	0.05	0.17	0.18	0.16	0.22

Options Expiration Week: 1980–2012				
Record (#Up–#Down)	17–16	19–14	18–15	19–14	17–16
Current streak	D1	D1	D1	D1	D1
Avg % Change	–0.29	–0.04	0.001	–0.05	0.10

Week After Options Expiration: 1980–2012				
Record (#Up–#Down)	12–21	10–23	14–19	10–22	11–22
Current streak	D2	D2	D2	D2	D2
Avg % Change	–0.73	–0.76	–0.89	–0.78	–1.37

First Trading Day Performance				
% of Time Up	60.3	61.9	54.8	50.0	50.0
Avg % Change	0.04	0.02	–0.01	–0.02	0.04

Last Trading Day Performance				
% of Time Up	38.1	41.3	47.6	47.1	61.8
Avg % Change	–0.14	–0.08	–0.05	–0.002	0.26

Dow & S&P 1950–April 2013, NASDAQ 1971–April 2013, Russell 1K & 2K 1979–April 2013.

September is when leaves and stocks tend to fall;
On Wall Street it's the worst month of all.

AUGUST

MONDAY
D 52.4
S 52.4
N 52.4
25

The four most expensive words in the English language, "This time it's different."
— Sir John Templeton (Founder Templeton Funds, philanthropist, 1912–2008)

TUESDAY
D 42.9
S 52.4
N 42.9
26

Bankruptcy was designed to forgive stupidity, not reward criminality.
— William P. Barr (Verizon General Counsel, calling for government liquidation of MCI-WorldCom in Chap. 7, 4/14/2003)

🐂WEDNESDAY
D 66.7
S 66.7
N 76.2
27

It isn't the incompetent who destroy an organization. It is those who have achieved something and want to rest upon their achievements who are forever clogging things up.
— Charles E. Sorenson (Danish-American engineer, officer, director of Ford Motor Co., 1907–1950, helped develop 1st auto assembly line, 1881–1968)

August's Next-to-Last Trading Day, S&P Down 14 of Last 17 Years

🐻THURSDAY
D 33.3
S 33.3
N 57.1
28

But how do we know when irrational exuberance has unduly escalated asset values, which then become subject to unexpected and prolonged contractions as they have in Japan over the past decade?
— Alan Greenspan (Fed Chairman 1987–2006, 12/5/96 speech to American Enterprise Institute, b. 1926)

FRIDAY
D 52.4
S 52.4
N 57.1
29

Mankind is divided into three classes: Those that are immovable, those that are movable, and those that move.
— Arabian proverb (also attributed to Benjamin Franklin)

SATURDAY
30

September Almanac Investor Seasonalities: See Pages 92, 94, and 96

SUNDAY
31

A CORRECTION FOR ALL SEASONS

While there's a rally for every season (page 70), almost always there's a decline or correction, too. Fortunately, corrections tend to be smaller than rallies, and that's what gives the stock market its long-term upward bias. In each season the average bounce outdoes the average setback. On average, the net gain between the rally and the correction is smallest in summer and fall.

The summer setback tends to be slightly outdone by the average correction in the fall. Tax selling and portfolio cleaning are the usual explanations—individuals sell to register a tax loss and institutions like to get rid of their losers before preparing year-end statements. The October jinx also plays a major part. Since 1964, there have been 18 fall declines of over 10%, and in 10 of them (1966, 1974, 1978, 1979, 1987, 1990, 1997, 2000, 2002, and 2008) much damage was done in October, where so many bear markets end. Recent October lows were also seen in 1998, 1999, 2004, 2005, and 2011. Most often, it has paid to buy after fourth quarter or late third quarter "waterfall declines" for a rally that may continue into January or even beyond. Anticipation of war in Iraq put the market down in 2003 Q1. Quick success rallied stocks through Q3. Financial crisis affected the pattern in 2008–2009, producing the worst winter decline since 1932. Easy monetary policy and strong corporate earnings spared Q1 2011 and 2012 from a seasonal slump.

SEASONAL CORRECTIONS IN DOW JONES INDUSTRIALS

	WINTER SLUMP Nov/Dec High to Q1 Low	SPRING SLUMP Feb/Mar High to Q2 Low	SUMMER SLUMP May/Jun High to Q3 Low	FALL SLUMP Aug/Sep High to Q4 Low
1964	−0.1%	−2.4%	−1.0%	−2.1%
1965	−2.5	−7.3	−8.3	−0.9
1966	−6.0	−13.2	−17.7	−12.7
1967	−4.2	−3.9	−5.5	−9.9
1968	−8.8	−0.3	−5.5	+0.4
1969	−8.7	−8.7	−17.2	−8.1
1970	−13.8	−20.2	−8.8	−2.5
1971	−1.4	−4.8	−10.7	−13.4
1972	−0.5	−2.6	−6.3	−5.3
1973	−11.0	−12.8	−10.9	−17.3
1974	−15.3	−10.8	−29.8	−27.6
1975	−6.3	−5.5	−9.9	−6.7
1976	−0.2	−5.1	−4.7	−8.9
1977	−8.5	−7.2	−11.5	−10.2
1978	−12.3	−4.0	−7.0	−13.5
1979	−2.5	−5.8	−3.7	−10.9
1980	−10.0	−16.0	−1.7	−6.8
1981	−6.9	−5.1	−18.6	−12.9
1982	−10.9	−7.5	−10.6	−3.3
1983	−4.1	−2.8	−6.8	−3.6
1984	−11.9	−10.5	−8.4	−6.2
1985	−4.8	−4.4	−2.8	−2.3
1986	−3.3	−4.7	−7.3	−7.6
1987	−1.4	−6.6	−1.7	−36.1
1988	−6.7	−7.0	−7.6	−4.5
1989	−1.7	−2.4	−3.1	−6.6
1990	−7.9	−4.0	−17.3	−18.4
1991	−6.3	−3.6	−4.5	−6.3
1992	+0.1	−3.3	−5.4	−7.6
1993	−2.7	−3.1	−3.0	−2.0
1994	−4.4	−9.6	−4.4	−7.1
1995	−0.8	−0.1	−0.2	−2.0
1996	−3.5	−4.6	−7.5	+0.2
1997	−1.8	−9.8	−2.2	−13.3
1998	−7.0	−3.1	−18.2	−13.1
1999	−2.7	−1.7	−8.0	−11.5
2000	−14.8	−7.4	−4.1	−11.8
2001	−14.5	−13.6	−27.4	−16.2
2002	−5.1	−14.2	−26.7	−19.5
2003	−15.8	−5.3	−3.1	−2.1
2004	−3.9	−7.7	−6.3	−5.7
2005	−4.5	−8.5	−3.3	−4.5
2006	−2.4	−5.4	−7.8	−0.4
2007	−3.7	−3.2	−6.1	−8.4
2008	−14.5	−11.0	−20.6	−35.9
2009	−32.0	−6.3	−7.4	−3.5
2010	−6.1	−10.4	−13.1	−1.0
2011	+0.2	−4.0	−16.3	−12.2
2012	+0.5	−8.7	−5.3	−7.8
2013	−0.2	−0.3*		
Totals	**−317.6%**	**−330.5%**	**−445.3%**	**−449.5%**
Average	**−6.4%**	**−6.6%**	**−9.1%**	**−9.2%**

* As of 5/17/2013

SEPTEMBER

Labor Day (Market Closed)

MONDAY

1

Take care of your employees and they'll take care of your customers.
— John W. Marriott (Founder Marriott International, 1900–1985)

First Trading Day in September, S&P Up 12 of Last 18, But Down 4 of Last 5
Day After Labor Day, Dow Up 13 of Last 19, 1997 Up 3.4%, 1998 Up 5.0%

TUESDAY

D 57.1
S 61.9
N 61.9

2

The universal line of distinction between the strong and the weak is that one persists, while the other hesitates, falters, trifles and at last collapses or caves in.
— Edwin Percy Whipple (American essayist, 1819–1886)

WEDNESDAY

D 61.9
S 42.9
N 57.1

3

The first panacea for a mismanaged nation is inflation of the currency; the second is war. Both bring a temporary prosperity; both bring a permanent ruin. But both are the refuge of political and economic opportunists.
— Ernest Hemingway (American writer, 1954 Nobel Prize, 1899–1961)

THURSDAY

D 57.1
S 52.4
N 57.1

4

No profession requires more hard work, intelligence, patience, and mental discipline than successful speculation.
— Robert Rhea (Economist, trader, *The Dow Theory*, 1887–1952)

FRIDAY

D 38.1
S 47.6
N 52.4

5

I invest in people, not ideas; I want to see fire in the belly and intellect.
— Arthur Rock (First venture capitalist)

SATURDAY

6

SUNDAY

7

FIRST-TRADING-DAY-OF-THE-MONTH PHENOMENON: DOW GAINS MORE ONE DAY THAN ALL OTHER DAYS

Over the last 16 years the Dow Jones Industrial Average has gained more points on the first trading days of all months than all other days combined. While the Dow has gained 7731.98 points between September 2, 1997 (7622.42) and May 17, 2013 (15354.40), it is incredible that 5671.44 points were gained on the first trading days of these 189 months. The remaining 3764 trading days combined gained 2060.54 points during the period. This averages out to gains of 30.01 points on first days, in contrast to just 0.55 points on all others.

Note September 1997 through October 2000 racked up a total gain of 2,632.39 Dow points on the first trading days of these 38 months (winners except for seven occasions). But between November 2000 and September 2002, when the 2000–2002 bear markets did the bulk of their damage, frightened investors switched from pouring money into the market on that day to pulling it out, fourteen months out of twenty-three, netting a 404.80 Dow point loss. The 2007–2009 bear market lopped off 964.14 Dow points on first days in 17 months, November 2007–March 2009. First days had their worst year in 2011, declining seven times for a total loss of 644.45 Dow points.

First days of June have performed worst. Triple-digit declines in four of the last five years have resulted in the biggest net loss. Due to persistent weakness, August is a net loser as well. In rising market trends first days perform much better as institutions are likely anticipating strong performance at each month's outset. S&P 500 first days differ slightly from the Dow's pattern as June and November are net losers. NASDAQ first days are not as strong with weakness in April, August, and October.

DOW POINTS GAINED FIRST DAY OF MONTH
SEPT 1997-MAY 17, 2013

	Jan	Feb	Mar	Apr	May	Jun	Jul	Aug	Sep	Oct	Nov	Dec	Totals
1997									257.36	70.24	232.31	189.98	749.89
1998	56.79	201.28	4.73	68.51	83.70	22.42	96.65	−96.55	288.36	−210.09	114.05	16.99	646.84
1999	2.84	−13.13	18.20	46.35	225.65	36.52	95.62	−9.19	108.60	−63.95	−81.35	120.58	486.74
2000	−139.61	100.52	9.62	300.01	77.87	129.87	112.78	84.97	23.68	49.21	−71.67	−40.95	636.30
2001	−140.70	96.27	−45.14	−100.85	163.37	78.47	91.32	−12.80	47.74	−10.73	188.76	−87.60	268.11
2002	51.90	−12.74	262.73	−41.24	113.41	−215.46	−133.47	−229.97	−355.45	346.86	120.61	−33.52	−126.34
2003	265.89	56.01	−53.22	77.73	−25.84	47.55	55.51	−79.83	107.45	194.14	57.34	116.59	819.32
2004	−44.07	11.11	94.22	15.63	88.43	14.20	−101.32	39.45	−5.46	112.38	26.92	162.20	413.69
2005	−53.58	62.00	63.77	−99.46	59.19	82.39	28.47	−17.76	−21.97	−33.22	−33.30	106.70	143.23
2006	129.91	89.09	60.12	35.62	−23.85	91.97	77.80	−59.95	83.00	−8.72	−49.71	−27.80	397.48
2007	11.37	51.99	−34.29	27.95	73.23	40.47	126.81	150.38	91.12	191.92	−362.14	−57.15	311.66
2008	−220.86	92.83	−7.49	391.47	189.87	−134.50	32.25	−51.70	−26.63	−19.59	−5.18	−679.95	−439.48
2009	258.30	−64.03	−299.64	152.68	44.29	221.11	57.06	114.95	−185.68	−203.00	76.71	126.74	299.49
2010	155.91	118.20	78.53	70.44	143.22	−112.61	−41.49	208.44	254.75	41.63	6.13	249.76	1172.91
2011	93.24	148.23	−168.32	56.99	−3.18	−279.65	168.43	−10.75	−119.96	−258.08	−297.05	25.65	−644.45
2012	179.82	83.55	28.23	52.45	65.69	−274.88	−8.70	−37.62	−54.90	77.98	136.16	−59.98	187.80
2013	308.41	149.21	35.17	−5.69	−138.85								348.25
Totals	915.56	1170.39	47.22	1048.59	1136.20	−252.13	657.72	−7.93	492.01	276.98	58.59	128.24	5671.44

SUMMARY FIRST DAYS VS. OTHER DAYS OF MONTH

	# of Days	Total Points Gained	Average Daily Point Gain
First days	189	5671.44	30.01
Other days	3764	2060.54	0.55

SEPTEMBER

MONDAY 8
D 61.9
S 57.1
N 57.1

Taxes are what we pay for civilized society.
— Oliver Wendell Holmes Jr. (U.S. Supreme Court Justice, 1902–1932, "The Great Dissenter," inscribed above IRS HQ entrance, 1841–1935)

TUESDAY 9
D 57.1
S 66.7
N 66.7

Don't compete. Create. Find out what everyone else is doing and then don't do it.
— Joel Weldon

WEDNESDAY 10
D 61.9
S 61.9
N 57.1

We may face more inflation pressure than currently shows up in formal data.
— William Poole (Economist, president Federal Reserve Bank St. Louis, 1998–2008, June 2006 speech, b. 1937)

2001 4-Day Market Closing, Longest Since
9-Day Banking Moratorium in March 1933

"In Memory"

THURSDAY 11
D 71.4
S 66.7
N 71.4

An economist is someone who sees something happen, and then wonders if it would work in theory.
— Ronald Reagan (40th U.S. President, 1911–2004)

FRIDAY 12
D 57.1
S 66.7
N 81.0

A president is elected and tries to get rid of the dirty stuff in the economy as quickly as possible, so that by the time the next election comes around, he looks like a hero. The stock market is reacting to what the politicians are doing.
— Yale Hirsch (Creator of *Stock Trader's Almanac*, *NY Times*, 10/10/2010, b. 1923)

SATURDAY 13

SUNDAY 14

MARKET BEHAVIOR THREE DAYS BEFORE AND THREE DAYS AFTER HOLIDAYS

The *Stock Trader's Almanac* has tracked holiday seasonality annually since the first edition in 1968. Stocks used to rise on the day before holidays and sell off the day after, but nowadays, each holiday moves to its own rhythm. Eight holidays are separated into seven groups. Average percentage changes for the Dow, S&P 500, NASDAQ, and Russell 2000 are shown.

The Dow and S&P consist of blue chips and the largest cap stocks, whereas NASDAQ and the Russell 2000 would be more representative of smaller-cap stocks. This is evident on the last day of the year with NASDAQ and the Russell 2000 having a field day, while their larger brethren in the Dow and S&P are showing losses on average.

Thanks to the Santa Claus Rally, the three days before and after New Year's Day and Christmas are best. NASDAQ and the Russell 2000 average gains of 1.3% to 1.8% over the six-day spans. However, trading around the first day of the year has been mixed. Traders have been selling more the first trading day of the year recently, pushing gains and losses into the New Year.

Bullishness before Labor Day and after Memorial Day is affected by strength the first day of September and June. The second worst day after a holiday is the day after Easter. Surprisingly, the following day is one of the best second days after a holiday, right up there with the second day after New Year's Day.

Presidents' Day is the least bullish of all the holidays, bearish the day before and three days after. NASDAQ has dropped 19 of the last 24 days before Presidents' Day (Dow, 16 of 24; S&P, 18 of 24; Russell 2000, 14 of 24).

HOLIDAYS: 3 DAYS BEFORE, 3 DAYS AFTER (Average % change 1980 - April 2013)

	−3	−2	−1	Mixed	+1	+2	+3
S&P 500	0.02	0.25	−0.09	**New Year's**	0.27	0.35	0.06
DJIA	−0.02	0.19	−0.17	**Day**	0.39	0.35	0.18
NASDAQ	0.09	0.30	0.23	1/1/14	0.27	0.66	0.21
Russell 2K	0.08	0.42	0.49		0.12	0.23	0.17
S&P 500	0.36	0.01	−0.24	Negative Before & After	−0.23	−0.07	−0.14
DJIA	0.35	0.02	−0.17	**Presidents'**	−0.14	−0.11	−0.17
NASDAQ	0.55	0.26	−0.39	**Day**	−0.59	−0.07	−0.09
Russell 2K	0.43	0.16	−0.12	2/17/14	−0.45	−0.18	−0.07
S&P 500	0.20	−0.06	0.40	Positive Before &	−0.24	0.32	0.11
DJIA	0.18	−0.09	0.31	Negative After	−0.16	0.31	0.11
NASDAQ	0.44	0.23	0.51	**Good Friday**	−0.37	0.33	0.21
Russell 2K	0.22	0.09	0.53	4/18/14	−0.36	0.19	0.13
S&P 500	0.04	0.06	−0.01	Positive After	0.34	0.13	0.24
DJIA	0.01	0.01	−0.07	**Memorial**	0.41	0.13	0.15
NASDAQ	0.10	0.24	0.01	**Day**	0.26	−0.03	0.48
Russell 2K	−0.03	0.31	0.08	5/26/14	0.25	0.04	0.41
S&P 500	0.11	0.09	0.05	Negative After	−0.16	0.04	0.05
DJIA	0.08	0.08	0.05	**Independence**	−0.10	0.07	0.04
NASDAQ	0.24	0.11	0.05	**Day**	−0.17	−0.09	0.21
Russell 2K	0.23	0.01	−0.04	7/4/14	−0.23	−0.01	0.02
S&P 500	0.17	−0.23	0.19	Positive Day Before	0.04	0.09	−0.09
DJIA	0.14	−0.29	0.19	**Labor**	0.08	0.15	−0.18
NASDAQ	0.38	−0.01	0.20	**Day**	−0.06	−0.05	0.07
Russell 2K	0.53	0.03	0.15	9/1/14	0.04	0.15	0.04
S&P 500	0.15	0.01	0.27	Positive Before & After	0.21	−0.43	0.30
DJIA	0.15	0.02	0.28	**Thanksgiving**	0.17	−0.37	0.32
NASDAQ	0.07	−0.24	0.40	11/27/14	0.47	−0.42	0.11
Russell 2K	0.13	−0.13	0.37		0.35	−0.46	0.27
S&P 500	0.17	0.18	0.23	**Christmas**	0.13	−0.01	0.32
DJIA	0.25	0.21	0.28	12/25/14	0.18	−0.01	0.27
NASDAQ	−0.11	0.42	0.42		0.10	0.05	0.38
Russell 2K	0.19	0.36	0.36		0.20	0.05	0.52

SEPTEMBER

Monday Before September Triple Witching, Russell 2000 Down 9 of Last 14

MONDAY
15

D 47.6
S 47.6
N 38.1

Every time everyone's talking about something, that's the time to sell.
— George Lindemann (Billionaire, *Forbes*)

FOMC Meeting (2 Days)

TUESDAY
16

D 57.1
S 61.9
N 66.7

If you create an act, you create a habit. If you create a habit, you create a character. If you create a character, you create a destiny.
— André Maurois (Novelist, biographer, essayist, 1885–1967)

Expiration Week 2001, Dow Lost 1370 Points (14.3%)
2nd Worst Weekly Point Loss Ever, 5th Worst Week Overall

WEDNESDAY
17

D 33.3
S 42.9
N 52.4

It is better to be out wishing you were in, than in wishing you were out.
— Albert W. Thomas (Trader, investor, *Over My Shoulder*, mutualfundmagic.com, *If It Doesn't Go Up, Don't Buy It!*, b. 1927)

THURSDAY
18

D 57.1
S 52.4
N 61.9

Benjamin Graham was correct in suggesting that while the stock market in the short run may be a voting mechanism, in the long run it is a weighing mechanism. True value will win out in the end.
— Burton G. Malkiel (Economist, April 2003 Princeton Paper, *A Random Walk Down Wall Street*, b. 1932)

September Triple Witching, Dow Up 9 of Last 11

FRIDAY
19

D 42.9
S 38.1
N 42.9

The greatest safety lies in putting all your eggs in one basket and watching the basket.
— Gerald M. Loeb (E.F. Hutton, *The Battle for Investment Survival*, predicted 1929 Crash, 1900–1974)

SATURDAY
20

SUNDAY
21

MARKET GAINS MORE ON SUPER-8 DAYS EACH MONTH THAN ON ALL 13 REMAINING DAYS COMBINED

For many years, the last day plus the first four days were the best days of the month. The market currently exhibits greater bullish bias from the last three trading days of the previous month through the first two days of the current month, and now shows significant bullishness during the middle three trading days, 9 to 11, due to 401(k) cash inflows (see pages 145 and 146). This pattern was not as pronounced during the boom years of the 1990s, with market strength all month long. It returned in 2000 with monthly bullishness at the ends, beginnings and middles of months versus weakness during the rest of the month. "Super Eight" performance in 2012, was on track as were most seasonal patterns and indicators.

SUPER-8 DAYS* DOW % CHANGES VS. REST OF MONTH

	Super 8 Days	Rest of Month	Super 8 Days	Rest of Month	Super 8 Days	Rest of Month
	2005		**2006**		**2007**	
Jan	−1.96%	−1.35%	−0.03%	0.34%	0.68%	−0.04%
Feb	1.76	−0.07	1.67	0.71	3.02	−1.72
Mar	0.31	−2.05	0.81	−0.03	−5.51	3.64
Apr	−4.62	1.46	1.69	−0.53	2.66	2.82
May	0.57	2.43	−0.66	0.08	2.21	0.95
Jun	1.43	−3.00	2.39	−4.87	3.84	−5.00
Jul	0.96	1.83	1.65	0.07	2.59	−1.47
Aug	1.36	−3.07	1.83	0.41	−2.94	−0.26
Sep	0.90	−0.31	1.13	1.64	4.36	1.18
Oct	1.14	−2.18	1.58	2.59	1.28	−1.05
Nov	1.67	3.89	−0.01	−0.31	−0.59	−5.63
Dec	0.57	−1.96	2.40	−0.05	−0.04	4.62
Totals	**4.09%**	**−4.37%**	**14.45%**	**0.04%**	**11.56%**	**−1.96%**
Average	**0.34%**	**−0.36%**	**1.20%**	**0.003%**	**0.96%**	**−0.163%**
	2008		**2009**		**2010**	
Jan	−4.76%	−4.11%	3.16%	−6.92%	0.66%	−3.92%
Feb	1.83	0.65	−6.05	−4.39	3.31	−2.38
Mar	−4.85	2.92	−4.37	12.84	1.91	3.51
Apr	−0.27	4.09	1.52	−0.24	1.13	0.18
May	2.19	−4.81	2.64	2.98	−3.08	−5.75
Jun	0.37	−6.30	1.71	−1.64	4.33	−3.26
Jul	−3.80	−1.99	2.30	5.03	−7.07	11.34
Aug	1.53	1.06	0.04	4.91	0.20	−5.49
Sep	−2.23	−1.19	−0.81	2.21	3.83	4.22
Oct	−3.39	−13.70	−0.05	2.40	−0.18	3.47
Nov	6.07	−11.90	0.00	5.57	−1.20	1.37
Dec	−2.54	3.49	0.62	0.46	1.98	1.45
Totals	**−9.85%**	**−31.79%**	**0.71%**	**23.21%**	**5.82%**	**4.74%**
Average	**−0.82%**	**−2.65%**	**0.06%**	**1.93%**	**0.49%**	**0.40%**
	2011		**2012**		**2013**	
Jan	1.70%	1.80%	1.90%	1.66%	2.28%	3.47%
Feb	0.45	0.57	−0.39	2.33	−0.27	−0.41
Mar	−1.40	2.21	2.22	−0.55	2.93	1.82
Apr	2.30	0.95	1.00	−1.80	0.11	1.65
May	1.03	−2.61	−0.38	−4.52		
Jun	−1.64	−1.19	−1.30	2.08		
Jul	3.52	0.31	5.11	−2.22		
Aug	2.04	−11.39	−0.40	2.09		
Sep	3.24	−3.96	−0.24	2.98		
Oct	−4.47	10.71	0.77	−3.60		
Nov	1.42	−6.66	−2.01	0.55		
Dec	5.74	3.58	0.49	1.35		
Totals	**13.93%**	**−5.68%**	**6.77%**	**0.35%**	**5.05%**	**6.53%**
Average	**1.16%**	**−0.47%**	**0.56%**	**0.03%**	**1.26%**	**1.63%**

	Super-8 Days*		**Rest of Month (13 Days)**	
100	**Net % Changes**	**52.53%**	**Net % Changes**	−8.92%
Month	**Average Period**	**0.53%**	**Average Period**	−0.09%
Totals	**Average Day**	**0.07%**	**Average Day**	−0.007%

Super-8 Days = Last 3 + First 2 + Middle 3

SEPTEMBER

Week After Sepetmber Triple Witching, Dow Down 18 of Last 23,
Average Loss Since 1990, 1.2%

MONDAY
D 38.1
S 38.1
N 38.1
22

Companies which do well generally tend to report (their quarterly earnings) earlier than those which do poorly.
— Alan Abelson (Financial journalist and editor, *Barron's*)

TUESDAY
D 28.6
S 33.3
N 42.9
23

There's no trick to being a humorist when you have the whole government working for you.
— Will Rogers (American humorist and showman, 1879–1935)

WEDNESDAY
D 47.6
S 42.9
N 42.9
24

It's not what you say. It's what they hear.
— (A sign in an advertising office)

Rosh Hashanah

THURSDAY
D 57.1
S 52.4
N 47.6
25

Anyone who has achieved excellence knows that it comes as a result of ceaseless concentration.
— Louise Brooks (Actress, 1906–1985)

End of September Prone to Weakness
From End-of-Q3 Institutional Portfolio Restructuring

FRIDAY
D 57.1
S 61.9
N 42.9
26

Innovation can't depend on trying to please the customer or the client. It is an elitist act by the inventor who acts alone and breaks rules.
— Dean Kamen (Inventor, President of DEKA R&D, *Business Week*, Feb. 12, 2001)

SATURDAY
27

October Almanac Investor Seasonalities: See Pages 92, 94, and 96

SUNDAY
28

GOOD MONTH !?!

OCTOBER ALMANAC

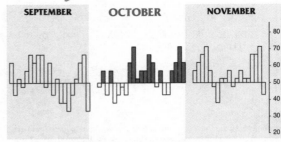

Market Probability Chart above is a graphic representation of the S&P 500 Recent Market Probability Calendar on page 124.

OCTOBER						
S	M	T	W	T	F	S
		1	2	3	4	
5	6	7	8	9	10	11
12	13	14	15	16	17	18
19	20	21	22	23	24	25
26	27	28	29	30	31	

NOVEMBER						
S	M	T	W	T	F	S
						1
2	3	4	5	6	7	8
9	10	11	12	13	14	15
16	17	18	19	20	21	22
23	24	25	26	27	28	29
30						

◆ Known as the jinx month because of crashes in 1929, 1987, the 554-point drop on October 27, 1997, back-to-back massacres in 1978 and 1979, Friday the 13th in 1989, and the meltdown in 2008 ◆ Yet October is a "bear killer" and turned the tide in 12 post-WWII bear markets: 1946, 1957, 1960, 1962, 1966, 1974, 1987, 1990, 1998, 2001, 2002, and 2011 ◆ First October Dow top in 2007, 20-year 1987 Crash anniversary −2.6% ◆ Worst six months of the year ends with October (page 48) ◆ No longer worst month (pages 44 & 56) ◆ Best Dow, S&P, and NASDAQ month from 1993 to 2007 ◆ Midterm election year Octobers since 1950, #1 Dow (+3.2%), #1 S&P (3.4%), and #1 NASDAQ (4.3) ◆ October is a great time to buy ◆ Big October gains five years 1999–2003 after atrocious Septembers ◆ Can get into Best Six Months earlier using MACD (page 50) ◆ October 2011, second month to gain 1000 Dow points.

October Vital Statistics

	DJIA		S&P 500		NASDAQ		Russell 1K		Russell 2K	
Rank	7		7		8		7		12	
Up	37		37		22		21		18	
Down	26		26		20		13		16	
Average % Change	0.5%		0.7%		0.5%		0.7%		−0.6%	
Midterm Year	3.2%		3.4%		4.3%		5.0%		3.5%	
Best & Worst October										
	% Change		% Change		% Change		% Change		% Change	
Best	1982	10.7	1974	16.3	1974	17.2	1982	11.3	2011	15.0
Worst	1987	−23.2	1987	−21.8	1987	−27.2	1987	−21.9	1987	−30.8
Best & Worst October Weeks										
Best	10/11/74	12.6	10/11/74	14.1	10/31/08	10.9	10/31/08	10.8	10/31/08	14.1
Worst	10/10/08	−18.2	10/10/08	−18.2	10/23/87	−19.2	10/10/08	−18.2	10/23/87	−20.4
Best & Worst October Days										
Best	10/13/08	11.1	10/13/08	11.6	10/13/08	11.8	10/13/08	11.7	10/13/08	9.3
Worst	10/19/87	−22.6	10/19/87	−20.5	10/19/87	−11.4	10/19/87	−19.0	10/19/87	−12.5
First Trading Day of Expiration Week: 1980–2012										
Record (#Up–#Down)	27–6		25–8		23–10		26–7		25–8	
Current streak	U1		U1		U1		U1		U1	
Avg % Change	0.82		0.80		0.63		0.77		0.44	
Options Expiration Day: 1980–2012										
Record (#Up–#Down)	14–19		16–17		17–16		16–17		14–19	
Current streak	D1		D1		D1		D1		D1	
Avg % Change	−0.23		−0.31		−0.20		−0.29		−0.22	
Options Expiration Week: 1980–2012										
Record (#Up–#Down)	23–10		23–10		18–15		23–10		19–14	
Current streak	U5		U5		D2		U5		D2	
Avg % Change	0.64		0.65		0.65		0.64		0.28	
Week After Options Expiration: 1980–2012										
Record (#Up–#Down)	14–19		13–20		16–17		13–20		17–19	
Current streak	D1		D1		D1		D1		D1	
Avg % Change	−0.53		−0.55		−0.60		−0.57		−0.73	
First Trading Day Performance										
% of Time Up	49.2		49.2		47.6		52.9		50.0	
Avg % Change	0.08		0.06		−0.15		0.25		−0.26	
Last Trading Day Performance										
% of Time Up	54.0		55.6		66.7		64.7		73.5	
Avg % Change	0.07		0.15		0.51		0.36		0.63	

Dow & S&P 1950–April 2013, NASDAQ 1971–April 2013, Russell 1K & 2K 1979–April 2013.

October has killed many a bear;
Buy techs and small caps and soon wear a grin ear to ear.

SEPTEMBER/OCTOBER

MONDAY
D 61.9
S 66.7
N 52.4
29

No other country can substitute for the U.S. The U.S. is still No. 1 in military, No. 1 in economy, No. 1 in promoting human rights and No. 1 in idealism. Only the U.S. can lead the world. No other country can.
— Senior Korean official (to Thomas L. Friedman, *NY Times* Foreign Affairs columnist, 2/25/2009)

Last Day of Q3, Dow Down 12 of Last 16, Massive 4.7% Rally in 2008

TUESDAY
D 33.3
S 33.3
N 33.3
30

When you get into a tight place and everything goes against you, till it seems as though you could not hang on a minute longer, never give up then, for that is just the place and time that the tide will turn.
— Harriet Beecher Stowe (American writer and abolitionist)

First Trading Day in October, Dow Down 5 of Last 8
Off 2.4% in 2011

WEDNESDAY
D 52.4
S 47.6
N 38.1
1

The usual bull market successfully weathers a number of tests until it is considered invulnerable, whereupon it is ripe for a bust.
— George Soros (Financier, philanthropist, political activist, author, and philosopher, b. 1930)

Start Looking for MACD BUY Signals (Pages 50, 58, and 60)
Almanac Investor Subscribers Emailed When It Triggers (See Insert)

THURSDAY
D 47.6
S 57.1
N 57.1
2

I'm not better than the next trader, just quicker at admitting my mistakes and moving on to the next opportunity.
— George Soros (Financier, philanthropist, political activist, author, and philosopher, b. 1930)

FRIDAY
D 47.6
S 42.9
N 52.4
3

Writing a book is an adventure. To begin with it is a toy, an amusement; then it is a mistress, and then a master, and then a tyrant.
— Winston Churchill (British statesman, 1874–1965)

Yom Kippur

SATURDAY
4

SUNDAY
5

SECTOR SEASONALITY: SELECTED PERCENTAGE PLAYS

Sector seasonality was featured in the first 1968 *Almanac*. A Merrill Lynch study showed that buying seven sectors around September or October and selling in the first few months of 1954–1964 tripled the gains of holding them for 10 years. Over the years we have honed this strategy significantly and now devote a large portion of our time and resources to investing and trading during positive and negative seasonal periods for different sectors with Exchange Traded Funds (ETFs).

Updated seasonalities appear in the table below. We specify whether the seasonality starts or finishes in the beginning third (B), middle third (M), or last third (E) of the month. These selected percentage plays are geared to take advantage of the bulk of seasonal sector strength or weakness.

By design, entry points are in advance of the major seasonal moves, providing traders ample opportunity to accumulate positions at favorable prices. Conversely, exit points have been selected to capture the majority of the move.

From the major seasonalities in the table below, we created the Sector Index Seasonality Strategy Calendar on pages 94 and 96. Note the concentration of bullish sector seasonalities during the Best Six Months, November to April, and bearish sector seasonalities during the Worst Six Months, May to October.

Almanac Investor newsletter subscribers receive specific entry and exit points for highly correlated ETFs and detailed analysis in our monthly ETF Scoreboard and ETF Trades. Visit *www.stocktradersalmanac.com,* or see the insert for additional details and a special offer for new subscribers.

SECTOR INDEX SEASONALITY TABLE

Ticker	Sector Index	Type	Start		Finish		15-Year	10-Year	5-Year
								Average % Return[†]	
XCI	Computer Tech	Short	January	B	March	B	−7.7	−6.5	−3.5
IIX	Internet	Short	January	B	February	E	−8.9	−4.3	−0.8
XNG	Natural Gas	Long	February	B	June	E	16.8	13.0	12.6
RXP	Healthcare Prod	Long	March	M	June	M	6.5	8.3	6.7
RXH	Healthcare Prov	Long	March	M	June	M	14.3	12.6	18.1
MSH	High-Tech	Long	March	M	July	B	9.3	10.6	8.0
UTY	Utilities	Long	March	M	October	B	10.7	10.8	7.9
XCI	Computer Tech	Long	April	M	July	M	9.1	6.7	4.3
IIX	Internet	Long	April	M	July	B	8.5	7.8	1.4
CYC	Cyclical	Short	May	M	October	E	−8.7	−2.7	−8.2
XAU	Gold & Silver	Short	May	M	June	E	−7.6	−4.2	−5.5
S5MATR*	Materials	Short	May	M	October	M	−9.6	−3.0	−7.7
BKX	Banking	Short	June	B	July	B	−5.6	−6.1	−9.4
XNG	Natural Gas	Short	June	M	July	E	−8.1	−4.2	−5.5
XAU	Gold & Silver	Long	July	E	December	E	15.8	16.9	7.8
DJT	Transports	Short	July	M	October	M	−9.6	−3.0	−4.9
BTK	Biotech	Long	August	B	March	B	28.9	16.0	15.7
RXP	Healthcare Prod	Long	August	B	February	B	10.7	9.6	9.6
MSH	High-Tech	Long	August	M	January	M	18.6	13.3	7.8
IIX	Internet	Long	August	B	January	B	28.6	17.1	8.6
SOX	Semiconductor	Short	August	M	October	E	−11.1	−6.0	−9.9
CMR	Consumer	Long	September	E	June	B	10.8	7.5	4.1
RXH	Healthcare Prov	Short	September	M	November	B	−6.8	−5.7	−8.8
XOI	Oil	Short	September	B	November	E	−4.8	−3.7	−6.8
BKX	Banking	Long	October	B	May	B	15.1	10.5	18.2
XBD	Broker/Dealer	Long	October	B	April	M	32.7	15.0	20.8
XCI	Computer Tech	Long	October	B	January	B	18.2	9.3	8.6
CYC	Cyclical	Long	October	B	May	M	21.9	18.2	21.6
RXH	Healthcare Prov	Long	October	E	January	M	13.3	12.7	15.1
S5MATR*	Materials	Long	October	M	May	M	17.0	13.5	10.4
DRG	Pharmaceutical	Long	October	M	January	M	7.1	6.4	7.5
RMZ	Real Estate	Long	October	E	May	B	14.2	13.2	18.7
SOX	Semiconductor	Long	October	E	December	B	16.6	9.5	8.1
XTC	Telecom	Long	October	M	December	B	10.4	5.6	5.1
DJT	Transports	Long	October	B	May	B	21.6	19.1	22.0
XOI	Oil	Long	December	M	July	B	12.2	12.0	2.4

[†]Average % Return based on full seasonality completion through May 17, 2013
* S5MATR Available @ bloomberg.com

MONDAY

D 66.7
S 57.1
N 66.7

6

Interviewer: How is it possible to fight an enemy willing and ready to die for his cause? Accommodate him!
— General Norman Schwartzkof (Ret. commander of allied forces in 1990–1991 Gulf War, December 2001)

October Ends Dow and S&P "Worst Six Months" (Pages 44, 48, 50, and 147)
And NASDAQ "Worst Four Months" (Pages 56, 58, and 148)

TUESDAY

D 38.1
S 38.1
N 47.6

7

Love your enemies, for they tell you your faults.
— Benjamin Franklin (U.S. Founding Father, diplomat, inventor, 1706–1790)

WEDNESDAY

D 42.9
S 42.9
N 57.1

8

People have difficulty in cutting losses, admitting an error, and moving on. I am rather frequently—and on occasion, quite spectacularly—wrong. However, if we expect to be wrong, then there should be no ego tied up in admitting the error, honoring the stop loss, selling the loser—and preserving your capital.
— Barry L. Ritholtz (CEO Fusion IQ, *Bailout Nation*, The Big Picture blog, 8/12/2010, b. 1961)

Dow Lost 1874 Points (18.2%) on the Week Ending 10/10/08
Worst Dow Week in the History of Wall Street

THURSDAY

D 47.6
S 47.6
N 57.1

9

Everything possible today was at one time impossible. Everything impossible today may at some time in the future be possible.
— Edward Lindaman (Apollo space project, president Whitworth College, 1920–1982)

FRIDAY

D 38.1
S 42.9
N 57.1

10

Politics ought to be the part-time profession of every citizen who would protect the rights and privileges of free people and who would preserve what is good and fruitful in our national heritage.
— Dwight D. Eisenhower (34th U.S. President, 1890–1969)

SATURDAY

11

SUNDAY

12

SECTOR INDEX SEASONALITY STRATEGY CALENDAR*

* Graphic representation of the Sector Index Seasonality Percentage Plays on page 92.
L = Long Trade, S = Short Trade, → = Start of Trade

(continued on page 96)

94

OCTOBER

Columbus Day (Bond Market Closed)
Monday Before October Expiration, Dow Up 27 of 33

MONDAY
D 57.1
S 61.9
N 71.4
13

I went to a restaurant that serves "breakfast at any time." So I ordered French toast during the Renaissance.
— Steven Wright (Comedian, b. 1955)

TUESDAY
D 76.2
S 71.4
N 66.7
14

If investing is entertaining, if you're having fun, you're probably not making any money. Good investing is boring.
— George Soros (Financier, philanthropist, political activist, author, and philosopher, b. 1930)

October 2011, Second Dow Month to Gain 1000 Points

WEDNESDAY
D 52.4
S 52.4
N 52.4
15

Your chances for success in any undertaking can be measured by your belief in yourself.
— Robert Collier (Direct marketing copywriter and author, 1885–1950)

THURSDAY
D 52.4
S 57.1
N 47.6
16

Knowledge born from actual experience is the answer to why one profits; lack of it is the reason one loses.
— Gerald M. Loeb (E.F. Hutton, *The Battle for Investment Survival*, predicted 1929 Crash, 1900–1974)

October Expiration Day, Dow Down 6 Straight 2005–2010 and 8 of Last 10
Crash of October 19, 1987, Dow down 22.6% in One Day

FRIDAY
D 47.6
S 57.1
N 42.9
17

To know values is to know the meaning of the market.
— Charles Dow (Co-founder Dow Jones & Co., 1851–1902)

SATURDAY
18

SUNDAY
19

(continued from page 94)

SECTOR INDEX SEASONALITY STRATEGY CALENDAR*

* Graphic representation of the Sector Index Seasonality Percentage Plays on page 92.
L = Long Trade, S = Short Trade, ➞ = Start of Trade

Jeffrey Hirsch Demonstrates
How He Uses Stock Market
Cycles to Time the Market in
This New Video Seminar

Available as DVD or
Online Video at WileyTrading.com

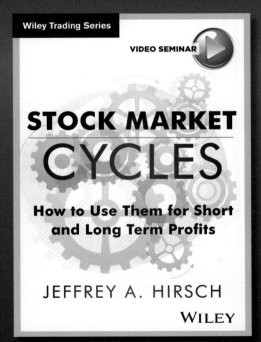

The Hirsch Organization has a long
history of accurate forecasts and
market-beating returns. In this new
video, Jeffrey Hirsch reveals how
to interpret stock market history
to forecast future movements. He
identifies major cycles, including
his Superboom forecast—a series of
converging factor that could result in
a six-fold market increase by 2025;
secular bull and bear markets; and
presidential term cycles.

He also discusses shorter term cycles,
including the "Best Six Months
Strategy," which has massively
outperformed the overall market for
many years. This video seminar
summarizes the STA investing approach
and provides a road map to profiting in
the market in the years ahead.

WILEY

Wiley is a registered trademark of John Wiley & Sons, Inc.

THE ULTIMATE GUIDE TO MARKET-BEATING RETURNS, FROM *STOCK TRADER'S ALMANAC* EDITOR-IN-CHIEF **JEFFREY HIRSCH**

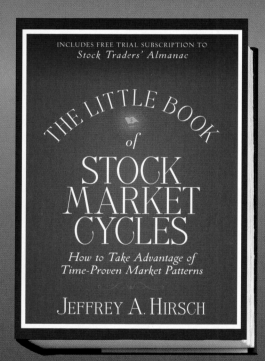

To profit from the stock market, you must be able to predict its patterns. *The Little Book of Stock Market Cycles* brings together everything you need to know about recurring trends in one insightful and accessible volume, backed by the wisdom of the pre-eminent authority on market cycles and seasonal patterns.

The perfect companion to the *Stock Trader's Almanac*, this little book is big on practical advice and proven strategies that you can put to use right away to consistently outperform the market.

Available wherever books and e-books are sold.
www.littlebook-series.com

Wiley is a registered trademark of John Wiley & Sons, Inc.

OCTOBER

Late October is Time to Buy Depressed Stocks
Especially Techs and Small Caps

MONDAY

D 61.9
S 66.7
N 66.7

20

Your organization will never get better unless you are willing to admit that there is something wrong with it.
— General Norman Schwartzkof (Ret. Commander of Allied Forces in 1990–1991 Gulf War)

TUESDAY

D 52.4
S 61.9
N 52.4

21

You must automate, emigrate, or evaporate.
— James A. Baker (*General Electric*)

WEDNESDAY

D 42.9
S 47.6
N 42.9

22

A person's greatest virtue is his ability to correct his mistakes and continually make a new person of himself.
— Yang-Ming Wang (Chinese philosopher, 1472–1529)

THURSDAY

D 52.4
S 57.1
N 57.1

23

I always keep these seasonal patterns in the back of my mind. My antennae start to purr at certain times of the year.
— Kenneth Ward (VP Hayden Stone, *General Technical Survey*, 1899–1976)

FRIDAY

D 47.6
S 42.9
N 42.9

24

Regardless of current economic conditions, it's always best to remember that the stock market is a barometer and not a thermometer.
— Yale Hirsch (Creator of *Stock Trader's Almanac*, b. 1923)

SATURDAY

25

SUNDAY

26

Good Month !!

NOVEMBER ALMANAC

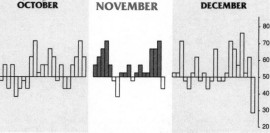

NOVEMBER						
S	M	T	W	T	F	S
						1
2	3	4	5	6	7	8
9	10	11	12	13	14	15
16	17	18	19	20	21	22
23	24	25	26	27	28	29
30						

DECEMBER						
S	M	T	W	T	F	S
	1	2	3	4	5	6
7	8	9	10	11	12	13
14	15	16	17	18	19	20
21	22	23	24	25	26	27
28	29	30	31			

Market Probability Chart above is a graphic representation of the S&P 500 Recent Market Probability Calendar on page 124.

◆ #3 S&P and Dow month since 1950, #4 on NASDAQ since 1971 (pages 44 & 56) ◆ Start of the "Best Six Months" of the year (page 48), NASDAQ's Best Eight Months and Best Three (pages 147 & 148) ◆ Simple timing indicator almost triples "Best Six Months" strategy (page 50), doubles NASDAQ's Best Eight (page 58) ◆ Day before and after Thanksgiving Day combined, only 13 losses in 61 years (page 104) ◆ Week before Thanksgiving Dow up 15 of last 20 ◆ Midterm election year Novembers rank #2 Dow, S&P, and NASDAQ.

November Vital Statistics

	DJIA		S&P 500		NASDAQ		Russell 1K		Russell 2K	
Rank	3		3		4		3		4	
Up	41		41		27		24		22	
Down	22		22		15		10		12	
Average % Change	1.5%		1.5%		1.5%		1.6%		1.8%	
Midterm Year	2.5%		2.7%		3.8%		2.7%		3.9%	
Best & Worst November										
	% Change		% Change		% Change		% Change		% Change	
Best	1962	10.1	1980	10.2	2001	14.2	1980	10.1	2002	8.8
Worst	1973	−14.0	1973	−11.4	2000	−22.9	2000	−9.3	2008	−12.0
Best & Worst November Weeks										
Best	11/28/08	9.7	11/28/08	12.0	11/28/08	10.9	11/28/08	12.5	11/28/08	16.4
Worst	11/21/08	−5.3	11/21/08	−8.4	11/10/00	−12.2	11/21/08	−8.8	11/21/08	−11.0
Best & Worst November Days										
Best	11/13/08	6.7	11/13/08	6.9	11/13/08	6.5	11/13/08	7.0	11/13/08	8.5
Worst	11/20/08	−5.6	11/20/08	−6.7	11/19/08	−6.5	11/20/08	−6.9	11/19/08	−7.9
First Trading Day of Expiration Week: 1980–2012										
Record (#Up–#Down)	16–17		14–19		12–21		15–18		14–19	
Current streak	D2		U1		D3		U1		D2	
Avg % Change	−0.05		−0.09		−0.16		−0.10		−0.11	
Options Expiration Day: 1980–2012										
Record (#Up–#Down)	21–12		19–14		17–16		19–14		16–16	
Current streak	U3		U1		U1		U1		U3	
Avg % Change	0.23		0.16		0.01		0.15		0.11	
Options Expiration Week: 1980–2012										
Record (#Up–#Down)	21–12		19–14		16–17		18–15		16–17	
Current streak	D2		D2		D5		D2		D2	
Avg % Change	0.22		−0.05		−0.11		−0.08		−0.37	
Week After Options Expiration: 1980–2012										
Record (#Up–#Down)	19–14		20–13		21–12		20–13		19–14	
Current streak	U1		U1		U1		U1		U1	
Avg % Change	0.72		0.70		0.78		0.70		0.78	
First Trading Day Performance										
% of Time Up	63.5		63.5		64.3		70.6		64.7	
Avg % Change	0.27		0.30		0.29		0.39		0.21	
Last Trading Day Performance										
% of Time Up	55.6		55.6		64.3		50.0		70.6	
Avg % Change	0.11		0.15		−0.08		0.03		0.22	

Dow & S&P 1950–April 2013, NASDAQ 1971–April 2013, Russell 1K & 2K 1979–April 2013.

Astute investors always smile and remember,
When stocks seasonally start soaring, and salute November.

OCTOBER/NOVEMBER

MONDAY
27

D 38.1
S 42.9
N 33.3

All you need to succeed is a yellow pad and a pencil.
— Andre Meyer (Top deal maker at Lazard Freres)

FOMC Meeting (2 Days)

TUESDAY
28

D 52.4
S 57.1
N 47.6

In the course of evolution and a higher civilization we might be able to get along comfortably without Congress, but without Wall Street, never.
— Henry Clews (1900)

85th Anniversary of 1929 Crash, Dow Down 23.0% in Two Days, October 28 and 29

WEDNESDAY
29

D 66.7
S 61.9
N 61.9

At a time of war, we need you to work for peace. At a time of inequality, we need you to work for opportunity. At a time of so much cynicism and so much doubt, we need you to make us believe again.
— Barack H. Obama (44th U.S. President, Commencement Wesleyan University, 5/28/2008, b. 1961)

THURSDAY
30

D 66.7
S 71.4
N 71.4

Your emotions are often a reverse indicator of what you ought to be doing.
— John F. Hindelong (Dillon, Reed)

Halloween

FRIDAY
31

D 52.4
S 61.9
N 66.7

History must repeat itself because we pay such little attention to it the first time.
— Blackie Sherrod (Sportswriter, b. 1919)

November Almanac Investor Seasonalities: See Pages 92, 94, and 96

SATURDAY
1

Daylight Saving Time Ends

SUNDAY
2

MIDTERM ELECTION TIME UNUSUALLY BULLISH

Presidential election years tend to produce high drama and frenetic campaigns. Midterm years with only local or state candidates running are less stressful. Could this be the reason for the bullishness that seems to occur in the five days before and three days after midterm congressional elections? We don't think so. So many bear markets seem to occur in midterm years, very often bottoming in October. Also, major military involvements began or were in their early stages in midterm years, such as World War II, Korea, Vietnam, Kuwait, and Iraq. Solidly bullish midterm years such as 1954, 1958, 1986, 2006, and 2010 were exceptions. With so many negative occurrences in midterm years, perhaps the opportunity for investors to make a change for the better by casting their votes translates into an inner bullish feeling before and after midterm elections.

An impressive 2.7% has been the average gain during the eight trading days surrounding midterm election days since 1934. This is equivalent to roughly 52 Dow points per day at present levels. There was only one losing period in 1994 when the Republicans took control of both the House and the Senate for the first time in 40 years. Four other midterm switches occurred in 1946, when control of Congress passed to the Republicans for just two years, in 1954, when Democrats took back control, in 2006, when Democrats regained control, and in 2010, when Republicans reclaimed the House.

There were 11 occasions when the percentage of House seats lost by the president's party was in double digits. The average market gain during the eight-day trading period was 2.1%. In contrast, in the eight occasions when there were no losses, or losses were in single digits, gains averaged 3.4%

BULLS WIN BATTLE BETWEEN ELEPHANTS AND DONKEYS

Midterm Year	Dow Jones Industrials 5 Trading Days Before E. Day	3 Trading Days After E. Day	% Change	President's Party % Seats Lost	President in Power
1934	93.36	99.02	6.1%	2.9%	Dem
1938	152.21	158.41	4.1	−21.3	Dem
1942	113.11	116.12	2.7	−16.9	Dem
1946	164.20	170.79	4.0	−22.6	Dem*
1950	225.69	229.29	1.6	−11.0	Dem
1954	356.32	366.00	2.7	−8.1	Rep*
1958	536.88	554.26	3.2	−23.9	Rep
1962	588.98	616.13	4.6	−1.5	Dem
1966	809.63	819.09	1.2	−15.9	Dem
1970	754.45	771.97	2.3	−6.3	Rep
1974	659.34	667.16	1.2	−25.0	Rep
1978	792.45	807.09	1.8	−5.1	Dem
1982	1006.07	1051.78	4.5	−13.5	Rep
1986	1845.47	1886.53	2.2	−2.7	Rep
1990	2448.02	2488.61	1.7	−4.6	Rep
1994	3863.37	3801.47	−1.6	−20.9	Dem*
1998	8366.04	8975.46	7.3	2.4	Dem
2002	8368.94	8537.13	2.0	3.6	Rep
2006	12080.73	12108.43	0.2	−12.9	Rep*
2010	11169.46	11444.08	2.5	−24.6	Dem*
		Total	**54.3%**		
		Average	**2.7%**		

*Control switches to other Party

First Trading Day in November, Dow Down 5 of Last 8

MONDAY

D 57.1
S 57.1
N 66.7

3

When a falling stock becomes a screaming buy because it cannot conceivably drop further, try to buy it 30 percent lower.
— Al Rizzo (1986)

Election Day

🐃 **TUESDAY**

D 52.4
S 61.9
N 61.9

4

Those who cast the votes decide nothing. Those who count the votes decide everything.
— Joseph Stalin (Ruler USSR, 1929–1953, 1879–1953)

🐃 **WEDNESDAY**

D 66.7
S 66.7
N 76.2

5

People somehow think you must buy at the bottom and sell at the top. That's nonsense. The idea is to buy when the probability is greatest that the market is going to advance.
— Martin Zweig (Fund manager, *Winning on Wall Street*, 1943–2013)

November Begins Dow and S&P "Best Six Months" (Pages 44, 48, 50, 147)
And NASDAQ "Best Eight Months" (Pages 56, 58, and 148)

🐃 **THURSDAY**

D 71.4
S 71.4
N 66.7

6

There is no great mystery to satisfying your customers. Build them a quality product and treat them with respect. It's that simple.
— Lee Iacocca (American industrialist, Former Chrysler CEO, b. 1924)

FRIDAY

D 57.1
S 57.1
N 61.9

7

The heights by great men reached and kept, were not attained by sudden flight, but they, while their companions slept, were toiling upward in the night.
— Henry Wadsworth Longfellow

SATURDAY

8

SUNDAY

9

FOURTH QUARTER MARKET MAGIC

Examining market performance on a quarterly basis reveals several intriguing and helpful patterns. Fourth-quarter market gains have been magical, providing the greatest and most consistent gains over the years. First-quarter performance runs a respectable second. This should not be surprising, as cash inflows, trading volume, and buying bias are generally elevated during these two quarters.

Positive market psychology hits a fever pitch as the holiday season approaches, and does not begin to wane until spring. Professionals drive the market higher, as they make portfolio adjustments to maximize year-end numbers. Bonuses are paid and invested around the turn of the year.

The market's sweet spot of the four-year cycle begins in the fourth quarter of the midterm year. The best two-quarter span runs from the fourth quarter of the midterm year through the first quarter of the pre-election year, averaging 15.3% for the Dow, 16.0% for the S&P 500, and an amazing 23.3% for NASDAQ.

Quarterly strength fades in the latter half of the pre-election year, but stays impressively positive through the election year. Losses dominate the first and third quarters of post-election years and the first and second quarters of midterm years.

QUARTERLY % CHANGES

	Q1	Q2	Q3	Q4	Year	Q2–Q3	Q4–Q1
Dow Jones Industrials (1949–March 2013)							
Average	2.3%	1.5%	0.5%	3.8%	8.2%	2.0%	6.4%
Post Election	−0.4%	1.6%	0.2%	3.4%	4.4%	1.8%	5.2%
Midterm	1.5%	−1.8%	−0.5%	7.3%	6.7%	−2.2%	15.3%
Pre-Election	7.5%	5.3%	1.6%	2.3%	16.9%	6.8%	3.2%
Election	0.8%	1.0%	0.6%	2.0%	4.8%	1.7%	1.7%
S&P 500 (1949-March 2013)							
Average	2.3%	1.6%	0.6%	4.0%	8.7%	2.3%	6.6%
Post Election	−0.6%	2.2%	0.4%	3.1%	4.8%	2.7%	4.3%
Midterm	1.0%	−2.8%	0.1%	8.0%	6.4%	−2.7%	16.0%
Pre-Election	7.5%	5.2%	1.1%	3.0%	17.1%	6.3%	4.6%
Election	1.4%	1.8%	0.9%	1.9%	6.6%	2.8%	1.6%
NASDAQ Composite (1971-March 2013)							
Average	4.4%	3.1%	−0.2%	4.3%	12.0%	3.1%	9.0%
Post Election	−2.2%	6.8%	1.3%	4.2%	8.4%	8.1%	6.3%
Midterm	2.1%	−3.4%	−5.2%	8.9%	1.7%	−8.1%	23.3%
Pre-Election	13.8%	8.0%	1.7%	5.1%	30.9%	9.8%	9.7%
Election	3.9%	0.8%	1.1%	− 0.8%	5.8%	2.2%	−2.4%

NOVEMBER

MONDAY
D 52.4
S 47.6
N 57.1
10

The political problem of mankind is to combine three things: economic efficiency, social justice, and individual liberty.
— John Maynard Keynes (British economist, 1883–1946)

Veterans' Day (Bond Market Closed)

TUESDAY
D 38.1
S 38.1
N 42.9
11

The test of success is not what you do when you are on top. Success is how high you bounce when you hit bottom.
— General George S. Patton, Jr. (U.S. Army field commander WWII, 1885–1945)

WEDNESDAY
D 52.4
S 52.4
N 52.4
12

The most dangerous thing that takes place [in companies] is that success breeds arrogance, and arrogance seems to make people stop listening to their customers and to their employees. And that is the beginning of the end. The challenge is not to be a great company; the challenge is to remain a great company.
— George Fisher (Motorola)

THURSDAY
D 57.1
S 52.4
N 57.1
13

We prefer to cut back exposure on what's going against us and add exposure where it's more favorable to our portfolio. This way, we're always attempting to tilt the odds in our favor. This is the exact opposite of a long investor that would average down. Averaging down is a very dangerous practice.
— John Del Vecchio and Brad Lamensdorf (Portfolio managers Active Bear ETF, 5/10/12 *Almanac Investor* Interview)

FRIDAY
D 61.9
S 57.1
N 57.1
14

I hate to be wrong. That has aborted many a tempting error, but not all of them. But I hate much more to stay wrong.
— Paul A. Samuelson (American economist, 12/23/03 University of Kansas interview, 1915–2009)

SATURDAY
15

SUNDAY
16

TRADING THE THANKSGIVING MARKET

For 35 years, the "holiday spirit" gave the Wednesday before Thanksgiving and the Friday after a great track record, except for two occasions. Publishing it in the 1987 *Almanac* was the "kiss of death." Wednesday, Friday, and Monday were all crushed, down 6.6% over the three days in 1987. Since 1988, Wednesday–Friday gained 15 of 25 times, with a total Dow point-gain of 672.37 versus Monday's total Dow point-loss of 661.38, down 10 of 15 since 1998. The best strategy appears to be coming into the week long and exiting into strength Friday. Greece's debt crisis cancelled Thanksgiving on Wall Street in 2011.

DOW JONES INDUSTRIALS BEFORE AND AFTER THANKSGIVING

	Tuesday Before	Wednesday Before		Friday After	Total Gain Dow Points	Dow Close	Next Monday
1952	−0.18	1.54		1.22	2.76	283.66	0.04
1953	1.71	0.65		2.45	3.10	280.23	1.14
1954	3.27	1.89		3.16	5.05	387.79	0.72
1955	4.61	0.71		0.26	0.97	482.88	−1.92
1956	−4.49	−2.16		4.65	2.49	472.56	−2.27
1957	−9.04	10.69		3.84	14.53	449.87	−2.96
1958	−4.37	8.63		8.31	16.94	557.46	2.61
1959	2.94	1.41		1.42	2.83	652.52	6.66
1960	−3.44	1.37		4.00	5.37	606.47	−1.04
1961	−0.77	1.10		2.18	3.28	732.60	−0.61
1962	6.73	4.31		7.62	11.93	644.87	−2.81
1963	32.03	−2.52	T	9.52	7.00	750.52	1.39
1964	−1.68	−5.21		−0.28	−5.49	882.12	−6.69
1965	2.56	N/C	H	−0.78	−0.78	948.16	−1.23
1966	−3.18	1.84		6.52	8.36	803.34	−2.18
1967	13.17	3.07	A	3.58	6.65	877.60	4.51
1968	8.14	−3.17		8.76	5.59	985.08	−1.74
1969	−5.61	3.23	N	1.78	5.01	812.30	−7.26
1970	5.21	1.98		6.64	8.62	781.35	12.74
1971	−5.18	0.66	K	17.96	18.62	816.59	13.14
1972	8.21	7.29		4.67	11.96	1025.21	−7.45
1973	−17.76	10.08	S	−0.98	9.10	854.00	−29.05
1974	5.32	2.03		−0.63	1.40	618.66	−15.64
1975	9.76	3.15		2.12	5.27	860.67	−4.33
1976	−6.57	1.66	G	5.66	7.32	956.62	−6.57
1977	6.41	0.78		1.12	1.90	844.42	−4.85
1978	−1.56	2.95	I	3.12	6.07	810.12	3.72
1979	−6.05	−1.80		4.35	2.55	811.77	16.98
1980	3.93	7.00	V	3.66	10.66	993.34	−23.89
1981	18.45	7.90		7.80	15.70	885.94	3.04
1982	−9.01	9.01	I	7.36	16.37	1007.36	−4.51
1983	7.01	−0.20		1.83	1.63	1277.44	−7.62
1984	9.83	6.40	N	18.78	25.18	1220.30	−7.95
1985	0.12	18.92		−3.56	15.36	1472.13	−14.22
1986	6.05	4.64	G	−2.53	2.11	1914.23	−1.55
1987	40.45	−16.58		−36.47	−53.05	1910.48	−76.93
1988	11.73	14.58	N	−17.60	−3.02	2074.68	6.76
1989	7.25	17.49		18.77	36.26	2675.55	19.42
1990	−35.15	9.16	G	−12.13	−2.97	2527.23	5.94
1991	14.08	−16.10		−5.36	−21.46	2894.68	40.70
1992	25.66	17.56		15.94	33.50	3282.20	22.96
1993	3.92	13.41		−3.63	9.78	3683.95	−6.15
1994	−91.52	−3.36		33.64	30.28	3708.27	31.29
1995	40.46	18.06	D	7.23*	25.29	5048.84	22.04
1996	−19.38	−29.07		22.36*	−6.71	6521.70	N/C
1997	41.03	−14.17	A	28.35*	14.18	7823.13	189.98
1998	−73.12	13.13		18.80*	31.93	9333.08	−216.53
1999	−93.89	12.54	Y	−19.26*	−6.72	10988.91	−40.99
2000	31.85	−95.18		70.91*	−24.27	10470.23	75.84
2001	−75.08	−66.70		125.03*	58.33	9959.71	23.04
2002	−172.98	255.26		−35.59*	219.67	8896.09	−33.52
2003	16.15	15.63		2.89*	18.52	9782.46	116.59
2004	3.18	27.71		1.92*	29.63	10522.23	−46.33
2005	51.15	44.66		15.53*	60.19	10931.62	−40.90
2006	5.05	5.36		−46.78*	−41.42	12280.17	−158.46
2007	51.70	−211.10		181.84*	−29.26	12980.88	−237.44
2008	36.08	247.14		102.43*	349.57	8829.04	−679.95
2009	−17.24	30.69		−154.48*	−123.79	10309.92	34.92
2010	−142.21	150.91		−95.28*	55.63	11092.00	−39.51
2011	−53.59	−236.17		−25.77*	−261.94	11231.78	291.23
2012	−7.45	48.38		172.79*	221.17	13009.68	−42.31

*Shortened trading day

Monday Before November Expiration, Dow Down 9 of Last 14

MONDAY

D 57.1
S 47.6
N 42.9

17

Of a stock's move, 31% can be attributed to the general stock market, 12% to the industry influence, 37% to the influence of other groupings, and the remaining 20% is peculiar to the one stock.
— Benjamin F. King (*Market and Industry Factors in Stock Price Behavior, Journal of Business*, January 1966)

TUESDAY

D 42.9
S 52.4
N 47.6

18

In this age of instant information, investors can experience both fear and greed at the exact same moment.
— Sam Stovall (Chief Investment Strategist Standard & Poor's, October 2003)

Week Before Thanksgiving, Dow Up 15 of Last 20,
2003 –1.4%, 2004 –0.8%, 2008 –5.3%, 2011 –2.9%, 2012 –1.8%

WEDNESDAY

D 52.4
S 57.1
N 52.4

19

If you don't know who you are, the stock market is an expensive place to find out.
— George Goodman (*Institutional Investor, New York*, "Adam Smith," *The Money Game*, b. 1930)

THURSDAY

D 52.4
S 52.4
N 57.1

20

Self-discipline is a form of freedom. Freedom from laziness and lethargy, freedom from expectations and demands of others, freedom from weakness and fear—and doubt.
— Harvey A. Dorfman (Sports psychologist, *The Mental ABC's of Pitching*, b. 1935)

November Expiration Day, Dow Up 9 of Last 11
Dow Surged in 2008, Up 494 Points (6.5%)

FRIDAY

D 57.1
S 52.4
N 57.1

21

In my experience, selling a put is much safer than buying a stock.
— Kyle Rosen (Boston Capital Mgmt., *Barron's*, 8/23/04)

SATURDAY

22

SUNDAY

23

MOST OF THE SO-CALLED "JANUARY EFFECT" TAKES PLACE IN THE LAST HALF OF DECEMBER

Over the years we reported annually on the fascinating January Effect, showing that small-cap stocks handily outperformed large-cap stocks during January 40 out of 43 years between 1953 and 1995. Readers saw that "Cats and Dogs" on average quadrupled the returns of blue chips in this period. Then, the January Effect disappeared over the next four years.

Looking at the graph on page 110, comparing the Russell 1000 index of large-capitalization stocks to the Russell 2000 smaller-capitalization stocks, shows small-cap stocks beginning to outperform the blue chips in mid-December. Narrowing the comparison down to half-month segments was an inspiration and proved to be quite revealing, as you can see in the table below.

26-YEAR AVERAGE RATES OF RETURN (DEC 1987 – FEB 2013)

From	Russell 1000		Russell 2000	
mid-Dec*	Change	Annualized	Change	Annualized
12/15–12/31	1.8%	50.5%	3.4%	115.1
12/15–01/15	2.2	28.3	4.0	56.7
12/15–01/31	2.5	22.2	4.3	40.8
12/15–02/15	3.4	22.2	5.9	41.1
12/15–02/28	2.7	14.4	5.6	31.6
end-Dec*				
12/31–01/15	0.5	11.0	0.6	13.4
12/31–01/31	0.7	8.7	0.9	11.4
12/31–02/15	1.6	13.3	2.4	20.5
12/31–02/28	0.9	5.8	2.1	14.0

34-YEAR AVERAGE RATES OF RETURN (DEC 1979 – FEB 2013)

From	Russell 1000		Russell 2000	
mid-Dec*	Change	Annualized	Change	Annualized
12/15–12/31	1.6%	43.9%	3.0%	96.8
12/15–01/15	2.4	31.2	4.4	63.8
12/15–01/31	2.8	25.2	4.8	46.4
12/15–02/15	3.5	22.9	6.3	44.3
12/15–02/28	3.0	15.7	6.1	34.0
end-Dec*				
12/31–01/15	0.8	18.2	1.4	33.9
12/31–01/31	1.2	15.4	1.7	22.4
12/31–02/15	1.9	16.0	3.2	28.2
12/31–02/28	1.5	9.6	3.0	19.9

Mid-month dates are the 11th trading day of the month, month end dates are monthly closes

Small-cap strength in the last half of December became even more magnified after the 1987 market crash. Note the dramatic shift in gains in the last half of December during the 26-year period starting in 1987, versus the 34 years from 1979 to 2013. With all the beaten-down small stocks being dumped for tax loss purposes, it generally pays to get a head start on the January Effect in mid-December. You don't have to wait until December either; the small-cap sector often begins to turn around toward the end of October and November.

NOVEMBER

Trading Thanksgiving Market: Long into Weakness Prior,
Exit into Strength After (Page 104)

🐃 **MONDAY**
D 66.7
S 66.7
N 57.1
24

If there is something you really want to do, make your plan and do it. Otherwise, you'll just regret it forever.
— Richard Rocco (PostNet franchisee, *Entrepreneur* magazine, 12/2006, b. 1946)

🐃 **TUESDAY**
D 61.9
S 66.7
N 61.9
25

Pullbacks near the 30-week moving average are often good times to take action.
— Michael L. Burke (*Investors Intelligence*)

🐃 **WEDNESDAY**
D 57.1
S 71.4
N 66.7
26

Never mind telling me what stocks to buy; tell me when to buy them.
— Humphrey B. Neill (Investor, analyst, author, *Neill Letters of Contrary Opinion*, 1895–1977)

Thanksgiving (Market Closed)

THURSDAY
27

Amongst democratic nations, each generation is a new people.
— Alexis de Tocqueville (Author, *Democracy in America*, 1840, 1805–1859)

(Shortened Trading Day)
Last Trading Day of November, S&P Up 6 of Last 7

FRIDAY
D 57.1
S 42.9
N 47.6
28

What investors really get paid for is holding dogs. Small stocks tend to have higher average returns than big stocks, and value stocks tend to have higher average returns than growth stocks.
— Kenneth R. French (Economist, Dartmouth, NBER, b. 1954)

SATURDAY
29

December Almanac Investor Seasonalities: See Pages 92, 94, and 96

SUNDAY
30

Good MONTH !!!

DECEMBER ALMANAC

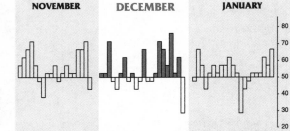

Market Probability Chart above is a graphic representation of the S&P 500 Recent Market Probability Calendar on page 124.

DECEMBER						
S	M	T	W	T	F	S
	1	2	3	4	5	6
7	8	9	10	11	12	13
14	15	16	17	18	19	20
21	22	23	24	25	26	27
28	29	30	31			

JANUARY						
S	M	T	W	T	F	S
				1	2	3
4	5	6	7	8	9	10
11	12	13	14	15	16	17
18	19	20	21	22	23	24
25	26	27	28	29	30	31

◆ #1 S&P (+1.7%) and #2 Dow (+1.7%) month since 1950 (page 44), #2 NASDAQ 2.0% since 1971 ◆ 2002 worst December since 1931, down over 6% Dow and S&P, –9.7% on NASDAQ (pages 152, 155, & 157) ◆ "Free lunch" served on Wall Street before Christmas (page 112) ◆ Small-caps start to outperform larger caps near middle of month (pages 106 & 110) ◆ "Santa Claus Rally" visible in graph above and on page 114 ◆ In 1998 was part of best fourth quarter since 1928 (page 167) ◆ Fourth quarter expiration week most bullish triple-witching week, Dow up 17 of last 22 (page 76) ◆ Midterm election years Decembers rankings: #3 Dow and S&P, #4 NASDAQ.

December Vital Statistics

	DJIA		S&P 500		NASDAQ		Russell 1K		Russell 2K	
Rank	2		1		2		2		1	
Up	45		48		25		27		27	
Down	18		15		17		7		7	
Average % Change	1.7%		1.7%		2.0%		1.7%		2.8%	
Midterm Year	1.6%		1.9%		0.8%		1.3%		1.6%	
Best & Worst December										
	% Change		% Change		% Change		% Change		% Change	
Best	1991	9.5	1991	11.2	1999	22.0	1991	11.2	1999	11.2
Worst	2002	–6.2	2002	–6.0	2002	–9.7	2002	–5.8	2002	–5.7
Best & Worst December Weeks										
Best	12/2/11	7.0	12/2/11	7.4	12/8/00	10.3	12/2/11	7.4	12/2/11	10.3
Worst	12/4/87	–7.5	12/6/74	–7.1	12/15/00	–9.1	12/4/87	–7.0	12/12/80	–6.5
Best & Worst December Days										
Best	12/16/08	4.2	12/16/08	5.1	12/5/00	10.5	12/16/08	5.2	12/16/08	6.7
Worst	12/1/08	–7.7	12/1/08	–8.9	12/1/08	–9.0	12/1/08	–9.1	12/1/08	–11.9
First Trading Day of Expiration Week: 1980–2012										
Record (#Up–#Down)	19–14		20–13		14–19		20–13		15–18	
Current streak	U1		U1		U1		U1		U1	
Avg % Change	0.17		0.14		–0.06		0.10		–0.17	
Options Expiration Day: 1980–2012										
Record (#Up–#Down)	21–12		24–9		23–10		24–9		21–12	
Current streak	D3		D1		D1		D1		D1	
Avg % Change	0.33		0.39		0.34		0.37		0.42	
Options Expiration Week: 1980–2012										
Record (#Up–#Down)	25–8		24–9		19–14		23–10		17–16	
Current streak	U1		U1		U1		U1		U1	
Avg % Change	0.65		0.68		0.16		0.62		0.52	
Week After Options Expiration: 1980–2012										
Record (#Up–#Down)	22–10		19–14		20–13		19–14		22–11	
Current streak	D1		D1		D1		D1		D1	
Avg % Change	0.71		0.44		0.63		0.47		0.78	
First Trading Day Performance										
% of Time Up	47.6		50.8		61.9		52.9		52.9	
Avg % Change	–0.06		–0.03		0.16		–0.04		–0.08	
Last Trading Day Performance										
% of Time Up	54.0		61.9		73.8		52.9		70.6	
Avg % Change	0.08		0.12		0.38		–0.04		0.49	

Dow & S&P 1950–April 2013, NASDAQ 1971–April 2013, Russell 1K & 2K 1979–April 2013.

If Santa Claus should fail to call,
Bears may come to Broad and Wall.

First Trading Day in December, NASDAQ Up 19 of 26
Down Three Straight 2006–2008

MONDAY

D 47.6
S 52.4
N 66.7

1

People with a sense of fulfillment think the world is good, while the frustrated blame the world for their failure.
— Eric Hoffer (*The True Believer*, 1951)

TUESDAY

D 47.6
S 52.4
N 61.9

2

It is tact that is golden, not silence.
— Samuel Butler (English writer, 1600–1680)

WEDNESDAY

D 66.7
S 71.4
N 61.9

3

Resentment is like taking poison and waiting for the other person to die.
— Malachy McCourt (*A Monk Swimming: A Memoir*)

THURSDAY

D 61.9
S 47.6
N 57.1

4

A government which robs Peter to pay Paul can always depend on the support of Paul.
— George Bernard Shaw (Irish dramatist, 1856–1950)

FRIDAY

D 47.6
S 42.9
N 33.3

5

The authority of a thousand is not worth the humble reasoning of a single individual.
— Galileo Galilei (Italian physicist and astronomer, 1564–1642)

SATURDAY

6

SUNDAY

7

JANUARY EFFECT NOW STARTS IN MID-DECEMBER

Small-cap stocks tend to outperform big caps in January. Known as the "January Effect," the tendency is clearly revealed by the graph below. Thirty-five years of daily data for the Russell 2000 index of smaller companies are divided by the Russell 1000 index of largest companies, and then compressed into a single year to show an idealized yearly pattern. When the graph is descending, big blue chips are outperforming smaller companies; when the graph is rising, smaller companies are moving up faster than their larger brethren.

In a typical year, the smaller fry stay on the sidelines while the big boys are on the field. Then, around late October, small stocks begin to wake up, and in mid-December, they take off. Anticipated year-end dividends, payouts, and bonuses could be a factor. Other major moves are quite evident just before Labor Day—possibly because individual investors are back from vacations—and off the low points in late October and November. Small caps hold the lead through the beginning of May.

RUSSELL 2000/RUSSELL 1000 ONE-YEAR SEASONAL PATTERN

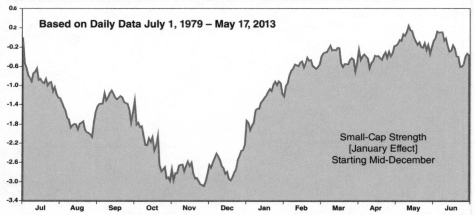

The bottom graph shows the actual ratio of the Russell 2000 divided by the Russell 1000 from 1979. Smaller companies had the upper hand for five years into 1983, as the last major bear trend wound to a close and the nascent bull market logged its first year. After falling behind for about eight years, they came back after the Persian Gulf War bottom in 1990, moving up until 1994, when big caps ruled the latter stages of the millennial bull. For six years, the picture was bleak for small fry, as the blue chips and tech stocks moved to stratospheric PE ratios. Small caps spiked in late 1999 and early 2000 and reached a peak in early 2006, as the four-year-old bull entered its final year. Note how the small-cap advantage has waned during major bull moves and intensified during weak market times.

RUSSELL 2000/RUSSELL 1000 (1979 TO APRIL 2013)

DECEMBER

MONDAY
8

D 52.4
S 52.4
N 57.1

There is a perfect inverse correlation between inflation rates and price/earnings ratios.... When inflation has been very high... P/E has been [low].
— Liz Ann Sonders (Chief Investment Strategist Charles Schwab, June 2006)

TUESDAY
9

D 61.9
S 61.9
N 57.1

Whenever a well-known bearish analyst is interviewed [Cover story] in the financial press, it usually coincides with an important near-term market bottom.
— Clif Droke (Clifdroke.com, 11/15/04)

WEDNESDAY
10

D 47.6
S 47.6
N 42.9

Lack of money is the root of all evil.
— George Bernard Shaw (Irish dramatist, 1856–1950)

Small-Cap Strength Starts in Mid-December (Page 106)

THURSDAY
11

D 47.6
S 52.4
N 42.9

You try to be greedy when others are fearful, and fearful when others are greedy.
— Warren Buffett (CEO Berkshire Hathaway, investor and philanthropist, b. 1930)

FRIDAY
12

D 47.6
S 42.9
N 38.1

Inflation is the modern way that governments default on their debt.
— Mike Epstein (MTA, MIT/Sloan Lab for Financial Engineering)

SATURDAY
13

SUNDAY
14

WALL STREET'S ONLY "FREE LUNCH" SERVED BEFORE CHRISTMAS

Investors tend to get rid of their losers near year-end for tax purposes, often hammering these stocks down to bargain levels. Over the years, the *Almanac* has shown that NYSE stocks selling at their lows on December 15 will usually outperform the market by February 15 in the following year. Preferred stocks, closed-end funds, splits, and new issues are eliminated. When there are a huge number of new lows, stocks down the most are selected, even though there are usually good reasons why some stocks have been battered.

BARGAIN STOCKS VS. THE MARKET*

Short Span* Late Dec–Jan/Feb	New Lows Late Dec	% Change Jan/Feb	% Change NYSE Composite	Bargain Stocks Advantage
1974–75	112	48.9%	22.1%	26.8%
1975–76	21	34.9	14.9	20.0
1976–77	2	1.3	−3.3	4.6
1977–78	15	2.8	−4.5	7.3
1978–79	43	11.8	3.9	7.9
1979–80	5	9.3	6.1	3.2
1980–81	14	7.1	−2.0	9.1
1981–82	21	−2.6	−7.4	4.8
1982–83	4	33.0	9.7	23.3
1983–84	13	−3.2	−3.8	0.6
1984–85	32	19.0	12.1	6.9
1985–86	4	−22.5	3.9	−26.4
1986–87	22	9.3	12.5	−3.2
1987–88	23	13.2	6.8	6.4
1988–89	14	30.0	6.4	23.6
1989–90	25	−3.1	−4.8	1.7
1990–91	18	18.8	12.6	6.2
1991–92	23	51.1	7.7	43.4
1992–93	9	8.7	0.6	8.1
1993–94	10	−1.4	2.0	−3.4
1994–95	25	14.6	5.7	8.9
1995–96	5	−11.3	4.5	−15.8
1996–97	16	13.9	11.2	2.7
1997–98	29	9.9	5.7	4.2
1998–99	40	−2.8	4.3	−7.1
1999–00	26	8.9	−5.4	14.3
2000–01	51	44.4	0.1	44.3
2001–02	12	31.4	−2.3	33.7
2002–03	33	28.7	3.9	24.8
2003–04	15	16.7	2.3	14.4
2004–05	36	6.8	−2.8	9.6
2005–06	71	12.0	2.6	9.4
2006–07	43	5.1	−0.5	5.6
2007–08	71	−3.2	−9.4	6.2
2008–09	88	11.4	−2.4	13.8
2009–10	25	1.8	−3.0	4.8
2010–11	20	8.3	3.4	4.9
2011–12	65	18.1	6.1	12.0
2012–13	17	20.9	3.4	17.5
39-Year Totals		**502.0%**	**122.9%**	**379.1%**
Average		**12.9%**	**3.2%**	**9.7%**

* Dec 15–Feb 15 (1974–1999), Dec 1999–2013 based on actual newsletter advice

In response to changing market conditions, we tweaked the strategy the last 14 years, adding selections from NASDAQ, AMEX, and the OTC Bulletin Board and selling in mid-January some years. We e-mail the list of stocks to our *Almanac Investor* newsletter subscribers. Visit *www.stocktradersalmanac.com,* or see the insert for additional details and a special offer for new subscribers.

We have come to the conclusion that the most prudent course of action is to compile our list from the stocks making new lows on Triple-Witching Friday before Christmas, capitalizing on the Santa Claus Rally (page 114). This also gives us the weekend to evaluate the issues in greater depth and weed out any glaringly problematic stocks. Subscribers will receive the list of stocks selected from the new lows made on December 20, 2013 and December 19, 2014 via e-mail.

This "Free Lunch" strategy is only an extremely short-term strategy reserved for the nimblest traders. It has performed better after market corrections and when there are more new lows to choose from. The object is to buy bargain stocks near their 52-week lows and sell any quick, generous gains, as these issues can often be real dogs.

DECEMBER

MONDAY

D 47.6
S 47.6
N 47.6

15

Change is the law of life. And those who look only to the past or present are certain to miss the future.
— John F. Kennedy (35th U.S. President, 1917–1963)

FOMC Meeting (2 Days)

TUESDAY

D 61.9
S 66.7
N 57.1

16

People's spending habits depend more on how wealthy they feel than with the actual amount of their current income.
— A.C. Pigou (English economist, *The Theory of Unemployment*, 1877–1959)

Chanukah

WEDNESDAY

D 42.9
S 47.6
N 38.1

17

Small volume is usually accompanied by a fall in price; large volume by a rise in price.
— Charles C. Ying ("Stock Market Prices and Volumes of Sales," *Econometrica*, July 1966)

December Triple Witching Week, S&P Up 23 of Last 29
2009 Broke 8-Year Bull Run

THURSDAY

D 47.6
S 47.6
N 57.1

18

We are nowhere near a capitulation point because it's at that point where it's despair, not hope, that reigns supreme, and there was scant evidence of any despair at any of the meetings I gave.
— David Rosenberg (Economist, Merrill Lynch, *Barron's*, 4/21/2008)

December Triple Witching, S&P Up 22 of 31, Average Gain 0.4%

FRIDAY

D 52.4
S 52.4
N 61.9

19

Don't worry about people stealing your ideas. If the ideas are any good, you'll have to ram them down people's throats.
— Howard Aiken (U.S. computer scientist, 1900–1973)

SATURDAY

20

The Only FREE LUNCH on Wall Street is Served (Page 112)
Almanac Investors Emailed Alert Before the Open, Monday (See Insert)

SUNDAY

21

IF SANTA CLAUS SHOULD FAIL TO CALL, BEARS MAY COME TO BROAD AND WALL

Santa Claus tends to come to Wall Street nearly every year, bringing a short, sweet, respectable rally within the last five days of the year and the first two in January. This has been good for an average 1.6% gain since 1969 (1.5% since 1950). Santa's failure to show tends to precede bear markets, or times stocks could be purchased later in the year at much lower prices. We discovered this phenomenon in 1972.

DAILY % CHANGE IN S&P 500 AT YEAR END

	Trading Days Before Year End						First Days in January			Rally % Change
	6	5	4	3	2	1	1	2	3	
1969	-0.4	1.1	0.8	-0.7	0.4	0.5	1.0	0.5	-0.7	3.6
1970	0.1	0.6	0.5	1.1	0.2	-0.1	-1.1	0.7	0.6	1.9
1971	-0.4	0.2	1.0	0.3	-0.4	0.3	-0.4	0.4	1.0	1.3
1972	-0.3	-0.7	0.6	0.4	0.5	1.0	0.9	0.4	-0.1	3.1
1973	-1.1	-0.7	3.1	2.1	-0.2	0.01	0.1	2.2	-0.9	6.7
1974	-1.4	1.4	0.8	-0.4	0.03	2.1	2.4	0.7	0.5	7.2
1975	0.7	0.8	0.9	-0.1	-0.4	0.5	0.8	1.8	1.0	4.3
1976	0.1	1.2	0.7	-0.4	0.5	0.5	-0.4	-1.2	-0.9	0.8
1977	0.8	0.9	N/C	0.1	0.2	0.2	-1.3	-0.3	-0.8	-0.3
1978	0.03	1.7	1.3	-0.9	-0.4	-0.2	0.6	1.1	0.8	3.3
1979	-0.6	0.1	0.1	0.2	-0.1	0.1	-2.0	-0.5	1.2	-2.2
1980	-0.4	0.4	0.5	-1.1	0.2	0.3	0.4	1.2	0.1	2.0
1981	-0.5	0.2	-0.2	-0.5	0.5	0.2	0.2	-2.2	-0.7	-1.8
1982	0.6	1.8	-1.0	0.3	-0.7	0.2	-1.6	2.2	0.4	1.2
1983	-0.2	-0.03	0.9	0.3	-0.2	0.05	-0.5	1.7	1.2	2.1
1984	-0.5	0.8	-0.2	-0.4	0.3	0.6	-1.1	-0.5	-0.5	-0.6
1985	-1.1	-0.7	0.2	0.9	0.5	0.3	-0.8	0.6	-0.1	1.1
1986	-1.0	0.2	0.1	-0.9	-0.5	-0.5	1.8	2.3	0.2	2.4
1987	1.3	-0.5	-2.6	-0.4	1.3	-0.3	3.6	1.1	0.1	2.2
1988	-0.2	0.3	-0.4	0.1	0.8	-0.6	-0.9	1.5	0.2	0.9
1989	0.6	0.8	-0.2	0.6	0.5	0.8	1.8	-0.3	-0.9	4.1
1990	0.5	-0.6	0.3	-0.8	0.1	0.5	-1.1	-1.4	-0.3	-3.0
1991	2.5	0.6	1.4	0.4	2.1	0.5	0.04	0.5	-0.3	5.7
1992	-0.3	0.2	-0.1	-0.3	0.2	-0.7	-0.1	-0.2	0.04	-1.1
1993	0.01	0.7	0.1	-0.1	-0.4	-0.5	-0.2	0.3	0.1	-0.1
1994	0.01	0.2	0.4	-0.3	0.1	-0.4	-0.03	0.3	-0.1	0.2
1995	0.8	0.2	0.4	0.04	-0.1	0.3	0.8	0.1	-0.6	1.8
1996	-0.3	0.5	0.6	0.1	-0.4	-1.7	-0.5	1.5	-0.1	0.1
1997	-1.5	-0.7	0.4	1.8	1.8	-0.04	0.5	0.2	-1.1	4.0
1998	2.1	-0.2	-0.1	1.3	-0.8	-0.2	-0.1	1.4	2.2	1.3
1999	1.6	-0.1	0.04	0.4	0.1	0.3	-1.0	-3.8	0.2	-4.0
2000	0.8	2.4	0.7	1.0	0.4	-1.0	-2.8	5.0	-1.1	5.7
2001	0.4	-0.02	0.4	0.7	0.3	-1.1	0.6	0.9	0.6	1.8
2002	0.2	-0.5	-0.3	-1.6	0.5	0.05	3.3	-0.05	2.2	1.2
2003	0.3	-0.2	0.2	1.2	0.01	0.2	-0.3	1.2	0.1	2.4
2004	0.1	-0.4	0.7	-0.01	0.01	-0.1	-0.8	-1.2	-0.4	-1.8
2005	0.4	0.04	-1.0	0.1	-0.3	-0.5	1.6	0.4	0.002	0.4
2006	-0.4	-0.5	0.4	0.7	-0.1	-0.5	-0.1	0.1	-0.6	0.003
2007	1.7	0.8	0.1	-1.4	0.1	-0.7	-1.4	N/C	-2.5	-2.5
2008	-1.0	0.6	0.5	-0.4	2.4	1.4	3.2	-0.5	0.8	7.4
2009	0.2	0.5	0.1	-0.1	0.02	-1.0	1.6	0.3	0.05	1.4
2010	-0.2	0.1	0.1	0.1	-0.2	-0.02	1.1	-0.1	0.5	1.1
2011	0.8	0.9	0.01	-1.3	1.1	-0.4	1.6	0.02	0.3	1.9
2012	-0.9	-0.2	-0.5	-0.1	-1.1	1.7	2.5	-0.2	0.5	2.0
Avg	0.09	0.32	0.27	0.05	0.20	0.05	0.27	0.41	0.05	1.6

The couplet above was certainly on the mark in 1999, as the period suffered a horrendous 4.0% loss. On January 14, 2000, the Dow started its 33-month 37.8% slide to the October 2002 midterm election year bottom. NASDAQ cracked eight weeks later, falling 37.3% in 10 weeks, eventually dropping 77.9% by October 2002. Saddam Hussein cancelled Christmas by invading Kuwait in 1990. Energy prices and Middle East terror woes may have grounded Santa in 2004. In 2007, the third worst reading since 1950 was recorded, as sub-prime mortgages and their derivatives led to a full-blown financial crisis and the second worst bear market in history. In 2012, a last-minute tax deal was reached and Christmas was saved.

DECEMBER

🐂 **MONDAY**
D 76.2
S 71.4
N 57.1
22

We go to the movies to be entertained, not see rape, ransacking, pillage and looting. We can get all that in the stock market.
— Kennedy Gammage (*The Richland Report*)

Watch for the Santa Claus Rally (Page 114)

🐂 **TUESDAY**
D 66.7
S 66.7
N 71.4
23

It was never my thinking that made the big money for me. It was always my sitting. Got that? My sitting tight!
— Jesse Livermore (Early 20th-century stock trader and speculator, *How to Trade in Stocks*, 1877–1940)

(Shortened Trading Day)
Last Trading Day Before Christmas, Dow Up 5 of Last 6 Years

WEDNESDAY
D 52.4
S 57.1
N 61.9
24

Short-term volatility is greatest at turning points and diminishes as a trend becomes established.
— George Soros (Financier, philanthropist, political activist, author, and philosopher, b. 1930)

Christmas Day (Market Closed)

THURSDAY
25

What the superior man seeks, is in himself. What the inferior man seeks, is in others.
— Confucius (Chinese philosopher, 551–478 B.C.)

🐂 **FRIDAY**
D 81.0
S 76.2
N 71.4
26

Brilliant men are often strikingly ineffectual; they fail to realize that the brilliant insight is not by itself achievement. They never have learned that insights become effectiveness only through hard systematic work.
— Peter Drucker (Austrian-born pioneer management theorist, 1909–2005)

SATURDAY
27

January Almanac Investor Seasonalities: See Pages 92, 94, and 96

SUNDAY
28

YEAR'S TOP INVESTMENT BOOKS

Mastering the Stock Market: High Probability Market Timing & Stock Selection Tools, John L. Person, Wiley, $90.00, http://www.personsplanet.com/. 2014 Best Investment Book of the Year.

Bailout: How Washington Abandoned Main Street While Rescuing Wall Street, Neil Barofsky, Free Press, $26.00. Saw Barofsky speak at Ritholtz's The Big Picture Conference. Ugly truth, seething exposé, scintillating read.

Broken Markets: How High Frequency Trading and Predatory Practices on Wall Street Are Destroying Investor Confidence, Sal L. Arnuk and Joseph C. Saluzzi, FT Press, $34.99. Team that runs institutional brokerage trading firm Themis Trading LLC gives the inside scoop on what's not working on Wall Street and how to fix it.

Diary of a Hedgehog: Biggs' Final Words on the Markets, Barton Biggs, Wiley, $29.95. More insights from the Wall Street legend. Finished just before his untimely passing.

Evolution of a Trader: Trading Basics, Swing and Day Trading, Fundamental Analysis and Position Trading, Thomas N. Bulkowski, Wiley, $75.00 each. Three-book series on four major trading styles. Like his *Encyclopedia of Chart Patterns,* which was one of our Top Books in 2006, this is an invaluable series.

George Lindsay's An Aid to Timing, Annotated by Ed Carlson, SeattleTA Press, $39.95. Previous book was 2012 Best Investment Book of the Year. Carlson delves deeper into Lindsay's market timing and analysis methodology. Also check out Carlson's two Lindsay DVDs.

Guide to Commodities: Producers, Players and Prices, Markets, Consumers and Trends (*The Economist*), Caroline Bain, Wiley, $40.00. Senior Commodities Editor for *The Economist Intelligence Unit* provides a comprehensive guide to the economics of the main commodities. Who, what, when, where, why, and how they are produced. Stats, trends, markets, trading, and outlooks.

Hedge Fund Market Wizards: How Winning Traders Win, Jack D. Schwager, Wiley, $40.00. Another beaut. Inspirational for us. The 40 Market Wizard Lessons in the back are worth the $40 cover price alone.

Plan Your Prosperity: The Only Retirement Guide You'll Ever Need, Starting Now—Whether You're 22, 52, or 82, Kenneth L. Fisher, Wiley, $26.95. Words of wisdom from one of the most successful investment managers of all time. Helps you invest smarter your whole life and plan retirement better.

Street Smarts: Adventures on the Road and in the Markets, Jim Rogers, Crown Business, $26.00. Another fun read from the guy who's seen it all. Mostly memoir, but why not? Chapter 9 is entitled after one of our favorite quotes, "Capitalism without bankruptcy is like Christianity without hell!"

Successful Stock Signals for Traders and Portfolio Managers: Integrating Technical Analysis with Fundamentals to Improve Performance + Website, Thomas K. Lloyd, Sr., Wiley, $85.00. We have been following Tom Lloyd's timely signals for decades. Tom pulls together a library's worth of the most effective technical analysis tools and market timing tricks of the trade. Trade like a pro with Tom's signals playbook.

Tap Dancing to Work: Warren Buffett on Practically Everything, 1966–2012: A Fortune Magazine Book, Carol J. Loomis, Portfolio/Penguin, $27.95. As advertised. A nostalgic trip down Buffett Memory Lane.

The Maxims of Wall Street: A Compendium of Financial Adages, Ancient Proverbs, and Worldly Wisdom (Second Edition), Mark Skousen, Eagle Publishing, $24.95. Warren Buffett says, "Loved your great little book. In fact, I plan to shamelessly steal some of the lines." We already have! Great stuff. Comes with handy built-in ribbon bookmark.

The Mindless Investor—Make Money in the Market by Overcoming Your Common Sense, R.Tyler Bollhorn, Stockscores Analytics Corp, $29.95. Got to love a self-published book by a self-made trader. Powerful tools help find stocks in uptrends that outperform. http://www.stockscores.com/mindless.asp.

The Wealth Code 2.0: How the Rich Stay Rich in Good Times and Bad, Jason Vanclef, Wiley, $40.00. Revised and expanded update of 2009 book. Diversify into oil/gas, equipment, notes, real estate, bullion, and rare coins the way the super-rich do. Pay off your home or pay cash for a car, or not. Pitfalls of insurance and variable/fixed/index annuities. Advanced income tax reduction strategies, discounted Roth IRA conversions, and asset-protection techniques.

Trade with the Odds: How to Construct Market-Beating Trading Systems + Website, Anthony Trongone, PhD, CFP, CTA, Bloomberg Press, $90.00. Met Trongone at NY Traders Expo. He's the real deal, a straight shooter. Great speaker and educator who will teach you exactly where to put a protective stop loss.

Wealth Regeneration at Retirement: Planning for a Lifetime of Leadership, Kaycee Krysty and Robert Moser, Bloomberg Press, $60.00. Handbook for life at and after retirement from two wealth management veterans.

MONDAY
D 52.4
S 52.4
N 52.4
29

[The Fed] is very smart, but [it] doesn't run the markets. In the end, the markets will run [the Fed]. The markets are bigger than any man or any group of men. The markets can even break a president.
— Richard Russell (*Dow Theory Letters*, 8/4/04)

TUESDAY
D 42.9
S 61.9
N 52.4
30

A good trader has to have three things: a chronic inability to accept things at face value, to feel continuously unsettled, and to have humility.
— Michael Steinhardt (Financier, philanthropist, political activist, chairman WisdomTree Investments, b. 1940)

Last Trading Day of the Year, NASDAQ Down 11 of last 13
NASDAQ Was Up 29 Years in a Row 1971–1999

WEDNESDAY
D 38.1
S 28.6
N 47.6
31

Whenever you see a successful business, someone once made a courageous decision.
— Peter Drucker (Austrian-born pioneer management theorist, 1909–2005)

New Year's Day (Market Closed)

THURSDAY
1

In order to be great writer (or "investor") a person must have a built-in, shockproof crap detector.
— Ernest Hemingway (American writer, 1954 Nobel Prize, 1899–1961)

Small Caps Punished First Trading Day of Year
Russell 2000 Down 14 of Last 24, But Up Last 5

FRIDAY
D 71.4
S 47.6
N 66.7
2

Financial genius is a rising stock market.
— John Kenneth Galbraith (Canadian/American economist and diplomat, 1908–2006)

SATURDAY
3

SUNDAY
4

2015 STRATEGY CALENDAR

(Option expiration dates circled)

	MONDAY	TUESDAY	WEDNESDAY	THURSDAY	FRIDAY	SATURDAY	SUNDAY
JANUARY	29	30	31	1 JANUARY New Year's Day	2	3	4
	5	6	7	8	9	10	11
	12	13	14	15	(16)	17	18
	19 Martin Luther King Day	20	21	22	23	24	25
	26	27	28	29	30	31	1 FEBRUARY
FEBRUARY	2	3	4	5	6	7	8
	9	10	11	12	13	14 ♥	15
	16 Presidents' Day	17	18 Ash Wednesday	19	(20)	21	22
	23	24	25	26	27	28	1 MARCH
MARCH	2	3	4	5	6	7	8 Daylight Saving Time Begins
	9	10	11	12	13	14	15
	16	17 ♣ St. Patrick's Day	18	19	(20)	21	22
	23	24	25	26	27	28	29
	30	31	1 APRIL	2	3 Good Friday	4	5 Easter
APRIL	6	7	8	9	10	11	12
	13	14	15 Tax Deadline Passover	16	(17)	18	19
	20	21	22	23	24	25	26
	27	28	29	30	1 MAY	2	3
MAY	4	5	6	7	8	9	10 Mother's Day
	11	12	13	14	(15)	16	17
	18	19	20	21	22	23	24
	25 Memorial Day	26	27	28	29	30	31
JUNE	1 JUNE	2	3	4	5	6	7
	8	9	10	11	12	13	14
	15	16	17	18	(19)	20	21 Father's Day
	22	23	24	25	26	27	28

Market closed on shaded weekdays; closes early when half-shaded.

2015 STRATEGY CALENDAR

(Option expiration dates circled)

MONDAY	TUESDAY	WEDNESDAY	THURSDAY	FRIDAY	SATURDAY	SUNDAY	
29	30	1 JULY	2	3	4 Independence Day	5	JULY
6	7	8	9	10	11	12	
13	14	15	16	(17)	18	19	
20	21	22	23	24	25	26	
27	28	29	30	31	1 AUGUST	2	
3	4	5	6	7	8	9	AUGUST
10	11	12	13	14	15	16	
17	18	19	20	(21)	22	23	
24	25	26	27	28	29	30	
31	1 SEPTEMBER	2	3	4	5	6	SEPTEMBER
7 Labor Day	8	9	10	11	12	13	
14 Rosh Hashanah	15	16	17	(18)	19	20	
21	22	23 Yom Kippur	24	25	26	27	
28	29	30	1 OCTOBER	2	3	4	OCTOBER
5	6	7	8	9	10	11	
12 Columbus Day	13	14	15	(16)	17	18	
19	20	21	22	23	24	25	
26	27	28	29	30	31	1 NOVEMBER Daylight Saving Time Ends	NOVEMBER
2	3 Election Day	4	5	6	7	8	
9	10	11 Veterans' Day	12	13	14	15	
16	17	18	19	(20)	21	22	
23	24	25	26 Thanksgiving	27	28	29	
30	1 DECEMBER	2	3	4	5	6	DECEMBER
7 Chanukah	8	9	10	11	12	13	
14	15	16	17	(18)	19	20	
21	22	23	24	25 Christmas	26	27	
28	29	30	31	1 JANUARY New Year's Day	2	3	

DIRECTORY OF TRADING PATTERNS AND DATABANK

CONTENTS

DOW JONES INDUSTRIALS MARKET PROBABILITY CALENDAR 2014

THE % CHANCE OF THE MARKET RISING ON ANY TRADING DAY OF THE YEAR*

(Based on the number of times the DJIA rose on a particular trading day during January 1954 to December 2012)

Date	Jan	Feb	Mar	Apr	May	Jun	Jul	Aug	Sep	Oct	Nov	Dec
1	H	S	S	61.0	57.6	S	62.7	44.1	H	47.5	S	45.8
2	57.6	S	S	59.3	64.4	55.9	59.3	S	57.6	57.6	S	52.5
3	72.9	59.3	64.4	54.2	S	52.5	59.3	S	57.6	52.5	61.0	64.4
4	S	54.2	62.7	57.6	S	52.5	H	45.8	59.3	S	50.8	59.3
5	S	39.0	59.3	S	49.2	57.6	S	50.8	45.8	S	67.8	47.5
6	49.2	54.2	47.5	S	49.2	50.8	S	50.8	S	62.7	59.3	S
7	55.9	49.2	45.8	52.5	44.1	S	55.9	55.9	S	45.8	47.5	S
8	47.5	S	S	57.6	50.8	S	62.7	45.8	47.5	50.8	S	45.8
9	49.2	S	S	62.7	49.2	45.8	54.2	S	44.1	42.4	S	55.9
10	47.5	42.4	54.2	64.4	S	37.3	50.8	S	57.6	39.0	59.3	57.6
11	S	47.5	59.3	54.2	S	57.6	40.7	47.5	61.0	S	50.8	44.1
12	S	61.0	54.2	S	52.5	59.3	S	49.2	47.5	S	59.3	52.5
13	49.2	45.8	55.9	S	45.8	59.3	S	44.1	S	52.5	47.5	S
14	55.9	49.2	52.5	71.2	52.5	S	64.4	64.4	S	59.3	49.2	S
15	55.9	S	S	66.1	54.2	50.8	49.2	57.6	52.5	52.5	S	45.8
16	61.0	S	S	55.9	44.1	50.8	45.8	S	54.2	50.8	S	57.6
17	39.0	H	59.3	55.9	S	47.5	50.8	S	39.0	42.4	55.9	47.5
18	S	54.2	61.0	H	S	50.8	50.8	52.5	50.8	S	49.2	54.2
19	S	40.7	59.3	S	52.5	44.1	S	49.2	45.8	S	50.8	55.9
20	H	49.2	52.5	S	44.1	45.8	S	54.2	S	61.0	50.8	S
21	35.6	50.8	50.8	55.9	40.7	S	42.4	47.5	S	50.8	57.6	S
22	40.7	S	S	50.8	33.9	S	45.8	54.2	42.4	47.5	S	59.3
23	57.6	S	S	52.5	50.8	40.7	47.5	S	39.0	42.4	S	50.8
24	47.5	35.6	39.0	52.5	S	37.3	47.5	S	50.8	47.5	62.7	59.3
25	S	44.1	49.2	57.6	S	47.5	61.0	49.2	54.2	S	59.3	H
26	S	57.6	45.8	S	H	45.8	S	45.8	50.8	S	52.5	71.2
27	57.6	47.5	54.2	S	44.1	54.2	S	59.3	S	27.1	H	S
28	57.6	52.5	44.1	54.2	47.5	S	50.8	40.7	S	54.2	52.5	S
29	50.8		S	49.2	55.9	S	45.8	62.7	50.8	54.2	S	49.2
30	57.6		S	50.8	59.3	52.5	61.0	S	39.0	61.0	S	55.9
31	59.3		42.4		S		50.8	S		54.2		54.2

* See new trends developing on pages 68, 88, 141–146

THE % CHANCE OF THE MARKET RISING ON ANY TRADING DAY OF THE YEAR*
(Based on the number of times the DJIA rose on a particular trading day during January 1992 to December 2012**)

Date	Jan	Feb	Mar	Apr	May	Jun	Jul	Aug	Sep	Oct	Nov	Dec
1	H	S	S	81.0	71.4	S	76.2	42.9	H	52.4	S	47.6
2	71.4	S	S	61.9	66.7	66.7	38.1	S	57.1	47.6	S	47.6
3	71.4	76.2	57.1	52.4	S	52.4	52.4	S	61.9	47.6	57.1	66.7
4	S	47.6	47.6	66.7	S	52.4	H	52.4	57.1	S	52.4	61.9
5	S	42.9	57.1	S	28.6	52.4	S	47.6	38.1	S	66.7	47.6
6	47.6	47.6	38.1	S	38.1	52.4	S	47.6	S	66.7	71.4	S
7	52.4	57.1	61.9	42.9	33.3	S	57.1	57.1	S	38.1	57.1	S
8	38.1	S	S	42.9	66.7	S	61.9	47.6	61.9	42.9	S	52.4
9	57.1	S	S	52.4	61.9	52.4	47.6	S	57.1	47.6	S	61.9
10	47.6	42.9	47.6	66.7	S	38.1	61.9	S	61.9	38.1	52.4	47.6
11	S	57.1	66.7	57.1	S	47.6	61.9	42.9	71.4	S	38.1	47.6
12	S	57.1	61.9	S	66.7	61.9	S	52.4	57.1	S	52.4	47.6
13	52.4	61.9	47.6	S	47.6	76.2	S	23.8	S	57.1	57.1	S
14	52.4	42.9	66.7	71.4	52.4	S	61.9	71.4	S	76.2	61.9	S
15	61.9	S	S	71.4	57.1	S	47.6	47.6	47.6	52.4	S	47.6
16	57.1	S	S	57.1	47.6	57.1	57.1	S	57.1	52.4	S	61.9
17	33.3	H	66.7	52.4	S	52.4	52.4	S	33.3	47.6	57.1	42.9
18	S	61.9	57.1	H	S	57.1	61.9	66.7	57.1	S	42.9	47.6
19	S	52.4	61.9	S	57.1	42.9	S	66.7	42.9	S	52.4	52.4
20	H	38.1	61.9	S	47.6	38.1	S	42.9	S	61.9	52.4	S
21	28.6	52.4	42.9	71.4	33.3	S	33.3	42.9	S	52.4	57.1	S
22	33.3	S	S	57.1	33.3	S	38.1	57.1	38.1	42.9	S	76.2
23	42.9	S	S	57.1	52.4	33.3	47.6	S	28.6	52.4	S	66.7
24	38.1	57.1	42.9	42.9	S	42.9	52.4	S	47.6	47.6	66.7	52.4
25	S	33.3	57.1	57.1	S	42.9	66.7	52.4	57.1	S	61.9	H
26	S	42.9	28.6	S	H	52.4	S	42.9	57.1	S	57.1	81.0
27	61.9	42.9	47.6	S	47.6	47.6	S	66.7	S	38.1	H	S
28	66.7	42.9	57.1	57.1	52.4	S	42.9	33.3	S	52.4	57.1	S
29	57.1		S	71.4	66.7	S	42.9	52.4	61.9	66.7	S	52.4
30	52.4		S	42.9	47.6	33.3	57.1	S	33.3	66.7	S	42.9
31	61.9		38.1		S		42.9	S		52.4		38.1

*See new trends developing on pages 68, 88, 141–146 ** Based on most recent 21-year period*

S&P 500 MARKET PROBABILITY CALENDAR 2014

THE % CHANCE OF THE MARKET RISING ON ANY TRADING DAY OF THE YEAR*
(Based on the number of times the S&P 500 rose on a particular trading day during January 1954 to December 2012)

Date	Jan	Feb	Mar	Apr	May	Jun	Jul	Aug	Sep	Oct	Nov	Dec
1	H	S	S	66.1	57.6	S	69.5	47.5	H	47.5	S	47.5
2	49.2	S	S	59.3	67.8	54.2	55.9	S	61.0	66.1	S	52.5
3	71.2	61.0	61.0	55.9	S	62.7	54.2	S	52.5	54.2	61.0	62.7
4	S	57.6	57.6	54.2	S	52.5	H	44.1	59.3	S	57.6	57.6
5	S	47.5	62.7	S	54.2	55.9	S	50.8	45.8	S	69.5	42.4
6	54.2	49.2	45.8	S	44.1	44.1	S	50.8	S	62.7	55.9	S
7	50.8	52.5	47.5	54.2	42.4	S	59.3	55.9	S	47.5	47.5	S
8	45.8	S	S	59.3	50.8	S	61.0	45.8	49.2	49.2	S	50.8
9	50.8	S	S	62.7	49.2	44.1	54.2	S	52.5	40.7	S	57.6
10	52.5	44.1	57.6	55.9	S	42.4	50.8	S	57.6	44.1	57.6	50.8
11	S	40.7	59.3	49.2	S	57.6	49.2	54.2	64.4	S	57.6	49.2
12	S	62.7	50.8	S	52.5	62.7	S	47.5	52.5	S	59.3	45.8
13	55.9	52.5	62.7	S	44.1	59.3	S	45.8	S	52.5	47.5	S
14	59.3	44.1	45.8	61.0	49.2	S	69.5	64.4	S	52.5	49.2	S
15	62.7	S	S	64.4	54.2	S	54.2	64.4	52.5	52.5	S	45.8
16	55.9	S	S	59.3	49.2	57.6	42.4	S	54.2	54.2	S	59.3
17	50.8	H	61.0	52.5	S	45.8	45.8	S	45.8	40.7	47.5	44.1
18	S	54.2	62.7	H	S	55.9	50.8	55.9	52.5	S	50.8	47.5
19	S	37.3	59.3	S	54.2	40.7	S	55.9	49.2	S	54.2	50.8
20	H	52.5	49.2	S	40.7	50.8	S	50.8	S	66.1	54.2	S
21	44.1	44.1	44.1	55.9	49.2	S	40.7	45.8	S	50.8	57.6	S
22	45.8	S	S	54.2	44.1	S	39.0	52.5	47.5	49.2	S	55.9
23	59.3	S	S	45.8	52.5	42.4	47.5	S	37.3	42.4	S	47.5
24	61.0	40.7	54.2	45.8	S	37.3	45.8	S	49.2	42.4	66.1	61.0
25	S	39.0	44.1	57.6	S	40.7	57.6	47.5	50.8	S	61.0	H
26	S	55.9	47.5	S	H	50.8	S	45.8	57.6	S	57.6	72.9
27	54.2	50.8	54.2	S	49.2	57.6	S	59.3	S	32.2	H	S
28	52.5	59.3	37.3	49.2	49.2	S	50.8	44.1	S	59.3	52.5	S
29	47.5		S	45.8	55.9	S	49.2	66.1	50.8	57.6	S	52.5
30	61.0		S	57.6	61.0	50.8	62.7	S	42.4	61.0	S	64.4
31	64.4		40.7		S		62.7	S		55.9		62.7

* See new trends developing on pages 68, 88, 141–146

RECENT S&P 500 MARKET PROBABILITY CALENDAR 2014

THE % CHANCE OF THE MARKET RISING ON ANY TRADING DAY OF THE YEAR*

(Based on the number of times the S&P 500 rose on a particular trading day during January 1992 to December 2012**)

Date	Jan	Feb	Mar	Apr	May	Jun	Jul	Aug	Sep	Oct	Nov	Dec
1	H	S	S	76.2	71.4	S	81.0	52.4	H	47.6	S	52.4
2	47.6	S	S	61.9	61.9	61.9	38.1	S	61.9	57.1	S	52.4
3	66.7	76.2	52.4	61.9	S	76.2	57.1	S	42.9	42.9	57.1	71.4
4	S	57.1	42.9	61.9	S	47.6	H	42.9	52.4	S	61.9	47.6
5	S	42.9	66.7	S	33.3	42.9	S	47.6	47.6	S	66.7	42.9
6	57.1	47.6	42.9	S	33.3	38.1	S	52.4	S	57.1	71.4	S
7	42.9	52.4	57.1	47.6	28.6	S	57.1	47.6	S	38.1	57.1	S
8	52.4	S	S	47.6	57.1	S	61.9	57.1	57.1	42.9	S	52.4
9	57.1	S	S	47.6	52.4	42.9	42.9	S	66.7	47.6	S	61.9
10	52.4	57.1	57.1	57.1	S	47.6	57.1	S	61.9	42.9	47.6	47.6
11	S	42.9	57.1	47.6	S	42.9	71.4	42.9	66.7	S	38.1	52.4
12	S	71.4	52.4	S	57.1	61.9	S	52.4	66.7	S	52.4	42.9
13	57.1	66.7	61.9	S	47.6	76.2	S	23.8	S	61.9	52.4	S
14	57.1	38.1	52.4	52.4	47.6	S	66.7	66.7	S	71.4	57.1	S
15	61.9	S	S	66.7	57.1	S	42.9	66.7	47.6	52.4	S	47.6
16	57.1	S	S	61.9	52.4	66.7	47.6	S	61.9	57.1	S	66.7
17	52.4	H	66.7	52.4	S	52.4	47.6	S	42.9	57.1	47.6	47.6
18	S	66.7	61.9	H	S	57.1	61.9	76.2	52.4	S	52.4	47.6
19	S	42.9	71.4	S	57.1	38.1	S	71.4	38.1	S	57.1	52.4
20	H	42.9	47.6	S	47.6	47.6	S	38.1	S	66.7	52.4	S
21	28.6	47.6	33.3	66.7	38.1	S	28.6	42.9	S	61.9	52.4	S
22	42.9	S	S	61.9	38.1	S	33.3	61.9	38.1	47.6	S	71.4
23	47.6	S	S	52.4	61.9	33.3	52.4	S	33.3	57.1	S	66.7
24	52.4	61.9	66.7	28.6	S	42.9	52.4	S	42.9	42.9	66.7	57.1
25	S	38.1	57.1	52.4	S	33.3	61.9	52.4	52.4	S	66.7	H
26	S	47.6	33.3	S	H	57.1	S	52.4	61.9	S	71.4	76.2
27	52.4	52.4	42.9	S	52.4	57.1	S	66.7	S	42.9	H	S
28	52.4	47.6	38.1	57.1	57.1	S	42.9	33.3	S	57.1	42.9	S
29	61.9		S	66.7	57.1	S	47.6	52.4	66.7	61.9	S	52.4
30	57.1		S	52.4	52.4	38.1	61.9	S	33.3	71.4	S	61.9
31	66.7		42.9		S		52.4	S		61.9		28.6

See new trends developing on pages 68, 88, 141–146 ** *Based on most recent 21-year period*

NASDAQ COMPOSITE MARKET PROBABILITY CALENDAR 2014

THE % CHANCE OF THE MARKET RISING ON ANY TRADING DAY OF THE YEAR*

(Based on the number of times the NASDAQ rose on a particular trading day during January 1972 to December 2012)

Date	Jan	Feb	Mar	Apr	May	Jun	Jul	Aug	Sep	Oct	Nov	Dec
1	H	S	S	46.3	63.4	S	58.5	51.2	H	46.3	S	61.0
2	56.1	S	S	61.0	70.7	56.1	48.8	S	53.7	61.0	S	63.4
3	70.7	70.7	61.0	65.9	S	75.6	43.9	S	58.5	56.1	65.9	63.4
4	S	68.3	53.7	53.7	S	56.1	H	41.5	58.5	S	56.1	61.0
5	S	56.1	65.9	S	58.5	58.5	S	51.2	56.1	S	70.7	39.0
6	58.5	63.4	51.2	S	53.7	46.3	S	58.5	S	63.4	58.5	S
7	63.4	58.5	51.2	46.3	53.7	S	51.2	56.1	S	58.5	51.2	S
8	53.7	S	S	58.5	63.4	S	61.0	39.0	53.7	61.0	S	53.7
9	61.0	S	S	61.0	53.7	43.9	61.0	S	51.2	51.2	S	48.8
10	56.1	51.2	56.1	63.4	S	43.9	58.5	S	53.7	48.8	53.7	43.9
11	S	48.8	56.1	51.2	S	53.7	70.7	53.7	63.4	S	56.1	41.5
12	S	63.4	51.2	S	39.0	61.0	S	48.8	63.4	S	63.4	41.5
13	61.0	58.5	70.7	S	56.1	68.3	S	53.7	S	75.6	53.7	S
14	63.4	61.0	51.2	58.5	53.7	S	73.2	58.5	S	63.4	51.2	S
15	65.9	S	S	53.7	56.1	S	65.9	58.5	36.6	53.7	S	43.9
16	68.3	S	S	58.5	56.1	58.5	48.8	S	51.2	51.2	S	58.5
17	61.0	H	51.2	56.1	S	43.9	56.1	S	51.2	39.0	41.5	46.3
18	S	58.5	61.0	H	S	53.7	56.1	51.2	63.4	S	46.3	53.7
19	S	48.8	61.0	S	51.2	48.8	S	61.0	53.7	S	53.7	53.7
20	H	56.1	61.0	S	41.5	46.3	S	51.2	S	70.7	56.1	S
21	39.0	39.0	58.5	56.1	46.3	S	41.5	51.2	S	46.3	58.5	S
22	43.9	S	S	56.1	48.8	S	41.5	51.2	51.2	58.5	S	58.5
23	48.8	S	S	53.7	53.7	46.3	51.2	S	48.8	46.3	S	65.9
24	58.5	48.8	58.5	48.8	S	43.9	51.2	S	51.2	41.5	56.1	68.3
25	S	53.7	48.8	46.3	S	46.3	58.5	53.7	46.3	S	65.9	H
26	S	61.0	43.9	S	H	61.0	S	53.7	46.3	S	63.4	70.7
27	46.3	53.7	51.2	S	53.7	65.9	S	63.4	S	31.7	H	S
28	65.9	53.7	51.2	70.7	61.0	S	48.8	61.0	S	46.3	63.4	S
29	65.9		S	63.4	56.1	S	46.3	70.7	48.8	58.5	S	48.8
30	53.7		S	68.3	70.7	65.9	56.1	S	46.3	61.0	S	65.9
31	65.9		63.4		S		51.2	S		65.9		73.2

* See new trends developing on pages 68, 88, 141–146

Based on NASDAQ composite, prior to Feb. 5, 1971, based on National Quotation Bureau indices

RECENT NASDAQ COMPOSITE MARKET PROBABILITY CALENDAR 2014

THE % CHANCE OF THE MARKET RISING ON ANY TRADING DAY OF THE YEAR*
(Based on the number of times the NASDAQ rose on a particular trading day during January 1992 to December 2012**)

Date	Jan	Feb	Mar	Apr	May	Jun	Jul	Aug	Sep	Oct	Nov	Dec
1	H	S	S	61.9	71.4	S	71.4	52.4	H	38.1	S	66.7
2	66.7	S	S	52.4	61.9	57.1	42.9	S	61.9	57.1	S	61.9
3	66.7	81.0	52.4	71.4	S	81.0	47.6	S	57.1	52.4	66.7	61.9
4	S	61.9	33.3	57.1	S	57.1	H	38.1	57.1	S	61.9	57.1
5	S	47.6	66.7	S	52.4	47.6	S	42.9	52.4	S	76.2	33.3
6	57.1	57.1	38.1	S	47.6	33.3	S	52.4	S	66.7	66.7	S
7	57.1	57.1	47.6	38.1	33.3	S	57.1	42.9	S	47.6	61.9	S
8	57.1	S	S	52.4	71.4	S	66.7	33.3	57.1	57.1	S	57.1
9	71.4	S	S	47.6	52.4	33.3	57.1	S	66.7	57.1	S	57.1
10	52.4	57.1	47.6	61.9	S	42.9	61.9	S	57.1	57.1	57.1	42.9
11	S	42.9	52.4	47.6	S	42.9	71.4	42.9	71.4	S	42.9	42.9
12	S	57.1	47.6	S	38.1	47.6	S	47.6	81.0	S	52.4	38.1
13	61.9	57.1	66.7	S	52.4	66.7	S	42.9	S	71.4	57.1	S
14	57.1	57.1	52.4	52.4	42.9	S	71.4	66.7	S	66.7	57.1	S
15	52.4	S	S	47.6	52.4	S	57.1	66.7	38.1	52.4	S	47.6
16	66.7	S	S	47.6	57.1	66.7	52.4	S	66.7	47.6	S	57.1
17	61.9	H	47.6	47.6	S	42.9	52.4	S	52.4	42.9	42.9	38.1
18	S	52.4	61.9	H	S	57.1	61.9	71.4	61.9	S	47.6	57.1
19	S	38.1	66.7	S	66.7	42.9	S	66.7	42.9	S	52.4	61.9
20	H	47.6	61.9	S	42.9	33.3	S	38.1	S	66.7	57.1	S
21	28.6	38.1	52.4	61.9	42.9	S	28.6	47.6	S	52.4	57.1	S
22	33.3	S	S	61.9	42.9	S	38.1	47.6	38.1	42.9	S	57.1
23	47.6	S	S	52.4	47.6	33.3	52.4	S	42.9	57.1	S	71.4
24	61.9	57.1	61.9	47.6	S	42.9	52.4	S	42.9	42.9	57.1	61.9
25	S	52.4	66.7	47.6	S	42.9	66.7	52.4	47.6	S	61.9	H
26	S	52.4	38.1	S	H	66.7	S	42.9	42.9	S	66.7	71.4
27	42.9	52.4	38.1	S	47.6	66.7	S	76.2	S	33.3	H	S
28	76.2	38.1	42.9	66.7	61.9	S	52.4	57.1	S	47.6	47.6	S
29	71.4		S	76.2	71.4	S	47.6	57.1	52.4	61.9	S	52.4
30	47.6		S	66.7	61.9	66.7	66.7	S	33.3	71.4	S	52.4
31	61.9		57.1		S		42.9	S		66.7		47.6

* See new trends developing on pages 68, 88, 141–146 ** Based on most recent 21-year period

RUSSELL 1000 INDEX MARKET PROBABILITY CALENDAR 2014

THE % CHANCE OF THE MARKET RISING ON ANY TRADING DAY OF THE YEAR*

(Based on the number of times the RUSSELL 1000 rose on a particular trading day during January 1980 to December 2012)

Date	Jan	Feb	Mar	Apr	May	Jun	Jul	Aug	Sep	Oct	Nov	Dec
1	H	S	S	63.6	57.6	S	72.7	45.5	H	54.5	S	54.5
2	42.4	S	S	60.6	63.6	54.5	42.4	S	51.5	57.6	S	54.5
3	60.6	66.7	57.6	54.5	S	60.6	42.4	S	48.5	51.5	69.7	63.6
4	S	60.6	45.5	54.5	S	48.5	H	39.4	51.5	S	57.6	42.4
5	S	57.6	60.6	S	51.5	54.5	S	51.5	39.4	S	63.6	42.4
6	60.6	48.5	39.4	S	39.4	30.3	S	48.5	S	60.6	60.6	S
7	51.5	63.6	42.4	48.5	39.4	S	57.6	54.5	S	42.4	48.5	S
8	51.5	S	S	63.6	54.5	S	57.6	54.5	48.5	54.5	S	48.5
9	60.6	S	S	54.5	57.6	42.4	48.5	S	57.6	39.4	S	57.6
10	54.5	48.5	57.6	54.5	S	42.4	57.6	S	60.6	39.4	51.5	45.5
11	S	39.4	54.5	45.5	S	51.5	66.7	48.5	66.7	S	45.5	45.5
12	S	66.7	45.5	S	51.5	57.6	S	48.5	60.6	S	60.6	42.4
13	57.6	63.6	60.6	S	54.5	63.6	S	39.4	S	66.7	57.6	S
14	57.6	42.4	45.5	57.6	51.5	S	78.8	60.6	S	66.7	51.5	S
15	69.7	S	S	69.7	54.5	S	48.5	63.6	51.5	60.6	S	51.5
16	69.7	S	S	57.6	54.5	60.6	51.5	S	48.5	51.5	S	63.6
17	42.4	H	57.6	48.5	S	48.5	48.5	S	42.4	39.4	45.5	48.5
18	S	63.6	60.6	H	S	63.6	60.6	63.6	48.5	S	48.5	45.5
19	S	36.4	60.6	S	54.5	36.4	S	66.7	42.4	S	63.6	51.5
20	H	45.5	48.5	S	48.5	51.5	S	60.6	S	72.7	51.5	S
21	30.3	42.4	45.5	54.5	48.5	S	36.4	48.5	S	54.5	57.6	S
22	45.5	S	S	51.5	42.4	S	33.3	57.6	45.5	54.5	S	69.7
23	54.5	S	S	54.5	60.6	39.4	48.5	S	39.4	48.5	S	57.6
24	51.5	45.5	51.5	42.4	S	36.4	39.4	S	42.4	36.4	66.7	60.6
25	S	45.5	54.5	54.5	S	39.4	75.8	42.4	48.5	S	72.7	H
26	S	57.6	36.4	S	H	51.5	S	54.5	63.6	S	63.6	69.7
27	51.5	57.6	48.5	S	60.6	57.6	S	57.6	S	33.3	H	S
28	63.6	57.6	42.4	57.6	60.6	S	51.5	45.5	S	54.5	51.5	S
29	60.6		S	54.5	54.5	S	45.5	60.6	57.6	54.5	S	57.6
30	57.6		S	57.6	57.6	48.5	63.6	S	48.5	66.7	S	66.7
31	63.6		48.5		S		57.6	S		66.7		51.5

See new trends developing on pages 68, 88, 141–146

RUSSELL 2000 INDEX MARKET PROBABILITY CALENDAR 2014

THE % CHANCE OF THE MARKET RISING ON ANY TRADING DAY OF THE YEAR*

(Based on the number of times the RUSSELL 2000 rose on a particular trading day during January 1980 to December 2012)

Date	Jan	Feb	Mar	Apr	May	Jun	Jul	Aug	Sep	Oct	Nov	Dec
1	H	S	S	51.5	60.6	S	63.6	48.5	H	51.5	S	54.5
2	45.5	S	S	60.6	63.6	60.6	51.5	S	51.5	48.5	S	63.6
3	63.6	69.7	63.6	48.5	S	69.7	39.4	S	60.6	48.5	63.6	66.7
4	S	63.6	57.6	51.5	S	51.5	H	45.5	54.5	S	69.7	60.6
5	S	54.5	66.7	S	60.6	54.5	S	48.5	63.6	S	69.7	42.4
6	60.6	66.7	54.5	S	57.6	51.5	S	48.5	S	69.7	60.6	S
7	60.6	66.7	60.6	42.4	51.5	S	51.5	48.5	S	42.4	54.5	S
8	60.6	S	S	57.6	54.5	S	51.5	42.4	51.5	48.5	S	57.6
9	63.6	S	S	60.6	60.6	33.3	57.6	S	60.6	48.5	S	48.5
10	54.5	60.6	51.5	63.6	S	48.5	51.5	S	60.6	54.5	51.5	48.5
11	S	42.4	54.5	48.5	S	54.5	63.6	57.6	66.7	S	48.5	36.4
12	S	69.7	39.4	S	48.5	57.6	S	48.5	57.6	S	69.7	42.4
13	69.7	60.6	60.6	S	57.6	69.7	S	45.5	S	69.7	51.5	S
14	63.6	63.6	51.5	57.6	48.5	S	63.6	72.7	S	60.6	51.5	S
15	66.7	S	S	63.6	45.5	S	54.5	63.6	33.3	60.6	S	36.4
16	72.7	S	S	54.5	54.5	57.6	51.5	S	48.5	42.4	S	60.6
17	72.7	H	48.5	48.5	S	48.5	51.5	S	39.4	45.5	45.5	60.6
18	S	54.5	57.6	H	S	42.4	48.5	63.6	42.4	S	21.2	60.6
19	S	51.5	69.7	S	51.5	39.4	S	60.6	48.5	S	60.6	63.6
20	H	42.4	54.5	S	51.5	42.4	S	48.5	S	69.7	48.5	S
21	30.3	36.4	60.6	60.6	45.5	S	36.4	45.5	S	57.6	57.6	S
22	45.5	S	S	63.6	51.5	S	39.4	60.6	51.5	54.5	S	63.6
23	51.5	S	S	51.5	57.6	45.5	42.4	S	42.4	48.5	S	66.7
24	57.6	51.5	51.5	51.5	S	42.4	48.5	S	45.5	39.4	60.6	75.8
25	S	57.6	54.5	60.6	S	48.5	63.6	54.5	33.3	S	63.6	H
26	S	57.6	42.4	S	H	57.6	S	60.6	51.5	S	66.7	66.7
27	45.5	63.6	51.5	S	51.5	69.7	S	63.6	S	36.4	H	S
28	66.7	60.6	48.5	66.7	72.7	S	63.6	60.6	S	39.4	69.7	S
29	63.6		S	60.6	66.7	S	45.5	72.7	60.6	54.5	S	54.5
30	54.5		S	69.7	72.7	66.7	54.5	S	63.6	57.6	S	63.6
31	78.8		81.8		S		63.6	S		75.8		69.7

* See new trends developing on pages 68, 88, 141–146

DECENNIAL CYCLE: A MARKET PHENOMENON

By arranging each year's market gain or loss so the first and succeeding years of each decade fall into the same column, certain interesting patterns emerge—strong fifth and eighth years; weak first, seventh, and zero years.

This fascinating phenomenon was first presented by Edgar Lawrence Smith in *Common Stocks and Business Cycles* (William-Frederick Press, 1959). Anthony Gaubis co-pioneered the decennial pattern with Smith.

When Smith first cut graphs of market prices into 10-year segments and placed them above one another, he observed that each decade tended to have three bull market cycles and that the longest and strongest bull markets seem to favor the middle years of a decade.

Don't place too much emphasis on the decennial cycle nowadays, other than the extraordinary fifth and zero years, as the stock market is more influenced by the quadrennial presidential election cycle, shown on page 130. Also, the last half-century, which has been the most prosperous in U.S. history, has distributed the returns among most years of the decade. Interestingly, NASDAQ suffered its worst bear market ever in a zero year.

Fourth years have the fourth best record within the Decennial Cycle, but 2014 is a midterm election year, which has the second worst record of the 4-year presidential election cycle. Of the last three midterm election years since the Depression that were also fourth years, only 1954 was impressive. As historical patterns continue to assert themselves, the likelihood of a banner 2014 is falling (see pages 24, 26, 30, 32, 74, and 130).

THE 10-YEAR STOCK MARKET CYCLE
Annual % Change in Dow Jones Industrial Average
Year of Decade

DECADES	1st	2nd	3rd	4th	5th	6th	7th	8th	9th	10th
1881–1890	3.0%	−2.9%	−8.5%	−18.8%	20.1%	12.4%	−8.4%	4.8%	5.5%	−14.1%
1891–1900	17.6	−6.6	−24.6	−0.6	2.3	−1.7	21.3	22.5	9.2	7.0
1901–1910	−8.7	−0.4	−23.6	41.7	38.2	−1.9	−37.7	46.6	15.0	−17.9
1911–1920	0.4	7.6	−10.3	−5.4	81.7	−4.2	−21.7	10.5	30.5	−32.9
1921–1930	12.7	21.7	−3.3	26.2	30.0	0.3	28.8	48.2	−17.2	−33.8
1931–1940	−52.7	−23.1	66.7	4.1	38.5	24.8	−32.8	28.1	−2.9	−12.7
1941–1950	−15.4	7.6	13.8	12.1	26.6	−8.1	2.2	−2.1	12.9	17.6
1951–1960	14.4	8.4	−3.8	44.0	20.8	2.3	−12.8	34.0	16.4	−9.3
1961–1970	18.7	−10.8	17.0	14.6	10.9	−18.9	15.2	4.3	−15.2	4.8
1971–1980	6.1	14.6	−16.6	−27.6	38.3	17.9	−17.3	−3.1	4.2	14.9
1981–1990	−9.2	19.6	20.3	−3.7	27.7	22.6	2.3	11.8	27.0	−4.3
1991–2000	20.3	4.2	13.7	2.1	33.5	26.0	22.6	16.1	25.2	−6.2
2001–2010	−7.1	−16.8	25.3	3.1	−0.6	16.3	6.4	−33.8	18.8	11.0
2011–2020	5.5	7.3								
Total % Change	5.6%	30.4%	66.1%	91.8%	368.0%	87.3%	−31.9%	187.9%	129.4%	−75.9%
Avg % Change	0.4%	2.2%	5.1%	7.1%	28.3%	6.8%	−2.5%	14.5%	10.0%	−5.8%
Up Years	9	8	6	8	12	8	7	10	10	5
Down Years	5	6	7	5	1	5	6	3	3	8

Based on annual close; Cowles indices 1881–1885; 12 Mixed Stocks, 10 Rails, 2 Inds 1886–1889;

20 Mixed Stocks, 18 Rails, 2 Inds 1890–1896; Railroad average 1897 (First industrial average published May 26, 1896).

PRESIDENTIAL ELECTION/STOCK MARKET CYCLE: THE 180-YEAR SAGA CONTINUES

It is no mere coincidence that the last two years (pre-election year and election year) of the 45 administrations since 1833 produced a total net market gain of 731.3%, dwarfing the 273.1% gain of the first two years of these administrations.

Presidential elections every four years have a profound impact on the economy and the stock market. Wars, recessions, and bear markets tend to start or occur in the first half of the term; prosperous times and bull markets, in the latter half. After nine straight annual Dow gains during the millennial bull, the four-year election cycle reasserted its overarching domination of market behavior the last 13 years. Despite European debt concerns, the Dow maintained its streak of no losses in pre-election years since 1939.

STOCK MARKET ACTION SINCE 1833
Annual % Change In Dow Jones Industrial Average[1]

4-Year Cycle Beginning	Elected President	Post-Election Year	Mid-Term Year	Pre-Election Year	Election Year
1833	Jackson (D)	−0.9	13.0	3.1	−11.7
1837	Van Buren (D)	−11.5	1.6	−12.3	5.5
1841*	W.H. Harrison (W)**	−13.3	−18.1	45.0	15.5
1845*	Polk (D)	8.1	−14.5	1.2	−3.6
1849*	Taylor (W)	N/C	18.7	−3.2	19.6
1853*	Pierce (D)	−12.7	−30.2	1.5	4.4
1857	Buchanan (D)	−31.0	14.3	−10.7	14.0
1861*	Lincoln (R)	−1.8	55.4	38.0	6.4
1865	Lincoln (R)**	−8.5	3.6	1.6	10.8
1869	Grant (R)	1.7	5.6	7.3	6.8
1873	Grant (R)	−12.7	2.8	−4.1	−17.9
1877	Hayes (R)	−9.4	6.1	43.0	18.7
1881	Garfield (R)**	3.0	−2.9	−8.5	−18.8
1885*	Cleveland (D)	20.1	12.4	−8.4	4.8
1889*	B. Harrison (R)	5.5	−14.1	17.6	−6.6
1893*	Cleveland (D)	−24.6	−0.6	2.3	−1.7
1897*	McKinley (R)	21.3	22.5	9.2	7.0
1901	McKinley (R)**	−8.7	−0.4	−23.6	41.7
1905	T. Roosevelt (R)	38.2	−1.9	−37.7	46.6
1909	Taft (R)	15.0	−17.9	0.4	7.6
1913*	Wilson (D)	−10.3	−5.4	81.7	−4.2
1917	Wilson (D)	−21.7	10.5	30.5	−32.9
1921*	Harding (R)**	12.7	21.7	−3.3	26.2
1925	Coolidge (R)	30.0	0.3	28.8	48.2
1929	Hoover (R)	−17.2	−33.8	−52.7	−23.1
1933*	F. Roosevelt (D)	66.7	4.1	38.5	24.8
1937	F. Roosevelt (D)	−32.8	28.1	−2.9	−12.7
1941	F. Roosevelt (D)	−15.4	7.6	13.8	12.1
1945	F. Roosevelt (D)**	26.6	−8.1	2.2	−2.1
1949	Truman (D)	12.9	17.6	14.4	8.4
1953*	Eisenhower (R)	−3.8	44.0	20.8	2.3
1957	Eisenhower (R)	−12.8	34.0	16.4	−9.3
1961*	Kennedy (D)**	18.7	−10.8	17.0	14.6
1965	Johnson (D)	10.9	−18.9	15.2	4.3
1969*	Nixon (R)	−15.2	4.8	6.1	14.6
1973	Nixon (R)***	−16.6	−27.6	38.3	17.9
1977*	Carter (D)	−17.3	−3.1	4.2	14.9
1981*	Reagan (R)	−9.2	19.6	20.3	−3.7
1985	Reagan (R)	27.7	22.6	2.3	11.8
1989	G. H. W. Bush (R)	27.0	−4.3	20.3	4.2
1993*	Clinton (D)	13.7	2.1	33.5	26.0
1997	Clinton (D)	22.6	16.1	25.2	−6.2
2001*	G. W. Bush (R)	−7.1	−16.8	25.3	3.1
2005	G. W. Bush (R)	−0.6	16.3	6.4	−33.8
2009*	Obama (D)	18.8	11.0	5.5	7.3
Total % Gain		**86.1%**	**187.0%**	**469.5%**	**261.8%**
Average % Gain		**2.0%**	**4.2%**	**10.4%**	**5.8%**
# Up		20	27	34	30
# Down		24	18	11	15

*Party in power ousted   **Death in office   ***Resigned   **D**–Democrat, **W**–Whig, **R**–Republican
[1] Based on annual close; Prior to 1886 based on Cowles and other indices; 12 Mixed Stocks, 10 Rails, 2 Inds 1886–1889; 20 Mixed Stocks, 18 Rails, 2 Inds 1890–1896; Railroad average 1897 (First industrial average published May 26, 1896).

DOW JONES INDUSTRIALS BULL AND BEAR MARKETS SINCE 1900

Bear markets begin at the end of one bull market and end at the start of the next bull market (7/17/90 to 10/11/90 as an example). The high at Dow 3978.36 on 1/31/94, was followed by a 9.7 percent correction. A 10.3 percent correction occurred between the 5/22/96 closing high of 5778 and the intraday low on 7/16/96. The longest bull market on record ended on 7/17/98, and the shortest bear market on record ended on 8/31/98, when the new bull market began. The greatest bull super cycle in history that began 8/12/82 ended in 2000 after the Dow gained 1409% and NASDAQ climbed 3072%. The Dow gained only 497% in the eight-year super bull from 1921 to the top in 1929. NASDAQ suffered its worst loss ever from the 2000 top to the 2002 bottom, down 77.9%, nearly as much as the 89.2% drop in the Dow from the 1929 top to the 1932 bottom. The third longest Dow bull since 1900 that began 10/9/02 ended on its fifth anniversary. The ensuing bear market was the second worst bear market since 1900, slashing the Dow 53.8%. European debt concerns in 2011 triggered a 16.8% Dow slide, ending the recovery bull shortly after its second anniversary. At press time, the current bull market was alive and well, making new all-time Dow highs. (See page 132 for S&P 500 and NASDAQ bulls and bears.)

DOW JONES INDUSTRIALS BULL AND BEAR MARKETS SINCE 1900

— Beginning —		— Ending —		Bull		Bear	
Date	DJIA	Date	DJIA	% Gain	Days	% Change	Days
9/24/00	38.80	6/17/01	57.33	47.8%	266	−46.1%	875
11/9/03	30.88	1/19/06	75.45	144.3	802	−48.5	665
11/15/07	38.83	11/19/09	73.64	89.6	735	−27.4	675
9/25/11	53.43	9/30/12	68.97	29.1	371	−24.1	668
7/30/14	52.32	11/21/16	110.15	110.5	845	−40.1	393
12/19/17	65.95	11/3/19	119.62	81.4	684	−46.6	660
8/24/21	63.90	3/20/23	105.38	64.9	573	−18.6	221
10/27/23	85.76	9/3/29	381.17	344.5	2138	−47.9	71
11/13/29	198.69	4/17/30	294.07	48.0	155	−86.0	813
7/8/32	41.22	9/7/32	79.93	93.9	61	−37.2	173
2/27/33	50.16	2/5/34	110.74	120.8	343	−22.8	171
7/26/34	85.51	3/10/37	194.40	127.3	958	−49.1	386
3/31/38	98.95	11/12/38	158.41	60.1	226	−23.3	147
4/8/39	121.44	9/12/39	155.92	28.4	157	−40.4	959
4/28/42	92.92	5/29/46	212.50	128.7	1492	−23.2	353
5/17/47	163.21	6/15/48	193.16	18.4	395	−16.3	363
6/13/49	161.60	1/5/53	293.79	81.8	1302	−13.0	252
9/14/53	255.49	4/6/56	521.05	103.9	935	−19.4	564
10/22/57	419.79	1/5/60	685.47	63.3	805	−17.4	294
10/25/60	566.05	12/13/61	734.91	29.8	414	−27.1	195
6/26/62	535.76	2/9/66	995.15	85.7	1324	−25.2	240
10/7/66	744.32	12/3/68	985.21	32.4	788	−35.9	539
5/26/70	631.16	4/28/71	950.82	50.6	337	−16.1	209
11/23/71	797.97	1/11/73	1051.70	31.8	415	−45.1	694
12/6/74	577.60	9/21/76	1014.79	75.7	655	−26.9	525
2/28/78	742.12	9/8/78	907.74	22.3	192	−16.4	591
4/21/80	759.13	4/27/81	1024.05	34.9	371	−24.1	472
8/12/82	776.92	11/29/83	1287.20	65.7	474	−15.6	238
7/24/84	1086.57	8/25/87	2722.42	150.6	1127	−36.1	55
10/19/87	1738.74	7/17/90	2999.75	72.5	1002	−21.2	86
10/11/90	2365.10	7/17/98	9337.97	294.8	2836	−19.3	45
8/31/98	7539.07	1/14/00	11722.98	55.5	501	−29.7	616
9/21/01	8235.81	3/19/02	10635.25	29.1	179	−31.5	204
10/9/02	7286.27	10/9/07	14164.53	94.4	1826	−53.8	517
3/9/09	6547.05	4/29/11	12810.54	95.7	781	−16.8	157
10/3/11	10655.30	5/3/13	14973.96	40.5*	578*	*At Press Time – not in averages	
		Average		**86.0%**	**756**	**− 31.1%**	**402**

Based on Dow Jones industrial average.
The NYSE was closed from 7/31/1914 to 12/11/1914 due to World War I.
DJIA figures were then adjusted back to reflect the composition change from 12 to 20 stocks in September 1916.

1900–2000 Data: Ned Davis Research

STANDARD & POOR'S 500 BULL AND BEAR MARKETS SINCE 1929 NASDAQ COMPOSITE SINCE 1971

A constant debate of the definition and timing of bull and bear markets permeates Wall Street like the bell that signals the open and close of every trading day. We have relied on the Ned Davis Research parameters for years to track bulls and bears on the Dow (see page 131). Standard & Poor's 500 index has been a stalwart indicator for decades and at times marched to a different beat than the Dow. The moves of the S&P 500 and NASDAQ have been correlated to the bull and bear dates on page 131. Many dates line up for the three indices, but you will notice quite a lag or lead on several occasions, including NASDAQ's independent cadence from 1975 to 1980.

STANDARD & POOR'S 500 BULL AND BEAR MARKETS

— Beginning —		— Ending —		Bull		Bear	
Date	S&P 500	Date	S&P 500	% Gain	Days	% Change	Days
11/13/29	17.66	4/10/30	25.92	46.8%	148	−83.0%	783
6/1/32	4.40	9/7/32	9.31	111.6	98	−40.6	173
2/27/33	5.53	2/6/34	11.82	113.7	344	−31.8	401
3/14/35	8.06	3/6/37	18.68	131.8	723	−49.0	390
3/31/38	8.50	11/9/38	13.79	62.2	223	−26.2	150
4/8/39	10.18	10/25/39	13.21	29.8	200	−43.5	916
4/28/42	7.47	5/29/46	19.25	157.7	1492	−28.8	353
5/17/47	13.71	6/15/48	17.06	24.4	395	−20.6	363
6/13/49	13.55	1/5/53	26.66	96.8	1302	−14.8	252
9/14/53	22.71	8/2/56	49.74	119.0	1053	−21.6	446
10/22/57	38.98	8/3/59	60.71	55.7	650	−13.9	449
10/25/60	52.30	12/12/61	72.64	38.9	413	−28.0	196
6/26/62	52.32	2/9/66	94.06	79.8	1324	−22.2	240
10/7/66	73.20	11/29/68	108.37	48.0	784	−36.1	543
5/26/70	69.29	4/28/71	104.77	51.2	337	−13.9	209
11/23/71	90.16	1/11/73	120.24	33.4	415	−48.2	630
10/3/74	62.28	9/21/76	107.83	73.1	719	−19.4	531
3/6/78	86.90	9/12/78	106.99	23.1	190	−8.2	562
3/27/80	98.22	11/28/80	140.52	43.1	246	−27.1	622
8/12/82	102.42	10/10/83	172.65	68.6	424	−14.4	288
7/24/84	147.82	8/25/87	336.77	127.8	1127	−33.5	101
12/4/87	223.92	7/16/90	368.95	64.8	955	−19.9	87
10/11/90	295.46	7/17/98	1186.75	301.7	2836	−19.3	45
8/31/98	957.28	3/24/00	1527.46	59.6	571	−36.8	546
9/21/01	965.80	1/4/02	1172.51	21.4	105	−33.8	278
10/9/02	776.76	10/9/07	1565.15	101.5	1826	−56.8	517
3/9/09	676.53	4/29/11	1363.61	101.6	781	−19.4	157
10/3/11	1099.23	5/3/13	1614.42	46.9*	578*	*At Press Time–not in averages	
			Average	**81.0%**	**729**	**−30.2%**	**379**

NASDAQ COMPOSITE BULL AND BEAR MARKETS

— Beginning —		— Ending —		Bull		Bear	
Date	NASDAQ	Date	NASDAQ	% Gain	Days	% Change	Days
11/23/71	100.31	1/11/73	136.84	36.4%	415	−59.9%	630
10/3/74	54.87	7/15/75	88.00	60.4	285	−16.2	63
9/16/75	73.78	9/13/78	139.25	88.7	1093	−20.4	62
11/14/78	110.88	2/8/80	165.25	49.0	451	−24.9	48
3/27/80	124.09	5/29/81	223.47	80.1	428	−28.8	441
8/13/82	159.14	6/24/83	328.91	106.7	315	−31.5	397
7/25/84	225.30	8/26/87	455.26	102.1	1127	−35.9	63
10/28/87	291.88	10/9/89	485.73	66.4	712	−33.0	372
10/16/90	325.44	7/20/98	2014.25	518.9	2834	−29.5	80
10/8/98	1419.12	3/10/00	5048.62	255.8	519	−71.8	560
9/21/01	1423.19	1/4/02	2059.38	44.7	105	−45.9	278
10/9/02	1114.11	10/31/07	2859.12	156.6	1848	−55.6	495
3/9/09	1268.64	4/29/11	2873.54	126.5	781	−18.7	157
10/3/11	2335.83	5/3/13	3378.63	44.6*	578*	*At Press Time– not in averages	
			Average	**130.2%**	**839**	**−36.3%**	**280**

JANUARY DAILY POINT CHANGES DOW JONES INDUSTRIALS

	2004	2005	2006	2007	2008	2009	2010	2011	2012	2013
Previous Month Close	10453.92	10783.01	10717.50	12463.15	13264.82	8776.39	10428.05	11577.51	12217.56	13104.14
1	H	S	S	H	H	H	H	S	S	H
2	−44.07	S	S	H*	−220.86	258.30	S	S	S	308.41
3	S	−53.58	129.91	11.37	12.76	S	S	93.24	179.82	−21.19
4	S	−98.65	32.74	6.17	−256.54	S	155.91	20.43	21.04	43.85
5	134.22	−32.95	2.00	−82.68	S	−81.80	−11.94	31.71	−2.72	S
6	−5.41	25.05	77.16	S	S	62.21	1.66	−25.58	−55.78	S
7	−9.63	−18.92	S	S	27.31	−245.40	33.18	−22.55	S	−50.92
8	63.41	S	S	25.48	−238.42	−27.24	11.33	S	S	−55.44
9	−133.55	S	52.59	−6.89	146.24	−143.28	S	S	32.77	61.66
10	S	17.07	−0.32	25.56	117.78	S	S	−37.31	69.78	80.71
11	S	−64.81	31.86	72.82	−246.79	S	45.80	34.43	−13.02	17.21
12	26.29	61.56	−81.08	41.10	S	−125.21	−36.73	83.56	21.57	S
13	−58.00	−111.95	−2.49	S	S	−25.41	53.51	−23.54	−48.96	S
14	111.19	52.17	S	S	171.85	−248.42	29.78	55.48	S	18.89
15	15.48	S	S	H	−277.04	12.35	−100.90	S	S	27.57
16	46.66	S	H	26.51	−34.95	68.73	S	S	H	−23.66
17	S	H	−63.55	−5.44	−306.95	S	S	H	60.01	84.79
18	S	70.79	−41.46	−9.22	−59.91	S	H	50.55	96.88	53.68
19	H	−88.82	25.85	−2.40	S	H	115.78	−12.64	45.03	S
20	−71.85	−68.50	−213.32	S	S	−332.13	−122.28	−2.49	96.50	S
21	94.96	−78.48	S	S	H	279.01	−213.27	49.04	S	H
22	−0.44	S	S	−88.37	−128.11	−105.30	−216.90	S	S	62.51
23	−54.89	S	21.38	56.64	298.98	−45.24	S	S	−11.66	67.12
24	S	−24.38	23.45	87.97	108.44	S	S	108.68	−33.07	46.00
25	S	92.95	−2.48	−119.21	−171.44	S	23.88	−3.33	81.21	70.65
26	134.22	37.03	99.73	−15.54	S	38.47	−2.57	8.25	−22.33	S
27	−92.59	−31.19	97.74	S	S	58.70	41.87	4.39	−74.17	S
28	−141.55	−40.20	S	S	176.72	200.72	−115.70	−166.13	S	−14.05
29	41.92	S	S	3.76	96.41	−226.44	−53.13	S	S	72.49
30	−22.22	S	−7.29	32.53	−37.47	−148.15	S	S	−6.74	−44.00
31	S	62.74	−35.06	98.38	207.53	S	S	68.23	−20.81	−49.84
Close	10488.07	10489.94	10864.86	12621.69	12650.36	8000.86	10067.33	11891.93	12632.91	13860.58
Change	34.15	−293.07	147.36	158.54	−614.46	−775.53	−360.72	314.42	415.35	756.44

* Ford funeral

FEBRUARY DAILY POINT CHANGES DOW JONES INDUSTRIALS

	2004	2005	2006	2007	2008	2009	2010	2011	2012	2013
Previous Month Close	10488.07	10489.94	10864.86	12621.69	12650.36	8000.86	10067.33	11891.93	12632.91	13860.58
1	S	62.00	89.09	51.99	92.83	S	118.20	148.23	83.55	149.21
2	11.11	44.85	−101.97	−20.19	S	−64.03	111.32	1.81	−11.05	S
3	6.00	−3.69	−58.36	S	S	141.53	−26.30	20.29	156.82	S
4	−34.44	123.03	S	S	−108.03	−121.70	−268.37	29.89	S	−129.71
5	24.81	S	S	8.25	−370.01	106.41	10.05	S	S	99.22
6	97.48	S	4.65	4.57	−65.03	217.52	S	S	−17.10	7.22
7	S	−0.37	−48.51	0.56	46.90	S	S	69.48	33.07	−42.47
8	S	8.87	108.86	−29.24	−64.87	S	−103.84	71.52	5.75	48.92
9	−14.00	−60.52	24.73	−56.80	S	−9.72	150.25	6.74	6.51	S
10	34.82	85.50	35.70	S	S	−381.99	−20.26	−10.60	−89.23	S
11	123.85	46.40	S	S	57.88	50.65	105.81	43.97	S	−21.73
12	−43.63	S	S	−28.28	133.40	−6.77	−45.05	S	S	47.46
13	−66.22	S	−26.73	102.30	178.83	−82.35	S	S	72.81	−35.79
14	S	−4.88	136.07	87.01	−175.26	S	S	−5.07	4.24	−9.52
15	S	46.19	30.58	23.15	−28.77	S	H	−41.55	−97.33	8.37
16	H	−2.44	61.71	2.56	S	H	169.67	61.53	123.13	S
17	87.03	−80.62	−5.36	S	S	−297.81	40.43	29.97	45.79	S
18	−42.89	30.96	S	S	H	3.03	83.66	73.11	S	H
19	−7.26	S	S	H	−10.99	−89.68	9.45	S	S	53.91
20	−45.70	S	H	19.07	90.04	−100.28	S	S	H	−108.13
21	S	H	−46.26	−48.23	−142.96	S	S	H	15.82	−46.92
22	S	−174.02	68.11	−52.39	96.72	S	−18.97	−178.46	−27.02	119.95
23	−9.41	62.59	−67.95	−38.54	S	−250.89	−100.97	−107.01	46.02	S
24	−43.25	75.00	−7.37	S	S	236.16	91.75	−37.28	−1.74	S
25	35.25	92.81	S	S	189.20	−80.05	−53.13	61.95	S	−216.40
26	−21.48	S	S	−15.22	114.70	−88.81	4.23	S	S	115.96
27	3.78	S	35.70	−416.02	9.36	−119.15	S	S	−1.44	175.24
28	S	−75.37	−104.14	52.39	−112.10	S	S	95.89	23.61	−20.88
29	—	—	—	—	−315.79	—	—	—	−53.05	—
Close	10583.92	10766.23	10993.41	12268.63	12266.39	7062.93	10325.26	12226.34	12952.07	14054.49
Change	95.85	276.29	128.55	−353.06	−383.97	−937.93	257.93	334.41	319.16	193.91

MARCH DAILY POINT CHANGES DOW JONES INDUSTRIALS

Previous Month Close	2004	2005	2006	2007	2008	2009	2010	2011	2012	2013
	10583.92	10766.23	10993.41	12268.63	12266.39	7062.93	10325.26	12226.34	12952.07	14054.49
1	94.22	63.77	60.12	-34.29	S	S	78.53	-168.32	28.23	35.17
2	-86.66	-18.03	-28.02	-120.24	S	-299.64	2.19	8.78	-2.73	S
3	1.63	21.06	-3.92	S	-7.49	-37.27	-9.22	191.40	S	S
4	-5.11	107.52	S	S	-45.10	149.82	47.38	-88.32	S	38.16
5	7.55	S	S	-63.69	41.19	-281.40	122.06	S	-14.76	125.95
6	S	S	-63.00	157.18	-214.60	32.50	S	S	-203.66	42.47
7	S	-3.69	22.10	-15.14	-146.70	S	S	-79.85	78.18	33.25
8	-66.07	-24.24	25.05	68.25	S	S	-13.68	124.35	70.61	67.58
9	-72.52	-107.00	-33.46	15.62	S	-79.89	11.86	-1.29	14.08	S
10	-160.07	45.89	104.06	S	-153.54	379.44	2.95	-228.48	S	S
11	-168.51	-77.15	S	S	416.66	3.91	44.51	59.79	S	50.22
12	111.70	S	S	42.30	-46.57	239.66	12.85	S	37.69	2.77
13	S	S	-0.32	-242.66	35.50	53.92	S	S	217.97	5.22
14	S	30.15	75.32	57.44	-194.65	S	S	-51.24	16.42	83.86
15	-137.19	-59.41	58.43	26.28	S	S	17.46	-137.74	58.66	-25.03
16	81.78	-112.03	43.47	-49.27	S	-7.01	43.83	-242.12	-20.14	S
17	115.63	-6.72	26.41	S	21.16	178.73	47.69	161.29	S	S
18	-4.52	3.32	S	S	420.41	90.88	45.50	83.93	S	-62.05
19	-109.18	S	S	115.76	-293.00	-85.78	-37.19	S	6.51	3.76
20	S	S	-5.12	61.93	261.66	-122.42	S	S	-68.94	55.91
21	S	-64.28	-39.06	159.42	H	S	S	178.01	-45.57	-90.24
22	-121.85	-94.88	81.96	13.62	S	S	43.91	-17.90	-78.48	90.54
23	-1.11	-14.49	-47.14	19.87	S	497.48	102.94	67.39	34.59	S
24	-15.41	-13.15	9.68	S	187.32	-115.89	-52.68	84.54	S	S
25	170.59	H	S	S	-16.04	89.84	5.06	50.03	S	-64.28
26	-5.85	S	S	-11.94	-109.74	174.75	9.15	S	160.90	111.90
27	S	S	-29.86	-71.78	-120.40	-148.38	S	S	-43.90	-33.49
28	S	42.78	-95.57	-96.93	-86.06	S	S	-22.71	-71.52	52.38
29	116.66	-79.95	61.16	48.39	S	S	45.50	81.13	19.61	H
30	52.07	135.23	-65.00	5.60	S	-254.16	11.56	71.60	66.22	S
31	-24.00	-37.17	-41.38	S	46.49	86.90	-50.79	-30.88	S	S
Close	10357.70	10503.76	11109.32	12354.35	12262.89	7608.92	10856.63	12319.73	13212.04	14578.54
Change	-226.22	-262.47	115.91	85.72	-3.50	545.99	531.37	93.39	259.97	524.05

APRIL DAILY POINT CHANGES DOW JONES INDUSTRIALS

Previous Month Close	2004	2005	2006	2007	2008	2009	2010	2011	2012	2013
	10357.70	10503.76	11109.32	12354.35	12262.89	7608.92	10856.63	12319.73	13212.04	14578.54
1	15.63	-99.46	S	S	391.47	152.68	70.44	56.99	S	-5.69
2	97.26	S	S	27.95	-48.53	216.48	H	S	52.45	89.16
3	S	S	35.62	128.00	20.20	39.51	S	S	-64.94	-111.66
4	S	16.84	58.91	19.75	-16.61	S	S	23.31	-124.80	55.76
5	87.78	37.32	35.70	30.15	S	S	46.48	-6.13	-14.61	-40.86
6	12.44	27.56	-23.05	H	S	-41.74	-3.56	32.85	H	S
7	-90.66	60.30	-96.46	S	3.01	-186.29	-72.47	-17.26	S	S
8	-38.12	-84.98	S	S	-35.99	47.55	29.55	-29.44	S	48.23
9	H	S	S	8.94	-49.18	246.27	70.28	S	-130.55	59.98
10	S	S	21.29	4.71	54.72	H	S	S	-213.66	128.78
11	S	-12.78	-51.70	-89.23	-256.56	S	S	1.06	89.46	62.90
12	73.53	59.41	40.34	68.34	S	S	8.62	-117.53	181.19	-0.08
13	-134.28	-104.04	7.68	59.17	S	-25.57	13.45	7.41	-136.99	S
14	-3.33	-125.18	H	S	-23.36	-137.63	103.69	14.16	S	S
15	19.51	-191.24	S	S	60.41	109.44	21.46	56.68	S	-265.86
16	54.51	S	S	108.33	256.80	95.81	-125.91	S	71.82	157.58
17	S	S	-63.87	52.58	1.22	5.90	S	S	194.13	-138.19
18	S	-16.26	194.99	30.80	228.87	S	S	-140.24	-82.79	-81.45
19	-14.12	56.16	10.00	4.79	S	S	73.39	65.16	-68.65	10.37
20	-123.35	-115.05	64.12	153.35	S	-289.60	25.01	186.79	65.16	S
21	2.77	206.24	4.56	S	-24.34	127.83	7.86	52.45	S	S
22	143.93	-60.89	S	S	-104.79	-82.99	9.37	H	S	19.66
23	11.64	S	S	-42.58	42.99	70.49	69.99	S	-102.09	152.29
24	S	S	-11.13	34.54	85.73	119.23	S	S	74.39	-43.16
25	S	84.76	-53.07	135.95	42.91	S	S	-26.11	89.16	24.50
26	-28.11	-91.34	71.24	15.61	S	S	0.75	115.49	113.90	11.75
27	33.43	47.67	28.02	15.44	S	-51.29	-213.04	95.59	23.69	S
28	-135.56	-128.43	-15.37	S	-20.11	-8.05	53.28	72.35	S	S
29	-70.33	122.14	S	S	-39.81	168.78	122.05	47.23	S	106.20
30	-46.70	S	S	-58.03	-11.81	-17.61	-158.71	S	-14.68	21.05
Close	10225.57	10192.51	11367.14	13062.91	12820.13	8168.12	11008.61	12810.54	13213.63	14839.80
Change	-132.13	-311.25	257.82	708.56	557.24	559.20	151.98	490.81	1.59	261.26

134

MAY DAILY POINT CHANGES DOW JONES INDUSTRIALS

Previous Month Close	2003	2004	2005	2006	2007	2008	2009	2010	2011	2012
	8480.09	10225.57	10192.51	11367.14	13062.91	12820.13	8168.12	11008.61	12810.54	13213.63
1	−25.84	S	S	−23.85	73.23	189.87	44.29	S	S	65.69
2	128.43	S	59.19	73.16	75.74	48.20	S	S	−3.18	−10.75
3	S	88.43	5.25	−16.17	29.50	S	S	143.22	0.15	−61.98
4	S	3.20	127.69	38.58	23.24	S	214.33	−225.06	−83.93	−168.32
5	−51.11	−6.25	−44.26	138.88	S	−88.66	−16.09	−58.65	−139.41	S
6	56.79	−69.69	5.02	S	S	51.29	101.63	−347.80	54.57	S
7	−27.73	−123.92	S	S	48.35	−206.48	−102.43	−139.89	S	−29.74
8	−69.41	S	S	6.80	−3.90	52.43	164.80	S	S	−76.44
9	113.38	S	38.94	55.23	53.80	−120.90	S	S	45.94	−97.03
10	S	−127.32	−103.23	2.88	−147.74	S	S	404.71	75.68	19.98
11	S	29.45	19.14	−141.92	111.09	S	−155.88	−36.88	−130.33	−34.44
12	122.13	25.69	−110.77	−119.74	S	130.43	50.34	148.65	65.89	S
13	−47.48	−34.42	−49.36	S	S	−44.13	−184.22	−113.96	−100.17	S
14	−31.43	2.13	S	S	20.56	66.20	46.43	−162.79	S	−125.25
15	65.32	S	S	47.78	37.06	94.28	−62.68	S	S	−63.35
16	−34.17	S	112.17	−8.88	103.69	−5.86	S	S	−47.38	−33.45
17	S	−105.96	79.59	−214.28	−10.81	S	S	5.67	−68.79	−156.06
18	S	61.60	132.57	−77.32	79.81	S	235.44	−114.88	80.60	−73.11
19	−185.58	−30.80	28.74	15.77	S	41.36	−29.23	−66.58	45.14	S
20	−2.03	−0.07	−21.28	S	S	−199.48	−52.81	−376.36	−93.28	S
21	25.07	29.10	S	S	−13.65	−227.49	−129.91	125.38	S	135.10
22	77.59	S	S	−18.73	−2.93	24.43	−14.81	S	S	−1.67
23	7.36	S	51.65	−26.98	−14.30	−145.99	S	S	−130.78	−6.66
24	S	−8.31	−19.88	18.97	−84.52	S	S	−126.82	−25.05	33.60
25	S	159.19	−45.88	93.73	66.15	S	H	−22.82	38.45	−74.92
26	H	−7.73	79.80	67.56	S	H	196.17	−69.30	8.10	S
27	179.97	95.31	4.95	S	S	68.72	−173.47	284.54	38.82	S
28	11.77	−16.75	S	S	H	45.68	103.78	−122.36	S	H
29	−81.94	S	S	S	14.06	52.19	96.53	S	S	125.86
30	139.08	S	S	H	111.74	−7.90	S	S	H	−160.83
31	S	H	−75.07	73.88	−5.44	S	S	H	128.21	−26.41
Close	8850.26	10188.45	10467.48	11168.31	13627.64	12638.32	8500.33	10136.63	12569.79	12393.45
Change	370.17	−37.12	274.97	−198.83	564.73	−181.81	332.21	−871.98	−240.75	−820.18

JUNE DAILY POINT CHANGES DOW JONES INDUSTRIALS

Previous Month Close	2003	2004	2005	2006	2007	2008	2009	2010	2011	2012
	8850.26	10188.45	10467.48	11168.31	13627.64	12638.32	8500.33	10136.63	12569.79	12393.45
1	S	14.20	82.39	91.97	40.47	S	221.11	−112.61	−279.65	−274.88
2	47.55	60.32	3.62	−12.41	S	−134.50	19.43	225.52	−41.59	S
3	25.14	−67.06	−92.52	S	S	−100.97	−65.59	5.74	−97.29	S
4	116.03	46.91	S	S	8.21	−12.37	74.96	−323.31	S	−17.11
5	2.32	S	S	−199.15	−80.86	213.97	12.89	S	S	26.49
6	21.49	S	6.06	−46.58	−129.79	−394.64	S	S	−61.30	286.84
7	S	148.26	16.04	−71.24	−198.94	S	S	−115.48	−19.15	46.17
8	S	41.44	−6.21	7.92	157.66	S	1.36	123.49	−21.87	93.24
9	−82.79	−64.08	26.16	−46.90	S	70.51	−1.43	−40.73	75.42	S
10	74.89	41.66	9.61	S	S	9.44	−24.04	273.28	−172.45	S
11	128.33	H*	S	S	0.57	−205.99	31.90	38.54	S	−142.97
12	13.33	S	S	−99.34	−129.95	57.81	28.34	S	S	162.57
13	−79.43	S	9.93	−86.44	187.34	165.77	S	S	1.06	−77.42
14	S	−75.37	25.01	110.78	71.37	S	S		123.14	155.53
15	S	45.70	18.80	198.27	85.76	S	−187.13	213.88	−178.84	115.26
16	201.84	−0.85	12.28	−0.64	S	−38.27	−107.46	4.69	64.25	S
17	4.06	−2.06	44.42	S	S	−108.78	−7.49	24.71	42.84	S
18	−29.22	38.89	S	S	−26.50	−131.24	58.42	16.47	S	−25.35
19	−114.27	S	S	−72.44	22.44	34.03	−15.87	S	S	95.51
20	21.22	S	−13.96	32.73	−146.00	−220.40	S	S	76.02	−12.94
21	S	−44.94	−9.44	104.62	56.42	S	S	−8.23	109.63	−250.82
22	S	23.60	−11.74	−60.35	−185.58	S	−200.72	−148.89	−80.34	67.21
23	−127.80	84.50	−166.49	−30.02	S	−0.33	−16.10	4.92	−59.67	S
24	36.90	−35.76	−123.60	S	S	−34.93	−23.05	−145.64	−115.42	S
25	−98.32	−71.97	S	S	−8.21	4.40	172.54	−8.99	S	−138.12
26	67.51	S	S	56.19	−14.39	−358.41	−34.01	S	S	32.01
27	−89.99	S	−7.06	−120.54	90.07	−106.91	S	S	108.98	92.34
28	S	−14.75	114.85	48.82	−5.45	S	S	−5.29	145.13	−24.75
29	S	56.34	−31.15	217.24	−13.66	S	90.99	−268.22	72.73	277.83
30	−3.61	22.05	−99.51	−40.58	S	3.50	−82.38	−96.28	152.92	S
Close	8985.44	10435.48	10274.97	11150.22	13408.62	11350.01	8447.00	9774.02	12414.34	12880.09
Change	135.18	247.03	−192.51	−18.09	−219.02	−1288.31	−53.33	−362.61	−155.45	486.64

* Reagan funeral

Previous Month Close	2003	2004	2005	2006	2007	2008	2009	2010	2011	2012
	8985.44	10435.48	10274.97	11150.22	13408.62	11350.01	8447.00	9774.02	12414.34	12880.09
1	55.51	-101.32	28.47	S	S	32.25	57.06	-41.49	168.43	S
2	101.89	-51.33	S	S	126.81	-166.75	-223.32	-46.05	S	-8.70
3	-72.63*	S	S	77.80*	41.87*	73.03*	H	S	S	72.43*
4	H	S	H	H	H	S	S	S	H	H
5	S	H	68.36	-76.20	-11.46	S	S	H	-12.90	-47.15
6	S	-63.49	-101.12	73.48	45.84	S	44.13	57.14	56.15	-124.20
7	146.58	20.95	31.61	-134.63	S	-56.58	-161.27	274.66	93.47	S
8	6.30	-68.73	146.85	S	S	152.25	14.81	120.71	-62.29	S
9	-66.88	41.66	S	S	38.29	-236.77	4.76	59.04	S	-36.18
10	-120.17	S	S	12.88	-148.27	81.58	-36.65	S	S	-83.17
11	83.55	S	70.58	31.22	76.17	-128.48	S	S	-151.44	-48.59
12	S	25.00	-5.83	-121.59	283.86	S	S	18.24	-58.88	-31.26
13	S	9.37	43.50	-166.89	45.52	S	185.16	146.75	44.73	203.82
14	57.56	-38.79	71.50	-106.94	S	-45.35	27.81	3.70	-54.49	S
15	-48.18	-45.64	11.94	S	S	-92.65	256.72	-7.41	42.61	S
16	-34.38	-23.38	S	S	43.73	276.74	95.61	-261.41	S	-49.88
17	-43.77	S	S	8.01	20.57	207.38	32.12	S	S	78.33
18	137.33	S	-65.84	51.87	-53.33	49.91	S	S	-94.57	103.16
19	S	-45.72	71.57	212.19	82.19	S	S	56.53	202.26	34.66
20	S	55.01	42.59	-83.32	-149.33	S	104.21	75.53	-15.51	-120.79
21	-91.46	-102.94	-61.38	-59.72	S	-29.23	67.79	-109.43	152.50	S
22	61.76	4.20	23.41	S	S	135.16	-34.68	201.77	-43.25	S
23	35.79	-88.11	S	S	92.34	29.88	188.03	102.32	S	-101.11
24	-81.73	S	S	182.67	-226.47	-283.10	23.95	S	S	-104.14
25	172.06	S	-54.70	52.66	68.12	21.41	S	S	-88.36	58.73
26	S	-0.30	-16.71	-1.20	-311.50	S	S	100.81	-91.50	211.88
27	S	123.22	57.32	-2.08	-208.10	S	15.27	12.26	-198.75	187.73
28	-18.06	31.93	68.46	119.27	S	-239.61	-11.79	-39.81	-62.44	S
29	-62.05	12.17	-64.64	S	S	266.48	-26.00	-30.72	-96.87	S
30	-4.41	10.47	S	S	92.84	186.13	83.74	-1.22	S	-2.65
31	33.75	S	S	-34.02	-146.32	-205.67	17.15	S	S	-64.33
Close	9233.80	10139.71	10640.91	11185.68	13211.99	11378.02	9171.61	10465.94	12143.24	13008.68
Change	248.36	-295.77	365.94	35.46	-196.63	28.01	724.61	691.92	-271.10	128.59

* Shortened trading day

Previous Month Close	2003	2004	2005	2006	2007	2008	2009	2010	2011	2012
	9233.80	10139.71	10640.91	11185.68	13211.99	11378.02	9171.61	10465.94	12143.24	13008.68
1	-79.83	S	-17.76	-59.95	150.38	-51.70	S	S	-10.75	-37.62
2	S	39.45	60.59	74.20	100.96	S	S	208.44	-265.87	-92.18
3	S	-58.92	13.85	42.66	-281.42	S	114.95	-38.00	29.82	217.29
4	32.07	6.27	-87.49	-2.24	S	-42.17	33.63	44.05	-512.76	S
5	-149.72	-163.48	-52.07	S	S	331.62	-39.22	-5.45	60.93	S
6	25.42	-147.70	S	S	286.87	40.30	-24.71	-21.42	S	21.34
7	64.71	S	S	-20.97	35.52	-224.64	113.81	S	S	51.09
8	64.64	S	-21.10	-45.79	153.56	302.89	S	S	-634.76	7.04
9	S	-0.67	78.74	-97.41	-387.18	S	S	45.19	429.92	-10.45
10	S	130.01	-21.26	48.19	-31.14	S	-32.12	-54.50	-519.83	42.76
11	26.26	-6.35	91.48	-36.34	S	48.03	-96.50	-265.42	423.37	S
12	92.71	-123.73	-85.58	S	S	-139.88	120.16	-58.88	125.71	S
13	-38.30	10.76	S	S	-3.01	-109.51	36.58	-16.80	S	-38.52
14	38.80	S	S	9.84	-207.61	82.97	-76.79	S	S	2.71
15	11.13	S	34.07	132.39	-167.45	43.97	S	S	213.88	-7.36
16	S	129.20	-120.93	96.86	-15.69	S	S	-1.14	-76.97	85.33
17	S	18.28	37.26	7.84	233.30	S	-186.06	103.84	4.28	25.09
18	90.76	110.32	4.22	46.51	S	-180.51	82.60	9.69	-419.63	S
19	16.45	-42.33	4.30	S	S	-130.84	61.22	-144.33	-172.93	S
20	-31.39	69.32	S	S	42.27	68.88	70.89	-57.59	S	-3.56
21	26.17	S	S	-36.42	-30.49	12.78	155.91	S	S	-68.06
22	-74.81	S	10.66	-5.21	145.27	197.85	S	S	37.00	-30.82
23	S	-37.09	-50.31	-41.94	-0.25	S	S	-39.21	322.11	-115.30
24	S	25.58	-84.71	6.56	142.99	S	3.32	-133.96	143.95	100.51
25	-31.23	83.11	15.76	-20.41	S	-241.81	30.01	19.61	-170.89	S
26	22.81	-8.33	-53.34	S	S	26.62	4.23	-74.25	134.72	S
27	-6.66	21.60	S	S	-56.74	89.64	37.11	164.84	S	-33.30
28	40.42	S	S	67.96	-280.28	212.67	-36.43	S	S	-21.68
29	41.61	S	65.76	17.93	247.44	-171.63	S	S	254.71	4.49
30	S	-72.49	-50.23	12.97	-50.56	S	S	-140.92	20.70	-106.77
31	S	51.40	68.78	-1.76	119.01	S	-47.92	4.99	53.58	90.13
Close	9415.82	10173.92	10481.60	11381.15	13357.74	11543.55	9496.28	10014.72	11613.53	13090.84
Change	182.02	34.21	-159.31	195.47	145.75	165.53	324.67	-451.22	-529.71	82.16

Previous Month	2003	2004	2005	2006	2007	2008	2009	2010	2011	2012
Close	9415.82	10173.92	10481.60	11381.15	13357.74	11543.55	9496.28	10014.72	11613.53	13090.84
1	H	−5.46	−21.97	83.00	S	H	−185.68	254.75	−119.96	S
2	107.45	121.82	−12.26	S	S	−26.63	−29.93	50.63	−253.31	S
3	45.19	−30.08	S	S	H	15.96	63.94	157.83	S	H
4	19.44	S	S	H	91.12	−344.65	96.66	S	S	−54.90
5	−84.56	S	H	5.13	−143.39	32.73	S	S	H	11.54
6	S	H	141.87	−63.08	57.88	S	S	H	−100.96	244.52
7	S	82.59	44.26	−74.76	−249.97	S	H	−137.24	275.56	14.64
8	82.95	−29.43	−37.57	60.67	S	289.78	56.07	46.32	−119.05	S
9	−79.09	−24.26	82.63	S	S	−280.01	49.88	28.23	−303.68	S
10	−86.74	23.97	S	4.73	14.47	38.19	80.26	47.53	S	−52.35
11	39.30	S	S	180.54	164.79	−22.07	S	S		69.07
12	11.79	S	4.38	101.25	−16.74	−11.72	S	S	68.99	9.99
13	S	1.69	−85.50	45.23	133.23	S	S	81.36	44.73	206.51
14	S	3.40	−52.54	−15.93	17.64	S	21.39	−17.64	140.88	53.51
15	−22.74	−86.80	13.85	33.38	S	−504.48	56.61	46.24	186.45	S
16	118.53	13.13	83.19	S	S	141.51	108.30	22.10	75.91	S
17	−21.69	39.97	S	−5.77	−39.10	−449.36	−7.79	13.02	S	−40.27
18	113.48	S	S	335.97	410.03	36.28	S	S		11.54
19	−14.31	S	−84.31	−14.09	76.17	368.75	S	S	−108.08	13.32
20	S	−79.57	−76.11	72.28	−48.86	S	S	145.77	7.65	18.97
21	S	40.04	−103.49	−79.96	53.49	S	−41.34	7.41	−283.82	−17.46
22	−109.41	−135.75	44.02	−25.13	S	−372.75	51.01	−21.72	−391.01	S
23	40.63	−70.28	−2.46	S	S	−161.52	−81.32	−76.89	37.65	S
24	−150.53	8.34	S	S	−61.13	−29.00	−41.11	197.84	S	−20.55
25	−81.55	S	S	67.71	19.59	196.89	−42.25	S	S	−101.37
26	−30.88	S	24.04	93.58	99.50	121.07	S	S	272.38	−44.04
27	S	−58.70	12.58	19.85	34.79	S	S	−48.22	146.83	72.46
28	S	88.86	16.88	29.21	−17.31	S	124.17	46.10	−179.79	−48.84
29	67.16	58.84	79.69	−39.38	S	−777.68	−47.16	−22.86	143.08	S
30	−105.18	−55.97	15.92	S	S	485.21	−29.92	−47.23	−240.60	S
Close	9275.06	10080.27	10568.70	11679.07	13895.63	10850.66	9712.28	10788.05	10913.38	13437.13
Change	−140.76	−93.65	87.10	297.92	537.89	−692.89	216.00	773.33	−700.15	346.29

Previous Month	2003	2004	2005	2006	2007	2008	2009	2010	2011	2012
Close	9275.06	10080.27	10568.70	11679.07	13895.63	10850.66	9712.28	10788.05	10913.38	13437.13
1	194.14	112.38	S	S	191.92	−19.59	−203.00	41.63	S	77.98
2	18.60	S	S	−8.72	−40.24	−348.22	−21.61	S	−258.08	−32.75
3	84.51	S	−33.22	56.99	−79.26	−157.47	S	S	153.41	12.25
4	S	23.89	−94.37	123.27	6.26	S	S	−78.41	131.24	80.75
5	S	−38.86	−123.75	16.08	91.70	S	112.08	193.45	131.24	34.79
6	22.67	62.24	−30.26	−16.48	S	−369.88	131.50	22.93	183.38	S
7	59.63	−114.52	5.21	S	S	−508.39	−5.67	−19.07	−20.21	S
8	−23.71	−70.20	S	S	−22.28	−189.01	61.29	57.90	S	−26.50
9	49.11	S	S	7.60	120.80	−678.91	78.07	S	S	−110.12
10	−5.33	S	−53.55	9.36	−85.84	−128.00	S	S	330.06	−128.56
11	S	26.77	14.41	−15.04	−63.57	S	S	3.86	−16.88	−18.58
12	S	−4.79	−36.26	95.57	77.96	S	20.86	10.06	102.55	2.46
13	89.70	−74.85	−0.32	12.81	S	936.42	−14.74	75.68	−40.72	S
14	48.60	−107.88	70.75	S	S	−76.62	144.80	−1.51	166.36	S
15	−9.93	38.93	S	S	−108.28	−733.08	47.08	−31.79	S	95.38
16	−11.33	S	S	20.09	−71.86	401.35	−67.03	S	S	127.55
17	−69.93	S	60.76	−30.58	−20.40	−127.04	S	S	−247.49	5.22
18	S	22.94	−62.84	42.66	−3.58	S	S	80.91	180.05	−8.06
19	S	−58.70	128.87	19.05	−366.94	S	96.28	−165.07	−72.43	−205.43
20	56.15	−10.69	−133.03	−9.36	S	413.21	−50.71	129.35	37.16	S
21	−30.30	−21.17	−65.88	S	S	−231.77	−92.12	38.60	267.01	S
22	−149.40	−107.95	S	S	44.95	−514.45	131.95	−14.01	S	2.38
23	14.89	S	S	114.54	109.26	172.04	−109.13	S	S	−243.36
24	−30.67	S	169.78	10.97	−0.98	−312.30	S	S	104.83	−25.19
25	S	−7.82	−7.13	6.80	−3.33	S	S	31.49	−207.00	26.34
26	S	138.49	−32.89	28.98	134.78	S	−104.22	5.41	162.42	3.53
27	25.70	113.55	−115.03	−73.40	S	−203.18	−119.48	−43.18	339.51	S
28	140.15	2.51	172.82	S	S	889.35	−119.48	−12.33	22.56	S
29	26.22	22.93	S	S	63.56	−74.16	199.89	4.54	S	H*
30	12.08	S	S	−3.76	−77.79	189.73	−249.85	S	S	H*
31	14.51	S	37.30	−5.77	137.54	144.32	S	S	−276.10	−10.75
Close	9801.12	10027.47	10440.07	12080.73	13930.01	9325.01	9712.73	11118.49	11955.01	13096.46
Change	526.06	−52.80	−128.63	401.66	34.38	−1525.65	0.45	330.44	1041.63	−340.67

* Hurricane Sandy

NOVEMBER DAILY POINT CHANGES DOW JONES INDUSTRIALS

	2003	2004	2005	2006	2007	2008	2009	2010	2011	2012
Previous Month Close	9801.12	10027.47	10440.07	12080.73	13930.01	9325.01	9712.73	11118.49	11955.01	13096.46
1	S	26.92	−33.30	−49.71	−362.14	S	S	6.13	−297.05	136.16
2	S	−18.66	65.96	−12.48	27.23	S	76.71	64.10	178.08	−139.46
3	57.34	101.32	49.86	−32.50	S	−5.18	−17.53	26.41	208.43	S
4	−19.63	177.71	8.17	S	S	305.45	30.23	219.71	−61.23	S
5	−18.00	72.78	S	S	−51.70	−486.01	203.82	9.24	S	19.28
6	36.14	S	S	119.51	117.54	−443.48	17.46	S	S	133.24
7	−47.18	S	55.47	51.22	−360.92	248.02	S	S	85.15	−312.95
8	S	3.77	−46.51	19.77	−33.73	S	S	−37.24	101.79	−121.41
9	S	−4.94	6.49	−73.24	−223.55	S	203.52	−60.09	−389.24	4.07
10	−53.26	−0.89	93.89	5.13	S	−73.27	20.03	10.29	112.85	S
11	−18.74	84.36	45.94	S	S	−176.58	44.29	−73.94	259.89	S
12	111.04	69.17	S	S	−55.19	−411.30	−93.79	−90.52	S	−0.31
13	−10.89	S	S	23.45	319.54	552.59	73.00	S	S	−58.90
14	−69.26	S	11.13	86.13	−76.08	−337.94	S	S	−74.70	−185.23
15	S	11.23	−10.73	33.70	−120.96	S	S	9.39	17.18	−28.57
16	S	−62.59	−11.68	54.11	66.74	S	136.49	−178.47	−190.57	45.93
17	−57.85	61.92	45.46	36.74	S	−223.73	30.46	−15.62	−134.86	S
18	−86.67	22.98	46.11	S	S	151.17	−11.11	173.35	25.43	S
19	66.30	−115.64	S	S	−218.35	−427.47	−93.87	22.32	S	207.65
20	−71.04	S	S	−26.02	51.70	−444.99	−14.28	S	S	−7.45
21	9.11	S	53.95	5.05	−211.10	494.13	S	S	−248.85	48.38
22	S	32.51	51.15	5.36	H	S	S	−24.97	−53.59	H
23	S	3.18	44.66	H	181.84*	S	132.79	−142.21	−236.17	172.79*
24	119.26	27.71	H	−46.78*	S	396.97	−17.24	150.91	H	S
25	16.15	H	15.53*	S	S	36.08	30.69	H	−25.77*	S
26	15.63	1.92*	S	S	−237.44	247.14	H	−95.28*	S	−42.31
27	H	S	S	−158.46	215.00	H	−154.48*	S	S	−89.24
28	2.89*	S	−40.90	14.74	331.01	102.43*	S	S	291.23	106.98
29	S	−46.33	−2.56	90.28	22.28	S	S	−39.51	32.62	36.71
30	S	−47.88	−82.29	−4.80	59.99	S	34.92	−46.47	490.05	3.76
Close	9782.46	10428.02	10805.87	12221.93	13371.72	8829.04	10344.84	11006.02	12045.68	13025.58
Change	−18.66	400.55	365.80	141.20	−558.29	−495.97	632.11	−112.47	90.67	−70.88

* Shortened trading day

DECEMBER DAILY POINT CHANGES DOW JONES INDUSTRIALS

	2003	2004	2005	2006	2007	2008	2009	2010	2011	2012
Previous Month Close	9782.46	10428.02	10805.87	12221.93	13371.72	8829.04	10344.84	11006.02	12045.68	13025.58
1	116.59	162.20	106.70	−27.80	S	−679.95	126.74	249.76	−25.65	S
2	−45.41	−5.10	−35.06	S	S	270.00	−18.90	106.63	−0.61	S
3	19.78	7.09	S	S	−57.15	172.60	−86.53	19.68	S	−59.98
4	57.40	S	S	89.72	−65.84	−215.45	22.75	S	S	−13.82
5	−68.14	S	−42.50	47.75	196.23	259.18	S	S	78.41	82.71
6	S	−45.15	21.85	−22.35	174.93	S	S	−19.90	52.30	39.55
7	S	−106.48	−45.95	−30.84	5.69	S	1.21	−3.03	46.24	81.09
8	102.59	53.65	−55.79	29.08	S	298.76	−104.14	13.32	−198.67	S
9	−41.85	58.59	23.46	S	S	−242.85	51.08	−2.42	186.56	S
10	−1.56	−9.60	S	S	101.45	70.09	68.78	40.26	S	14.75
11	86.30	S	S	20.99	−294.26	−196.33	65.67	S	S	78.56
12	34.00	S	−10.81	−12.90	41.13	64.59	S	S	−162.87	−2.99
13	S	95.10	55.95	1.92	44.06	S	S	18.24	−66.45	−74.73
14	S	38.13	59.79	99.26	−178.11	S	29.55	47.98	−131.46	−35.71
15	−19.34	15.00	−1.84	28.76	S	−65.15	−49.05	−19.07	45.33	S
16	106.74	14.19	−6.08	S	S	359.61	−10.88	41.78	−2.42	S
17	15.70	−55.72	S	S	−172.65	−99.80	−132.86	−7.34	S	100.38
18	102.82	S	S	−4.25	65.27	−219.35	20.63	S	S	115.57
19	30.14	S	−39.06	30.05	−25.20	−25.88	S	S	−100.13	−98.99
20	S	11.68	−30.98	−7.45	38.37	S	S	−13.78	337.32	59.75
21	S	97.83	28.18	−42.62	205.01	S	85.25	55.03	4.16	−120.88
22	59.78	56.46	55.71	−78.03	S	−59.34	50.79	26.33	61.91	S
23	3.26	11.23	−6.17	S	S	−100.28	1.51	14.00	124.35	S
24	−36.07*	H	S	S	98.68*	48.99*	53.66*	H	S	−51.76*
25	H	S	S	H	H	H	H	S	S	H
26	19.48*	S	H	64.41	2.36	47.07	S	S	H	−24.49
27	S	−50.99	−105.50	102.94	−192.08	S	S	−18.46	−2.65	−18.28
28	S	78.41	18.49	−9.05	6.26	S	26.98	20.51	−139.94	−158.20
29	125.33	−25.35	−11.44	−38.37	S	−31.62	−1.67	13.65	135.63	S
30	−24.96	−28.89	−67.32	S	S	184.46	3.10	−15.67	−69.48	S
31	28.88	−17.29	S	S	−101.05	108.00	−120.46	7.80	S	166.03
Close	10453.92	10783.01	10717.50	12463.15	13264.82	8776.39	10428.05	11577.51	12217.56	13104.14
Change	671.46	354.99	−88.37	241.22	−106.90	−52.65	83.21	571.49	171.88	78.56

* Shortened trading day

A TYPICAL DAY IN THE MARKET

Half-hourly data became available for the Dow Jones Industrial Average starting in January 1987. The NYSE switched 10:00 a.m. openings to 9:30 a.m. in October 1985. Below is the comparison between half-hourly performance from January 1987 to May 3, 2013 and hourly performance from November 1963 to June 1985. Stronger openings and closings in a more bullish climate are evident. Morning and afternoon weaknesses appear an hour earlier.

MARKET % PERFORMANCE EACH HALF-HOUR OF THE DAY
(January 1987 to May 3, 2013)

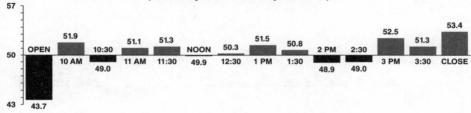

Based on the number of times the Dow Jones Industrial Average increased over previous half-hour.

MARKET % PERFORMANCE EACH HOUR OF THE DAY
(November 1963 to June 1985)

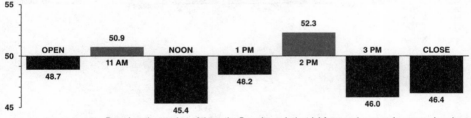

Based on the number of times the Dow Jones Industrial Average increased over previous hour.

On the next page, half-hourly movements since January 1987 are separated by day of the week. From 1953 to 1989, Monday was the worst day of the week, especially during long bear markets, but times changed. Monday reversed positions and became the best day of the week and on the plus side eleven years in a row from 1990 to 2000.

During the last 13 years (2001–May 10, 2013) Monday and Friday are net losers. Tuesday and Wednesday are solid gainers, Tuesday the best (page 68). On all days stocks do tend to firm up near the close with weakness early morning and from 2 to 2:30 frequently.

THROUGH THE WEEK ON A HALF-HOURLY BASIS

From the chart showing the percentage of times the Dow Jones Industrial Average rose over the preceding half-hour (January 1987 to May 3, 2013*), the typical week unfolds.

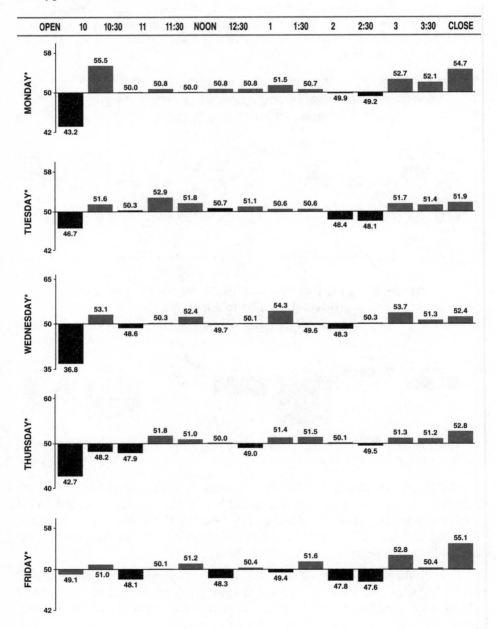

*Monday denotes first trading day of the week, Friday denotes last trading day of the week.

TUESDAY MOST PROFITABLE DAY OF WEEK

Between 1952 and 1989, Monday was the worst trading day of the week. The first trading day of the week (including Tuesday, when Monday is a holiday) rose only 44.3% of the time, while the other trading days closed higher 54.8% of the time. (NYSE Saturday trading was discontinued June 1952.)

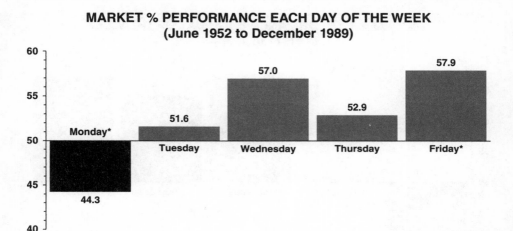

MARKET % PERFORMANCE EACH DAY OF THE WEEK
(June 1952 to December 1989)

A dramatic reversal occurred in 1990—Monday became the most powerful day of the week. However, during the last twelve and a third years, Tuesday has produced the most gains. Since the top in 2000, traders have not been inclined to stay long over the weekend nor buy up equities at the outset of the week. This is not uncommon during uncertain market times. Monday was the worst day during the 2007–2009 bear, and only Tuesday was a net gainer. Since the March 2009 bottom, Thursday is best. See pages 68 and 143.

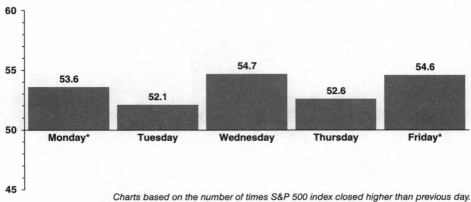

MARKET % PERFORMANCE EACH DAY OF THE WEEK
(January 1990 to May 4, 2013)

Charts based on the number of times S&P 500 index closed higher than previous day.
*Monday denotes first trading day of the week, Friday denotes last trading day of the week.

NASDAQ STRONGEST LAST 3 DAYS OF WEEK

Despite 20 years less data, daily trading patterns on NASDAQ through 1989 appear to be fairly similar to the S&P on page 141, except for more bullishness on Thursdays. During the mostly flat markets of the 1970s and early 1980s, it would appear that apprehensive investors decided to throw in the towel over weekends and sell on Mondays and Tuesdays.

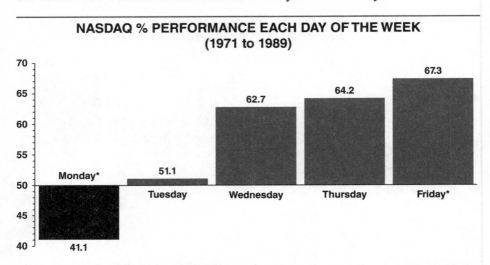

NASDAQ % PERFORMANCE EACH DAY OF THE WEEK
(1971 to 1989)

Notice the vast difference in the daily trading pattern between NASDAQ and S&P from January 1, 1990, to recent times. The reason for so much more bullishness is that NASDAQ moved up 1010%, over three times as much during the 1990 to 2000 period. The gain for the S&P was 332% and for the Dow Jones industrials, 326%. NASDAQ's weekly patterns are beginning to move in step with the rest of the market. Notice the similarities to the S&P since 2001 on pages 143 and 144—Monday and Friday weakness, midweek strength.

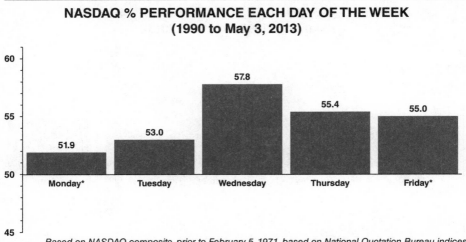

NASDAQ % PERFORMANCE EACH DAY OF THE WEEK
(1990 to May 3, 2013)

Based on NASDAQ composite, prior to February 5, 1971, based on National Quotation Bureau indices.
*Monday denotes first trading day of the week, Friday denotes last trading day of the week.

S&P DAILY PERFORMANCE EACH YEAR SINCE 1952

To determine if market trend alters performance of different days of the week, we separated 22 bear years—1953, '56, '57, '60, '62, '66, '69, '70, '73, '74, '77, '78, '81, '84, '87, '90, '94, 2000, 2001, 2002, 2008, and 2011—from 39 bull market years. While Tuesday and Thursday did not vary much between bull and bear years, Mondays and Fridays were sharply affected. There was a swing of 10.5 percentage points in Monday's and 9.3 in Friday's performance. Tuesday is developing a reputation as the best day of the week based upon total points gained. See page 68.

PERCENTAGE OF TIMES MARKET CLOSED HIGHER THAN PREVIOUS DAY
(June 1952 to May 3, 2013)

	Monday*	Tuesday	Wednesday	Thursday	Friday*
1952	48.4%	55.6%	58.1%	51.9%	66.7%
1953	32.7	50.0	54.9	57.5	56.6
1954	50.0	57.5	63.5	59.2	73.1
1955	50.0	45.7	63.5	60.0	78.9
1956	36.5	39.6	46.9	50.0	59.6
1957	25.0	54.0	66.7	48.9	44.2
1958	59.6	52.0	59.6	68.1	72.6
1959	42.3	53.1	55.8	48.9	69.8
1960	34.6	50.0	44.2	54.0	59.6
1961	52.9	54.4	64.7	56.0	67.3
1962	28.3	52.1	54.0	51.0	50.0
1963	46.2	63.3	51.0	57.5	69.2
1964	40.4	48.0	61.5	58.7	77.4
1965	44.2	57.5	55.8	51.0	71.2
1966	36.5	47.8	53.9	42.0	57.7
1967	38.5	50.0	60.8	64.0	69.2
1968†	49.1	57.5	64.3	42.6	54.9
1969	30.8	45.8	50.0	67.4	50.0
1970	38.5	46.0	63.5	48.9	52.8
1971	44.2	64.6	57.7	55.1	51.9
1972	38.5	60.9	57.7	51.0	67.3
1973	32.1	51.1	52.9	44.9	44.2
1974	32.7	57.1	51.0	36.7	30.8
1975	53.9	38.8	61.5	56.3	55.8
1976	55.8	55.3	55.8	40.8	58.5
1977	40.4	40.4	46.2	53.1	53.9
1978	51.9	43.5	59.6	54.0	48.1
1979	54.7	53.2	58.8	66.0	44.2
1980	55.8	54.2	71.7	35.4	59.6
1981	44.2	38.8	55.8	53.2	47.2
1982	46.2	39.6	44.2	44.9	50.0
1983	55.8	46.8	61.5	52.0	55.8
1984	39.6	63.8	31.4	46.0	44.2
1985	44.2	61.2	54.9	56.3	53.9
1986	51.9	44.9	67.3	58.3	55.8
1987	51.9	57.1	63.5	61.7	49.1
1988	51.9	61.7	51.9	48.0	59.6
1989	51.9	47.8	69.2	58.0	69.2
1990	67.9	53.2	52.9	40.0	51.9
1991	44.2	46.9	52.9	49.0	51.9
1992	51.9	49.0	53.9	56.3	45.3
1993	65.4	41.7	55.8	44.9	48.1
1994	55.8	46.8	52.9	48.0	59.6
1995	63.5	56.5	63.5	62.0	63.5
1996	54.7	44.9	51.0	57.1	63.5
1997	67.3	67.4	42.3	41.7	57.7
1998	57.7	62.5	57.7	38.3	60.4
1999	46.2	29.8	67.3	53.1	57.7
2000	51.9	43.5	40.4	56.0	46.2
2001	45.3	51.1	44.0	59.2	43.1
2002	40.4	37.5	56.9	38.8	48.1
2003	59.6	62.5	42.3	58.3	50.0
2004	51.9	61.7	59.6	52.1	52.8
2005	59.6	47.8	59.6	56.0	55.8
2006	55.8	55.6	67.3	52.0	48.1
2007	47.2	50.0	64.0	50.0	61.5
2008	42.3	50.0	41.5	60.4	55.8
2009	53.9	50.0	57.7	63.8	52.8
2010	61.5	57.5	55.8	53.1	57.7
2011	48.1	56.5	55.8	56.0	57.7
2012	52.8	48.9	50.0	58.0	53.9
2013‡	41.2	80.0	66.7	58.8	66.7
Average	**48.0%**	**51.3%**	**55.9%**	**52.7%**	**56.4%**
39 Bull Years	**51.8%**	**52.7%**	**58.2%**	**53.5%**	**59.8%**
22 Bear Years	**41.2%**	**48.9%**	**51.8%**	**51.3%**	**50.5%**

Based on S&P 500

† Most Wednesdays closed last 7 months of 1968   ‡ Through 5/3/2013 only, not included in averages
*Monday denotes first trading day of the week, Friday denotes last trading day of the week.

NASDAQ DAILY PERFORMANCE EACH YEAR SINCE 1971

After dropping a hefty 77.9% from its 2000 high (versus −37.8% on the Dow and −49.1% on the S&P 500), NASDAQ tech stocks still outpace the blue chips and big caps—but not by nearly as much as they did. From January 1, 1971 through May 3, 2013, NASDAQ, moved up an impressive 3670%. The Dow (up 1685%) and the S&P (up 1652%) gained less than half as much.

Monday's performance on NASDAQ was lackluster during the three-year bear market of 2000–2002. As NASDAQ rebounded (up 50% in 2003), strength returned to Monday during 2003–2006. During the bear market from late 2007 to early 2009, weakness was most consistent on Monday and Friday.

PERCENTAGE OF TIMES NASDAQ CLOSED HIGHER THAN PREVIOUS DAY
(1971 to May 3, 2013)

	Monday*	Tuesday	Wednesday	Thursday	Friday*
1971	51.9%	52.1%	59.6%	65.3%	71.2%
1972	30.8	60.9	63.5	57.1	78.9
1973	34.0	48.9	52.9	53.1	48.1
1974	30.8	44.9	52.9	51.0	42.3
1975	44.2	42.9	63.5	64.6	63.5
1976	50.0	63.8	67.3	59.2	58.5
1977	51.9	40.4	53.9	63.3	73.1
1978	48.1	47.8	73.1	72.0	84.6
1979	45.3	53.2	64.7	86.0	82.7
1980	46.2	64.6	84.9	52.1	73.1
1981	42.3	32.7	67.3	76.6	69.8
1982	34.6	47.9	59.6	51.0	63.5
1983	42.3	44.7	67.3	68.0	73.1
1984	22.6	53.2	35.3	52.0	51.9
1985	36.5	59.2	62.8	68.8	66.0
1986	38.5	55.1	65.4	72.9	75.0
1987	42.3	49.0	65.4	68.1	66.0
1988	50.0	55.3	61.5	66.0	63.5
1989	38.5	54.4	71.2	72.0	75.0
1990	54.7	42.6	60.8	46.0	55.8
1991	51.9	59.2	66.7	65.3	51.9
1992	44.2	53.1	59.6	60.4	45.3
1993	55.8	56.3	69.2	57.1	67.3
1994	51.9	46.8	54.9	52.0	55.8
1995	50.0	52.2	63.5	64.0	63.5
1996	50.9	57.1	64.7	61.2	63.5
1997	65.4	59.2	53.9	52.1	55.8
1998	59.6	58.3	65.4	44.7	58.5
1999	61.5	40.4	63.5	57.1	65.4
2000	40.4	41.3	42.3	60.0	57.7
2001	41.5	57.8	52.0	55.1	47.1
2002	44.2	37.5	56.9	46.9	46.2
2003	57.7	60.4	40.4	60.4	46.2
2004	57.7	59.6	53.9	50.0	50.9
2005	61.5	47.8	51.9	48.0	59.6
2006	55.8	51.1	65.4	50.0	44.2
2007	47.2	63.0	66.0	56.0	57.7
2008	34.6	52.1	49.1	54.2	42.3
2009	51.9	54.2	63.5	63.8	50.9
2010	61.5	53.2	61.5	55.1	61.5
2011	50.0	56.5	50.0	64.0	53.9
2012	49.1	53.3	50.0	54.0	51.9
2013†	47.1	60.0	61.1	52.9	66.7
Average	**47.1%**	**52.0%**	**59.9%**	**59.4%**	**60.3%**
30 Bull Years	**49.7%**	**54.0%**	**62.6%**	**60.6%**	**63.2%**
12 Bear Years	**40.8%**	**46.9%**	**53.3%**	**56.6%**	**53.1%**

Based on NASDAQ composite; prior to February 5, 1971, based on National Quotation Bureau indices.
† Through 5/3/2013 only, not included in averages.
*Monday denotes first trading day of the week, Friday denotes last trading day of the week.

MONTHLY CASH INFLOWS INTO S&P STOCKS

For many years, the last trading day of the month, plus the first four of the following month, were the best market days of the month. This pattern is quite clear in the first chart, showing these five consecutive trading days towering above the other 16 trading days of the average month in the 1953–1981 period. The rationale was that individuals and institutions tended to operate similarly, causing a massive flow of cash into stocks near beginnings of months.

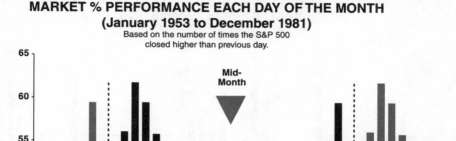

MARKET % PERFORMANCE EACH DAY OF THE MONTH
(January 1953 to December 1981)
Based on the number of times the S&P 500
closed higher than previous day.

Clearly "front-running" traders took advantage of this phenomenon, drastically altering the previous pattern. The second chart from 1982 onward shows the trading shift caused by these "anticipators" to the last three trading days of the month, plus the first two. Another astonishing development shows the ninth, tenth, and eleventh trading days rising strongly as well. Perhaps the enormous growth of 401(k) retirement plans (participants' salaries are usually paid twice monthly) is responsible for this mid-month bulge. First trading days of the month have produced the greatest gains in recent years (see page 84).

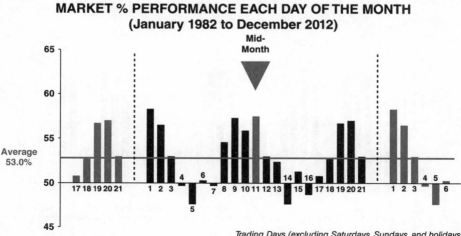

MARKET % PERFORMANCE EACH DAY OF THE MONTH
(January 1982 to December 2012)

Trading Days (excluding Saturdays, Sundays, and holidays).

MONTHLY CASH INFLOWS INTO NASDAQ STOCKS

NASDAQ stocks moved up 58.1% of the time through 1981 compared to 52.6% for the S&P on page 145. Ends and beginnings of the month are fairly similar, specifically the last plus the first four trading days. But notice how investors piled into NASDAQ stocks until mid-month. NASDAQ rose 118.6% from January 1, 1971, to December 31, 1981, compared to 33.0% for the S&P.

NASDAQ % PERFORMANCE EACH DAY OF THE MONTH
(January 1971 to December 1981)
Based on the number of times the NASDAQ composite closed higher than previous day.

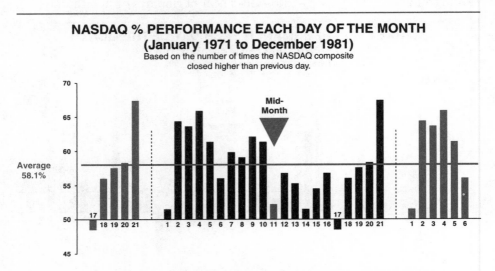

After the air was let out of the tech market 2000–2002, S&P's 1064% gain over the last 31 years is more evenly matched with NASDAQ's 1442% gain. Last three, first four, and middle ninth and tenth days rose the most. Where the S&P has five days of the month that go down more often than up, NASDAQ has none. NASDAQ exhibits the most strength on the last trading day of the month; however, over the past 16 years, last days have weakened considerably, down more often then not.

NASDAQ % PERFORMANCE EACH DAY OF THE MONTH
(January 1982 to December 2012)

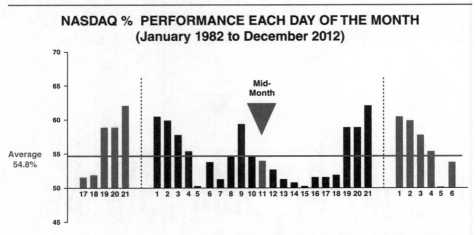

Trading Days (excluding Saturdays, Sundays, and holidays).
Based on NASDAQ composite, prior to February 5, 1971, based on National Quotation Bureau indices.

NOVEMBER, DECEMBER, AND JANUARY: YEAR'S BEST THREE-MONTH SPAN

The most important observation to be made from a chart showing the average monthly percent change in market prices since 1950 is that institutions (mutual funds, pension funds, banks, etc.) determine the trading patterns in today's market.

The "investment calendar" reflects the annual, semi-annual and quarterly operations of institutions during January, April and July. October, besides being the last campaign month before elections, is also the time when most bear markets seem to end, as in 1946, 1957, 1960, 1966, 1974, 1987, 1990, 1998 and 2002. (August and September tend to combine to make the worst consecutive two-month period.)

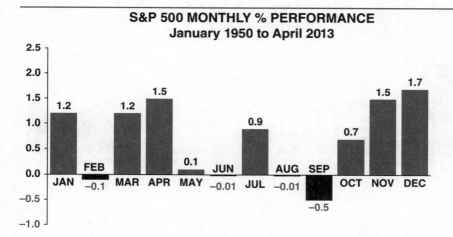

S&P 500 MONTHLY % PERFORMANCE
January 1950 to April 2013

Average month-to-month % change in S&P 500
(Based on monthly closing prices.)

Unusual year-end strength comes from corporate and private pension funds, producing a 4.4% gain on average between November 1 and January 31. In 2007–2008, these three months were all down for the fourth time since 1930; previously in 1931–1932, 1940–1941, and 1969–1970, also bear markets. September's dismal performance makes it the worst month of the year. However, in the last 18 years it has been up eleven times—down five in a row 1999–2003.

In midterm election years since 1950, the best three months are October +3.4% (12–4), November +2.7% (12–4), and December +1.9% (12–4). February, March, April, and July are gainers while January, May, June, August, and September are losers. June is worst, −2.1% (5–11).

See page 44 for monthly performance tables for the S&P 500 and the Dow Jones industrials. See pages 48, 50, and 60 for unique switching strategies.

On page 62, you can see how the first month of the first three quarters far outperforms the second and the third months since 1950, and note the improvement in May's and October's performance since 1991.

NOVEMBER THROUGH JUNE: NASDAQ'S EIGHT-MONTH RUN

The two-and-a-half-year plunge of 77.9% in NASDAQ stocks, between March 10, 2000, and October 9, 2002, brought several horrendous monthly losses (the two greatest were November 2000, −22.9%, and February 2001, −22.4%), which trimmed average monthly performance over the $42^1/_3$-year period. Ample Octobers in ten of the last 15 years, including three huge turnarounds in 2001 (+12.8%), 2002 (+13.5%), and 2011 (+11.1%) have put bear-killing October in the number one spot since 1998. January's 3.0% average gain is still awesome, and twice S&P's 1.2% January average since 1971.

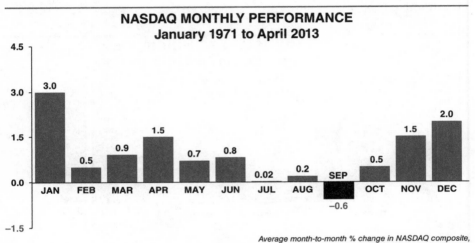

NASDAQ MONTHLY PERFORMANCE
January 1971 to April 2013

Average month-to-month % change in NASDAQ composite, prior to February 5, 1971, based on National Quotation Bureau indices. (Based on monthly closing prices.)

Bear in mind, when comparing NASDAQ to the S&P on page 147, that there are 22 fewer years of data here. During this $42^1/_3$-year (1971–April 2013) period, NASDAQ gained 3615%, while the S&P and the Dow rose only 1669% and 1634%, respectively. On page 56 you can see a statistical monthly comparison between NASDAQ and the Dow.

Year-end strength is even more pronounced in NASDAQ, producing a 6.5% gain on average between November 1 and January 31—1.5 times greater than that of the S&P 500 on page 147. September is the worst month of the year for the over-the-counter index as well, posting an average loss of −0.6%. These extremes underscore NASDAQ's higher volatility—and potential for moves of greater magnitude.

In midterm election years since 1971, the best three months are October +4.3% (8–2), November +3.8% (6–4), and March +2.1% (7–3). February, April, and December also provide modest gains. January, May, June, July, August, and September are net losers with July the worst, averaging −2.4% (3–7).

DOW JONES INDUSTRIALS ANNUAL HIGHS, LOWS, & CLOSES SINCE 1901

YEAR	HIGH DATE	HIGH CLOSE	LOW DATE	LOW CLOSE	YEAR CLOSE	YEAR	HIGH DATE	HIGH CLOSE	LOW DATE	LOW CLOSE	YEAR CLOSE
1901	6/17	57.33	12/24	45.07	47.29	1958	12/31	583.65	2/25	436.89	583.65
1902	4/24	50.14	12/15	43.64	47.10	1959	12/31	679.36	2/9	574.46	679.36
1903	2/16	49.59	11/9	30.88	35.98	1960	1/5	685.47	10/25	566.05	615.89
1904	12/5	53.65	3/12	34.00	50.99	1961	12/13	734.91	1/3	610.25	731.14
1905	12/29	70.74	1/25	50.37	70.47	1962	1/3	726.01	6/26	535.76	652.10
1906	1/19	75.45	7/13	62.40	69.12	1963	12/18	767.21	1/2	646.79	762.95
1907	1/7	70.60	11/15	38.83	43.04	1964	11/18	891.71	1/2	766.08	874.13
1908	11/13	64.74	2/13	42.94	63.11	1965	12/31	969.26	6/28	840.59	969.26
1909	11/19	73.64	2/23	58.54	72.56	1966	2/9	995.15	10/7	744.32	785.69
1910	1/3	72.04	7/26	53.93	59.60	1967	9/25	943.08	1/3	786.41	905.11
1911	6/19	63.78	9/25	53.43	59.84	1968	12/3	985.21	3/21	825.13	943.75
1912	9/30	68.97	2/10	58.72	64.37	1969	5/14	968.85	12/17	769.93	800.36
1913	1/9	64.88	6/11	52.83	57.71	1970	12/29	842.00	5/26	631.16	838.92
1914	3/20	61.12	7/30	52.32	54.58	1971	4/28	950.82	11/23	797.97	890.20
1915	12/27	99.21	2/24	54.22	99.15	1972	12/11	1036.27	1/26	889.15	1020.02
1916	11/21	110.15	4/22	84.96	95.00	1973	1/11	1051.70	12/5	788.31	850.86
1917	1/3	99.18	12/19	65.95	74.38	1974	3/13	891.66	12/6	577.60	616.24
1918	10/18	89.07	1/15	73.38	82.20	1975	7/15	881.81	1/2	632.04	852.41
1919	11/3	119.62	2/8	79.15	107.23	1976	9/21	1014.79	1/2	858.71	1004.65
1920	1/3	109.88	12/21	66.75	71.95	1977	1/3	999.75	11/2	800.85	831.17
1921	12/15	81.50	8/24	63.90	81.10	1978	9/8	907.74	2/28	742.12	805.01
1922	10/14	103.43	1/10	78.59	98.73	1979	10/5	897.61	11/7	796.67	838.74
1923	3/20	105.38	10/27	85.76	95.52	1980	11/20	1000.17	4/21	759.13	963.99
1924	12/31	120.51	5/20	88.33	120.51	1981	4/27	1024.05	9/25	824.01	875.00
1925	11/6	159.39	3/30	115.00	156.66	1982	12/27	1070.55	8/12	776.92	1046.54
1926	8/14	166.64	3/30	135.20	157.20	1983	11/29	1287.20	1/3	1027.04	1258.64
1927	12/31	202.40	1/25	152.73	202.40	1984	1/6	1286.64	7/24	1086.57	1211.57
1928	12/31	300.00	2/20	191.33	300.00	1985	12/16	1553.10	1/4	1184.96	1546.67
1929	9/3	381.17	11/13	198.69	248.48	1986	12/2	1955.57	1/22	1502.29	1895.95
1930	4/17	294.07	12/16	157.51	164.58	1987	8/25	2722.42	10/19	1738.74	1938.83
1931	2/24	194.36	12/17	73.79	77.90	1988	10/21	2183.50	1/20	1879.14	2168.57
1932	3/8	88.78	7/8	41.22	59.93	1989	10/9	2791.41	1/3	2144.64	2753.20
1933	7/18	108.67	2/27	50.16	99.90	1990	7/17	2999.75	10/11	2365.10	2633.66
1934	2/5	110.74	7/26	85.51	104.04	1991	12/31	3168.83	1/9	2470.30	3168.83
1935	11/19	148.44	3/14	96.71	144.13	1992	6/1	3413.21	10/9	3136.58	3301.11
1936	11/17	184.90	1/6	143.11	179.90	1993	12/29	3794.33	1/20	3241.95	3754.09
1937	3/10	194.40	11/24	113.64	120.85	1994	1/31	3978.36	4/4	3593.35	3834.44
1938	11/12	158.41	3/31	98.95	154.76	1995	12/13	5216.47	1/30	3832.08	5117.12
1939	9/12	155.92	4/8	121.44	150.24	1996	12/27	6560.91	1/10	5032.94	6448.27
1940	1/3	152.80	6/10	111.84	131.13	1997	8/6	8259.31	4/11	6391.69	7908.25
1941	1/10	133.59	12/23	106.34	110.96	1998	11/23	9374.27	8/31	7539.07	9181.43
1942	12/26	119.71	4/28	92.92	119.40	1999	12/31	11497.12	1/22	9120.67	11497.12
1943	7/14	145.82	1/8	119.26	135.89	2000	1/14	11722.98	3/7	9796.03	10786.85
1944	12/16	152.53	2/7	134.22	152.32	2001	5/21	11337.92	9/21	8235.81	10021.50
1945	12/11	195.82	1/24	151.35	192.91	2002	3/19	10635.25	10/9	7286.27	8341.63
1946	5/29	212.50	10/9	163.12	177.20	2003	12/31	10453.92	3/11	7524.06	10453.92
1947	7/24	186.85	5/17	163.21	181.16	2004	12/28	10854.54	10/25	9749.99	10783.01
1948	6/15	193.16	3/16	165.39	177.30	2005	3/4	10940.55	4/20	10012.36	10717.50
1949	12/30	200.52	6/13	161.60	200.13	2006	12/27	12510.57	1/20	10667.39	12463.15
1950	11/24	235.47	1/13	196.81	235.41	2007	10/9	14164.53	3/5	12050.41	13264.82
1951	9/13	276.37	1/3	238.99	269.23	2008	5/2	13058.20	11/20	7552.29	8776.39
1952	12/30	292.00	5/1	256.35	291.90	2009	12/30	10548.51	3/9	6547.05	10428.05
1953	1/5	293.79	9/14	255.49	280.90	2010	12/29	11585.38	7/2	9686.48	11577.51
1954	12/31	404.39	1/11	279.87	404.39	2011	4/29	12810.54	10/3	10655.30	12217.56
1955	12/30	488.40	1/17	388.20	488.40	2012	10/5	13610.15	6/4	12101.46	13104.14
1956	4/6	521.05	1/23	462.35	499.47	2013*	5/3	14973.96	1/8	13328.85	At Press Time
1957	7/12	520.77	10/22	419.79	435.69						

*Through May 3, 2013

149

S&P 500 ANNUAL HIGHS, LOWS, & CLOSES SINCE 1930

YEAR	HIGH DATE	HIGH CLOSE	LOW DATE	LOW CLOSE	YEAR CLOSE
1930	4/10	25.92	12/16	14.44	15.34
1931	2/24	18.17	12/17	7.72	8.12
1932	9/7	9.31	6/1	4.40	6.89
1933	7/18	12.20	2/27	5.53	10.10
1934	2/6	11.82	7/26	8.36	9.50
1935	11/19	13.46	3/14	8.06	13.43
1936	11/9	17.69	1/2	13.40	17.18
1937	3/6	18.68	11/24	10.17	10.55
1938	11/9	13.79	3/31	8.50	13.21
1939	1/4	13.23	4/8	10.18	12.49
1940	1/3	12.77	6/10	8.99	10.58
1941	1/10	10.86	12/29	8.37	8.69
1942	12/31	9.77	4/28	7.47	9.77
1943	7/14	12.64	1/2	9.84	11.67
1944	12/16	13.29	2/7	11.56	13.28
1945	12/10	17.68	1/23	13.21	17.36
1946	5/29	19.25	10/9	14.12	15.30
1947	2/8	16.20	5/17	13.71	15.30
1948	6/15	17.06	2/14	13.84	15.20
1949	12/30	16.79	6/13	13.55	16.76
1950	12/29	20.43	1/14	16.65	20.41
1951	10/15	23.85	1/3	20.69	23.77
1952	12/30	26.59	2/20	23.09	26.57
1953	1/5	26.66	9/14	22.71	24.81
1954	12/31	35.98	1/11	24.80	35.98
1955	11/14	46.41	1/17	34.58	45.48
1956	8/2	49.74	1/23	43.11	46.67
1957	7/15	49.13	10/22	38.98	39.99
1958	12/31	55.21	1/2	40.33	55.21
1959	8/3	60.71	2/9	53.58	59.89
1960	1/5	60.39	10/25	52.30	58.11
1961	12/12	72.64	1/3	57.57	71.55
1962	1/3	71.13	6/26	52.32	63.10
1963	12/31	75.02	1/2	62.69	75.02
1964	11/20	86.28	1/2	75.43	84.75
1965	11/15	92.63	6/28	81.60	92.43
1966	2/9	94.06	10/7	73.20	80.33
1967	9/25	97.59	1/3	80.38	96.47
1968	11/29	108.37	3/5	87.72	103.86
1969	5/14	106.16	12/17	89.20	92.06
1970	1/5	93.46	5/26	69.29	92.15
1971	4/28	104.77	11/23	90.16	102.09
1972	12/11	119.12	1/3	101.67	118.05
1973	1/11	120.24	12/5	92.16	97.55
1974	1/3	99.80	10/3	62.28	68.56
1975	7/15	95.61	1/8	70.04	90.19
1976	9/21	107.83	1/2	90.90	107.46
1977	1/3	107.00	11/2	90.71	95.10
1978	9/12	106.99	3/6	86.90	96.11
1979	10/5	111.27	2/27	96.13	107.94
1980	11/28	140.52	3/27	98.22	135.76
1981	1/6	138.12	9/25	112.77	122.55
1982	11/9	143.02	8/12	102.42	140.64
1983	10/10	172.65	1/3	138.34	164.93
1984	11/6	170.41	7/24	147.82	167.24
1985	12/16	212.02	1/4	163.68	211.28
1986	12/2	254.00	1/22	203.49	242.17
1987	8/25	336.77	12/4	223.92	247.08
1988	10/21	283.66	1/20	242.63	277.72
1989	10/9	359.80	1/3	275.31	353.40
1990	7/16	368.95	10/11	295.46	330.22
1991	12/31	417.09	1/9	311.49	417.09
1992	12/18	441.28	4/8	394.50	435.71
1993	12/28	470.94	1/8	429.05	466.45
1994	2/2	482.00	4/4	438.92	459.27
1995	12/13	621.69	1/3	459.11	615.93
1996	11/25	757.03	1/10	598.48	740.74
1997	12/5	983.79	1/2	737.01	970.43
1998	12/29	1241.81	1/9	927.69	1229.23
1999	12/31	1469.25	1/14	1212.19	1469.25
2000	3/24	1527.46	12/20	1264.74	1320.28
2001	2/1	1373.47	9/21	965.80	1148.08
2002	1/4	1172.51	10/9	776.76	879.82
2003	12/31	1111.92	3/11	800.73	1111.92
2004	12/30	1213.55	8/12	1063.23	1211.92
2005	12/14	1272.74	4/20	1137.50	1248.29
2006	12/15	1427.09	6/13	1223.69	1418.30
2007	10/9	1565.15	3/5	1374.12	1468.36
2008	1/2	1447.16	11/20	752.44	903.25
2009	12/28	1127.78	3/9	676.53	1115.10
2010	12/29	1259.78	7/2	1022.58	1257.64
2011	4/29	1363.61	10/3	1099.23	1257.60
2012	9/14	1465.77	1/3	1277.06	1426.19
2013*	5/3	1614.42	1/8	1457.15	At Press Time

*Through May 3, 2013

NASDAQ ANNUAL HIGHS, LOWS, & CLOSES SINCE 1971

YEAR	HIGH DATE	HIGH CLOSE	LOW DATE	LOW CLOSE	YEAR CLOSE	YEAR	HIGH DATE	HIGH CLOSE	LOW DATE	LOW CLOSE	YEAR CLOSE
1971	12/31	114.12	1/5	89.06	114.12	1993	10/15	787.42	4/26	645.87	776.80
1972	12/8	135.15	1/3	113.65	133.73	1994	3/18	803.93	6/24	693.79	751.96
1973	1/11	136.84	12/24	88.67	92.19	1995	12/4	1069.79	1/3	743.58	1052.13
1974	3/15	96.53	10/3	54.87	59.82	1996	12/9	1316.27	1/15	988.57	1291.03
1975	7/15	88.00	1/2	60.70	77.62	1997	10/9	1745.85	4/2	1201.00	1570.35
1976	12/31	97.88	1/2	78.06	97.88	1998	12/31	2192.69	10/8	1419.12	2192.69
1977	12/30	105.05	4/5	93.66	105.05	1999	12/31	4069.31	1/4	2208.05	4069.31
1978	9/13	139.25	1/11	99.09	117.98	2000	3/10	5048.62	12/20	2332.78	2470.52
1979	10/5	152.29	1/2	117.84	151.14	2001	1/24	2859.15	9/21	1423.19	1950.40
1980	11/28	208.15	3/27	124.09	202.34	2002	1/4	2059.38	10/9	1114.11	1335.51
1981	5/29	223.47	9/28	175.03	195.84	2003	12/30	2009.88	3/11	1271.47	2003.37
1982	12/8	240.70	8/13	159.14	232.41	2004	12/30	2178.34	8/12	1752.49	2175.44
1983	6/24	328.91	1/3	230.59	278.60	2005	12/2	2273.37	4/28	1904.18	2205.32
1984	1/6	287.90	7/25	225.30	247.35	2006	11/22	2465.98	7/21	2020.39	2415.29
1985	12/16	325.16	1/2	245.91	324.93	2007	10/31	2859.12	3/5	2340.68	2652.28
1986	7/3	411.16	1/9	323.01	349.33	2008	1/2	2609.63	11/20	1316.12	1577.03
1987	8/26	455.26	10/28	291.88	330.47	2009	12/30	2291.28	3/9	1268.64	2269.15
1988	7/5	396.11	1/12	331.97	381.38	2010	12/22	2671.48	7/2	2091.79	2652.87
1989	10/9	485.73	1/3	378.56	454.82	2011	4/29	2873.54	10/3	2335.83	2605.15
1990	7/16	469.60	10/16	325.44	373.84	2012	9/14	3183.95	1/4	2648.36	3019.51
1991	12/31	586.34	1/14	355.75	586.34	2013*	5/3	3378.63	1/8	3091.81	At Press-time
1992	12/31	676.95	6/26	547.84	676.95						

RUSSELL 1000 ANNUAL HIGHS, LOWS, & CLOSES SINCE 1979

YEAR	HIGH DATE	HIGH CLOSE	LOW DATE	LOW CLOSE	YEAR CLOSE	YEAR	HIGH DATE	HIGH CLOSE	LOW DATE	LOW CLOSE	YEAR CLOSE
1979	10/5	61.18	2/27	51.83	59.87	1997	12/5	519.72	4/11	389.03	513.79
1980	11/28	78.26	3/27	53.68	75.20	1998	12/29	645.36	1/9	490.26	642.87
1981	1/6	76.34	9/25	62.03	67.93	1999	12/31	767.97	2/9	632.53	767.97
1982	11/9	78.47	8/12	55.98	77.24	2000	9/1	813.71	12/20	668.75	700.09
1983	10/10	95.07	1/3	76.04	90.38	2001	1/30	727.35	9/21	507.98	604.94
1984	1/6	92.80	7/24	79.49	90.31	2002	3/19	618.74	10/9	410.52	466.18
1985	12/16	114.97	1/4	88.61	114.39	2003	12/31	594.56	3/11	425.31	594.56
1986	7/2	137.87	1/22	111.14	130.00	2004	12/30	651.76	8/13	566.06	650.99
1987	8/25	176.22	12/4	117.65	130.02	2005	12/14	692.09	4/20	613.37	679.42
1988	10/21	149.94	1/20	128.35	146.99	2006	12/15	775.08	6/13	665.81	770.08
1989	10/9	189.93	1/3	145.78	185.11	2007	10/9	852.32	3/5	749.85	799.82
1990	7/16	191.56	10/11	152.36	171.22	2008	1/2	788.62	11/20	402.91	487.77
1991	12/31	220.61	1/9	161.94	220.61	2009	12/28	619.22	3/9	367.55	612.01
1992	12/18	235.06	4/8	208.87	233.59	2010	12/29	698.11	7/2	562.58	696.90
1993	10/15	252.77	1/8	229.91	250.71	2011	4/29	758.45	10/3	604.42	693.36
1994	2/1	258.31	4/4	235.38	244.65	2012	9/14	809.01	1/4	703.72	789.90
1995	12/13	331.18	1/3	244.41	328.89	2013*	5/3	895.34	1/8	807.95	At Press-time
1996	12/2	401.21	1/10	318.24	393.75						

RUSSELL 2000 ANNUAL HIGHS, LOWS, & CLOSES SINCE 1979

YEAR	HIGH DATE	HIGH CLOSE	LOW DATE	LOW CLOSE	YEAR CLOSE	YEAR	HIGH DATE	HIGH CLOSE	LOW DATE	LOW CLOSE	YEAR CLOSE
1979	12/31	55.91	1/2	40.81	55.91	1997	10/13	465.21	4/25	335.85	437.02
1980	11/28	77.70	3/27	45.36	74.80	1998	4/21	491.41	10/8	310.28	421.96
1981	6/15	85.16	9/25	65.37	73.67	1999	12/31	504.75	3/23	383.37	504.75
1982	12/8	91.01	8/12	60.33	88.90	2000	3/9	606.05	12/20	443.80	483.53
1983	6/24	126.99	1/3	88.29	112.27	2001	5/22	517.23	9/21	378.89	488.50
1984	1/12	116.69	7/25	93.95	101.49	2002	4/16	522.95	10/9	327.04	383.09
1985	12/31	129.87	1/2	101.21	129.87	2003	12/30	565.47	3/12	345.94	556.91
1986	7/3	155.30	1/9	128.23	135.00	2004	12/28	654.57	8/12	517.10	651.57
1987	8/25	174.44	10/28	106.08	120.42	2005	12/2	690.57	4/28	575.02	673.22
1988	7/15	151.42	1/12	121.23	147.37	2006	12/27	797.73	7/21	671.94	787.66
1989	10/9	180.78	1/3	146.79	168.30	2007	7/13	855.77	11/26	735.07	766.03
1990	6/15	170.90	10/30	118.82	132.16	2008	6/5	763.27	11/20	385.31	499.45
1991	12/31	189.94	1/15	125.25	189.94	2009	12/24	634.07	3/9	343.26	625.39
1992	12/31	221.01	7/8	185.81	221.01	2010	12/27	792.35	2/8	586.49	783.65
1993	11/2	260.17	2/23	217.55	258.59	2011	4/29	865.29	10/3	609.49	740.92
1994	3/18	271.08	12/9	235.16	250.36	2012	9/14	864.70	6/4	737.24	849.35
1995	9/14	316.12	1/30	246.56	315.97	2013*	5/3	954.42	1/3	872.60	At Press-time
1996	5/22	364.61	1/16	301.75	362.61						

*Through May 3, 2013

DOW JONES INDUSTRIALS MONTHLY PERCENT CHANGE SINCE 1950

	Jan	Feb	Mar	Apr	May	Jun	Jul	Aug	Sep	Oct	Nov	Dec	Year's Change
1950	0.8	0.8	1.3	4.0	4.2	-6.4	0.1	3.6	4.4	-0.6	1.2	3.4	17.6
1951	5.7	1.3	-1.6	4.5	-3.7	-2.8	6.3	4.8	0.3	-3.2	-0.4	3.0	14.4
1952	0.5	-3.9	3.6	-4.4	2.1	4.3	1.9	-1.6	-1.6	-0.5	5.4	2.9	8.4
1953	-0.7	-1.9	-1.5	-1.8	-0.9	-1.5	2.7	-5.1	1.1	4.5	2.0	-0.2	-3.8
1954	4.1	0.7	3.0	5.2	2.6	1.8	4.3	-3.5	7.3	-2.3	9.8	4.6	44.0
1955	1.1	0.7	-0.5	3.9	-0.2	6.2	3.2	0.5	-0.3	-2.5	6.2	1.1	20.8
1956	-3.6	2.7	5.8	0.8	-7.4	3.1	5.1	-3.0	-5.3	1.0	-1.5	5.6	2.3
1957	-4.1	-3.0	2.2	4.1	2.1	-0.3	1.0	-4.8	-5.8	-3.3	2.0	-3.2	-12.8
1958	3.3	-2.2	1.6	2.0	1.5	3.3	5.2	1.1	4.6	2.1	2.6	4.7	34.0
1959	1.8	1.6	-0.3	3.7	3.2	-0.03	4.9	-1.6	-4.9	2.4	1.9	3.1	16.4
1960	-8.4	1.2	-2.1	-2.4	4.0	2.4	-3.7	1.5	-7.3	0.04	2.9	3.1	-9.3
1961	5.2	2.1	2.2	0.3	2.7	-1.8	3.1	2.1	-2.6	0.4	2.5	1.3	18.7
1962	-4.3	1.1	-0.2	-5.9	-7.8	-8.5	6.5	1.9	-5.0	1.9	10.1	0.4	-10.8
1963	4.7	-2.9	3.0	5.2	1.3	-2.8	-1.6	4.9	0.5	3.1	-0.6	1.7	17.0
1964	2.9	1.9	1.6	-0.3	1.2	1.3	1.2	-0.3	4.4	-0.3	0.3	-0.1	14.6
1965	3.3	0.1	-1.6	3.7	-0.5	-5.4	1.6	1.3	4.2	3.2	-1.5	2.4	10.9
1966	1.5	-3.2	-2.8	1.0	-5.3	-1.6	-2.6	-7.0	-1.8	4.2	-1.9	-0.7	-18.9
1967	8.2	-1.2	3.2	3.6	-5.0	0.9	5.1	-0.3	2.8	-5.1	-0.4	3.3	15.2
1968	-5.5	-1.7	0.02	8.5	-1.4	-0.1	-1.6	1.5	4.4	1.8	3.4	-4.2	4.3
1969	0.2	-4.3	3.3	1.6	-1.3	-6.9	-6.6	2.6	-2.8	5.3	-5.1	-1.5	-15.2
1970	-7.0	4.5	1.0	-6.3	-4.8	-2.4	7.4	4.1	-0.5	-0.7	5.1	5.6	4.8
1971	3.5	1.2	2.9	4.1	-3.6	-1.8	-3.7	4.6	-1.2	-5.4	-0.9	7.1	6.1
1972	1.3	2.9	1.4	1.4	0.7	-3.3	-0.5	4.2	-1.1	0.2	6.6	0.2	14.6
1973	-2.1	-4.4	-0.4	-3.1	-2.2	-1.1	3.9	-4.2	6.7	1.0	-14.0	3.5	-16.6
1974	0.6	0.6	-1.6	-1.2	-4.1	0.03	-5.6	-10.4	-10.4	9.5	-7.0	-0.4	-27.6
1975	14.2	5.0	3.9	6.9	1.3	5.6	-5.4	0.5	-5.0	5.3	2.9	-1.0	38.3
1976	14.4	-0.3	2.8	-0.3	-2.2	2.8	-1.8	-1.1	1.7	-2.6	-1.8	6.1	17.9
1977	-5.0	-1.9	-1.8	0.8	-3.0	2.0	-2.9	-3.2	-1.7	-3.4	1.4	0.2	-17.3
1978	-7.4	-3.6	2.1	10.6	0.4	-2.6	5.3	1.7	-1.3	-8.5	0.8	0.7	-3.1
1979	4.2	-3.6	6.6	-0.8	-3.8	2.4	0.5	4.9	-1.0	-7.2	0.8	2.0	4.2
1980	4.4	-1.5	-9.0	4.0	4.1	2.0	7.8	-0.3	-0.02	-0.9	7.4	-3.0	14.9
1981	-1.7	2.9	3.0	-0.6	-0.6	-1.5	-2.5	-7.4	-3.6	0.3	4.3	-1.6	-9.2
1982	-0.4	-5.4	-0.2	3.1	-3.4	-0.9	-0.4	11.5	-0.6	10.7	4.8	0.7	19.6
1983	2.8	3.4	1.6	8.5	-2.1	1.8	-1.9	1.4	1.4	-0.6	4.1	-1.4	20.3
1984	-3.0	-5.4	0.9	0.5	-5.6	2.5	-1.5	9.8	-1.4	0.1	-1.5	1.9	-3.7
1985	6.2	-0.2	-1.3	-0.7	4.6	1.5	0.9	-1.0	-0.4	3.4	7.1	5.1	27.7
1986	1.6	8.8	6.4	-1.9	5.2	0.9	-6.2	6.9	-6.9	6.2	1.9	-1.0	22.6
1987	13.8	3.1	3.6	-0.8	0.2	5.5	6.3	3.5	-2.5	-23.2	-8.0	5.7	2.3
1988	1.0	5.8	-4.0	2.2	-0.1	5.4	-0.6	-4.6	4.0	1.7	-1.6	2.6	11.8
1989	8.0	-3.6	1.6	5.5	2.5	-1.6	9.0	2.9	-1.6	-1.8	2.3	1.7	27.0
1990	-5.9	1.4	3.0	-1.9	8.3	0.1	0.9	-10.0	-6.2	-0.4	4.8	2.9	-4.3
1991	3.9	5.3	1.1	-0.9	4.8	-4.0	4.1	0.6	-0.9	1.7	-5.7	9.5	20.3
1992	1.7	1.4	-1.0	3.8	1.1	-2.3	2.3	-4.0	0.4	-1.4	2.4	-0.1	4.2
1993	0.3	1.8	1.9	-0.2	2.9	-0.3	0.7	3.2	-2.6	3.5	0.1	1.9	13.7
1994	6.0	-3.7	-5.1	1.3	2.1	-3.5	3.8	4.0	-1.8	1.7	-4.3	2.5	2.1
1995	0.2	4.3	3.7	3.9	3.3	2.0	3.3	-2.1	3.9	-0.7	6.7	0.8	33.5
1996	5.4	1.7	1.9	-0.3	1.3	0.2	-2.2	1.6	4.7	2.5	8.2	-1.1	26.0
1997	5.7	0.9	-4.3	6.5	4.6	4.7	7.2	-7.3	4.2	-6.3	5.1	1.1	22.6
1998	-0.02	8.1	3.0	3.0	-1.8	0.6	-0.8	-15.1	4.0	9.6	6.1	0.7	16.1
1999	1.9	-0.6	5.2	10.2	-2.1	3.9	-2.9	1.6	-4.5	3.8	1.4	5.7	25.2
2000	-4.8	-7.4	7.8	-1.7	-2.0	-0.7	0.7	6.6	-5.0	3.0	-5.1	3.6	-6.2
2001	0.9	-3.6	-5.9	8.7	1.6	-3.8	0.2	-5.4	-11.1	2.6	8.6	1.7	-7.1
2002	-1.0	1.9	2.9	-4.4	-0.2	-6.9	-5.5	-0.8	-12.4	10.6	5.9	-6.2	-16.8
2003	-3.5	-2.0	1.3	6.1	4.4	1.5	2.8	2.0	-1.5	5.7	-0.2	6.9	25.3
2004	0.3	0.9	-2.1	-1.3	-0.4	2.4	-2.8	0.3	-0.9	-0.5	4.0	3.4	3.1
2005	-2.7	2.6	-2.4	-3.0	2.7	-1.8	3.6	-1.5	0.8	-1.2	3.5	-0.8	-0.6
2006	1.4	1.2	1.1	2.3	-1.7	-0.2	0.3	1.7	2.6	3.4	1.2	2.0	16.3
2007	1.3	-2.8	0.7	5.7	4.3	-1.6	-1.5	1.1	4.0	0.2	-4.0	-0.8	6.4
2008	-4.6	-3.0	-0.03	4.5	-1.4	-10.2	0.2	1.5	-6.0	-14.1	-5.3	-0.6	-33.8
2009	-8.8	-11.7	7.7	7.3	4.1	-0.6	8.6	3.5	2.3	0.005	6.5	0.8	18.8
2010	-3.5	2.6	5.1	1.4	-7.9	-3.6	7.1	-4.3	7.7	3.1	-1.0	5.2	11.0
2011	2.7	2.8	0.8	4.0	-1.9	-1.2	-2.2	-4.4	-6.0	9.5	0.8	1.4	5.5
2012	3.4	2.5	2.0	0.01	-6.2	3.9	1.0	0.6	2.6	-2.5	-0.5	0.6	7.3
2013	5.8	1.4	3.7	1.8									
TOTALS	72.2	4.2	71.8	126.0	-5.2	-19.0	73.1	-4.2	-50.5	30.0	92.8	106.5	
AVG.	1.1	0.1	1.1	2.0	-0.1	-0.3	1.2	-0.1	-0.8	0.5	1.5	1.7	
# Up	42	37	42	42	31	29	39	36	25	37	41	45	
# Down	22	27	22	22	32	34	24	27	38	26	22	18	

DOW JONES INDUSTRIALS MONTHLY POINT CHANGES SINCE 1950

	Jan	Feb	Mar	Apr	May	Jun	Jul	Aug	Sep	Oct	Nov	Dec	Year's Close
1950	1.66	1.65	2.61	8.28	9.09	– 14.31	0.29	7.47	9.49	– 1.35	2.59	7.81	235.41
1951	13.42	3.22	– 4.11	11.19	– 9.48	– 7.01	15.22	12.39	0.91	– 8.81	– 1.08	7.96	269.23
1952	1.46	– 10.61	9.38	– 11.83	5.31	11.32	5.30	– 4.52	– 4.43	– 1.38	14.43	8.24	291.90
1953	– 2.13	– 5.50	– 4.40	– 5.12	– 2.47	– 4.02	7.12	– 14.16	2.82	11.77	5.56	– 0.47	280.90
1954	11.49	2.15	8.97	15.82	8.16	6.04	14.39	– 12.12	24.66	– 8.32	34.63	17.62	404.39
1955	4.44	3.04	– 2.17	15.95	– 0.79	26.52	14.47	2.33	– 1.56	– 11.75	28.39	5.14	488.40
1956	– 17.66	12.91	28.14	4.33	– 38.07	14.73	25.03	– 15.77	– 26.79	4.60	– 7.07	26.69	499.47
1957	– 20.31	– 14.54	10.19	19.55	10.57	– 1.64	5.23	– 24.17	– 28.05	– 15.26	8.83	– 14.18	435.69
1958	14.33	– 10.10	6.84	9.10	6.84	15.48	24.81	5.64	23.46	11.13	14.24	26.19	583.65
1959	10.31	9.54	– 1.79	22.04	20.04	– 0.19	31.28	– 10.47	– 32.73	14.92	12.58	20.18	679.36
1960	– 56.74	7.50	– 13.53	– 14.89	23.80	15.12	– 23.89	9.26	– 45.85	0.22	16.86	18.67	615.89
1961	32.31	13.88	14.55	2.08	18.01	– 12.76	21.41	14.57	– 18.73	2.71	17.68	9.54	731.14
1962	– 31.14	8.05	– 1.10	– 41.62	– 51.97	– 52.08	36.65	11.25	– 30.20	10.79	59.53	2.80	652.10
1963	30.75	– 19.91	19.58	35.18	9.26	– 20.08	– 11.45	33.89	3.47	22.44	– 4.71	12.43	762.95
1964	22.39	14.80	13.15	– 2.52	9.79	10.94	9.60	– 2.62	36.89	– 2.29	2.35	– 1.30	874.13
1965	28.73	0.62	– 14.43	33.26	– 4.27	– 50.01	13.71	11.36	37.48	30.24	– 14.11	22.55	969.26
1966	14.25	– 31.62	– 27.12	8.91	– 49.61	– 13.97	– 22.72	– 58.97	– 14.19	32.85	– 15.48	– 5.90	785.69
1967	64.20	– 10.52	26.61	31.07	– 44.49	7.70	43.98	– 2.95	25.37	– 46.92	– 3.93	29.30	905.11
1968	– 49.64	– 14.97	0.17	71.55	– 13.22	– 1.20	– 14.80	13.01	39.78	16.60	32.69	– 41.33	943.75
1969	2.30	– 40.84	30.27	14.70	– 12.62	– 64.37	– 57.72	21.25	– 23.63	42.90	– 43.69	– 11.94	800.36
1970	– 56.30	33.53	7.98	– 49.50	– 35.63	– 16.91	50.59	30.46	– 3.90	– 5.07	38.48	44.83	838.92
1971	29.58	10.33	25.54	37.38	– 33.94	– 16.67	– 32.71	39.64	– 10.88	– 48.19	– 7.66	58.86	890.20
1972	11.97	25.96	12.57	13.47	6.55	– 31.69	– 4.29	38.99	– 10.46	2.25	62.69	1.81	1020.02
1973	– 21.00	– 43.95	– 4.06	– 29.58	– 20.02	– 9.70	34.69	– 38.83	59.53	9.48	– 134.33	28.61	850.86
1974	4.69	4.98	– 13.85	– 9.93	– 34.58	0.24	– 44.98	– 78.85	– 70.71	57.65	– 46.86	– 2.42	616.24
1975	87.45	35.36	29.10	53.19	10.95	46.70	– 47.48	3.83	– 41.46	42.16	24.63	– 8.26	852.41
1976	122.87	– 2.67	26.84	– 2.60	– 21.62	27.55	– 18.14	– 10.90	16.45	– 25.26	– 17.71	57.43	1004.65
1977	– 50.28	– 17.95	– 17.29	7.77	– 28.24	17.64	– 26.23	– 28.58	– 14.38	– 28.76	11.35	1.47	831.17
1978	– 61.25	– 27.80	15.24	79.96	3.29	– 21.66	43.32	14.55	– 11.00	– 73.37	6.58	5.98	805.01
1979	34.21	– 30.40	53.36	– 7.28	– 32.57	19.65	4.44	41.21	– 9.05	– 62.88	6.65	16.39	838.74
1980	37.11	– 12.71	– 77.39	31.31	33.79	17.07	67.40	– 2.73	– 0.17	– 7.93	68.85	– 29.35	963.99
1981	– 16.72	27.31	29.29	– 6.12	– 6.00	– 14.87	– 24.54	– 70.87	– 31.49	2.57	36.43	– 13.98	875.00
1982	– 3.90	– 46.71	– 1.62	25.59	– 28.82	– 7.61	– 3.33	92.71	– 5.06	95.47	47.56	7.26	1046.54
1983	29.16	36.92	17.41	96.17	– 26.22	21.98	– 22.74	16.94	16.97	– 7.93	50.82	– 17.38	1258.64
1984	– 38.06	– 65.95	10.26	5.86	– 65.90	27.55	– 17.12	109.10	– 17.67	0.67	– 18.44	22.63	1211.57
1985	75.20	– 2.76	– 17.23	– 8.72	57.35	20.05	11.99	– 13.44	– 5.38	45.68	97.82	74.54	1546.67
1986	24.32	138.07	109.55	– 34.63	92.73	16.01	– 117.41	123.03	– 130.76	110.23	36.42	– 18.28	1895.95
1987	262.09	65.95	80.70	– 18.33	5.21	126.96	153.54	90.88	– 66.67	– 602.75	– 159.98	105.28	1938.83
1988	19.39	113.40	– 83.56	44.27	– 1.21	110.59	– 12.98	– 97.08	81.26	35.74	– 34.14	54.06	2168.57
1989	173.75	– 83.93	35.23	125.18	61.35	– 40.09	220.60	76.61	– 44.45	– 47.74	61.19	46.93	2753.20
1990	– 162.66	36.71	79.96	– 50.45	219.90	4.03	24.51	– 290.84	– 161.88	– 10.15	117.32	74.01	2633.66
1991	102.73	145.79	31.68	– 25.99	139.63	– 120.75	118.07	18.78	– 26.83	52.33	– 174.42	274.15	3168.83
1992	54.56	44.28	– 32.20	123.65	37.76	– 78.36	75.26	– 136.43	14.31	– 45.38	78.88	– 4.05	3301.11
1993	8.92	60.78	64.30	– 7.56	99.88	– 11.35	23.39	111.78	– 96.13	125.47	3.36	70.14	3754.09
1994	224.27	– 146.34	– 196.06	45.73	76.68	– 133.41	139.54	148.92	– 70.23	64.93	– 168.89	95.21	3834.44
1995	9.42	167.19	146.64	163.58	143.87	90.96	152.37	– 97.91	178.52	– 33.60	319.01	42.63	5117.12
1996	278.18	90.32	101.52	– 18.06	74.10	11.45	– 125.72	87.30	265.96	147.21	492.32	– 73.43	6448.27
1997	364.82	64.65	– 294.26	425.51	322.05	341.75	549.82	– 600.19	322.84	– 503.18	381.05	85.12	7908.25
1998	– 1.75	639.22	254.09	263.56	– 163.42	52.07	– 68.73	– 1344.22	303.55	749.48	524.45	64.88	9181.43
1999	177.40	– 52.25	479.58	1002.88	– 229.30	411.06	– 315.65	174.13	– 492.33	392.91	147.95	619.31	11497.12
2000	– 556.59	– 812.22	793.61	– 188.01	– 211.58	– 74.44	74.09	693.12	– 564.18	320.22	– 556.65	372.36	10786.85
2001	100.51	– 392.08	– 616.50	856.19	176.97	– 409.54	20.41	– 573.06	– 1102.19	227.58	776.42	169.94	10021.50
2002	– 101.50	186.13	297.81	– 457.72	– 20.97	– 681.99	– 506.67	– 73.09	– 1071.57	805.10	499.06	– 554.46	8341.63
2003	– 287.82	– 162.73	101.05	487.96	370.17	135.18	248.36	182.02	– 140.76	526.06	– 18.66	671.46	10453.92
2004	34.15	95.85	– 226.22	– 132.13	– 37.12	247.03	– 295.77	34.21	– 93.65	– 52.80	400.55	354.99	10783.01
2005	– 293.07	276.29	– 262.47	– 311.25	274.97	– 192.51	365.94	– 159.31	87.10	– 128.63	365.80	– 88.37	10717.50
2006	147.36	128.55	115.91	257.82	– 198.83	– 18.09	35.46	195.47	297.92	401.66	141.20	241.22	12463.15
2007	158.54	– 353.06	85.72	708.56	564.73	– 219.02	– 196.63	145.75	537.89	34.38	– 558.29	– 106.90	13264.82
2008	– 614.46	– 383.97	– 3.50	557.24	– 181.81	– 1288.31	28.01	165.53	– 692.69	– 1525.65	– 495.97	– 52.65	8776.39
2009	– 775.53	– 937.93	545.99	559.20	332.21	– 53.33	724.61	324.67	216.00	0.45	632.11	83.21	10428.05
2010	– 360.72	257.93	531.37	151.98	– 871.98	– 362.61	691.92	– 451.22	773.33	330.44	– 112.47	571.49	11577.51
2011	314.42	334.41	93.39	490.81	– 240.75	– 155.45	– 271.10	– 529.71	– 700.15	1041.63	90.67	171.88	12217.56
2012	415.35	319.16	259.97	1.59	– 820.18	486.64	128.59	82.16	346.29	– 340.67	– 70.88	78.56	13104.14
2013	756.44	193.91	524.05	261.26									
TOTALS	731.67	– 123.68	3215.31	5746.84	– 312.67	– 1859.99	1972.61	– 1558.80	– 2190.19	2176.90	3104.56	3737.11	
# Up	42	37	42	42	31	29	39	36	25	37	41	45	
# Down	22	27	22	22	32	34	24	27	38	26	22	18	

153

DOW JONES INDUSTRIALS MONTHLY CLOSING PRICES SINCE 1950

	Jan	Feb	Mar	Apr	May	Jun	Jul	Aug	Sep	Oct	Nov	Dec
1950	201.79	203.44	206.05	214.33	223.42	209.11	209.40	216.87	226.36	225.01	227.60	235.41
1951	248.83	252.05	247.94	259.13	249.65	242.64	257.86	270.25	271.16	262.35	261.27	269.23
1952	270.69	260.08	269.46	257.63	262.94	274.26	279.56	275.04	270.61	269.23	283.66	291.90
1953	289.77	284.27	279.87	274.75	272.28	268.26	275.38	261.22	264.04	275.81	281.37	280.90
1954	292.39	294.54	303.51	319.33	327.49	333.53	347.92	335.80	360.46	352.14	386.77	404.39
1955	408.83	411.87	409.70	425.65	424.86	451.38	465.85	468.18	466.62	454.87	483.26	488.40
1956	470.74	483.65	511.79	516.12	478.05	492.78	517.81	502.04	475.25	479.85	472.78	499.47
1957	479.16	464.62	474.81	494.36	504.93	503.29	508.52	484.35	456.30	441.04	449.87	435.69
1958	450.02	439.92	446.76	455.86	462.70	478.18	502.99	508.63	532.09	543.22	557.46	583.65
1959	593.96	603.50	601.71	623.75	643.79	643.60	674.88	664.41	631.68	646.60	659.18	679.36
1960	622.62	630.12	616.59	601.70	625.50	640.62	616.73	625.99	580.14	580.36	597.22	615.89
1961	648.20	662.08	676.63	678.71	696.72	683.96	705.37	719.94	701.21	703.92	721.60	731.14
1962	700.00	708.05	706.95	665.33	613.36	561.28	597.93	609.18	578.98	589.77	649.30	652.10
1963	682.85	662.94	682.52	717.70	726.96	706.88	695.43	729.32	732.79	755.23	750.52	762.95
1964	785.34	800.14	813.29	810.77	820.56	831.50	841.10	838.48	875.37	873.08	875.43	874.13
1965	902.86	903.48	889.05	922.31	918.04	868.03	881.74	893.10	930.58	960.82	946.71	969.26
1966	983.51	951.89	924.77	933.68	884.07	870.10	847.38	788.41	774.22	807.07	791.59	785.69
1967	849.89	839.37	865.98	897.05	852.56	860.26	904.24	901.29	926.66	879.74	875.81	905.11
1968	855.47	840.50	840.67	912.22	899.00	897.80	883.00	896.01	935.79	952.39	985.08	943.75
1969	946.05	905.21	935.48	950.18	937.56	873.19	815.47	836.72	813.09	855.99	812.30	800.36
1970	744.06	777.59	785.57	736.07	700.44	683.53	734.12	764.58	760.68	755.61	794.09	838.92
1971	868.50	878.83	904.37	941.75	907.81	891.14	858.43	898.07	887.19	839.00	831.34	890.20
1972	902.17	928.13	940.70	954.17	960.72	929.03	924.74	963.73	953.27	955.52	1018.21	1020.02
1973	999.02	955.07	951.01	921.43	901.41	891.71	926.40	887.57	947.10	956.58	822.25	850.86
1974	855.55	860.53	846.68	836.75	802.17	802.41	757.43	678.58	607.87	665.52	618.66	616.24
1975	703.69	739.05	768.15	821.34	832.29	878.99	831.51	835.34	793.88	836.04	860.67	852.41
1976	975.28	972.61	999.45	996.85	975.23	1002.78	984.64	973.74	990.19	964.93	947.22	1004.65
1977	954.37	936.42	919.13	926.90	898.66	916.30	890.07	861.49	847.11	818.35	829.70	831.17
1978	769.92	742.12	757.36	837.32	840.61	818.95	862.27	876.82	865.82	792.45	799.03	805.01
1979	839.22	808.82	862.18	854.90	822.33	841.98	846.42	887.63	878.58	815.70	822.35	838.74
1980	875.85	863.14	785.75	817.06	850.85	867.92	935.32	932.59	932.42	924.49	993.34	963.99
1981	947.27	974.58	1003.87	997.75	991.75	976.88	952.34	881.47	849.98	852.55	888.98	875.00
1982	871.10	824.39	822.77	848.36	819.54	811.93	808.60	901.31	896.25	991.72	1039.28	1046.54
1983	1075.70	1112.62	1130.03	1226.20	1199.98	1221.96	1199.22	1216.16	1233.13	1225.20	1276.02	1258.64
1984	1220.58	1154.63	1164.89	1170.75	1104.85	1132.40	1115.28	1224.38	1206.71	1207.38	1188.94	1211.57
1985	1286.77	1284.01	1266.78	1258.06	1315.41	1335.46	1347.45	1334.01	1328.63	1374.31	1472.13	1546.67
1986	1570.99	1709.06	1818.61	1783.98	1876.71	1892.72	1775.31	1898.34	1767.58	1877.81	1914.23	1895.95
1987	2158.04	2223.99	2304.69	2286.36	2291.57	2418.53	2572.07	2662.95	2596.28	1993.53	1833.55	1938.83
1988	1958.22	2071.62	1988.06	2032.33	2031.12	2141.71	2128.73	2031.65	2112.91	2148.65	2114.51	2168.57
1989	2342.32	2258.39	2293.62	2418.80	2480.15	2440.06	2660.66	2737.27	2692.82	2645.08	2706.27	2753.20
1990	2590.54	2627.25	2707.21	2656.76	2876.66	2880.69	2905.20	2614.36	2452.48	2442.33	2559.65	2633.66
1991	2736.39	2882.18	2913.86	2887.87	3027.50	2906.75	3024.82	3043.60	3016.77	3069.10	2894.68	3168.83
1992	3223.39	3267.67	3235.47	3359.12	3396.88	3318.52	3393.78	3257.35	3271.66	3226.28	3305.16	3301.11
1993	3310.03	3370.81	3435.11	3427.55	3527.43	3516.08	3539.47	3651.25	3555.12	3680.59	3683.95	3754.09
1994	3978.36	3832.02	3635.96	3681.69	3758.37	3624.96	3764.50	3913.42	3843.19	3908.12	3739.23	3834.44
1995	3843.86	4011.05	4157.69	4321.27	4465.14	4556.10	4708.47	4610.56	4789.08	4755.48	5074.49	5117.12
1996	5395.30	5485.62	5587.14	5569.08	5643.18	5654.63	5528.91	5616.21	5882.17	6029.38	6521.70	6448.27
1997	6813.09	6877.74	6583.48	7008.99	7331.04	7672.79	8222.61	7622.42	7945.26	7442.08	7823.13	7908.25
1998	7906.50	8545.72	8799.81	9063.37	8899.95	8952.02	8883.29	7539.07	7842.62	8592.10	9116.55	9181.43
1999	9358.83	9306.58	9786.16	10789.04	10559.74	10970.80	10655.15	10829.28	10336.95	10729.86	10877.81	11497.12
2000	10940.53	10128.31	10921.92	10733.91	10522.33	10447.89	10521.98	11215.10	10650.92	10971.14	10414.49	10786.85
2001	10887.36	10495.28	9878.78	10734.97	10911.94	10502.40	10522.81	9949.75	8847.56	9075.14	9851.56	10021.50
2002	9920.00	10106.13	10403.94	9946.22	9925.25	9243.26	8736.59	8663.50	7591.93	8397.03	8896.09	8341.63
2003	8053.81	7891.08	7992.13	8480.09	8850.26	8985.44	9233.80	9415.82	9275.06	9801.12	9782.46	10453.92
2004	10488.07	10583.92	10357.70	10225.57	10188.45	10435.48	10139.71	10173.92	10080.27	10027.47	10428.02	10783.01
2005	10489.94	10766.23	10503.76	10192.51	10467.48	10274.97	10640.91	10481.60	10568.70	10440.07	10805.87	10717.50
2006	10864.86	10993.41	11109.32	11367.14	11168.31	11150.22	11185.68	11381.15	11679.07	12080.73	12221.93	12463.15
2007	12621.69	12268.63	12354.35	13062.91	13627.64	13408.62	13211.99	13357.74	13895.63	13930.01	13371.72	13264.82
2008	12650.36	12266.39	12262.89	12820.13	12638.32	11350.01	11378.02	11543.55	10850.66	9325.01	8829.04	8776.39
2009	8000.86	7062.93	7608.92	8168.12	8500.33	8447.00	9171.61	9496.28	9712.28	9712.73	10344.84	10428.05
2010	10067.33	10325.26	10856.63	11008.61	10136.63	9774.02	10465.94	10014.72	10788.05	11118.49	11006.02	11577.51
2011	11891.93	12226.34	12319.73	12810.54	12569.79	12414.34	12143.24	11613.53	10913.38	11955.01	12045.68	12217.56
2012	12632.91	12952.07	13212.04	13213.63	12393.45	12880.09	13008.68	13090.84	13437.13	13096.46	13025.58	13104.14
2013	13860.58	14054.49	14578.54	14839.80								

154

STANDARD & POOR'S 500 MONTHLY PERCENT CHANGES SINCE 1950

	Jan	Feb	Mar	Apr	May	Jun	Jul	Aug	Sep	Oct	Nov	Dec	Year's Change
1950	1.7	1.0	0.4	4.5	3.9	-5.8	0.8	3.3	5.6	0.4	-0.1	4.6	21.8
1951	6.1	0.6	-1.8	4.8	-4.1	-2.6	6.9	3.9	-0.1	-1.4	-0.3	3.9	16.5
1952	1.6	-3.6	4.8	-4.3	2.3	4.6	1.8	-1.5	-2.0	-0.1	4.6	3.5	11.8
1953	-0.7	-1.8	-2.4	-2.6	-0.3	-1.6	2.5	-5.8	0.1	5.1	0.9	0.2	-6.6
1954	5.1	0.3	3.0	4.9	3.3	0.1	5.7	-3.4	8.3	-1.9	8.1	5.1	45.0
1955	1.8	0.4	-0.5	3.8	-0.1	8.2	6.1	-0.8	1.1	-3.0	7.5	-0.1	26.4
1956	-3.6	3.5	6.9	-0.2	-6.6	3.9	5.2	-3.8	-4.5	0.5	-1.1	3.5	2.6
1957	-4.2	-3.3	2.0	3.7	3.7	-0.1	1.1	-5.6	-6.2	-3.2	1.6	-4.1	-14.3
1958	4.3	-2.1	3.1	3.2	1.5	2.6	4.3	1.2	4.8	2.5	2.2	5.2	38.1
1959	0.4	-0.02	0.1	3.9	1.9	-0.4	3.5	-1.5	-4.6	1.1	1.3	2.8	8.5
1960	-7.1	0.9	-1.4	-1.8	2.7	2.0	-2.5	2.6	-6.0	-0.2	4.0	4.6	-3.0
1961	6.3	2.7	2.6	0.4	1.9	-2.9	3.3	2.0	-2.0	2.8	3.9	0.3	23.1
1962	-3.8	1.6	-0.6	-6.2	-8.6	-8.2	6.4	1.5	-4.8	0.4	10.2	1.3	-11.8
1963	4.9	-2.9	3.5	4.9	1.4	-2.0	-0.3	4.9	-1.1	3.2	-1.1	2.4	18.9
1964	2.7	1.0	1.5	0.6	1.1	1.6	1.8	-1.6	2.9	0.8	-0.5	0.4	13.0
1965	3.3	-0.1	-1.5	3.4	-0.8	-4.9	1.3	2.3	3.2	2.7	-0.9	0.9	9.1
1966	0.5	-1.8	-2.2	2.1	-5.4	-1.6	-1.3	-7.8	-0.7	4.8	0.3	-0.1	-13.1
1967	7.8	0.2	3.9	4.2	-5.2	1.8	4.5	-1.2	3.3	-2.9	0.1	2.6	20.1
1968	-4.4	-3.1	0.9	8.2	1.1	0.9	-1.8	1.1	3.9	0.7	4.8	-4.2	7.7
1969	-0.8	-4.7	3.4	2.1	-0.2	-5.6	-6.0	4.0	-2.5	4.4	-3.5	-1.9	-11.4
1970	-7.6	5.3	0.1	-9.0	-6.1	-5.0	7.3	4.4	3.3	-1.1	4.7	5.7	0.1
1971	4.0	0.9	3.7	3.6	-4.2	0.1	-4.1	3.6	-0.7	-4.2	-0.3	8.6	10.8
1972	1.8	2.5	0.6	0.4	1.7	-2.2	0.2	3.4	-0.5	0.9	4.6	1.2	15.6
1973	-1.7	-3.7	-0.1	-4.1	-1.9	-0.7	3.8	-3.7	4.0	-0.1	-11.4	1.7	-17.4
1974	-1.0	-0.4	-2.3	-3.9	-3.4	-1.5	-7.8	-9.0	-11.9	16.3	-5.3	-2.0	-29.7
1975	12.3	6.0	2.2	4.7	4.4	4.4	-6.8	-2.1	-3.5	6.2	2.5	-1.2	31.5
1976	11.8	-1.1	3.1	-1.1	-1.4	4.1	-0.8	-0.5	2.3	-2.2	-0.8	5.2	19.1
1977	-5.1	-2.2	-1.4	0.02	-2.4	4.5	-1.6	-2.1	-0.2	-4.3	2.7	0.3	-11.5
1978	-6.2	-2.5	2.5	8.5	0.4	-1.8	5.4	2.6	-0.7	-9.2	1.7	1.5	1.1
1979	4.0	-3.7	5.5	0.2	-2.6	3.9	0.9	5.3	N/C	-6.9	4.3	1.7	12.3
1980	5.8	-0.4	-10.2	4.1	4.7	2.7	6.5	0.6	2.5	1.6	10.2	-3.4	25.8
1981	-4.6	1.3	3.6	-2.3	-0.2	-1.0	-0.2	-6.2	-5.4	4.9	3.7	-3.0	-9.7
1982	-1.8	-6.1	-1.0	4.0	-3.9	-2.0	-2.3	11.6	0.8	11.0	3.6	1.5	14.8
1983	3.3	1.9	3.3	7.5	-1.2	3.5	-3.3	1.1	1.0	-1.5	1.7	-0.9	17.3
1984	-0.9	-3.9	1.3	0.5	-5.9	1.7	-1.6	10.6	-0.3	-0.01	-1.5	2.2	1.4
1985	7.4	0.9	-0.3	-0.5	5.4	1.2	-0.5	-1.2	-3.5	4.3	6.5	4.5	26.3
1986	0.2	7.1	5.3	-1.4	5.0	1.4	-5.9	7.1	-8.5	5.5	2.1	-2.8	14.6
1987	13.2	3.7	2.6	-1.1	0.6	4.8	4.8	3.5	-2.4	-21.8	-8.5	7.3	2.0
1988	4.0	4.2	-3.3	0.9	0.3	4.3	-0.5	-3.9	4.0	2.6	-1.9	1.5	12.4
1989	7.1	-2.9	2.1	5.0	3.5	-0.8	8.8	1.6	-0.7	-2.5	1.7	2.1	27.3
1990	-6.9	0.9	2.4	-2.7	9.2	-0.9	-0.5	-9.4	-5.1	-0.7	6.0	2.5	-6.6
1991	4.2	6.7	2.2	0.03	3.9	-4.8	4.5	2.0	-1.9	1.2	-4.4	11.2	26.3
1992	-2.0	1.0	-2.2	2.8	0.1	-1.7	3.9	-2.4	0.9	0.2	3.0	1.0	4.5
1993	0.7	1.0	1.9	-2.5	2.3	0.1	-0.5	3.4	-1.0	1.9	-1.3	1.0	7.1
1994	3.3	-3.0	-4.6	1.2	1.2	-2.7	3.1	3.8	-2.7	2.1	-4.0	1.2	-1.5
1995	2.4	3.6	2.7	2.8	3.6	2.1	3.2	-0.03	4.0	-0.5	4.1	1.7	34.1
1996	3.3	0.7	0.8	1.3	2.3	0.2	-4.6	1.9	5.4	2.6	7.3	-2.2	20.3
1997	6.1	0.6	-4.3	5.8	5.9	4.3	7.8	-5.7	5.3	-3.4	4.5	1.6	31.0
1998	1.0	7.0	5.0	0.9	-1.9	3.9	-1.2	-14.6	6.2	8.0	5.9	5.6	26.7
1999	4.1	-3.2	3.9	3.8	-2.5	5.4	-3.2	-0.6	-2.9	6.3	1.9	5.8	19.5
2000	-5.1	-2.0	9.7	-3.1	-2.2	2.4	-1.6	6.1	-5.3	-0.5	-8.0	0.4	-10.1
2001	3.5	-9.2	-6.4	7.7	0.5	-2.5	-1.1	-6.4	-8.2	1.8	7.5	0.8	-13.0
2002	-1.6	-2.1	3.7	-6.1	-0.9	-7.2	-7.9	0.5	-11.0	8.6	5.7	-6.0	-23.4
2003	-2.7	-1.7	1.0	8.0	5.1	1.1	1.6	1.8	-1.2	5.5	0.7	5.1	26.4
2004	1.7	1.2	-1.6	-1.7	1.2	1.8	-3.4	0.2	0.9	1.4	3.9	3.2	9.0
2005	-2.5	1.9	-1.9	-2.0	3.0	-0.01	3.6	-1.1	0.7	-1.8	3.5	-0.1	3.0
2006	2.5	0.05	1.1	1.2	-3.1	0.01	0.5	2.1	2.5	3.2	1.6	1.3	13.6
2007	1.4	-2.2	1.0	4.3	3.3	-1.8	-3.2	1.3	3.6	1.5	-4.4	-0.9	3.5
2008	-6.1	-3.5	-0.6	4.8	1.1	-8.6	-1.0	1.2	-9.1	-16.9	-7.5	0.8	-38.5
2009	-8.6	-11.0	8.5	9.4	5.3	0.02	7.4	3.4	3.6	-2.0	5.7	1.8	23.5
2010	-3.7	2.9	5.9	1.5	-8.2	-5.4	6.9	-4.7	8.8	3.7	-0.2	6.5	12.8
2011	2.3	3.2	-0.1	2.8	-1.4	-1.8	-2.1	-5.7	-7.2	10.8	-0.5	0.9	-0.003
2012	4.4	4.1	3.1	-0.7	-6.3	4.0	1.3	2.0	2.4	-2.0	0.3	0.7	13.4
2013	5.0	1.1	3.6	1.8									
TOTALS	74.6	-6.3	77.8	97.0	7.8	-0.5	59.1	-0.4	-33.0	47.2	93.6	106.5	
AVG.	1.2	-0.1	1.2	1.5	0.1	-0.01	0.9	-0.01	-0.5	0.7	1.5	1.7	
# Up	40	35	42	44	35	33	34	35	28	37	41	48	
# Down	24	29	22	20	28	30	29	28	34	26	22	15	

STANDARD & POOR'S 500 MONTHLY CLOSING PRICES SINCE 1950

	Jan	Feb	Mar	Apr	May	Jun	Jul	Aug	Sep	Oct	Nov	Dec
1950	17.05	17.22	17.29	18.07	18.78	17.69	17.84	18.42	19.45	19.53	19.51	20.41
1951	21.66	21.80	21.40	22.43	21.52	20.96	22.40	23.28	23.26	22.94	22.88	23.77
1952	24.14	23.26	24.37	23.32	23.86	24.96	25.40	25.03	24.54	24.52	25.66	26.57
1953	26.38	25.90	25.29	24.62	24.54	24.14	24.75	23.32	23.35	24.54	24.76	24.81
1954	26.08	26.15	26.94	28.26	29.19	29.21	30.88	29.83	32.31	31.68	34.24	35.98
1955	36.63	36.76	36.58	37.96	37.91	41.03	43.52	43.18	43.67	42.34	45.51	45.48
1956	43.82	45.34	48.48	48.38	45.20	46.97	49.39	47.51	45.35	45.58	45.08	46.67
1957	44.72	43.26	44.11	45.74	47.43	47.37	47.91	45.22	42.42	41.06	41.72	39.99
1958	41.70	40.84	42.10	43.44	44.09	45.24	47.19	47.75	50.06	51.33	52.48	55.21
1959	55.42	55.41	55.44	57.59	58.68	58.47	60.51	59.60	56.88	57.52	58.28	59.89
1960	55.61	56.12	55.34	54.37	55.83	56.92	55.51	56.96	53.52	53.39	55.54	58.11
1961	61.78	63.44	65.06	65.31	66.56	64.64	66.76	68.07	66.73	68.62	71.32	71.55
1962	68.84	69.96	69.55	65.24	59.63	54.75	58.23	59.12	56.27	56.52	62.26	63.10
1963	66.20	64.29	66.57	69.80	70.80	69.37	69.13	72.50	71.70	74.01	73.23	75.02
1964	77.04	77.80	78.98	79.46	80.37	81.69	83.18	81.83	84.18	84.86	84.42	84.75
1965	87.56	87.43	86.16	89.11	88.42	84.12	85.25	87.17	89.96	92.42	91.61	92.43
1966	92.88	91.22	89.23	91.06	86.13	84.74	83.60	77.10	76.56	80.20	80.45	80.33
1967	86.61	86.78	90.20	94.01	89.08	90.64	94.75	93.64	96.71	93.90	94.00	96.47
1968	92.24	89.36	90.20	97.59	98.68	99.58	97.74	98.86	102.67	103.41	108.37	103.86
1969	103.01	98.13	101.51	103.69	103.46	97.71	91.83	95.51	93.12	97.24	93.81	92.06
1970	85.02	89.50	89.63	81.52	76.55	72.72	78.05	81.52	84.21	83.25	87.20	92.15
1971	95.88	96.75	100.31	103.95	99.63	99.70	95.58	99.03	98.34	94.23	93.99	102.09
1972	103.94	106.57	107.20	107.67	109.53	107.14	107.39	111.09	110.55	111.58	116.67	118.05
1973	116.03	111.68	111.52	106.97	104.95	104.26	108.22	104.25	108.43	108.29	95.96	97.55
1974	96.57	96.22	93.98	90.31	87.28	86.00	79.31	72.15	63.54	73.90	69.97	68.56
1975	76.98	81.59	83.36	87.30	91.15	95.19	88.75	86.88	83.87	89.04	91.24	90.19
1976	100.86	99.71	102.77	101.64	100.18	104.28	103.44	102.91	105.24	102.90	102.10	107.46
1977	102.03	99.82	98.42	98.44	96.12	100.48	98.85	96.77	96.53	92.34	94.83	95.10
1978	89.25	87.04	89.21	96.83	97.24	95.53	100.68	103.29	102.54	93.15	94.70	96.11
1979	99.93	96.28	101.59	101.76	99.08	102.91	103.81	109.32	109.32	101.82	106.16	107.94
1980	114.16	113.66	102.09	106.29	111.24	114.24	121.67	122.38	125.46	127.47	140.52	135.76
1981	129.55	131.27	136.00	132.81	132.59	131.21	130.92	122.79	116.18	121.89	126.35	122.55
1982	120.40	113.11	111.96	116.44	111.88	109.61	107.09	119.51	120.42	133.71	138.54	140.64
1983	145.30	148.06	152.96	164.42	162.39	168.11	162.56	164.40	166.07	163.55	166.40	164.93
1984	163.41	157.06	159.18	160.05	150.55	153.18	150.66	166.68	166.10	166.09	163.58	167.24
1985	179.63	181.18	180.66	179.83	189.55	191.85	190.92	188.63	182.08	189.82	202.17	211.28
1986	211.78	226.92	238.90	235.52	247.35	250.84	236.12	252.93	231.32	243.98	249.22	242.17
1987	274.08	284.20	291.70	288.36	290.10	304.00	318.66	329.80	321.83	251.79	230.30	247.08
1988	257.07	267.82	258.89	261.33	262.16	273.50	272.02	261.52	271.91	278.97	273.70	277.72
1989	297.47	288.86	294.87	309.64	320.52	317.98	346.08	351.45	349.15	340.36	345.99	353.40
1990	329.08	331.89	339.94	330.80	361.23	358.02	356.15	322.56	306.05	304.00	322.22	330.22
1991	343.93	367.07	375.22	375.35	389.83	371.16	387.81	395.43	387.86	392.46	375.22	417.09
1992	408.79	412.70	403.69	414.95	415.35	408.14	424.21	414.03	417.80	418.68	431.35	435.71
1993	438.78	443.38	451.67	440.19	450.19	450.53	448.13	463.56	458.93	467.83	461.79	466.45
1994	481.61	467.14	445.77	450.91	456.50	444.27	458.26	475.49	462.69	472.35	453.69	459.27
1995	470.42	487.39	500.71	514.71	533.40	544.75	562.06	561.88	584.41	581.50	605.37	615.93
1996	636.02	640.43	645.50	654.17	669.12	670.63	639.95	651.99	687.31	705.27	757.02	740.74
1997	786.16	790.82	757.12	801.34	848.28	885.14	954.29	899.47	947.28	914.62	955.40	970.43
1998	980.28	1049.34	1101.75	1111.75	1090.82	1133.84	1120.67	957.28	1017.01	1098.67	1163.63	1229.23
1999	1279.64	1238.33	1286.37	1335.18	1301.84	1372.71	1328.72	1320.41	1282.71	1362.93	1388.91	1469.25
2000	1394.46	1366.42	1498.58	1452.43	1420.60	1454.60	1430.83	1517.68	1436.51	1429.40	1314.95	1320.28
2001	1366.01	1239.94	1160.33	1249.46	1255.82	1224.42	1211.23	1133.58	1040.94	1059.78	1139.45	1148.08
2002	1130.20	1106.73	1147.39	1076.92	1067.14	989.82	911.62	916.07	815.28	885.76	936.31	879.82
2003	855.70	841.15	849.18	916.92	963.59	974.50	990.31	1008.01	995.97	1050.71	1058.20	1111.92
2004	1131.13	1144.94	1126.21	1107.30	1120.68	1140.84	1101.72	1104.24	1114.58	1130.20	1173.82	1211.92
2005	1181.27	1203.60	1180.59	1156.85	1191.50	1191.33	1234.18	1220.33	1228.81	1207.01	1249.48	1248.29
2006	1280.08	1280.66	1294.83	1310.61	1270.09	1270.20	1276.66	1303.82	1335.85	1377.94	1400.63	1418.30
2007	1438.24	1406.82	1420.86	1482.37	1530.62	1503.35	1455.27	1473.99	1526.75	1549.38	1481.14	1468.36
2008	1378.55	1330.63	1322.70	1385.59	1400.38	1280.00	1267.38	1282.83	1166.36	968.75	896.24	903.25
2009	825.88	735.09	797.87	872.81	919.14	919.32	987.48	1020.62	1057.08	1036.19	1095.63	1115.10
2010	1073.87	1104.49	1169.43	1186.69	1089.41	1030.71	1101.60	1049.33	1141.20	1183.26	1180.55	1257.64
2011	1286.12	1327.22	1325.83	1363.61	1345.20	1320.64	1292.28	1218.89	1131.42	1253.30	1246.96	1257.60
2012	1312.41	1365.68	1408.47	1397.91	1310.33	1362.16	1379.32	1406.58	1440.67	1412.16	1416.18	1426.19
2013	1498.11	1514.68	1569.19	1597.57								

NASDAQ COMPOSITE MONTHLY PERCENT CHANGES SINCE 1971

	Jan	Feb	Mar	Apr	May	Jun	Jul	Aug	Sep	Oct	Nov	Dec	Year's Change
1971	10.2	2.6	4.6	6.0	-3.6	-0.4	-2.3	3.0	0.6	-3.6	-1.1	9.8	27.4
1972	4.2	5.5	2.2	2.5	0.9	-1.8	-1.8	1.7	-0.3	0.5	2.1	0.6	17.2
1973	-4.0	-6.2	-2.4	-8.2	-4.8	-1.6	7.6	-3.5	6.0	-0.9	-15.1	-1.4	-31.1
1974	3.0	-0.6	-2.2	-5.9	-7.7	-5.3	-7.9	-10.9	-10.7	17.2	-3.5	-5.0	-35.1
1975	16.6	4.6	3.6	3.8	5.8	4.7	-4.4	-5.0	-5.9	3.6	2.4	-1.5	29.8
1976	12.1	3.7	0.4	-0.6	-2.3	2.6	1.1	-1.7	1.7	-1.0	0.9	7.4	26.1
1977	-2.4	-1.0	-0.5	1.4	0.1	4.3	0.9	-0.5	0.7	-3.3	5.8	1.8	7.3
1978	-4.0	0.6	4.7	8.5	4.4	0.05	5.0	6.9	-1.6	-16.4	3.2	2.9	12.3
1979	6.6	-2.6	7.5	1.6	-1.8	5.1	2.3	6.4	-0.3	-9.6	6.4	4.8	28.1
1980	7.0	-2.3	-17.1	6.9	7.5	4.9	8.9	5.7	3.4	2.7	8.0	-2.8	33.9
1981	-2.2	0.1	6.1	3.1	3.1	-3.5	-1.9	-7.5	-8.0	8.4	3.1	-2.7	-3.2
1982	-3.8	-4.8	-2.1	5.2	-3.3	-4.1	-2.3	6.2	5.6	13.3	9.3	0.04	18.7
1983	6.9	5.0	3.9	8.2	5.3	3.2	-4.6	-3.8	1.4	-7.4	4.1	-2.5	19.9
1984	-3.7	-5.9	-0.7	-1.3	-5.9	2.9	-4.2	10.9	-1.8	-1.2	-1.8	2.0	-11.2
1985	12.7	2.0	-1.7	0.5	3.6	1.9	1.7	-1.2	-5.8	4.4	7.3	3.5	31.4
1986	3.3	7.1	4.2	2.3	4.4	1.3	-8.4	3.1	-8.4	2.9	-0.3	-2.8	7.5
1987	12.2	8.4	1.2	-2.8	-0.3	2.0	2.4	4.6	-2.3	-27.2	-5.6	8.3	-5.4
1988	4.3	6.5	2.1	1.2	-2.3	6.6	-1.9	-2.8	3.0	-1.4	-2.9	2.7	15.4
1989	5.2	-0.4	1.8	5.1	4.4	-2.4	4.3	3.4	0.8	-3.7	0.1	-0.3	19.3
1990	-8.6	2.4	2.3	-3.6	9.3	0.7	-5.2	-13.0	-9.6	-4.3	8.9	4.1	-17.8
1991	10.8	9.4	6.5	0.5	4.4	-6.0	5.5	4.7	0.2	3.1	-3.5	11.9	56.8
1992	5.8	2.1	-4.7	-4.2	1.1	-3.7	3.1	-3.0	3.6	3.8	7.9	3.7	15.5
1993	2.9	-3.7	2.9	-4.2	5.9	0.5	0.1	5.4	2.7	2.2	-3.2	3.0	14.7
1994	3.0	-1.0	-6.2	-1.3	0.2	-4.0	2.3	6.0	-0.2	1.7	-3.5	0.2	-3.2
1995	0.4	5.1	3.0	3.3	2.4	8.0	7.3	1.9	2.3	-0.7	2.2	-0.7	39.9
1996	0.7	3.8	0.1	8.1	4.4	-4.7	-8.8	5.6	7.5	-0.4	5.8	-0.1	22.7
1997	6.9	-5.1	-6.7	3.2	11.1	3.0	10.5	-0.4	6.2	-5.5	0.4	-1.9	21.6
1998	3.1	9.3	3.7	1.8	-4.8	6.5	-1.2	-19.9	13.0	4.6	10.1	12.5	39.6
1999	14.3	-8.7	7.6	3.3	-2.8	8.7	-1.8	3.8	0.2	8.0	12.5	22.0	85.6
2000	-3.2	19.2	-2.6	-15.6	-11.9	16.6	-5.0	11.7	-12.7	-8.3	-22.9	-4.9	-39.3
2001	12.2	-22.4	-14.5	15.0	-0.3	2.4	-6.2	-10.9	-17.0	12.8	14.2	1.0	-21.1
2002	-0.8	-10.5	6.6	-8.5	-4.3	-9.4	-9.2	-1.0	-10.9	13.5	11.2	-9.7	-31.5
2003	-1.1	1.3	0.3	9.2	9.0	1.7	6.9	4.3	-1.3	8.1	1.5	2.2	50.0
2004	3.1	-1.8	-1.8	-3.7	3.5	3.1	-7.8	-2.6	3.2	4.1	6.2	3.7	8.6
2005	-5.2	-0.5	-2.6	-3.9	7.6	-0.5	6.2	-1.5	-0.02	-1.5	5.3	-1.2	1.4
2006	4.6	-1.1	2.6	-0.7	-6.2	-0.3	-3.7	4.4	3.4	4.8	2.7	-0.7	9.5
2007	2.0	-1.9	0.2	4.3	3.1	-0.05	-2.2	2.0	4.0	5.8	-6.9	-0.3	9.8
2008	-9.9	-5.0	0.3	5.9	4.6	-9.1	1.4	1.8	-11.6	-17.7	-10.8	2.7	-40.5
2009	-6.4	-6.7	10.9	12.3	3.3	3.4	7.8	1.5	5.6	-3.6	4.9	5.8	43.9
2010	-5.4	4.2	7.1	2.6	-8.3	-6.5	6.9	-6.2	12.0	5.9	-0.4	6.2	16.9
2011	1.8	3.0	-0.04	3.3	-1.3	-2.2	-0.6	-6.4	-6.4	11.1	-2.4	-0.6	-1.8
2012	8.0	5.4	4.2	-1.5	-7.2	3.8	0.2	4.3	1.6	-4.5	1.1	0.3	15.9
2013	4.1	0.6	3.4	1.9									
TOTALS	127.3	19.7	38.2	65.0	30.3	32.4	1.0	7.5	-26.1	20.3	63.7	84.0	
AVG.	3.0	0.5	0.9	1.5	0.7	0.8	0.02	0.2	-0.6	0.5	1.5	2.0	
# Up	29	23	28	28	24	24	21	23	23	22	27	25	
# Down	14	20	15	15	18	18	21	19	19	20	15	17	

Based on NASDAQ composite; prior to February 5, 1971, based on National Quotation Bureau indices.

NASDAQ COMPOSITE MONTHLY CLOSING PRICES SINCE 1971

	Jan	Feb	Mar	Apr	May	Jun	Jul	Aug	Sep	Oct	Nov	Dec
1971	98.77	101.34	105.97	112.30	108.25	107.80	105.27	108.42	109.03	105.10	103.97	114.12
1972	118.87	125.38	128.14	131.33	132.53	130.08	127.75	129.95	129.61	130.24	132.96	133.73
1973	128.40	120.41	117.46	107.85	102.64	100.98	108.64	104.87	111.20	110.17	93.51	92.19
1974	94.93	94.35	92.27	86.86	80.20	75.96	69.99	62.37	55.67	65.23	62.95	59.82
1975	69.78	73.00	75.66	78.54	83.10	87.02	83.19	79.01	74.33	76.99	78.80	77.62
1976	87.05	90.26	90.62	90.08	88.04	90.32	91.29	89.70	91.26	90.35	91.12	97.88
1977	95.54	94.57	94.13	95.48	95.59	99.73	100.65	100.10	100.85	97.52	103.15	105.05
1978	100.84	101.47	106.20	115.18	120.24	120.30	126.32	135.01	132.89	111.12	114.69	117.98
1979	125.82	122.56	131.76	133.82	131.42	138.13	141.33	150.44	149.98	135.53	144.26	151.14
1980	161.75	158.03	131.00	139.99	150.45	157.78	171.81	181.52	187.76	192.78	208.15	202.34
1981	197.81	198.01	210.18	216.74	223.47	215.75	211.63	195.75	180.03	195.24	201.37	195.84
1982	188.39	179.43	175.65	184.70	178.54	171.30	167.35	177.71	187.65	212.63	232.31	232.41
1983	248.35	260.67	270.80	293.06	308.73	318.70	303.96	292.42	296.65	274.55	285.67	278.60
1984	268.43	252.57	250.78	247.44	232.82	239.65	229.70	254.64	249.94	247.03	242.53	247.35
1985	278.70	284.17	279.20	280.56	290.80	296.20	301.29	297.71	280.33	292.54	313.95	324.93
1986	335.77	359.53	374.72	383.24	400.16	405.51	371.37	382.86	350.67	360.77	359.57	349.33
1987	392.06	424.97	430.05	417.81	416.54	424.67	434.93	454.97	444.29	323.30	305.16	330.47
1988	344.66	366.95	374.64	379.23	370.34	394.66	387.33	376.55	387.71	382.46	371.45	381.38
1989	401.30	399.71	406.73	427.55	446.17	435.29	453.84	469.33	472.92	455.63	456.09	454.82
1990	415.81	425.83	435.54	420.07	458.97	462.29	438.24	381.21	344.51	329.84	359.06	373.84
1991	414.20	453.05	482.30	484.72	506.11	475.92	502.04	525.68	526.88	542.98	523.90	586.34
1992	620.21	633.47	603.77	578.68	585.31	563.60	580.83	563.12	583.27	605.17	652.73	676.95
1993	696.34	670.77	690.13	661.42	700.53	703.95	704.70	742.84	762.78	779.26	754.39	776.80
1994	800.47	792.50	743.46	733.84	735.19	705.96	722.16	765.62	764.29	777.49	750.32	751.96
1995	755.20	793.73	817.21	843.98	864.58	933.45	1001.21	1020.11	1043.54	1036.06	1059.20	1052.13
1996	1059.79	1100.05	1101.40	1190.52	1243.43	1185.02	1080.59	1141.50	1226.92	1221.51	1292.61	1291.03
1997	1379.85	1309.00	1221.70	1260.76	1400.32	1442.07	1593.81	1587.32	1685.69	1593.61	1600.55	1570.35
1998	1619.36	1770.51	1835.68	1868.41	1778.87	1894.74	1872.39	1499.25	1693.84	1771.39	1949.54	2192.69
1999	2505.89	2288.03	2461.40	2542.85	2470.52	2686.12	2638.49	2739.35	2746.16	2966.43	3336.16	4069.31
2000	3940.35	4696.69	4572.83	3860.66	3400.91	3966.11	3766.99	4206.35	3672.82	3369.63	2597.93	2470.52
2001	2772.73	2151.83	1840.26	2116.24	2110.49	2160.54	2027.13	1805.43	1498.80	1690.20	1930.58	1950.40
2002	1934.03	1731.49	1845.35	1688.23	1615.73	1463.21	1328.26	1314.85	1172.06	1329.75	1478.78	1335.51
2003	1320.91	1337.52	1341.17	1464.31	1595.91	1622.80	1735.02	1810.45	1786.94	1932.21	1960.26	2003.37
2004	2066.15	2029.82	1994.22	1920.15	1986.74	2047.79	1887.36	1838.10	1896.84	1974.99	2096.81	2175.44
2005	2062.41	2051.72	1999.23	1921.65	2068.22	2056.96	2184.83	2152.09	2151.69	2120.30	2232.82	2205.32
2006	2305.82	2281.39	2339.79	2322.57	2178.88	2172.09	2091.47	2183.75	2258.43	2366.71	2431.77	2415.29
2007	2463.93	2416.15	2421.64	2525.09	2604.52	2603.23	2545.57	2596.36	2701.50	2859.12	2660.96	2652.28
2008	2389.86	2271.48	2279.10	2412.80	2522.66	2292.98	2325.55	2367.52	2091.88	1720.95	1535.57	1577.03
2009	1476.42	1377.84	1528.59	1717.30	1774.33	1835.04	1978.50	2009.06	2122.42	2045.11	2144.60	2269.15
2010	2147.35	2238.26	2397.96	2461.19	2257.04	2109.24	2254.70	2114.03	2368.62	2507.41	2498.23	2652.87
2011	2700.08	2782.27	2781.07	2873.54	2835.30	2773.52	2756.38	2579.46	2415.40	2684.41	2620.34	2605.15
2012	2813.84	2966.89	3091.57	3046.36	2827.34	2935.05	2939.52	3066.96	3116.23	2977.23	3010.24	3019.51
2013	3142.13	3160.19	3267.52	3328.79								

Based on NASDAQ composite; prior to February 5, 1971, based on National Quotation Bureau indices.

RUSSELL 1000 INDEX MONTHLY PERCENT CHANGES SINCE 1979

	Jan	Feb	Mar	Apr	May	Jun	Jul	Aug	Sep	Oct	Nov	Dec	Year's Change
1979	4.2	-3.5	6.0	0.3	-2.2	4.3	1.1	5.6	0.02	-7.1	5.1	2.1	16.1
1980	5.9	-0.5	-11.5	4.6	5.0	3.2	6.4	1.1	2.6	1.8	10.1	-3.9	25.6
1981	-4.6	1.0	3.8	-1.9	0.2	-1.2	-0.1	-6.2	-6.4	5.4	4.0	-3.3	-9.7
1982	-2.7	-5.9	-1.3	3.9	-3.6	-2.6	-2.3	11.3	1.2	11.3	4.0	1.3	13.7
1983	3.2	2.1	3.2	7.1	-0.2	3.7	-3.2	0.5	1.3	-2.4	2.0	-1.2	17.0
1984	-1.9	-4.4	1.1	0.3	-5.9	2.1	-1.8	10.8	-0.2	-0.1	-1.4	2.2	-0.1
1985	7.8	1.1	-0.4	-0.3	5.4	1.6	-0.8	-1.0	-3.9	4.5	6.5	4.1	26.7
1986	0.9	7.2	5.1	-1.3	5.0	1.4	-5.9	6.8	-8.5	5.1	1.4	-3.0	13.6
1987	12.7	4.0	1.9	-1.8	0.4	4.5	4.2	3.8	-2.4	-21.9	-8.0	7.2	0.02
1988	4.3	4.4	-2.9	0.7	0.2	4.8	-0.9	-3.3	3.9	2.0	-2.0	1.7	13.1
1989	6.8	-2.5	2.0	4.9	3.8	-0.8	8.2	1.7	-0.5	-2.8	1.5	1.8	25.9
1990	-7.4	1.2	2.2	-2.8	8.9	-0.7	-1.1	-9.6	-5.3	-0.8	6.4	2.7	-7.5
1991	4.5	6.9	2.5	-0.1	3.8	-4.7	4.6	2.2	-1.5	1.4	-4.1	11.2	28.8
1992	-1.4	0.9	-2.4	2.3	0.3	-1.9	4.1	-2.5	1.0	0.7	3.5	1.4	5.9
1993	0.7	0.6	2.2	-2.8	2.4	0.4	-0.4	3.5	-0.5	1.2	-1.7	1.6	7.3
1994	2.9	-2.9	-4.5	1.1	1.0	-2.9	3.1	3.9	-2.6	1.7	-3.9	1.2	-2.4
1995	2.4	3.8	2.3	2.5	3.5	2.4	3.7	0.5	3.9	-0.6	4.2	1.4	34.4
1996	3.1	1.1	0.7	1.4	2.1	-0.1	-4.9	2.5	5.5	2.1	7.1	-1.8	19.7
1997	5.8	0.2	-4.6	5.3	6.2	4.0	8.0	-4.9	5.4	-3.4	4.2	1.9	30.5
1998	0.6	7.0	4.9	0.9	-2.3	3.6	-1.3	-15.1	6.5	7.8	6.1	6.2	25.1
1999	3.5	-3.3	3.7	4.2	-2.3	5.1	-3.2	-1.0	-2.8	6.5	2.5	6.0	19.5
2000	-4.2	-0.4	8.9	-3.3	-2.7	2.5	-1.8	7.4	-4.8	-1.2	-9.3	1.1	-8.8
2001	3.2	-9.5	-6.7	8.0	0.5	-2.4	-1.4	-6.2	-8.6	2.0	7.5	0.9	-13.6
2002	-1.4	-2.1	4.0	-5.8	-1.0	-7.5	-7.5	0.3	-10.9	8.1	5.7	-5.8	-22.9
2003	-2.5	-1.7	0.9	7.9	5.5	1.2	1.8	1.9	-1.2	5.7	1.0	4.6	27.5
2004	1.8	1.2	-1.5	-1.9	1.3	1.7	-3.6	0.3	1.1	1.5	4.1	3.5	9.5
2005	-2.6	2.0	-1.7	-2.0	3.4	0.3	3.8	-1.1	0.8	-1.9	3.5	0.01	4.4
2006	2.7	0.01	1.3	1.1	-3.2	0.003	0.1	2.2	2.3	3.3	1.9	1.1	13.3
2007	1.8	-1.9	0.9	4.1	3.4	-2.0	-3.2	1.2	3.7	1.6	-4.5	-0.8	3.9
2008	-6.1	-3.3	-0.8	5.0	1.6	-8.5	-1.3	1.2	-9.7	-17.6	-7.9	1.3	-39.0
2009	-8.3	-10.7	8.5	10.0	5.3	0.1	7.5	3.4	3.9	-2.3	5.6	2.3	25.5
2010	-3.7	3.1	6.0	1.8	-8.1	-5.7	6.8	-4.7	9.0	3.8	0.1	6.5	13.9
2011	2.3	3.3	0.1	2.9	-1.3	-1.9	-2.3	-6.0	-7.6	11.1	-0.5	0.7	-0.5
2012	4.8	4.1	3.0	-0.7	-6.4	3.7	1.1	2.2	2.4	-1.8	0.5	0.8	13.9
2013	5.3	1.1	3.7	1.7									
TOTALS	44.4	3.7	40.6	57.3	30.0	7.7	17.5	12.7	-22.9	24.7	55.2	57.0	
AVG.	1.3	0.1	1.2	1.6	0.9	0.2	0.5	0.4	-0.7	0.7	1.6	1.7	
# Up	23	21	24	23	22	20	15	22	17	21	24	27	
# Down	12	14	11	12	12	14	19	12	17	13	10	7	

RUSSELL 1000 INDEX MONTHLY CLOSING PRICES SINCE 1979

	Jan	Feb	Mar	Apr	May	Jun	Jul	Aug	Sep	Oct	Nov	Dec
1979	53.76	51.88	54.97	55.15	53.92	56.25	56.86	60.04	60.05	55.78	58.65	59.87
1980	63.40	63.07	55.79	58.38	61.31	63.27	67.30	68.05	69.84	71.08	78.26	75.20
1981	71.75	72.49	75.21	73.77	73.90	73.01	72.92	68.42	64.06	67.54	70.23	67.93
1982	66.12	62.21	61.43	63.85	61.53	59.92	58.54	65.14	65.89	73.34	76.28	77.24
1983	79.75	81.45	84.06	90.04	89.89	93.18	90.18	90.65	91.85	89.69	91.50	90.38
1984	88.69	84.76	85.73	86.00	80.94	82.61	81.13	89.87	89.67	89.62	88.36	90.31
1985	97.31	98.38	98.03	97.72	103.02	104.65	103.78	102.76	98.75	103.16	109.91	114.39
1986	115.39	123.71	130.07	128.44	134.82	136.75	128.74	137.43	125.70	132.11	133.97	130.00
1987	146.48	152.29	155.20	152.39	152.94	159.84	166.57	172.95	168.83	131.89	121.28	130.02
1988	135.55	141.54	137.45	138.37	138.66	145.31	143.99	139.26	144.68	147.55	144.59	146.99
1989	156.93	152.98	155.99	163.63	169.85	168.49	182.27	185.33	184.40	179.17	181.85	185.11
1990	171.44	173.43	177.28	172.32	187.66	186.29	184.32	166.69	157.83	156.62	166.69	171.22
1991	179.00	191.34	196.15	195.94	203.32	193.78	202.67	207.18	204.02	206.96	198.46	220.61
1992	217.52	219.50	214.29	219.13	219.71	215.60	224.37	218.86	221.15	222.65	230.44	233.59
1993	235.25	236.67	241.80	235.13	240.80	241.78	240.78	249.23	247.95	250.97	246.70	250.71
1994	258.08	250.52	239.19	241.71	244.13	237.11	244.44	254.04	247.49	251.62	241.82	244.65
1995	250.52	260.08	266.11	272.81	282.48	289.29	299.98	301.40	313.28	311.37	324.36	328.89
1996	338.97	342.56	345.01	349.84	357.35	357.10	339.44	347.79	366.77	374.38	401.05	393.75
1997	416.77	417.46	398.19	419.15	445.06	462.95	499.89	475.33	500.78	483.86	504.25	513.79
1998	517.02	553.14	580.31	585.46	572.16	592.57	584.97	496.66	529.11	570.63	605.31	642.87
1999	665.64	643.67	667.49	695.25	679.10	713.61	690.51	683.27	663.83	707.19	724.66	767.97
2000	736.08	733.04	797.99	771.58	750.98	769.68	755.57	811.17	772.60	763.06	692.40	700.09
2001	722.55	654.25	610.36	658.90	662.39	646.64	637.43	597.67	546.46	557.29	599.32	604.94
2002	596.66	583.88	607.35	572.04	566.18	523.72	484.39	486.08	433.22	468.51	495.00	466.18
2003	454.30	446.37	450.35	486.09	512.92	518.94	528.53	538.40	532.15	562.51	568.32	594.56
2004	605.21	612.58	603.42	591.83	599.40	609.31	587.21	589.09	595.66	604.51	629.26	650.99
2005	633.99	646.93	635.78	623.32	644.28	645.92	670.26	663.13	668.53	656.09	679.35	679.42
2006	697.79	697.83	706.74	714.37	691.78	691.80	692.59	707.55	723.48	747.30	761.43	770.08
2007	784.11	768.92	775.97	807.82	835.14	818.17	792.11	801.22	830.59	844.20	806.44	799.82
2008	750.97	726.42	720.32	756.03	768.28	703.22	694.07	702.17	634.08	522.47	481.43	487.77
2009	447.32	399.61	433.67	476.84	501.95	502.27	539.88	558.21	579.97	566.52	598.41	612.01
2010	589.41	607.45	643.79	655.06	601.79	567.37	606.09	577.68	629.78	653.57	654.24	696.90
2011	712.97	736.24	737.07	758.45	748.75	734.48	717.77	674.79	623.45	692.41	688.77	693.36
2012	726.33	756.42	778.92	773.50	724.12	750.61	758.60	775.07	793.74	779.35	783.37	789.90
2013	831.74	840.97	872.11	886.89								

	Jan	Feb	Mar	Apr	May	Jun	Jul	Aug	Sep	Oct	Nov	Dec	Year's Change
1979	9.0	-3.2	9.7	2.3	-1.8	5.3	2.9	7.8	-0.7	-11.3	8.1	6.6	38.0
1980	8.2	-2.1	-18.5	6.0	8.0	4.0	11.0	6.5	2.9	3.9	7.0	-3.7	33.8
1981	-0.6	0.3	7.7	2.5	3.0	-2.5	-2.6	-8.0	-8.6	8.2	2.8	-2.0	-1.5
1982	-3.7	-5.3	-1.5	5.1	-3.2	-4.0	-1.7	7.5	3.6	14.1	8.8	1.1	20.7
1983	7.5	6.0	2.5	7.2	7.0	4.4	-3.0	-4.0	1.6	-7.0	5.0	-2.1	26.3
1984	-1.8	-5.9	0.4	-0.7	-5.4	2.6	-5.0	11.5	-1.0	-2.0	-2.9	1.4	-9.6
1985	13.1	2.4	-2.2	-1.4	3.4	1.0	2.7	-1.2	-6.2	3.6	6.8	4.2	28.0
1986	1.5	7.0	4.7	1.4	3.3	-0.2	-9.5	3.0	-6.3	3.9	-0.5	-3.1	4.0
1987	11.5	8.2	2.4	-3.0	-0.5	2.3	2.8	2.9	-2.0	-30.8	-5.5	7.8	-10.8
1988	4.0	8.7	4.4	2.0	-2.5	7.0	-0.9	-2.8	2.3	-1.2	-3.6	3.8	22.4
1989	4.4	0.5	2.2	4.3	4.2	-2.4	4.2	2.1	0.01	-6.0	0.4	0.1	14.2
1990	-8.9	2.9	3.7	-3.4	6.8	0.1	-4.5	-13.6	-9.2	-6.2	7.3	3.7	-21.5
1991	9.1	11.0	6.9	-0.2	4.5	-6.0	3.1	3.7	0.6	2.7	-4.7	7.7	43.7
1992	8.0	2.9	-3.5	-3.7	1.2	-5.0	3.2	-3.1	2.2	3.1	7.5	3.4	16.4
1993	3.2	-2.5	3.1	-2.8	4.3	0.5	1.3	4.1	2.7	2.5	-3.4	3.3	17.0
1994	3.1	-0.4	-5.4	0.6	-1.3	-3.6	1.6	5.4	-0.5	-0.4	-4.2	2.5	-3.2
1995	-1.4	3.9	1.6	2.1	1.5	5.0	5.7	1.9	1.7	-4.6	4.2	2.4	26.2
1996	-0.2	3.0	1.8	5.3	3.9	-4.2	-8.8	5.7	3.7	-1.7	4.0	2.4	14.8
1997	1.9	-2.5	-4.9	0.1	11.0	4.1	4.6	2.2	7.2	-4.5	-0.8	1.7	20.5
1998	-1.6	7.4	4.1	0.5	-5.4	0.2	-8.2	-19.5	7.6	4.0	5.2	6.1	-3.4
1999	1.2	-8.2	1.4	8.8	1.4	4.3	-2.8	-3.8	-0.1	0.3	5.9	11.2	19.6
2000	-1.7	16.4	-6.7	-6.1	-5.9	8.6	-3.2	7.4	-3.1	-4.5	-10.4	8.4	-4.2
2001	5.1	-6.7	-5.0	7.7	2.3	3.3	-5.4	-3.3	-13.6	5.8	7.6	6.0	1.0
2002	-1.1	-2.8	7.9	0.8	-4.5	-5.1	-15.2	-0.4	-7.3	3.1	8.8	-5.7	-21.6
2003	-2.9	-3.1	1.1	9.4	10.6	1.7	6.2	4.5	-2.0	8.3	3.5	1.9	45.4
2004	4.3	0.8	0.8	-5.2	1.5	4.1	-6.8	-0.6	4.6	1.9	8.6	2.8	17.0
2005	-4.2	1.6	-3.0	-5.8	6.4	3.7	6.3	-1.9	0.2	-3.2	4.7	-0.6	3.3
2006	8.9	-0.3	4.7	-0.1	-5.7	0.5	-3.3	2.9	0.7	5.7	2.5	0.2	17.0
2007	1.6	-0.9	0.9	1.7	4.0	-1.6	-6.9	2.2	1.6	2.8	-7.3	-0.2	-2.7
2008	-6.9	-3.8	0.3	4.1	4.5	-7.8	3.6	3.5	-8.1	-20.9	-12.0	5.6	-34.8
2009	-11.2	-12.3	8.7	15.3	2.9	1.3	9.5	2.8	5.6	-6.9	3.0	7.9	25.2
2010	-3.7	4.4	8.0	5.6	-7.7	-7.9	6.8	-7.5	12.3	4.0	3.4	7.8	25.3
2011	-0.3	5.4	2.4	2.6	-2.0	-2.5	-3.7	-8.8	-11.4	15.0	-0.5	0.5	-5.5
2012	7.0	2.3	2.4	-1.6	-6.7	4.8	-1.4	3.2	3.1	-2.2	0.4	3.3	14.6
2013	6.2	1.0	4.4	-0.4									
TOTALS	68.6	36.1	47.5	61.0	43.1	16.0	-17.4	12.3	-15.9	-20.5	59.7	96.4	
AVG.	2.0	1.0	1.4	1.7	1.3	0.5	-0.5	0.4	-0.5	-0.6	1.8	2.8	
# Up	20	20	26	22	21	21	16	20	19	18	22	27	
# Down	15	15	9	13	13	13	18	14	15	16	12	7	

	Jan	Feb	Mar	Apr	May	Jun	Jul	Aug	Sep	Oct	Nov	Dec
1979	44.18	42.78	46.94	48.00	47.13	49.62	51.08	55.05	54.68	48.51	52.43	55.91
1980	60.50	59.22	48.27	51.18	55.26	57.47	63.81	67.97	69.94	72.64	77.70	74.80
1981	74.33	74.52	80.25	82.25	84.72	82.56	80.41	73.94	67.55	73.06	75.14	73.67
1982	70.96	67.21	66.21	69.59	67.39	64.67	63.59	68.38	70.84	80.86	87.96	88.90
1983	95.53	101.23	103.77	111.20	118.94	124.17	120.43	115.60	117.43	109.17	114.66	112.27
1984	110.21	103.72	104.10	103.34	97.75	100.30	95.25	106.21	105.17	103.07	100.11	101.49
1985	114.77	117.54	114.92	113.35	117.26	118.38	121.56	120.10	112.65	116.73	124.62	129.87
1986	131.78	141.00	147.63	149.66	154.61	154.23	139.65	143.83	134.73	139.95	139.26	135.00
1987	150.48	162.84	166.79	161.82	161.02	164.75	169.42	174.25	170.81	118.26	111.70	120.42
1988	125.24	136.10	142.15	145.01	141.37	151.30	149.89	145.74	149.08	147.25	142.01	147.37
1989	153.84	154.56	157.89	164.68	171.53	167.42	174.50	178.20	178.21	167.47	168.17	168.30
1990	153.27	157.72	163.63	158.09	168.91	169.04	161.51	139.52	126.70	118.83	127.50	132.16
1991	144.17	160.00	171.01	170.61	178.34	167.61	172.76	179.11	180.16	185.00	176.37	189.94
1992	205.16	211.15	203.69	196.25	198.52	188.64	194.74	188.79	192.92	198.90	213.81	221.01
1993	228.12	222.41	229.21	222.68	232.19	233.35	236.46	246.19	252.95	259.18	250.41	258.59
1994	266.52	265.53	251.06	252.55	249.28	240.29	244.06	257.32	256.12	255.02	244.25	250.36
1995	246.85	256.57	260.77	266.17	270.25	283.63	299.72	305.31	310.38	296.25	308.58	315.97
1996	315.38	324.93	330.77	348.28	361.85	346.61	316.00	333.88	346.39	340.57	354.11	362.61
1997	369.45	360.05	342.56	343.00	380.76	396.37	414.48	423.43	453.82	433.26	429.92	437.02
1998	430.05	461.83	480.68	482.89	456.62	457.39	419.75	337.95	363.59	378.16	397.75	421.96
1999	427.22	392.26	397.63	432.81	438.68	457.68	444.77	427.83	427.30	428.64	454.08	504.75
2000	496.23	577.71	539.09	506.25	476.18	517.23	500.64	537.89	521.37	497.68	445.94	483.53
2001	508.34	474.37	450.53	485.32	496.50	512.64	484.78	468.56	404.87	428.17	460.78	488.50
2002	483.10	469.36	506.46	510.67	487.47	462.64	392.42	390.96	362.27	373.50	406.35	383.09
2003	372.17	360.52	364.54	398.68	441.00	448.37	476.02	497.42	487.68	528.22	546.51	556.91
2004	580.76	585.56	590.31	559.80	568.28	591.52	551.29	547.93	572.94	583.79	633.77	651.57
2005	624.02	634.06	615.07	579.38	616.71	639.66	679.75	666.51	667.80	646.61	677.29	673.22
2006	733.20	730.64	765.14	764.54	721.01	724.67	700.56	720.53	725.59	766.84	786.12	787.66
2007	800.34	793.30	800.71	814.57	847.19	833.69	776.13	792.86	805.45	828.02	767.77	766.03
2008	713.30	686.18	687.97	716.18	748.28	689.66	714.52	739.50	679.58	537.52	473.14	499.45
2009	443.53	389.02	422.75	487.56	501.58	508.28	556.71	572.07	604.28	562.77	579.73	625.39
2010	602.04	628.56	678.64	716.60	661.61	609.49	650.89	602.06	676.14	703.35	727.01	783.65
2011	781.25	823.45	843.55	865.29	848.30	827.43	797.03	726.81	644.16	741.06	737.42	740.92
2012	792.82	810.94	830.30	816.88	761.82	798.49	786.94	812.09	837.45	818.73	821.92	849.35
2013	902.09	911.11	951.54	947.46								

160

The Seasonal & Sector Swing Trader Delivers the Best-Performing Trades in Every Major Market Four Times a Year

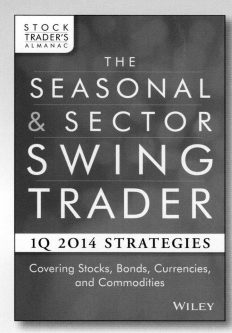

Seasonal tendencies and cycles provide a foundation for informed trading. From the powerhouse team of Jeffrey Hirsch, Editor-in-Chief of Stock Trader's Almanac, and John Person, President of PersonsPlanet.com comes the trading industry's most authoritative analysis of seasonal tendencies.

This digital-only, quarterly report provides timely, actionable trading analysis on stocks, bonds, currencies, energy, metals, grains, soft commodities, and meats; precise entry and exit dates for dozens of seasonal trade that have a record of 70% or more accuracy; and major trades and in-depth analysis on the historic price patterns of the underlying market.

The Seasonal & Sector Swing Trader will equip serious traders with the information they need to compare current market conditions against historic tendencies and make informed trading decisions.

- **Provides precise entry/exit dates for dozens of seasonal trades that have a record of 70% or more accuracy**

- **PREMIER SEASONAL ANALYSIS:** The trading industry's most authoritative analysis of seasonal tendencies of every major market: stocks, bonds, currencies, and commodities

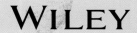

Wiley is a registered trademark of John Wiley & Sons, Inc.

v Stock Trader's Almanac

@AlmanacTrader

Stock Trader's Almanac

Stock Trader's Almanac Group

STA Blog: http://blog.stocktradersalmanac.com/

Follow Wiley Trading

@Wiley_Trading

Wiley Trading

Wiley Trading Group

Website: WileyTrading.com

10 **BEST** DAYS BY PERCENT AND POINT

	BY PERCENT CHANGE				BY POINT CHANGE		
DAY	CLOSE	PNT CHANGE	% CHANGE	DAY	CLOSE	PNT CHANGE	% CHANGE
DJIA 1901 TO 1949							
3/15/33	62.10	8.26	15.3	10/30/29	258.47	28.40	12.3
10/6/31	99.34	12.86	14.9	11/14/29	217.28	18.59	9.4
10/30/29	258.47	28.40	12.3	10/5/29	341.36	16.19	5.0
9/21/32	75.16	7.67	11.4	10/31/29	273.51	15.04	5.8
8/3/32	58.22	5.06	9.5	10/6/31	99.34	12.86	14.9
2/11/32	78.60	6.80	9.5	11/15/29	228.73	11.45	5.3
11/14/29	217.28	18.59	9.4	6/19/30	228.97	10.13	4.6
12/18/31	80.69	6.90	9.4	9/5/39	148.12	10.03	7.3
2/13/32	85.82	7.22	9.2	11/22/28	290.34	9.81	3.5
5/6/32	59.01	4.91	9.1	10/1/30	214.14	9.24	4.5
DJIA 1950 TO APRIL 2013							
10/13/08	9387.61	936.42	11.1	10/13/08	9387.61	936.42	11.1
10/28/08	9065.12	889.35	10.9	10/28/08	9065.12	889.35	10.9
10/21/87	2027.85	186.84	10.2	11/13/08	8835.25	552.59	6.7
3/23/09	7775.86	497.48	6.8	3/16/00	10630.60	499.19	4.9
11/13/08	8835.25	552.59	6.7	3/23/09	7775.86	497.48	6.8
11/21/08	8046.42	494.13	6.5	11/21/08	8046.42	494.13	6.5
7/24/02	8191.29	488.95	6.4	11/30/11	12045.68	490.05	4.2
10/20/87	1841.01	102.27	5.9	7/24/02	8191.29	488.95	6.4
3/10/09	6926.49	379.44	5.8	9/30/08	10850.66	485.21	4.7
7/29/02	8711.88	447.49	5.4	7/29/02	8711.88	447.49	5.4
S&P 500 1930 TO APRIL 2013							
3/15/33	6.81	0.97	16.6	10/13/08	1003.35	104.13	11.6
10/6/31	9.91	1.09	12.4	10/28/08	940.51	91.59	10.8
9/21/32	8.52	0.90	11.8	3/16/00	1458.47	66.32	4.8
10/13/08	1003.35	104.13	11.6	1/3/01	1347.56	64.29	5.0
10/28/08	940.51	91.59	10.8	9/30/08	1166.36	59.97	5.4
2/16/35	10.00	0.94	10.4	11/13/08	911.29	58.99	6.9
8/17/35	11.70	1.08	10.2	3/23/09	822.92	54.38	7.1
3/16/35	9.05	0.82	10.0	3/18/08	1330.74	54.14	4.2
9/12/38	12.06	1.06	9.6	8/9/11	1172.53	53.07	4.7
9/5/39	12.64	1.11	9.6	8/11/11	1172.64	51.88	4.6
NASDAQ 1971 TO APRIL 2013							
1/3/01	2616.69	324.83	14.2	1/3/01	2616.69	324.83	14.2
10/13/08	1844.25	194.74	11.8	12/5/00	2889.80	274.05	10.5
12/5/00	2889.80	274.05	10.5	4/18/00	3793.57	254.41	7.2
10/28/08	1649.47	143.57	9.5	5/30/00	3459.48	254.37	7.9
4/5/01	1785.00	146.20	8.9	10/19/00	3418.60	247.04	7.8
4/18/01	2079.44	156.22	8.1	10/13/00	3316.77	242.09	7.9
5/30/00	3459.48	254.37	7.9	6/2/00	3813.38	230.88	6.4
10/13/00	3316.77	242.09	7.9	4/25/00	3711.23	228.75	6.6
10/19/00	3418.60	247.04	7.8	4/17/00	3539.16	217.87	6.6
5/8/02	1696.29	122.47	7.8	10/13/08	1844.25	194.74	11.8
RUSSELL 1000 1979 TO APRIL 2013							
10/13/08	542.98	56.75	11.7	10/13/08	542.98	56.75	11.7
10/28/08	503.74	47.68	10.5	10/28/08	503.74	47.68	10.5
10/21/87	135.85	11.15	8.9	3/16/00	777.86	36.60	4.9
3/23/09	446.90	29.36	7.0	1/3/01	712.63	35.74	5.3
11/13/08	489.83	31.99	7.0	11/13/08	489.83	31.99	7.0
11/24/08	456.14	28.26	6.6	9/30/08	634.08	31.74	5.3
3/10/09	391.01	23.46	6.4	8/9/11	647.85	30.57	5.0
11/21/08	427.88	24.97	6.2	12/5/00	728.44	30.36	4.4
7/24/02	448.05	23.87	5.6	3/23/09	446.90	29.36	7.0
7/29/02	477.61	24.69	5.5	8/11/11	649.44	29.14	4.7
RUSSELL 2000 1979 TO APRIL 2013							
10/13/08	570.89	48.41	9.3	10/13/08	570.89	48.41	9.3
11/13/08	491.23	38.43	8.5	9/18/08	723.68	47.30	7.0
3/23/09	433.72	33.61	8.4	8/9/11	696.16	45.20	6.9
10/21/87	130.65	9.26	7.6	11/30/11	737.42	41.32	5.9
10/28/08	482.55	34.15	7.6	10/4/11	648.64	39.15	6.4
11/24/08	436.80	30.26	7.4	11/13/08	491.23	38.43	8.5
3/10/09	367.75	24.49	7.1	10/27/11	765.43	38.28	5.3
9/18/08	723.68	47.30	7.0	5/10/10	689.61	36.61	5.6
8/9/11	696.16	45.20	6.9	8/11/11	695.89	35.68	5.4
10/16/08	536.57	34.46	6.9	10/16/08	536.57	34.46	6.9

10 <u>WORST</u> DAYS BY PERCENT AND POINT

	BY PERCENT CHANGE				BY POINT CHANGE		
DAY	CLOSE	PNT CHANGE	% CHANGE	DAY	CLOSE	PNT CHANGE	% CHANGE
DJIA 1901 to 1949							
10/28/29	260.64	–38.33	–12.8	10/28/29	260.64	–38.33	–12.8
10/29/08	230.07	–30.57	–11.7	10/29/29	230.07	–30.57	–11.7
11/6/29	232.13	–25.55	–9.9	11/6/29	232.13	–25.55	–9.9
8/12/32	63.11	–5.79	–8.4	10/23/29	305.85	–20.66	–6.3
3/14/07	55.84	–5.05	–8.3	11/11/29	220.39	–16.14	–6.8
7/21/33	88.71	–7.55	–7.8	11/4/29	257.68	–15.83	–5.8
10/18/37	125.73	–10.57	–7.8	12/12/29	243.14	–15.30	–5.9
2/1/17	88.52	–6.91	–7.2	10/3/29	329.95	–14.55	–4.2
10/5/32	66.07	–5.09	–7.2	6/16/30	230.05	–14.20	–5.8
9/24/31	107.79	–8.20	–7.1	8/9/29	337.99	–14.11	–4.0
DJIA 1950 to APRIL 2013							
10/19/87	1738.74	–508.00	–22.6	9/29/08	10365.45	–777.68	–7.0
10/26/87	1793.93	–156.83	–8.0	10/15/08	8577.91	–733.08	–7.9
10/15/08	8577.91	–733.08	–7.9	9/17/01	8920.70	–684.81	–7.1
12/1/08	8149.09	–679.95	–7.7	12/1/08	8149.09	–679.95	–7.7
10/9/08	8579.19	–678.91	–7.3	10/9/08	8579.19	–678.91	–7.3
10/27/97	7161.15	–554.26	–7.2	8/8/11	10809.85	–634.76	–5.6
9/17/01	8920.70	–684.81	–7.1	4/14/00	10305.77	–617.78	–5.7
9/29/08	10365.45	–777.68	–7.0	10/27/97	7161.15	–554.26	–7.2
10/13/89	2569.26	–190.58	–6.9	8/10/11	10719.94	–519.83	–4.6
1/8/88	1911.31	–140.58	–6.9	10/22/08	8519.21	–514.45	–5.7
S&P 500 1930 to APRIL 2013							
10/19/87	224.84	–57.86	–20.5	9/29/08	1106.39	–106.62	–8.8
3/18/35	8.14	–0.91	–10.1	10/15/08	907.84	–90.17	–9.0
4/16/35	8.22	–0.91	–10.0	4/14/00	1356.56	–83.95	–5.8
9/3/46	15.00	–1.65	–9.9	12/1/08	816.21	–80.03	–8.9
10/18/37	10.76	–1.10	–9.3	8/8/11	1119.46	–79.92	–6.7
10/15/08	907.84	–90.17	–9.0	10/9/08	909.92	–75.02	–7.6
12/1/08	816.21	–80.03	–8.9	8/31/98	957.28	–69.86	–6.8
7/20/33	10.57	–1.03	–8.9	10/27/97	876.99	–64.65	–6.9
9/29/08	1106.39	–106.62	–8.8	10/7/08	996.23	–60.66	–5.7
7/21/33	9.65	–0.92	–8.7	8/4/11	1200.07	–60.27	–4.8
NASDAQ 1971 to APRIL 2013							
10/19/87	360.21	–46.12	–11.4	4/14/00	3321.29	–355.49	–9.7
4/14/00	3321.29	–355.49	–9.7	4/3/00	4223.68	–349.15	–7.6
9/29/08	1983.73	–199.61	–9.1	4/12/00	3769.63	–286.27	–7.1
10/26/87	298.90	–29.55	–9.0	4/10/00	4188.20	–258.25	–5.8
10/20/87	327.79	–32.42	–9.0	1/4/00	3901.69	–229.46	–5.6
12/1/08	1398.07	–137.50	–9.0	3/14/00	4706.63	–200.61	–4.1
8/31/98	1499.25	–140.43	–8.6	5/10/00	3384.73	–200.28	–5.6
10/15/08	1628.33	–150.68	–8.5	5/23/00	3164.55	–199.66	–5.9
4/3/00	4223.68	–349.15	–7.6	9/29/08	1983.73	–199.61	–9.1
1/2/01	2291.86	–178.66	–7.2	10/25/00	3229.57	–190.22	–5.6
RUSSELL 1000 1979 to APRIL 2013							
10/19/87	121.04	–28.40	–19.0	9/29/08	602.34	–57.35	–8.7
10/15/08	489.71	–49.11	–9.1	10/15/08	489.71	–49.11	–9.1
12/1/08	437.75	–43.68	–9.1	4/14/00	715.20	–45.74	–6.0
9/29/08	602.34	–57.35	–8.7	8/8/11	617.28	–45.56	–6.9
10/26/87	119.45	–10.74	–8.3	12/1/08	437.75	–43.68	–9.1
10/9/08	492.13	–40.05	–7.5	10/9/08	492.13	–40.05	–7.5
8/8/11	617.28	–45.56	–6.9	8/31/98	496.66	–35.77	–6.7
11/20/08	402.91	–29.62	–6.9	8/4/11	664.65	–34.92	–5.0
8/31/98	496.66	–35.77	–6.7	10/27/97	465.44	–32.96	–6.6
10/27/97	465.44	–32.96	–6.6	10/7/08	538.15	–32.64	–5.7
RUSSELL 2000 1979 to APRIL 2013							
10/19/87	133.60	–19.14	–12.5	8/8/11	650.96	–63.67	–8.9
12/1/08	417.07	–56.07	–11.9	12/1/08	417.07	–56.07	–11.9
10/15/08	502.11	–52.54	–9.5	10/15/08	502.11	–52.54	–9.5
10/26/87	110.33	–11.26	–9.3	10/9/08	499.20	–47.37	–8.7
10/20/87	121.39	–12.21	–9.1	9/29/08	657.72	–47.07	–6.7
8/8/11	650.96	–63.67	–8.9	8/4/11	726.80	–45.98	–6.0
10/9/08	499.20	–47.37	–8.7	8/18/11	662.51	–41.52	–5.9
11/19/08	412.38	–35.13	–7.9	10/7/08	558.95	–36.96	–6.2
4/14/00	453.72	–35.50	–7.3	11/9/11	718.86	–36.41	–4.8
11/14/08	456.52	–34.71	–7.1	8/10/11	660.21	–35.95	–5.2

10 BEST WEEKS BY PERCENT AND POINT

	BY PERCENT CHANGE				BY POINT CHANGE		
WEEK ENDS	CLOSE	PNT CHANGE	% CHANGE	WEEK ENDS	CLOSE	PNT CHANGE	% CHANGE
DJIA 1901 to 1949							
8/6/32	66.56	12.30	22.7	12/7/29	263.46	24.51	10.3
6/25/38	131.94	18.71	16.5	6/25/38	131.94	18.71	16.5
2/13/32	85.82	11.37	15.3	6/27/31	156.93	17.97	12.9
4/22/33	72.24	9.36	14.9	11/22/29	245.74	17.01	7.4
10/10/31	105.61	12.84	13.8	8/17/29	360.70	15.86	4.6
7/30/32	54.26	6.42	13.4	12/22/28	285.94	15.22	5.6
6/27/31	156.93	17.97	12.9	8/24/29	375.44	14.74	4.1
9/24/32	74.83	8.39	12.6	2/21/29	310.06	14.21	4.8
8/27/32	75.61	8.43	12.6	5/10/30	272.01	13.70	5.3
3/18/33	60.56	6.72	12.5	11/15/30	186.68	13.54	7.8
DJIA 1950 to APRIL 2013							
10/11/74	658.17	73.61	12.6	10/31/08	9325.01	946.06	11.3
10/31/08	9325.01	946.06	11.3	12/2/11	12019.42	787.64	7.0
8/20/82	869.29	81.24	10.3	11/28/08	8829.04	782.62	9.7
11/28/08	8829.04	782.62	9.7	3/17/00	10595.23	666.41	6.7
3/13/09	7223.98	597.04	9.0	3/21/03	8521.97	662.26	8.4
10/8/82	986.85	79.11	8.7	7/1/11	12582.77	648.19	5.4
3/21/03	8521.97	662.26	8.4	9/28/01	8847.56	611.75	7.4
8/3/84	1202.08	87.46	7.9	7/17/09	8743.94	597.42	7.3
9/28/01	8847.56	611.75	7.4	3/13/09	7223.98	597.04	9.0
7/17/09	8743.94	597.42	7.3	7/2/99	11139.24	586.68	5.6
S&P 500 1930 to APRIL 2013							
8/6/32	7.22	1.12	18.4	6/2/00	1477.26	99.24	7.2
6/25/38	11.39	1.72	17.8	11/28/08	896.24	96.21	12.0
7/30/32	6.10	0.89	17.1	10/31/08	968.75	91.98	10.5
4/22/33	7.75	1.09	16.4	12/2/11	1244.28	85.61	7.4
10/11/74	71.14	8.80	14.1	4/20/00	1434.54	77.98	5.8
2/13/32	8.80	1.08	14.0	7/2/99	1391.22	75.91	5.8
9/24/32	8.52	1.02	13.6	3/3/00	1409.17	75.81	5.7
10/10/31	10.64	1.27	13.6	9/28/01	1040.94	75.14	7.8
8/27/32	8.57	1.01	13.4	3/13/09	756.55	73.17	10.7
3/18/33	6.61	0.77	13.2	10/16/98	1056.42	72.10	7.3
NASDAQ 1971 to APRIL 2013							
6/2/00	3813.38	608.27	19.0	6/2/00	3813.38	608.27	19.0
4/12/01	1961.43	241.07	14.0	2/4/00	4244.14	357.07	9.2
11/28/08	1535.57	151.22	10.9	3/3/00	4914.79	324.29	7.1
10/31/08	1720.95	168.92	10.9	4/20/00	3643.88	322.59	9.7
3/13/09	1431.50	137.65	10.6	12/8/00	2917.43	272.14	10.3
4/20/01	2163.41	201.98	10.3	4/12/01	1961.43	241.07	14.0
12/8/00	2917.43	272.14	10.3	7/14/00	4246.18	222.98	5.5
4/20/00	3643.88	322.59	9.7	1/12/01	2626.50	218.85	9.1
10/11/74	60.42	5.26	9.5	4/28/00	3860.66	216.78	6.0
2/4/00	4244.14	357.07	9.0	12/23/99	3969.44	216.38	5.8
RUSSELL 1000 1979 to APRIL 2013							
11/28/08	481.43	53.55	12.5	6/2/00	785.02	57.93	8.0
10/31/08	522.47	50.94	10.8	11/28/08	481.43	53.55	12.5
3/13/09	411.10	39.88	10.7	10/31/08	522.47	50.94	10.8
8/20/82	61.51	4.83	8.5	12/2/11	687.44	47.63	7.4
6/2/00	785.02	57.93	8.0	4/20/00	757.32	42.12	5.9
9/28/01	546.46	38.48	7.6	3/3/00	756.41	41.55	5.8
10/16/98	546.09	38.45	7.6	3/13/09	411.10	39.88	10.7
8/3/84	87.43	6.13	7.5	7/1/11	745.21	39.46	5.6
12/2/11	687.44	47.63	7.4	10/14/11	675.52	38.87	6.1
3/21/03	474.58	32.69	7.4	7/2/99	723.25	38.80	5.7
RUSSELL 2000 1979 to APRIL 2013							
11/28/08	473.14	66.60	16.4	12/2/11	735.02	68.86	10.3
10/31/08	537.52	66.40	14.1	11/28/08	473.14	66.60	16.4
6/2/00	513.03	55.66	12.2	10/31/08	537.52	66.40	14.1
3/13/09	393.09	42.04	12.0	10/14/11	712.46	56.25	8.6
12/2/11	735.02	68.86	10.3	6/2/00	513.03	55.66	12.2
10/14/11	712.46	56.25	8.6	10/28/11	761.00	48.58	6.8
7/17/09	519.22	38.24	8.0	1/4/13	879.15	47.05	5.7
10/16/98	342.87	24.47	7.7	7/1/11	840.04	42.25	5.3
12/18/87	116.94	8.31	7.7	3/13/09	393.09	42.04	12.0
3/3/00	597.88	41.14	7.4	2/1/08	730.50	41.90	6.1

10 <u>WORST</u> WEEKS BY PERCENT AND POINT

	BY PERCENT CHANGE				BY POINT CHANGE		
WEEK ENDS	CLOSE	PNT CHANGE	% CHANGE	WEEK ENDS	CLOSE	PNT CHANGE	% CHANGE
DJIA 1901 to 1949							
7/22/33	88.42	−17.68	−16.7	11/8/29	236.53	−36.98	−13.5
5/18/40	122.43	−22.42	−15.5	12/8/28	257.33	−33.47	−11.5
10/8/32	61.17	−10.92	−15.2	6/21/30	215.30	−28.95	−11.9
10/3/31	92.77	−14.59	−13.6	10/19/29	323.87	−28.82	−8.2
11/8/29	236.53	−36.98	−13.5	5/3/30	258.31	−27.15	−9.5
9/17/32	66.44	−10.10	−13.2	10/31/29	273.51	−25.46	−8.5
10/21/33	83.64	−11.95	−12.5	10/26/29	298.97	−24.90	−7.7
12/12/31	78.93	−11.21	−12.4	5/18/40	122.43	−22.42	−15.5
5/8/15	62.77	−8.74	−12.2	2/8/29	301.53	−18.23	−5.7
6/21/30	215.30	−28.95	−11.9	10/11/30	193.05	−18.05	−8.6
DJIA 1950 to APRIL 2013							
10/10/08	8451.19	−1874.19	−18.2	10/10/08	8451.19	−1874.19	−18.2
9/21/01	8235.81	−1369.70	−14.3	9/21/01	8235.81	−1369.70	−14.3
10/23/87	1950.76	−295.98	−13.2	3/16/01	9823.41	−821.21	−7.7
10/16/87	2246.74	−235.47	−9.5	10/3/08	10325.38	−817.75	−7.3
10/13/89	2569.26	−216.26	−7.8	4/14/00	10305.77	−805.71	−7.3
3/16/01	9823.41	−821.21	−7.7	9/23/11	10771.48	−737.61	−6.4
7/19/02	8019.26	−665.27	−7.7	8/5/11	11444.61	−698.63	−5.8
12/4/87	1766.74	−143.74	−7.5	7/12/02	8684.53	−694.97	−7.4
9/13/74	627.19	−50.69	−7.5	7/19/02	8019.26	−665.27	−7.7
9/12/86	1758.72	−141.03	−7.4	10/15/99	10019.71	−630.05	−5.9
S&P 500 1930 to APRIL 2013							
7/22/33	9.71	−2.20	−18.5	10/10/08	899.22	−200.01	−18.2
10/10/08	899.22	−200.01	−18.2	4/14/00	1356.56	−159.79	−10.5
5/18/40	9.75	−2.05	−17.4	9/21/01	965.80	−126.74	−11.6
10/8/32	6.77	−1.38	−16.9	10/3/08	1099.23	−113.78	−9.4
9/17/32	7.50	−1.28	−14.6	8/5/11	1199.38	−92.90	−7.2
10/21/33	8.57	−1.31	−13.3	10/15/99	1247.41	−88.61	−6.6
10/3/31	9.37	−1.36	−12.7	3/16/01	1150.53	−82.89	−6.7
10/23/87	248.22	−34.48	−12.2	1/28/00	1360.16	−81.20	−5.6
12/12/31	8.20	−1.13	−12.1	9/23/11	1136.43	−79.58	−6.5
3/26/38	9.20	−1.21	−11.6	1/18/08	1325.19	−75.83	−5.4
NASDAQ 1971 to APRIL 2013							
4/14/00	3321.29	−1125.16	−25.3	4/14/00	3321.29	−1125.16	−25.3
10/23/87	328.45	−77.88	−19.2	7/28/00	3663.00	−431.45	−10.5
9/21/01	1423.19	−272.19	−16.1	11/10/00	3028.99	−422.59	−12.2
10/10/08	1649.51	−297.88	−15.3	3/31/00	4572.83	−390.20	−7.9
11/10/00	3028.99	−422.59	−12.2	1/28/00	3887.07	−348.33	−8.2
10/3/08	1947.39	−235.95	−10.8	10/6/00	3361.01	−311.81	−8.5
7/28/00	3663.00	−431.45	−10.5	10/10/08	1649.51	−297.88	−15.3
10/24/08	1552.03	−159.26	−9.3	5/12/00	3529.06	−287.76	−7.5
12/15/00	2653.27	−264.16	−9.1	9/21/01	1423.19	−272.19	−16.1
12/1/00	2645.29	−259.09	−8.9	12/15/00	2653.27	−264.16	−9.1
RUSSELL 1000 1979 to APRIL 2013							
10/10/08	486.23	−108.31	−18.2	10/10/08	486.23	−108.31	−18.2
10/23/87	130.19	−19.25	−12.9	4/14/00	715.20	−90.39	−11.2
9/21/01	507.98	−67.59	−11.7	9/21/01	507.98	−67.59	−11.7
4/14/00	715.20	−90.39	−11.2	10/3/08	594.54	−65.15	−9.9
10/3/08	594.54	−65.15	−9.9	8/5/11	662.84	−54.93	−7.7
10/16/87	149.44	−14.42	−8.8	9/23/11	627.56	−45.42	−6.8
11/21/08	427.88	−41.15	−8.8	10/15/99	646.79	−43.89	−6.4
9/12/86	124.95	−10.87	−8.0	3/16/01	605.71	−43.88	−6.8
8/5/11	662.84	−54.93	−7.7	5/7/10	611.63	−43.43	−6.6
7/19/02	450.64	−36.13	−7.4	7/27/07	793.72	−41.97	−5.0
RUSSELL 2000 1979 to APRIL 2013							
10/23/87	121.59	−31.15	−20.4	10/10/08	522.48	−96.92	−15.7
4/14/00	453.72	−89.27	−16.4	4/14/00	453.72	−89.27	−16.4
10/10/08	522.48	−96.92	−15.7	10/3/08	619.40	−85.39	−12.1
9/21/01	378.89	−61.84	−14.0	8/5/11	714.63	−82.40	−10.3
10/3/08	619.40	−85.39	−12.1	5/7/10	653.00	−63.60	−8.9
11/21/08	406.54	−49.98	−11.0	9/23/11	652.43	−61.88	−8.7
10/24/08	471.12	−55.31	−10.5	9/21/01	378.89	−61.84	−14.0
8/5/11	714.63	−82.40	−10.3	7/27/07	777.83	−58.61	−7.0
3/6/09	351.05	−37.97	−9.8	10/24/08	471.12	−55.31	−10.5
11/14/08	456.52	−49.27	−9.7	11/25/11	666.16	−53.26	−7.4

164

10 **BEST** MONTHS BY PERCENT AND POINT

	BY PERCENT CHANGE				BY POINT CHANGE		
MONTH	CLOSE	PNT CHANGE	% CHANGE	MONTH	CLOSE	PNT CHANGE	% CHANGE
DJIA 1901 to 1949							
APR-1933	77.66	22.26	40.2	NOV-1928	293.38	41.22	16.3
AUG-1932	73.16	18.90	34.8	JUN-1929	333.79	36.38	12.2
JUL-1932	54.26	11.42	26.7	AUG-1929	380.33	32.63	9.4
JUN-1938	133.88	26.14	24.3	JUN-1938	133.88	26.14	24.3
APR-1915	71.78	10.95	18.0	AUG-1928	240.41	24.41	11.3
JUN-1931	150.18	21.72	16.9	APR-1933	77.66	22.26	40.2
NOV-1928	293.38	41.22	16.3	FEB-1931	189.66	22.11	13.2
NOV-1904	52.76	6.59	14.3	JUN-1931	150.18	21.72	16.9
MAY-1919	105.50	12.62	13.6	AUG-1932	73.16	18.90	34.8
SEP-1939	152.54	18.13	13.5	JAN-1930	267.14	18.66	7.5
DJIA 1950 to APRIL 2013							
JAN-1976	975.28	122.87	14.4	OCT-2011	11955.01	1041.63	9.5
JAN-1975	703.69	87.45	14.2	APR-1999	10789.04	1002.88	10.2
JAN-1987	2158.04	262.09	13.8	APR-2001	10734.97	856.19	8.7
AUG-1982	901.31	92.71	11.5	OCT-2002	8397.03	805.10	10.6
OCT-1982	991.72	95.47	10.7	MAR-2000	10921.92	793.61	7.8
OCT-2002	8397.03	805.10	10.6	NOV-2001	9851.56	776.42	8.6
APR-1978	837.32	79.96	10.6	SEP-2010	10788.05	773.33	7.7
APR-1999	10789.04	1002.88	10.2	JAN-2013	13860.58	756.44	5.8
NOV-1962	649.30	59.53	10.1	OCT-1998	8592.10	749.48	9.6
NOV-1954	386.77	34.63	9.8	JUL-2009	9171.61	724.61	8.6
S&P 500 1930 to APRIL 2013							
APR-1933	8.32	2.47	42.2	MAR-2000	1498.58	132.16	9.7
JUL-1932	6.10	1.67	37.7	OCT-2011	1253.30	121.88	10.8
AUG-1932	8.39	2.29	37.5	SEP-2010	1141.20	91.87	8.8
JUN-1938	11.56	2.29	24.7	APR-2001	1249.46	89.13	7.7
SEP-1939	13.02	1.84	16.5	AUG-2000	1517.68	86.85	6.1
OCT-1974	73.90	10.36	16.3	OCT-1998	1098.67	81.66	8.0
MAY-1933	9.64	1.32	15.9	DEC-1999	1469.25	80.34	5.8
APR-1938	9.70	1.20	14.1	OCT-1997	1362.93	80.22	6.3
JUN-1931	14.83	1.81	13.9	NOV-2001	1139.45	79.67	7.5
JAN-1987	274.08	31.91	13.2	DEC-2010	1257.64	77.09	6.5
NASDAQ 1971 to APRIL 2013							
DEC-1999	4069.31	733.15	22.0	FEB-2000	4696.69	756.34	19.2
FEB-2000	4696.69	756.34	19.2	DEC-1999	4069.31	733.15	22.0
OCT-1974	65.23	9.56	17.2	JUN-2000	3966.11	565.20	16.6
JAN-1975	69.78	9.96	16.6	AUG-2000	4206.35	439.36	11.7
JUN-2000	3966.11	565.20	16.6	NOV-1999	3336.16	369.73	12.5
APR-2001	2116.24	275.98	15.0	JAN-1999	2505.89	313.20	14.3
JAN-1999	2505.89	313.20	14.3	JAN-2001	2772.73	302.21	12.2
NOV-2001	1930.58	240.38	14.2	APR-2001	2116.24	275.98	15.0
OCT-2002	1329.75	157.69	13.5	OCT-2011	2684.41	269.01	11.1
OCT-1982	212.63	24.98	13.3	SEP-2010	2368.62	254.59	12.0
RUSSELL 1000 1979 to APRIL 2013							
JAN-1987	146.48	16.48	12.7	OCT-2011	692.41	68.96	11.1
OCT-1982	73.34	7.45	11.3	MAR-2000	797.99	64.95	8.9
AUG-1982	65.14	6.60	11.3	AUG-2000	811.17	55.60	7.4
DEC-1991	220.61	22.15	11.2	SEP-2010	629.78	52.10	9.0
OCT-2011	692.41	68.96	11.1	APR-2001	658.90	48.54	8.0
AUG-1984	89.87	8.74	10.8	OCT-1999	707.19	43.36	6.5
NOV-1980	78.26	7.18	10.1	DEC-1999	767.97	43.31	6.0
APR-2009	476.84	43.17	10.0	APR-2009	476.84	43.17	10.0
SEP-2010	629.78	52.10	9.0	DEC-2010	696.90	42.66	6.5
MAY-1990	187.66	15.34	8.0	NOV-2001	599.32	42.03	7.0
RUSSELL 2000 1979 to APRIL 2013							
FEB-2000	577.71	81.48	16.4	OCT-2011	741.06	96.90	15.0
APR-2009	487.56	64.81	15.3	FEB-2000	577.71	81.48	16.4
OCT-2011	741.06	96.90	15.0	SEP-2010	676.14	74.08	12.3
OCT-1982	80.86	10.02	14.1	APR-2009	487.56	64.81	15.3
JAN-1985	114.77	13.28	13.1	JAN-2006	733.20	59.98	8.9
SEP-2010	676.14	74.08	12.3	DEC-2010	783.65	56.64	7.8
AUG-1984	106.21	10.96	11.5	JAN-2013	902.09	52.74	6.2
JAN-1987	150.48	15.48	11.5	JAN-2012	792.82	51.90	7.0
DEC-1999	504.75	50.67	11.2	DEC-1999	504.75	50.67	11.2
JUL-1980	63.81	6.34	11.0	MAR-2010	678.64	50.08	8.0

10 <u>WORST</u> MONTHS BY PERCENT AND POINT

	BY PERCENT CHANGE				BY POINT CHANGE		
MONTH	CLOSE	PNT CHANGE	% CHANGE	MONTH	CLOSE	PNT CHANGE	% CHANGE
DJIA 1901 to 1949							
SEP-1931	96.61	−42.80	−30.7	OCT-1929	273.51	−69.94	−20.4
MAR-1938	98.95	−30.69	−23.7	JUN-1930	226.34	−48.73	−17.7
APR-1932	56.11	−17.17	−23.4	SEP-1931	96.61	−42.80	−30.7
MAY-1940	116.22	−32.21	−21.7	SEP-1929	343.45	−36.88	−9.7
OCT-1929	273.51	−69.94	−20.4	SEP-1930	204.90	−35.52	−14.8
MAY-1932	44.74	−11.37	−20.3	NOV-1929	238.95	−34.56	−12.6
JUN-1930	226.34	−48.73	−17.7	MAY-1940	116.22	−32.21	−21.7
DEC-1931	77.90	−15.97	−17.0	MAR-1938	98.95	−30.69	−23.7
FEB-1933	51.39	−9.51	−15.6	SEP-1937	154.57	−22.84	−12.9
MAY-1931	128.46	−22.73	−15.0	MAY-1931	128.46	−22.73	−15.0
DJIA 1950 to APRIL 2013							
OCT-1987	1993.53	−602.75	−23.2	OCT-2008	9325.01	−1525.65	−14.1
AUG-1998	7539.07	−1344.22	−15.1	AUG-1998	7539.07	−1344.22	−15.1
OCT-2008	9325.01	−1525.65	−14.1	JUN-2008	11350.01	−1288.31	−10.2
NOV-1973	822.25	−134.33	−14.0	SEP-2001	8847.56	−1102.19	−11.1
SEP-2002	7591.93	−1071.57	−12.4	SEP-2002	7591.93	−1071.57	−12.4
FEB-2009	7062.93	−937.93	−11.7	FEB-2009	7062.93	−937.93	−11.7
SEP-2001	8847.56	−1102.19	−11.1	MAY-2010	10136.63	−871.98	−7.9
SEP-1974	607.87	−70.71	−10.4	MAY-2012	12393.45	−820.18	−6.2
AUG-1974	678.58	−78.85	−10.4	FEB-2000	10128.31	−812.22	−7.4
JUN-2008	11350.01	−1288.31	−10.2	JAN-2009	8000.86	−775.53	−8.8
S&P 500 1930 to APRIL 2013							
SEP-1931	9.71	−4.15	−29.9	OCT-2008	968.75	−197.61	−16.9
MAR-1938	8.50	−2.84	−25.0	AUG-1998	957.28	−163.39	−14.6
MAY-1940	9.27	−2.92	−24.0	FEB-2001	1239.94	−126.07	−9.2
MAY-1932	4.47	−1.36	−23.3	JUN-2008	1280.00	−120.38	−8.6
OCT-1987	251.79	−70.04	−21.8	SEP-2008	1166.36	−116.47	−9.1
APR-1932	5.83	−1.48	−20.2	NOV-2000	1314.95	−114.45	−8.0
FEB-1933	5.66	−1.28	−18.4	SEP-2002	815.28	−100.79	−11.0
OCT-2008	968.75	−197.61	−16.9	MAY-2010	1089.41	−97.28	−8.2
JUN-1930	20.46	−4.03	−16.5	SEP-2001	1040.94	−92.64	−8.2
AUG-1998	957.28	−163.39	−14.6	FEB-2009	735.09	−90.79	−11.0
NASDAQ 1971 to APRIL 2013							
OCT-1987	323.30	−120.99	−27.2	NOV-2000	2597.93	−771.70	−22.9
NOV-2000	2597.93	−771.70	−22.9	APR-2000	3860.66	−712.17	−15.6
FEB-2001	2151.83	−620.90	−22.4	FEB-2001	2151.83	−620.90	−22.4
AUG-1998	1499.25	−373.14	−19.9	SEP-2000	3672.82	−533.53	−12.7
OCT-2008	1720.95	−370.93	−17.7	MAY-2000	3400.91	−459.75	−11.9
MAR-1980	131.00	−27.03	−17.1	AUG-1998	1499.25	−373.14	−19.9
SEP-2001	1498.80	−306.63	−17.0	OCT-2008	1720.95	−370.93	−17.7
OCT-1978	111.12	−21.77	−16.4	MAR-2001	1840.26	−311.57	−14.5
APR-2000	3860.66	−712.17	−15.6	SEP-2001	1498.80	−306.63	−17.0
NOV-1973	93.51	−16.66	−15.1	OCT-2000	3369.63	−303.19	−8.3
RUSSELL 1000 1979 to APRIL 2013							
OCT-1987	131.89	−36.94	−21.9	OCT-2008	522.47	−111.61	−17.6
OCT-2008	522.47	−111.61	−17.6	AUG-1998	496.66	−88.31	−15.1
AUG-1998	496.66	−88.31	−15.1	NOV-2000	692.40	−70.66	−9.3
MAR-1980	55.79	−7.28	−11.5	FEB-2001	654.25	−68.30	−9.5
SEP-2002	433.22	−52.86	−10.9	SEP-2008	634.08	−68.09	−9.7
FEB-2009	399.61	−47.71	−10.7	JUN-2008	703.22	−65.06	−8.5
SEP-2008	634.08	−68.09	−9.7	MAY-2010	601.79	−53.27	−8.1
AUG-1990	166.69	−17.63	−9.6	SEP-2002	433.22	−52.86	−10.9
FEB-2001	654.25	−68.30	−9.5	SEP-2011	623.45	−51.34	−7.6
NOV-2000	692.40	−70.66	−9.3	SEP-2001	546.46	−51.21	−8.6
RUSSELL 2000 1979 to APRIL 2013							
OCT-1987	118.26	−52.55	−30.8	OCT-2008	537.52	−142.06	−20.9
OCT-2008	537.52	−142.06	−20.9	SEP-2011	644.16	−82.65	−11.4
AUG-1998	337.95	−81.80	−19.5	AUG-1998	337.95	−81.80	−19.5
MAR-1980	48.27	−10.95	−18.5	JUL-2002	392.42	−70.22	−15.2
JUL-2002	392.42	−70.22	−15.2	AUG-2011	726.81	−70.22	−8.8
AUG-1990	139.52	−21.99	−13.6	NOV-2008	473.14	−64.38	−12.0
SEP-2001	404.87	−63.69	−13.6	SEP-2001	404.87	−63.69	−13.6
FEB-2009	389.02	−54.51	−12.3	NOV-2007	767.77	−60.25	−7.3
NOV-2008	473.14	−64.38	−12.0	SEP-2008	679.58	−59.92	−8.1
SEP-2011	644.16	−82.65	−11.4	JUN-2008	689.66	−58.62	−7.8

10 <u>BEST</u> QUARTERS BY PERCENT AND POINT

	BY PERCENT CHANGE				BY POINT CHANGE		
QUARTER	CLOSE	PNT CHANGE	% CHANGE	QUARTER	CLOSE	PNT CHANGE	% CHANGE
			DJIA 1901 to 1949				
JUN-1933	98.14	42.74	77.1	DEC-1928	300.00	60.57	25.3
SEP-1932	71.56	28.72	67.0	JUN-1933	98.14	42.74	77.1
JUN-1938	133.88	34.93	35.3	MAR-1930	286.10	37.62	15.1
SEP-1915	90.58	20.52	29.3	JUN-1938	133.88	34.93	35.3
DEC-1928	300.00	60.57	25.3	SEP-1927	197.59	31.36	18.9
DEC-1904	50.99	8.80	20.9	SEP-1928	239.43	28.88	13.7
JUN-1919	106.98	18.13	20.4	SEP-1932	71.56	28.72	67.0
SEP-1927	197.59	31.36	18.9	JUN-1929	333.79	24.94	8.1
DEC-1905	70.47	10.47	17.4	SEP-1939	152.54	21.91	16.8
JUN-1935	118.21	17.40	17.3	SEP-1915	90.58	20.52	29.3
			DJIA 1950 to APRIL 2013				
MAR-1975	768.15	151.91	24.7	MAR-2013	14578.54	1474.40	11.3
MAR-1987	2304.69	408.74	21.6	DEC-1998	9181.43	1338.81	17.1
MAR-1986	1818.61	271.94	17.6	DEC-2011	12217.56	1304.18	12.0
MAR-1976	999.45	147.04	17.2	SEP-2009	9712.28	1265.28	15.0
DEC-1998	9181.43	1338.81	17.1	JUN-1999	10970.80	1184.64	12.1
DEC-1982	1046.54	150.29	16.8	DEC-2003	10453.92	1178.86	12.7
JUN-1997	7672.79	1089.31	16.5	DEC-2001	10021.50	1173.94	13.3
DEC-1985	1546.67	218.04	16.4	DEC-1999	11497.12	1160.17	11.2
SEP-2009	9712.28	1265.28	15.0	JUN-1997	7672.79	1089.31	16.5
JUN-1975	878.99	110.84	14.4	JUN-2007	13408.62	1054.27	8.5
			S&P 500 1930 to APRIL 2013				
JUN-1933	10.91	5.06	86.5	DEC-1998	1229.23	212.22	20.9
SEP-1932	8.08	3.65	82.4	DEC-1999	1469.25	186.54	14.5
JUN-1938	11.56	3.06	36.0	MAR-2012	1408.47	150.87	12.0
MAR-1975	83.36	14.80	21.6	MAR-2013	1569.19	143.00	10.0
DEC-1998	1229.23	212.22	20.9	SEP-2009	1057.08	137.76	15.0
JUN-1935	10.23	1.76	20.8	MAR-1998	1101.75	131.32	13.5
MAR-1987	291.70	49.53	20.5	JUN-1997	885.14	128.02	16.9
SEP-1939	13.02	2.16	19.9	DEC-2011	1257.60	126.18	11.2
MAR-1943	11.58	1.81	18.5	JUN-2003	974.50	125.32	14.8
MAR-1930	25.14	3.69	17.2	JUN-2009	919.32	121.45	15.2
			NASDAQ 1971 to APRIL 2013				
DEC-1999	4069.31	1323.15	48.2	DEC-1999	4069.31	1323.15	48.2
DEC-2001	1950.40	451.60	30.1	MAR-2000	4572.83	503.52	12.4
DEC-1998	2192.69	498.85	29.5	DEC-1998	2192.69	498.85	29.5
MAR-1991	482.30	108.46	29.0	MAR-2012	3091.57	486.42	18.7
MAR-1975	75.66	15.84	26.5	DEC-2001	1950.40	451.60	30.1
DEC-1982	232.41	44.76	23.9	JUN-2001	2160.54	320.28	17.4
MAR-1987	430.05	80.72	23.1	JUN-2009	1835.04	306.45	20.0
JUN-2003	1622.80	281.63	21.0	SEP-2009	2122.42	287.38	15.7
JUN-1980	157.78	26.78	20.4	DEC-2010	2652.87	284.25	12.0
JUN-2009	1835.04	306.45	20.0	JUN-2003	1622.80	281.63	21.0
			RUSSELL 1000 1979 to APRIL 2013				
DEC-1998	642.87	113.76	21.5	DEC-1998	642.87	113.76	21.5
MAR-1987	155.20	25.20	19.4	DEC-1999	767.97	104.14	15.7
DEC-1982	77.24	11.35	17.2	MAR-2012	778.92	85.56	12.3
JUN-1997	462.95	64.76	16.3	MAR-2013	872.11	82.21	10.4
DEC-1985	114.39	15.64	15.8	SEP-2009	579.97	77.70	15.5
JUN-2009	502.27	68.60	15.8	DEC-2011	693.36	69.91	11.2
DEC-1999	767.97	104.14	15.7	JUN-2009	502.27	68.60	15.8
SEP-2009	579.97	77.70	15.5	JUN-2003	518.94	68.59	15.2
JUN-2003	518.94	68.59	15.2	DEC-2010	696.90	67.12	10.7
MAR-1991	196.15	24.93	14.6	MAR-1998	580.31	66.52	12.9
			RUSSELL 2000 1979 to APRIL 2013				
MAR-1991	171.01	38.85	29.4	DEC-2010	783.65	107.51	15.9
DEC-1982	88.90	18.06	25.5	MAR-2013	951.54	102.19	12.0
MAR-1987	166.79	31.79	23.5	DEC-2011	740.92	96.76	15.0
JUN-2003	448.37	83.83	23.0	SEP-2009	604.28	96.00	18.9
SEP-1980	69.94	12.47	21.7	MAR-2006	765.14	91.92	13.7
DEC-2001	488.50	83.63	20.7	MAR-2012	830.30	89.38	12.1
JUN-1983	124.17	20.40	19.7	JUN-2009	508.28	85.53	20.2
JUN-1980	57.47	9.20	19.1	JUN-2003	448.37	83.83	23.0
DEC-1999	504.75	77.45	18.1	DEC-2001	488.50	83.63	20.7
SEP-2009	604.28	96.00	18.9	DEC-2004	651.57	78.63	13.7

10 <u>WORST</u> QUARTERS BY PERCENT AND POINT

	BY PERCENT CHANGE				BY POINT CHANGE		
QUARTER	CLOSE	PNT CHANGE	% CHANGE	QUARTER	CLOSE	PNT CHANGE	% CHANGE
DJIA 1901 to 1949							
JUN-1932	42.84	−30.44	−41.5	DEC-1929	248.48	−94.97	−27.7
SEP-1931	96.61	−53.57	−35.7	JUN-1930	226.34	−59.76	−20.9
DEC-1929	248.48	−94.97	−27.7	SEP-1931	96.61	−53.57	−35.7
SEP-1903	33.55	−9.73	−22.5	DEC-1930	164.58	−40.32	−19.7
DEC-1937	120.85	−33.72	−21.8	DEC-1937	120.85	−33.72	−21.8
JUN-1930	226.34	−59.76	−20.9	SEP-1946	172.42	−33.20	−16.1
DEC-1930	164.58	−40.32	−19.7	JUN-1932	42.84	−30.44	−41.5
DEC-1931	77.90	−18.71	−19.4	JUN-1940	121.87	−26.08	−17.6
MAR-1938	98.95	−21.90	−18.1	MAR-1939	131.84	−22.92	−14.8
JUN-1940	121.87	−26.08	−17.6	JUN-1931	150.18	−22.18	−12.9
DJIA 1950 to APRIL 2013							
DEC-1987	1938.83	−657.45	−25.3	DEC-2008	8776.39	−2074.27	−19.1
SEP-1974	607.87	−194.54	−24.2	SEP-2001	8847.56	−1654.84	−15.8
JUN-1962	561.28	−145.67	−20.6	SEP-2002	7591.93	−1651.33	−17.9
DEC-2008	8776.39	−2074.27	−19.1	SEP-2011	10913.38	−1500.96	−12.1
SEP-2002	7591.93	−1651.33	−17.9	MAR-2009	7608.92	−1167.47	−13.3
SEP-2001	8847.56	−1654.84	−15.8	JUN-2002	9243.26	−1160.68	−11.2
SEP-1990	2452.48	−428.21	−14.9	SEP-1998	7842.62	−1109.40	−12.4
MAR-2009	7608.92	−1167.47	−13.3	JUN-2010	9774.02	−1082.61	−10.0
SEP-1981	849.98	−126.90	−13.0	MAR-2008	12262.89	−1001.93	−7.6
JUN-1970	683.53	−102.04	−13.0	JUN-2008	11350.01	−912.88	−7.4
S&P 500 1930 to APRIL 2013							
JUN-1932	4.43	−2.88	−39.4	DEC-2008	903.25	−263.11	−22.6
SEP-1931	9.71	−5.12	−34.5	SEP-2011	1131.42	−189.22	−14.3
SEP-1974	63.54	−22.46	−26.1	SEP-2001	1040.94	−183.48	−15.0
DEC-1937	10.55	−3.21	−23.3	SEP-2002	815.28	−174.54	−17.6
DEC-1987	247.08	−74.75	−23.2	MAR-2001	1160.33	−159.95	−12.1
DEC-2008	903.25	−263.11	−22.6	JUN-2002	989.82	−157.57	−13.7
JUN-1962	54.75	−14.80	−21.3	MAR-2008	1322.70	−145.66	−9.9
MAR-1938	8.50	−2.05	−19.4	JUN-2010	1030.71	−138.72	−11.9
JUN-1970	72.72	−16.91	−18.9	SEP-1998	1017.01	−116.83	−10.3
SEP-1946	14.96	−3.47	−18.8	DEC-2000	1320.28	−116.23	−8.1
NASDAQ 1971 to APRIL 2013							
DEC-2000	2470.52	−1202.30	−32.7	DEC-2000	2470.52	−1202.30	−32.7
SEP-2001	1498.80	−661.74	−30.6	SEP-2001	1498.80	−661.74	−30.6
SEP-1974	55.67	−20.29	−26.7	MAR-2001	1840.26	−630.26	−25.5
DEC-1987	330.47	−113.82	−25.6	JUN-2000	3966.11	−606.72	−13.3
MAR-2001	1840.26	−630.26	−25.5	DEC-2008	1577.03	−514.85	−24.6
SEP-1990	344.51	−117.78	−25.5	JUN-2002	1463.21	−382.14	−20.7
DEC-2008	1577.03	−514.85	−24.6	MAR-2008	2279.10	−373.18	−14.1
JUN-2002	1463.21	−382.14	−20.7	SEP-2011	2415.40	−358.12	−12.9
SEP-2002	1172.06	−291.15	−19.9	SEP-2000	3672.82	−293.29	−7.4
JUN-1974	75.96	−16.31	−17.7	SEP-2002	1172.06	−291.15	−19.9
RUSSELL 1000 1979 to APRIL 2013							
DEC-2008	487.77	−146.31	−23.1	DEC-2008	487.77	−146.31	−23.1
DEC-1987	130.02	−38.81	−23.0	SEP-2011	623.45	−111.03	−15.1
SEP-2002	433.22	−90.50	−17.3	SEP-2001	546.46	−100.18	−15.5
SEP-2001	546.46	−100.18	−15.5	SEP-2002	433.22	−90.50	−17.3
SEP-1990	157.83	−28.46	−15.3	MAR-2001	610.36	−89.73	−12.8
SEP-2011	623.45	−111.03	−15.1	JUN-2002	523.72	−83.63	−13.8
JUN-2002	523.72	−83.63	−13.8	MAR-2008	720.32	−79.50	−9.9
MAR-2001	610.36	−89.73	−12.8	JUN-2010	567.37	−76.42	−11.9
SEP-1981	64.06	−8.95	−12.3	DEC-2000	700.09	−72.51	−9.4
JUN-2010	567.37	−76.42	−11.9	SEP-2008	634.08	−69.14	−9.8
RUSSELL 2000 1979 to APRIL 2013							
DEC-1987	120.42	−50.39	−29.5	SEP-2011	644.16	−183.27	−22.1
DEC-2008	499.45	−180.13	−26.5	DEC-2008	499.45	−180.13	−26.5
SEP-1990	126.70	−42.34	−25.0	SEP-2001	404.87	−107.77	−21.0
SEP-2011	644.16	−183.27	−22.1	SEP-2002	362.27	−100.37	−21.7
SEP-2002	362.27	−100.37	−21.7	SEP-1998	363.59	−93.80	−20.5
SEP-2001	404.87	−107.77	−21.0	MAR-2008	687.97	−78.06	−10.2
SEP-1998	363.59	−93.80	−20.5	MAR-2009	422.75	−76.70	−15.4
SEP-1981	67.55	−15.01	−18.2	JUN-2010	609.49	−69.15	−10.2
MAR-2009	422.75	−76.70	−15.4	DEC-1987	120.42	−50.39	−29.5
MAR-1980	48.27	−7.64	−13.7	JUN-2002	462.64	−43.82	−8.7

168

10 BEST YEARS BY PERCENT AND POINT

	BY PERCENT CHANGE				BY POINT CHANGE		
YEAR	CLOSE	PNT CHANGE	% CHANGE	YEAR	CLOSE	PNT CHANGE	% CHANGE
DJIA 1901 to 1949							
1915	99.15	44.57	81.7	1928	300.00	97.60	48.2
1933	99.90	39.97	66.7	1927	202.40	45.20	28.8
1928	300.00	97.60	48.2	1915	99.15	44.57	81.7
1908	63.11	20.07	46.6	1945	192.91	40.59	26.6
1904	50.99	15.01	41.7	1935	144.13	40.09	38.5
1935	144.13	40.09	38.5	1933	99.90	39.97	66.7
1905	70.47	19.48	38.2	1925	156.66	36.15	30.0
1919	107.23	25.03	30.5	1936	179.90	35.77	24.8
1925	156.66	36.15	30.0	1938	154.76	33.91	28.1
1927	202.40	45.20	28.8	1919	107.23	25.03	30.5
DJIA 1950 to APRIL 2013							
1954	404.39	123.49	44.0	1999	11497.12	2315.69	25.2
1975	852.41	236.17	38.3	2003	10453.92	2112.29	25.3
1958	583.65	147.96	34.0	2006	12463.15	1745.65	16.3
1995	5117.12	1282.68	33.5	2009	10428.05	1651.66	18.8
1985	1546.67	335.10	27.7	1997	7908.25	1459.98	22.6
1989	2753.20	584.63	27.0	1996	6448.27	1331.15	26.0
1996	6448.27	1331.15	26.0	1995	5117.12	1282.68	33.5
2003	10453.92	2112.29	25.3	1998	9181.43	1273.18	16.1
1999	11497.12	2315.69	25.2	2010	11577.51	1149.46	11.0
1997	7908.25	1459.98	22.6	2012	13104.14	886.58	7.3
S&P 500 1930 to APRIL 2013							
1933	10.10	3.21	46.6	1998	1229.23	258.80	26.7
1954	35.98	11.17	45.0	1999	1469.25	240.02	19.5
1935	13.43	3.93	41.4	2003	1111.92	232.10	26.4
1958	55.21	15.22	38.1	1997	970.43	229.69	31.0
1995	615.93	156.66	34.1	2009	1115.10	211.85	23.5
1975	90.19	21.63	31.5	2006	1418.30	170.01	13.6
1997	970.43	229.69	31.0	2012	1426.19	168.59	13.4
1945	17.36	4.08	30.7	1995	615.93	156.66	34.1
1936	17.18	3.75	27.9	2010	1257.64	142.54	12.8
1989	353.40	75.68	27.3	1996	740.74	124.81	20.3
NASDAQ 1971 to APRIL 2013							
1999	4069.31	1876.62	85.6	1999	4069.31	1876.62	85.6
1991	586.34	212.50	56.8	2009	2269.15	692.12	43.9
2003	2003.37	667.86	50.0	2003	2003.37	667.86	50.0
2009	2269.15	692.12	43.9	1998	2192.69	622.34	39.6
1995	1052.13	300.17	39.9	2012	3019.51	414.36	15.9
1998	2192.69	622.34	39.6	2010	2652.87	383.72	16.9
1980	202.34	51.20	33.9	1995	1052.13	300.17	39.9
1985	324.93	77.58	31.4	1997	1570.35	279.32	21.6
1975	77.62	17.80	29.8	1996	1291.03	238.90	22.7
1979	151.14	33.16	28.1	2007	2652.28	236.99	9.8
RUSSELL 1000 1979 to APRIL 2013							
1995	328.89	84.24	34.4	1998	642.87	129.08	25.1
1997	513.79	120.04	30.5	2003	594.56	128.38	27.5
1991	220.61	49.39	28.8	1999	767.97	125.10	19.5
2003	594.56	128.38	27.5	2009	612.01	124.24	25.5
1985	114.39	24.08	26.7	1997	513.79	120.04	30.5
1989	185.11	38.12	25.9	2012	789.90	96.54	13.9
1980	75.20	15.33	25.6	2006	770.08	90.66	13.3
2009	612.01	124.24	25.5	2010	696.90	84.89	13.9
1998	642.87	129.08	25.1	1995	328.89	84.24	34.4
1996	393.75	64.86	19.7	1996	393.75	64.86	19.7
RUSSELL 2000 1979 to APRIL 2013							
2003	556.91	173.82	45.4	2003	556.91	173.82	45.4
1991	189.94	57.78	43.7	2010	783.65	158.26	25.3
1979	55.91	15.39	38.0	2009	625.39	125.94	25.2
1980	74.80	18.89	33.8	2006	787.66	114.44	17.0
1985	129.87	28.38	28.0	2012	849.35	108.43	14.6
1983	112.27	23.37	26.3	2004	651.57	94.66	17.0
1995	315.97	65.61	26.2	1999	504.75	82.79	19.6
2010	783.65	158.26	25.3	1997	437.02	74.41	20.5
2009	625.39	125.94	25.2	1995	315.97	65.61	26.2
1988	147.37	26.95	22.4	1991	189.94	57.78	43.7

10 WORST YEARS BY PERCENT AND POINT

	BY PERCENT CHANGE				BY POINT CHANGE		
YEAR	CLOSE	PNT CHANGE	% CHANGE	YEAR	CLOSE	PNT CHANGE	% CHANGE
DJIA 1901 to 1949							
1931	77.90	–86.68	–52.7	1931	77.90	–86.68	–52.7
1907	43.04	–26.08	–37.7	1930	164.58	–83.90	–33.8
1930	164.58	–83.90	–33.8	1937	120.85	–59.05	–32.8
1920	71.95	–35.28	–32.9	1929	248.48	–51.52	–17.2
1937	120.85	–59.05	–32.8	1920	71.95	–35.28	–32.9
1903	35.98	–11.12	–23.6	1907	43.04	–26.08	–37.7
1932	59.93	–17.97	–23.1	1917	74.38	–20.62	–21.7
1917	74.38	–20.62	–21.7	1941	110.96	–20.17	–15.4
1910	59.60	–12.96	–17.9	1940	131.13	–19.11	–12.7
1929	248.48	–51.52	–17.2	1932	59.93	–17.97	–23.1
DJIA 1950 to APRIL 2013							
2008	8776.39	–4488.43	–33.8	2008	8776.39	–4488.43	–33.8
1974	616.24	–234.62	–27.6	2002	8341.63	–1679.87	–16.8
1966	785.69	–183.57	–18.9	2001	10021.50	–765.35	–7.1
1977	831.17	–173.48	–17.3	2000	10786.85	–710.27	–6.2
2002	8341.63	–1679.87	–16.8	1974	616.24	–234.62	–27.6
1973	850.86	–169.16	–16.6	1966	785.69	–183.57	–18.9
1969	800.36	–143.39	–15.2	1977	831.17	–173.48	–17.3
1957	435.69	–63.78	–12.8	1973	850.86	–169.16	–16.6
1962	652.10	–79.04	–10.8	1969	800.36	–143.39	–15.2
1960	615.89	–63.47	–9.3	1990	2633.66	–119.54	–4.3
S&P 500 1930 to APRIL 2013							
1931	8.12	–7.22	–47.1	2008	903.25	–565.11	–38.5
1937	10.55	–6.63	–38.6	2002	879.82	–268.26	–23.4
2008	903.25	–565.11	–38.5	2001	1148.08	–172.20	–13.0
1974	68.56	–28.99	–29.7	2000	1320.28	–148.97	–10.1
1930	15.34	–6.11	–28.5	1974	68.56	–28.99	–29.7
2002	879.82	–268.26	–23.4	1990	330.22	–23.18	–6.6
1941	8.69	–1.89	–17.9	1973	97.55	–20.50	–17.4
1973	97.55	–20.50	–17.4	1981	122.55	–13.21	–9.7
1940	10.58	–1.91	–15.3	1977	95.10	–12.36	–11.5
1932	6.89	–1.23	–15.1	1966	80.33	–12.10	–13.1
NASDAQ 1971 to APRIL 2013							
2008	1577.03	–1075.25	–40.5	2000	2470.52	–1598.79	–39.3
2000	2470.52	–1598.79	–39.3	2008	1577.03	–1075.25	–40.5
1974	59.82	–32.37	–35.1	2002	1335.51	–614.89	–31.5
2002	1335.51	–614.89	–31.5	2001	1950.40	–520.12	–21.1
1973	92.19	–41.54	–31.1	1990	373.84	–80.98	–17.8
2001	1950.40	–520.12	–21.1	2011	2605.15	–47.72	–1.8
1990	373.84	–80.98	–17.8	1973	92.19	–41.54	–31.1
1984	247.35	–31.25	–11.2	1974	59.82	–32.37	–35.1
1987	330.47	–18.86	–5.4	1984	247.35	–31.25	–11.2
1981	195.84	–6.50	–3.2	1994	751.96	–24.84	–3.2
RUSSELL 1000 1979 to APRIL 2013							
2008	487.77	–312.05	–39.0	2008	487.77	–312.05	–39.0
2002	466.18	–138.76	–22.9	2002	466.18	–138.76	–22.9
2001	604.94	–95.15	–13.6	2001	604.94	–95.15	–13.6
1981	67.93	–7.27	–9.7	2000	700.09	–67.88	–8.8
2000	700.09	–67.88	–8.8	1990	171.22	–13.89	–7.5
1990	171.22	–13.89	–7.5	1981	67.93	–7.27	–9.7
1994	244.65	–6.06	–2.4	1994	244.65	–6.06	–2.4
2011	693.36	–3.54	–0.5	2011	693.36	–3.54	–0.5
1984	90.31	–0.07	–0.1	1984	90.31	–0.07	–0.1
1987	130.02	0.02	0.02	1987	130.02	0.02	0.02
RUSSELL 2000 1979 to APRIL 2013							
2008	499.45	–266.58	–34.8	2008	499.45	–266.58	–34.8
2002	383.09	–105.41	–21.6	2002	383.09	–105.41	–21.6
1990	132.16	–36.14	–21.5	2011	740.92	–42.73	–5.5
1987	120.42	–14.58	–10.8	1990	132.16	–36.14	–21.5
1984	101.49	–10.78	–9.6	2007	766.03	–21.63	–2.7
2011	740.92	–42.73	–5.5	2000	483.53	–21.22	–4.2
2000	483.53	–21.22	–4.2	1998	421.96	–15.06	–3.4
1998	421.96	–15.06	–3.4	1987	120.42	–14.58	–10.8
1994	250.36	–8.23	–3.2	1984	101.49	–10.78	–9.6
2007	766.03	–21.63	–2.7	1994	250.36	–8.23	–3.2

DOW JONES INDUSTRIALS ONE-YEAR SEASONAL PATTERN CHARTS SINCE 1901

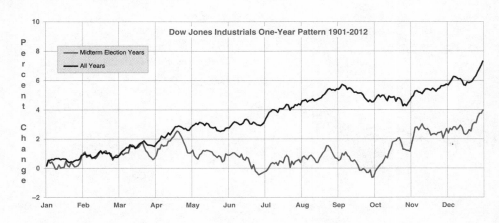

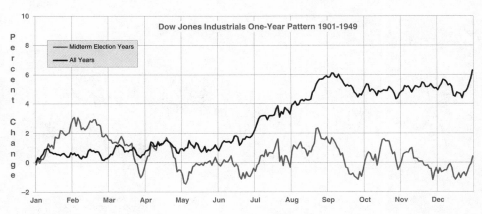

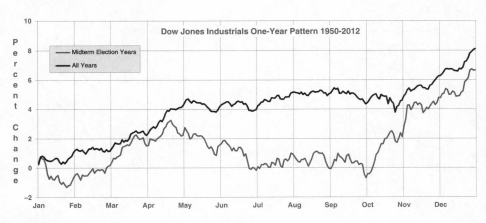

S&P 500 ONE-YEAR SEASONAL PATTERN CHARTS SINCE 1930

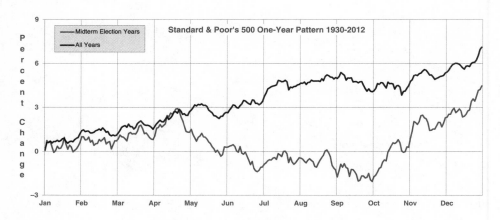

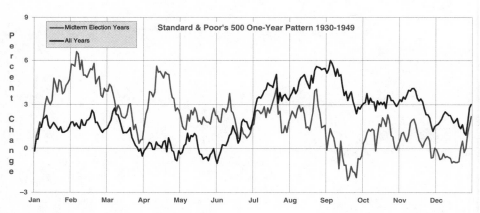

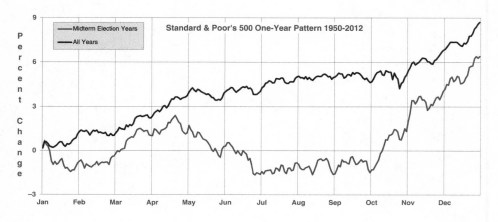

NASDAQ, RUSSELL 1000 & 2000 ONE-YEAR SEASONAL PATTERN CHARTS SINCE 1971

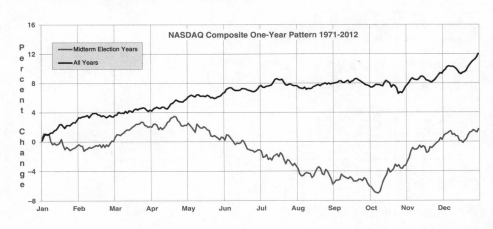

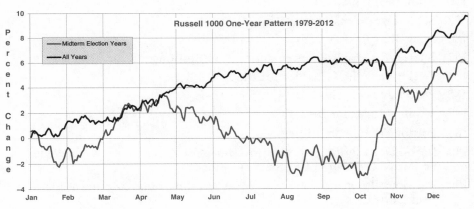

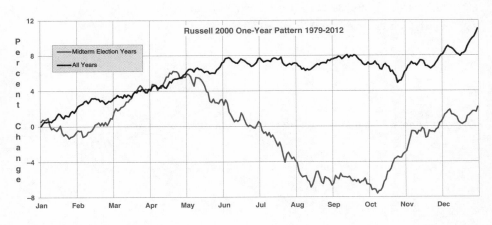

STRATEGY
PLANNING
AND RECORD
SECTION

CONTENTS

These forms are available at our website www.stocktradersalmanac.com.

PORTFOLIO AT START OF 2014

DATE ACQUIRED	NO. OF SHARES	SECURITY	PRICE	TOTAL COST	PAPER PROFITS	PAPER LOSSES

ADDITIONAL PURCHASES

DATE ACQUIRED	NO. OF SHARES	SECURITY	PRICE	TOTAL COST	REASON FOR PURCHASE PRIME OBJECTIVE, ETC.

ADDITIONAL PURCHASES

DATE ACQUIRED	NO. OF SHARES	SECURITY	PRICE	TOTAL COST	REASON FOR PURCHASE PRIME OBJECTIVE, ETC.

SHORT-TERM TRANSACTIONS

Pages 178–181 can accompany next year's income tax return (Schedule D). Enter transactions as completed to avoid last-minute pressures.

NO. OF SHARES	SECURITY	DATE ACQUIRED	DATE SOLD	SALE PRICE	COST	LOSS	GAIN

TOTALS: Carry over to next page

SHORT-TERM TRANSACTIONS *(continued)*

NO. OF SHARES	SECURITY	DATE ACQUIRED	DATE SOLD	SALE PRICE	COST	LOSS	GAIN

TOTALS:

LONG-TERM TRANSACTIONS

Pages 178–181 can accompany next year's income tax return (Schedule D). Enter transactions as completed to avoid last-minute pressures.

NO. OF SHARES	SECURITY	DATE ACQUIRED	DATE SOLD	SALE PRICE	COST	LOSS	GAIN

TOTALS:
Carry over to next page

LONG-TERM TRANSACTIONS *(continued)*

NO. OF SHARES	SECURITY	DATE ACQUIRED	DATE SOLD	SALE PRICE	COST	LOSS	GAIN

TOTALS:

INTEREST/DIVIDENDS RECEIVED DURING 2014

SHARES	STOCK/BOND	FIRST QUARTER		SECOND QUARTER		THIRD QUARTER		FOURTH QUARTER	
		$		$		$		$	

BROKERAGE ACCOUNT DATA 2014

	MARGIN INTEREST	TRANSFER TAXES	CAPITAL ADDED	CAPITAL WITHDRAWN
JAN				
FEB				
MAR				
APR				
MAY				
JUN				
JUL				
AUG				
SEP				
OCT				
NOV				
DEC				

WEEKLY PORTFOLIO PRICE RECORD 2014 (FIRST HALF)

Place purchase price above stock name and weekly closes below.

STOCKS Week Ending	1	2	3	4	5	6	7	8	9	10
JANUARY 3										
10										
17										
24										
31										
FEBRUARY 7										
14										
21										
28										
MARCH 7										
14										
21										
28										
APRIL 4										
11										
18										
25										
MAY 2										
9										
16										
23										
30										
JUNE 6										
13										
20										
27										

WEEKLY PORTFOLIO PRICE RECORD 2014 (SECOND HALF)

Place purchase price above stock name and weekly closes below.

STOCKS / Week Ending	1	2	3	4	5	6	7	8	9	10
JULY										
4										
11										
18										
25										
AUGUST										
1										
8										
15										
22										
29										
SEPTEMBER										
5										
12										
19										
26										
OCTOBER										
3										
10										
17										
24										
31										
NOVEMBER										
7										
14										
21										
28										
DECEMBER										
5										
12										
19										
26										
2										

WEEKLY INDICATOR DATA 2014 (FIRST HALF)

	Week Ending	Dow Jones Industrial Average	Net Change for Week	Net Change on Friday	Net Change Next Monday	S&P or NASDAQ	NYSE Advances	NYSE De- clines	New Highs	New Lows	CBOE Put/Call Ratio	90-Day Treas. Rate	Moody's AAA Rate
JANUARY	3												
	10												
	17												
	24												
	31												
FEBRUARY	7												
	14												
	21												
	28												
MARCH	7												
	14												
	21												
	28												
APRIL	4												
	11												
	18												
	25												
MAY	2												
	9												
	16												
	23												
	30												
JUNE	6												
	13												
	20												
	27												

WEEKLY INDICATOR DATA 2014 (SECOND HALF)

	Week Ending	Dow Jones Industrial Average	Net Change for Week	Net Change on Friday	Net Change Next Monday	S&P or NASDAQ	NYSE Advances	NYSE Declines	New Highs	New Lows	CBOE Put/Call Ratio	90-Day Treas. Rate	Moody's AAA Rate
JULY	4												
	11												
	18												
	25												
AUGUST	1												
	8												
	15												
	22												
	29												
SEPTEMBER	5												
	12												
	19												
	26												
OCTOBER	3												
	10												
	17												
	24												
	31												
NOVEMBER	7												
	14												
	21												
	28												
DECEMBER	5												
	12												
	19												
	26												
	2												

MONTHLY INDICATOR DATA 2014

	DJIA% Last 3 + 1st 2 Days	DJIA% 9th to 11th Trading Days	DJIA% Change Rest of Month	DJIA% Change Whole Month	% Change Your Stocks	Gross Domestic Product	Prime Rate	Trade Deficit $ Billion	CPI % Change	% Unem- ployment Rate
JAN										
FEB										
MAR										
APR										
MAY										
JUN										
JUL										
AUG										
SEP										
OCT										
NOV										
DEC										

INSTRUCTIONS:

Weekly Indicator Data (pages 185–186). Keeping data on several indicators may give you a better feel of the market. In addition to the closing DJIA and its net change for the week, post the net change for Friday's Dow and also the following Monday's. A series of "down Fridays" followed by "down Mondays" often precedes a downswing. Tracking either the S&P or NASDAQ composite, and advances and declines, will help prevent the Dow from misleading you. New highs and lows and put/call ratios (www.cboe.com) are also useful indicators. All these weekly figures appear in weekend papers or *Barron's*. Data for 90-day Treasury Rate and Moody's AAA Bond Rate are quite important for tracking short- and long-term interest rates. These figures are available from:

> Weekly U.S. Financial Data
> Federal Reserve Bank of St. Louis
> P.O. Box 442
> St. Louis MO 63166
> **http://research.stlouisfed.org**

Monthly Indicator Data. The purpose of the first three columns is to enable you to track the market's bullish bias near the end, beginning, and middle of the month, which has been shifting lately (see pages 88, 145, and 146). Market direction, performance of your stocks, gross domestic product, prime rate, trade deficit, Consumer Price Index, and unemployment rate are worthwhile indicators to follow. Or, readers may wish to gauge other data.

187

PORTFOLIO AT END OF 2014

DATE ACQUIRED	NO. OF SHARES	SECURITY	PRICE	TOTAL COST	PAPER PROFITS	PAPER LOSSES

IF YOU DON'T PROFIT FROM YOUR INVESTMENT MISTAKES, SOMEONE ELSE WILL

No matter how much we may deny it, almost every successful person in Wall Street pays a great deal of attention to trading suggestions—especially when they come from "the right sources."

One of the hardest things to learn is to distinguish between good tips and bad ones. Usually, the best tips have a logical reason in back of them, which accompanies the tip. Poor tips usually have no reason to support them.

The important thing to remember is that the market discounts. It does not review, it does not reflect. The Street's real interest in "tips," inside information, buying and selling suggestions, and everything else of this kind emanates from a desire to find out just what the market has on hand to discount. The process of finding out involves separating the wheat from the chaff—and there is plenty of chaff.

HOW TO MAKE USE OF STOCK "TIPS"

- The source should be **reliable**. (By listing all "tips" and suggestions on a Performance Record of Recommendations, such as the form below, and then periodically evaluating the outcomes, you will soon know the "batting average" of your sources.)

- The story should make sense. Would the merger violate antitrust laws? Are there too many computers on the market already? How many years will it take to become profitable?

- The stock should not have had a recent sharp run-up. Otherwise, the story may already be discounted, and confirmation or denial in the press would most likely be accompanied by a sell-off in the stock.

PERFORMANCE RECORD OF RECOMMENDATIONS

STOCK RECOMMENDED	BY WHOM	DATE	PRICE	REASON FOR RECOMMENDATION	SUBSEQUENT ACTION OF STOCK

INDIVIDUAL RETIREMENT ACCOUNTS: MOST AWESOME INVESTMENT INCENTIVE EVER DEVISED

MAX IRA INVESTMENTS OF $5,000* A YEAR COMPOUNDED AT VARIOUS INTEREST RATES OF RETURN FOR DIFFERENT PERIODS

Annual Rate	5 Yrs	10 Yrs	15 Yrs	20 Yrs	25 Yrs	30 Yrs	35 Yrs	40 Yrs	45 Yrs	50 Yrs
1%	$28,336	$58,118	$89,418	$122,316	$156,891	$193,230	$231,423	$271,564	$313,752	$358,093
2%	29,195	61,428	97,016	136,308	179,690	227,587	280,469	338,855	403,318	474,490
3%	30,076	64,943	105,363	152,221	206,542	269,515	342,518	427,148	525,258	638,994
4%	30,981	68,675	114,535	170,331	238,215	320,806	421,291	543,546	692,288	873,256
5%	31,911	72,637	124,616	190,956	275,624	383,684	521,600	697,619	922,268	1,208,985
6%	32,864	76,844	135,699	214,460	319,860	460,909	649,665	902,262	1,240,295	1,692,658
7%	33,843	81,310	147,884	241,258	372,221	555,902	813,524	1,174,853	1,681,635	2,392,423
8%	34,848	86,050	161,284	271,826	434,249	672,902	1,023,562	1,538,796	2,295,843	3,408,195
9%	35,878	91,082	176,019	306,705	507,782	817,164	1,293,186	2,025,605	3,152,523	4,886,426
10%	36,936	96,421	192,224	346,514	595,000	995,189	1,639,697	2,677,685	4,349,374	7,041,647
11%	38,021	102,088	210,045	391,958	698,493	1,215,022	2,085,404	3,552,048	6,023,428	10,187,848
12%	39,134	108,100	229,643	443,843	821,337	1,486,609	2,659,047	4,725,283	8,366,697	14,784,112
13%	40,275	114,479	251,195	503,085	967,176	1,822,233	3,397,621	6,300,172	11,647,933	21,500,837
14%	41,445	121,245	274,892	570,726	1,140,330	2,237,054	4,348,701	8,414,497	16,242,841	31,315,649
15%	42,646	128,421	300,946	647,956	1,345,916	2,749,763	5,573,401	11,252,746	22,675,938	45,652,055
16%	43,876	136,031	329,588	736,123	1,589,985	3,383,389	7,150,149	15,061,631	31,678,448	66,579,439
17%	45,138	144,100	361,069	836,762	1,879,695	4,166,271	9,179,470	20,170,648	44,268,235	97,100,943
18%	46,431	152,653	395,665	951,616	2,223,497	5,133,252	11,790,069	27,019,253	61,859,935	141,566,978
19%	47,756	161,720	433,676	1,082,661	2,631,368	6,327,131	15,146,529	36,192,731	86,416,412	206,267,876
20%	49,115	171,327	475,432	1,232,141	3,115,075	7,800,418	19,459,052	48,469,462	120,656,646	300,281,459

* At Press Time, 2014 Contribution Limit will be indexed to inflation

G. M. LOEB'S "BATTLE PLAN" FOR INVESTMENT SURVIVAL

LIFE IS CHANGE: Nothing can ever be the same a minute from now as it was a minute ago. Everything you own is changing in price and value. You can find that last price of an active security on the stock ticker, but you cannot find the next price anywhere. The value of your money is changing. Even the value of your home is changing, though no one walks in front of it with a sandwich board consistently posting the changes.

RECOGNIZE CHANGE: Your basic objective should be to profit from change. The art of investing is being able to recognize change and to adjust investment goals accordingly.

WRITE THINGS DOWN: You will score more investment success and avoid more investment failures if you write things down. Very few investors have the drive and inclination to do this.

KEEP A CHECKLIST: If you aim to improve your investment results, get into the habit of keeping a checklist on every issue you consider buying. Before making a commitment, it will pay you to write down the answers to at least some of the basic questions—How much am I investing in this company? How much do I think I can make? How much do I have to risk? How long do I expect to take to reach my goal?

HAVE A SINGLE RULING REASON: Above all, writing things down is the best way to find "the ruling reason." When all is said and done, there is invariably a single reason that stands out above all others, why a particular security transaction can be expected to show a profit. All too often, many relatively unimportant statistics are allowed to obscure this single important point.

Any one of a dozen factors may be the point of a particular purchase or sale. It could be a technical reason—an increase in earnings or dividend not yet discounted in the market price—a change of management—a promising new product—an expected improvement in the market's valuation of earnings—or many others. But, in any given case, one of these factors will almost certainly be more important than all the rest put together.

CLOSING OUT A COMMITMENT: If you have a loss, the solution is automatic, provided you decide what to do at the time you buy. Otherwise, the question divides itself into two parts. Are we in a bull or bear market? Few of us really know until it is too late. For the sake of the record, if you think it is a bear market, just put that consideration first and sell as much as your conviction suggests and your nature allows.

If you think it is a bull market, or at least a market where some stocks move up, some mark time, and only a few decline, do not sell unless:

✓ You see a bear market ahead.
✓ You see trouble for a particular company in which you own shares.
✓ Time and circumstances have turned up a new and seemingly far better buy than the issue you like least in your list.
✓ Your shares stop going up and start going down.

A subsidiary question is, which stock to sell first? Two further observations may help:

✓ Do not sell solely because you think a stock is "overvalued."
✓ If you want to sell some of your stocks and not all, in most cases it is better to go against your emotional inclinations and sell first the issues with losses, small profits, or none at all, the weakest, the most disappointing, etc.

Mr. Loeb is the author of *The Battle for Investment Survival*, John Wiley & Sons.

G. M. LOEB'S INVESTMENT SURVIVAL CHECKLIST

OBJECTIVES AND RISKS

Security		Price	Shares	Date

"Ruling reason" for commitment	Amount of commitment $_____
	% of my investment capital _____%

Price objective	Est. time to achieve it	I will risk _____ points	Which would be $_____

TECHNICAL POSITION

Price action of stock:

❑ Hitting new highs   ❑ In a trading range

❑ Pausing in an uptrend   ❑ Moving up from low ground

❑ Acting stronger than market   ❑ _____

Dow Jones Industrial Average

Trend of market

SELECTED YARDSTICKS

	Price Range		Earnings Per Share Actual or Projected	Price/Earnings Ratio Actual or Projected
	High	Low		
Current year Previous year				

Merger possibilities	Years for earnings to double in past
Comment on future	Years for market price to double in past

PERIODIC RE-CHECKS

Date	Stock Price	DJIA	Comment	Action taken, if any

COMPLETED TRANSACTIONS

Date closed	Period of time held	Profit or loss

Reason for profit or loss